AF594642

PRAISE FOR SPARE THESE STONES

"In a day and age of polish and sanding of rough edges in our sport, these pages contain something wholly unique to its core. Andrew Kornylak's words and images capture the spirit of a movement."
—Fitz Cahall, founder of Duct Tape Then Beer

"Andrew Kornylak is a uniquely gifted visual storyteller whose skills extend to the written word. This stunning compilation of people, place, sport, culture, legend, and lore embodies the spirit of ascension in the Southeast and calls you to embrace and care for the community and landscape. For climbers and non-climbers alike, *Spare These Stones* offers a gripping journey that draws you in and inspires you to seek out—and then hold on tight to—all the good that surrounds us."
—Jennifer Pharr Davis, author of *Becoming Odyssa* and *The Pursuit of Endurance*

"*Spare These Stones* is a love letter to Southern climbing—the sandstone, the soul, and the rugged, humble characters who call it home. Andrew Kornylak brings a singular visual voice to this deeply personal and definitive work. Through stunning imagery and intimate stories, he captures not just the routes and crags, but the heart of a community whose ambition is matched only by its generosity. This is more than a climbing book—it's a portrait of a place and its people, rendered with honesty, grit, and reverence."
—Andrew Bisharat, cohost of *The Runout* podcast and publisher of Evening Sends

"Part time capsule, art installation, and motivational speech, *Spare These Stones* is a magical journey through rock climbing in the American Southeast. Andrew Kornylak has long been one of the region's most dedicated climbing photographers, and this book showcases his best work. Steep cliffs are the backdrop, but the true subject is the strong and colorful community."
—Jeff Achey, former editor of *Climbing*

"In *Spare These Stones,* Andrew Kornylak takes a bare-knuckle approach to documenting the intrepid souls who would cross the River Styx and thrash through the brambles to revel in the glory of Southeast climbing."
—John Sherman

"*Spare These Stones* documents cutting-edge climbs—bone-breaking highballs, runout trad, and hard sport—that continue to be established by the sport's elite. . . . These shots capture climbers on challenging routes and stunning landscapes, forests, rocks, and even ordinary people whose presence feels perfectly placed."
—Chris Van Leuven, editor for Yosemite Climbing Association and former editor of *Alpinist*

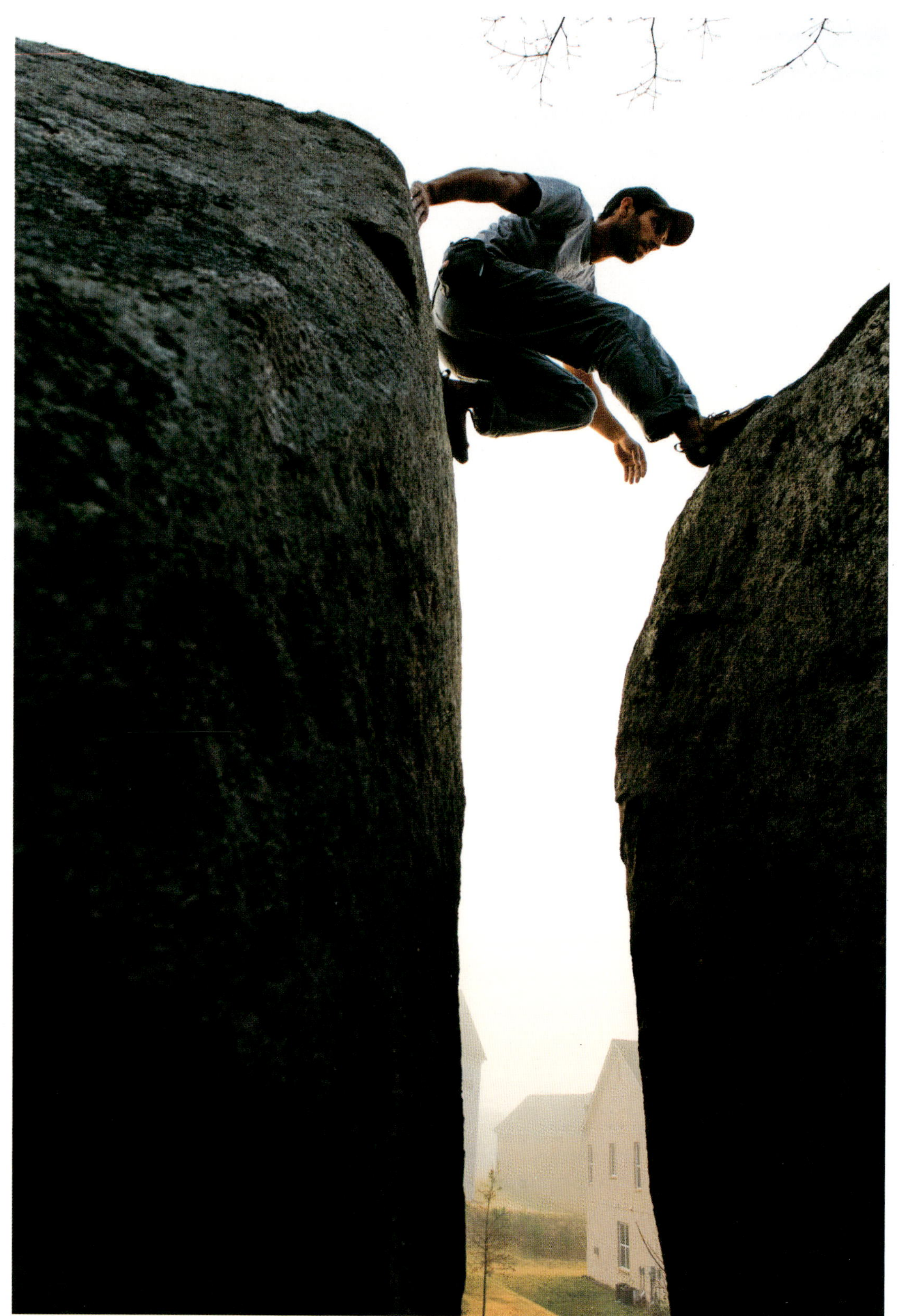

SPARE THESE STONES

A Journey Through Southern Climbing Culture

Andrew Kornylak

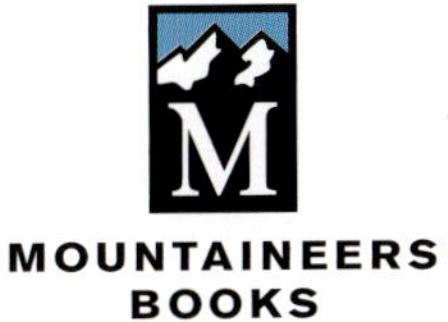

MOUNTAINEERS BOOKS

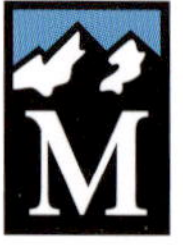

MOUNTAINEERS BOOKS is dedicated
to the exploration, preservation, and enjoyment
of outdoor and wilderness areas.

1001 SW Klickitat Way, Suite 201, Seattle, WA 98134
800-553-4453, www.mountaineersbooks.org

Printed in China

28 27 26 25 1 2 3 4 5

Design and layout: Melissa McFeeters
Map maker: Joey Henson
All photographs by the author unless credited otherwise
Cover photographs, front: *Sunrise through Twin Arches, Big South Fork National River and Recreation Area, Tennessee;* back, *Lisa Rands topping out on Mystery Machine Boulder at Stone Fort near Chattanooga, Tennessee*
Frontispiece: *Daniel Paulete at Boat Rock in southwestern Atlanta*
Photograph on page 208: *Taylor McNeill after his repeat of* Inner Mounting Flame *at the Viaduct Boulders near Boone, North Carolina*

Library of Congress Cataloging-in-Publication data is available at https://lccn.loc.gov/2024059872

Mountaineers Books titles may be purchased for corporate, educational, or other promotional sales, and our authors are available for a wide range of events. For information on special discounts or booking an author, contact our customer service at 800-553-4453 or mbooks@mountaineersbooks.org.

Printed on FSC®-certified materials

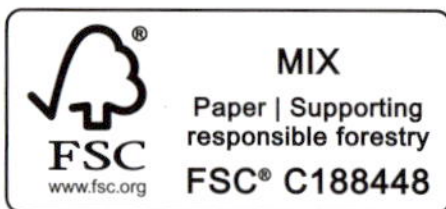

ISBN (hardcover): 978-1-68051-822-1

An independent nonprofit publisher since 1960

To Vera,
who showed me
the ropes

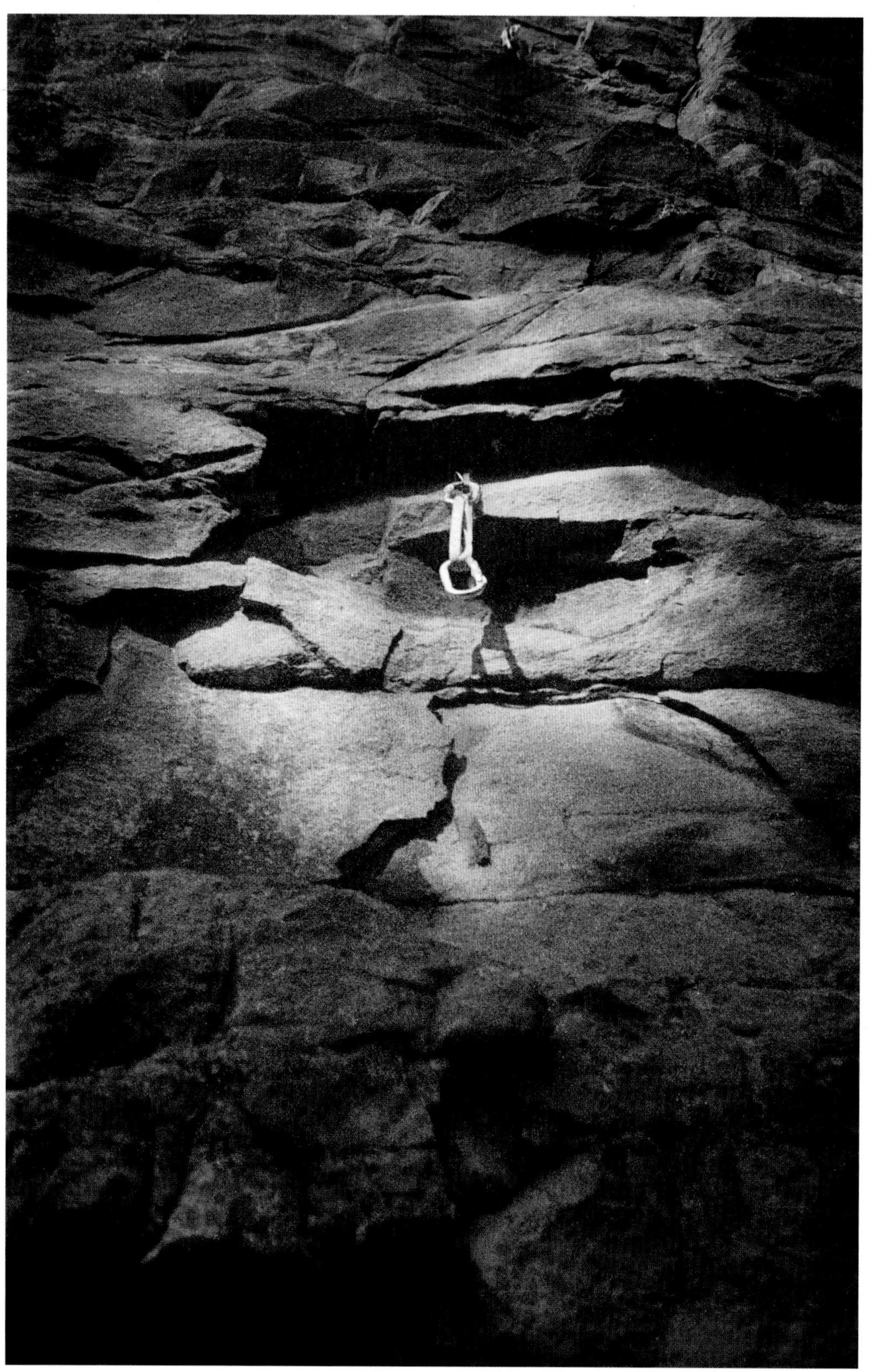

Foster Falls,
Tennessee

CONTENTS

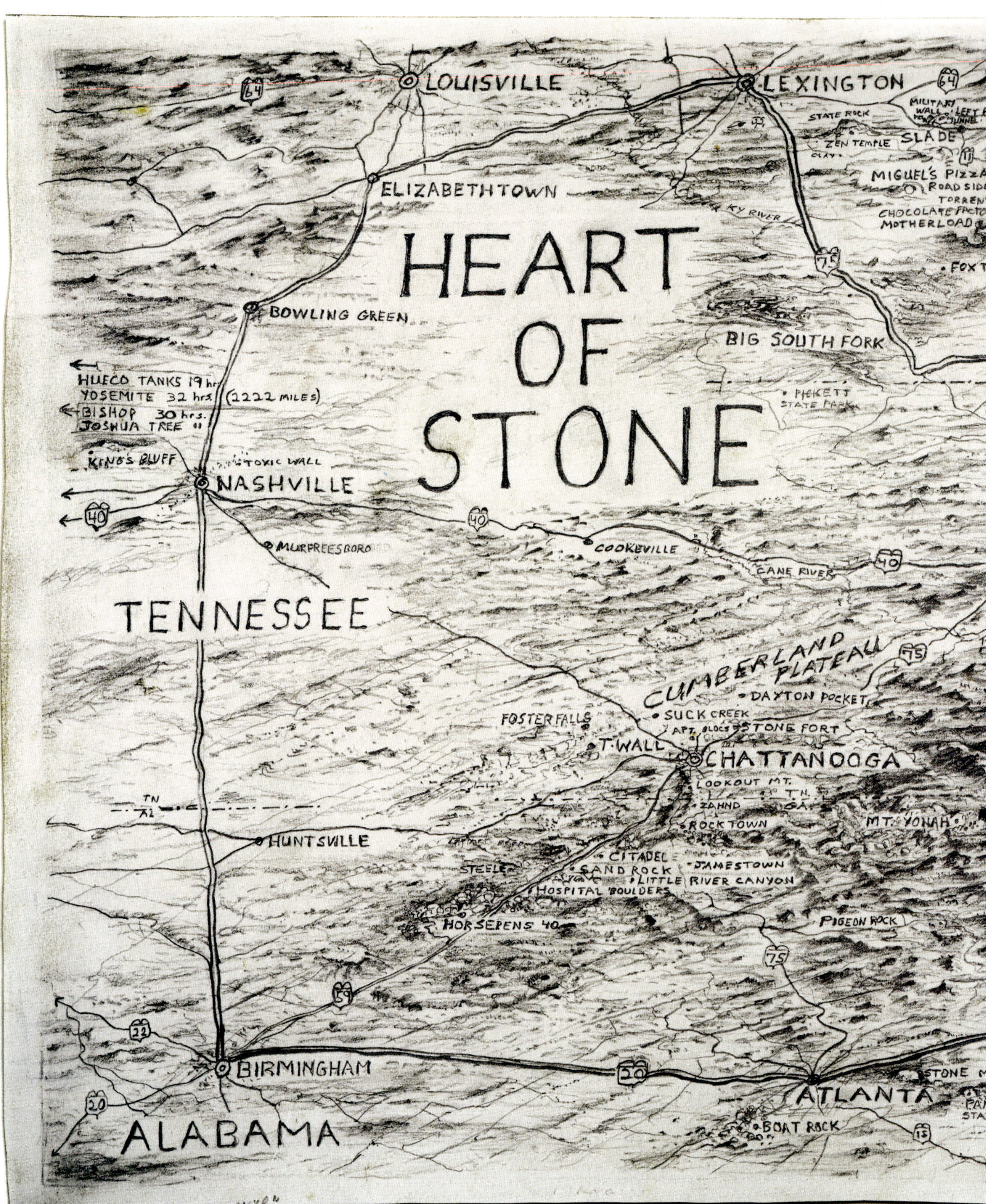
HEART OF STONE
LOUISVILLE
LEXINGTON
ELIZABETHTOWN
KY RIVER
STATE ROCK
ZEN TEMPLE
SLADE
MIGUEL'S PIZZA
ROAD SIDE
TORRENT
CHOCOLATE FACTORY
MOTHERLOAD
FOX TO
BOWLING GREEN
BIG SOUTH FORK
PICKETT STATE PARK
HUECO TANKS 19 hr
YOSEMITE 32 hrs. (2222 MILES)
BISHOP 30 hrs.
JOSHUA TREE "
KING'S BLUFF
TOXIC WALL
NASHVILLE
MURFREESBORO
COOKEVILLE
CANE RIVER
TENNESSEE
CUMBERLAND PLATEAU
DAYTON POCKET
SUCK CREEK
STONE FORT
FOSTER FALLS
T-WALL
CHATTANOOGA
LOOKOUT MT.
TN
GA
ZAHND
ROCK TOWN
MT. YONAH
TN
AL
HUNTSVILLE
CITADEL
SAND ROCK
JAMESTOWN
STEELE
LITTLE RIVER CANYON
HOSPITAL BOULDERS
HORSEPENS 40
PIGEON ROCK
BIRMINGHAM
ATLANTA
STONE MT.
BOAT ROCK
ALABAMA
64
75
40
59
20
22
15

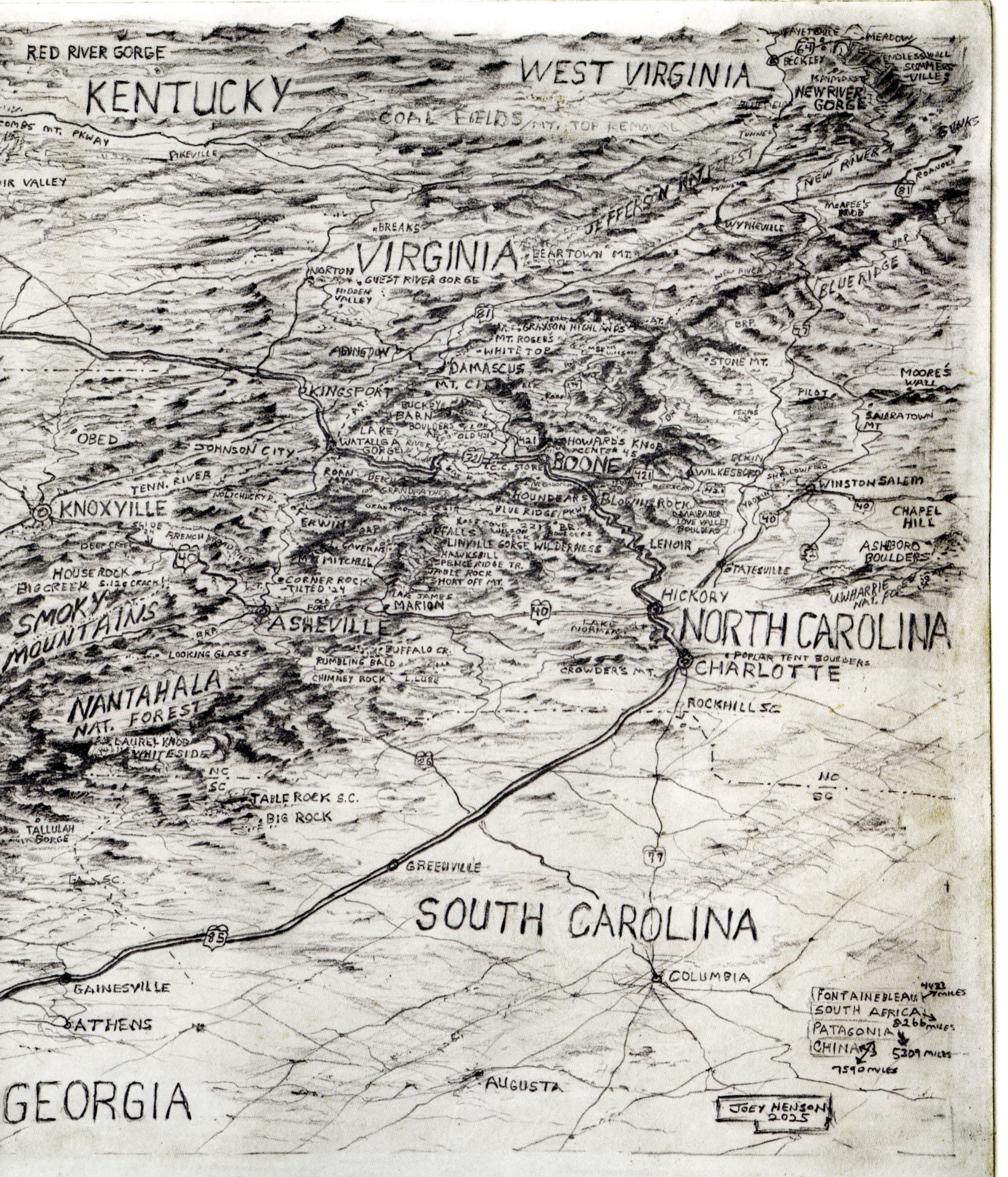
RED RIVER GORGE
KENTUCKY
WEST VIRGINIA
COAL FIELDS
MT. TOP REMOVAL
PIKEVILLE
NEW RIVER GORGE
SUMMERSVILLE
NEW RIVER
JEFFERSON NAT. FOREST
BREAKS
VIRGINIA
BEARTOWN MT.
NORTON
GUEST RIVER GORGE
HIDDEN VALLEY
WYTHEVILLE
BLUE RIDGE
GRAYSON HIGHLANDS
MT. ROGERS
WHITE TOP
ABINGDON
DAMASCUS
STONE MT.
MOORE'S WALL
PILOT
SAURATOWN MT.
KINGSPORT
OBED
JOHNSON CITY
WATAUGA RIVER GORGE
HOWARD'S KNOB
BOONE
WILKESBORO
WINSTON SALEM
CHAPEL HILL
TENN. RIVER
KNOXVILLE
HOUNDEARS
BLUE RIDGE PKWY
BLOWING ROCK
ERWIN
LINVILLE GORGE WILDERNESS
HAWKSBILL
TABLE ROCK
SHORT OFF MT.
LENOIR
ASHBORO BOULDERS
STATESVILLE
HOUSE ROCK
SMOKY MOUNTAINS
MT. MITCHELL
CORNER ROCK
MARION
HICKORY
UWHARRIE NAT. FOREST
ASHEVILLE
NORTH CAROLINA
LOOKING GLASS
BUFFALO CR.
RUMBLING BALD
CHIMNEY ROCK
CROWDERS MT.
POPLAR TENT BOULDERS
CHARLOTTE
NANTAHALA NAT. FOREST
LAUREL KNOB
WHITESIDE
ROCKHILL SC
NC
SC
TABLE ROCK S.C.
BIG ROCK
TALLULAH GORGE
GREENVILLE
SOUTH CAROLINA
85
77
26
40
81
GAINESVILLE
ATHENS
COLUMBIA
FONTAINEBLEAU
SOUTH AFRICA
PATAGONIA
CHINA
AUGUSTA
GEORGIA
JOEY HENSON 2025

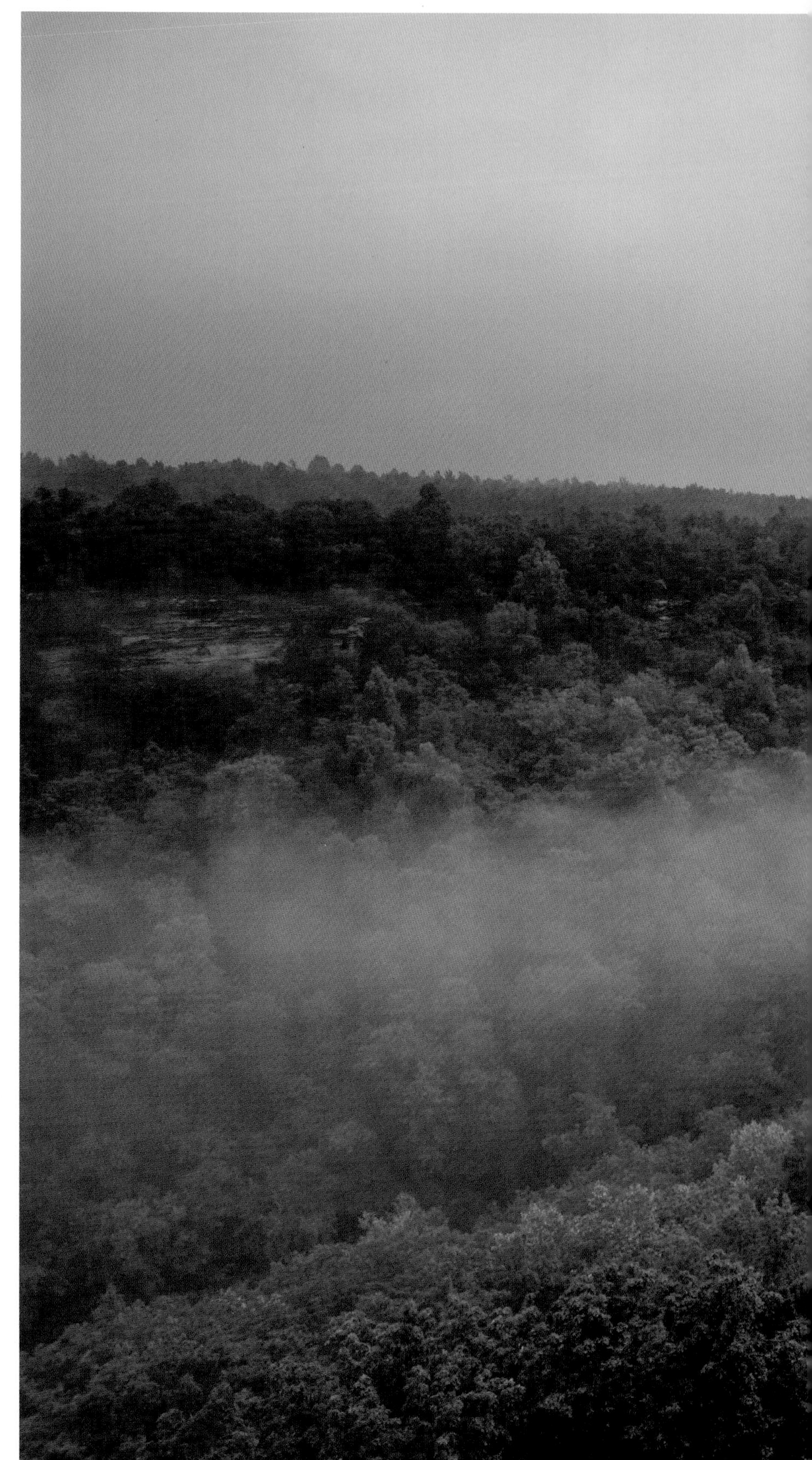

Fog envelops Alabama's Little River Canyon National Preserve at sunrise

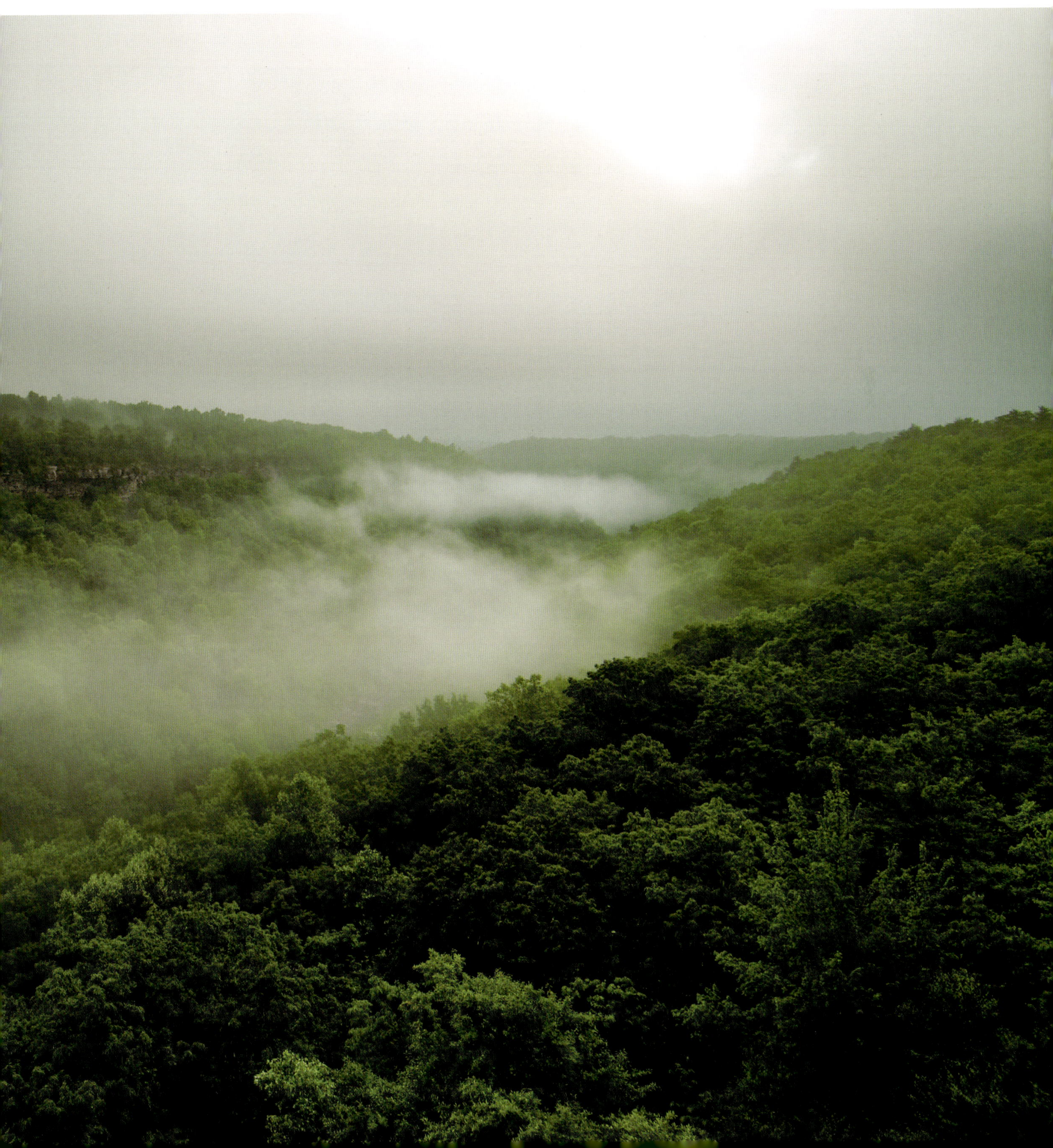

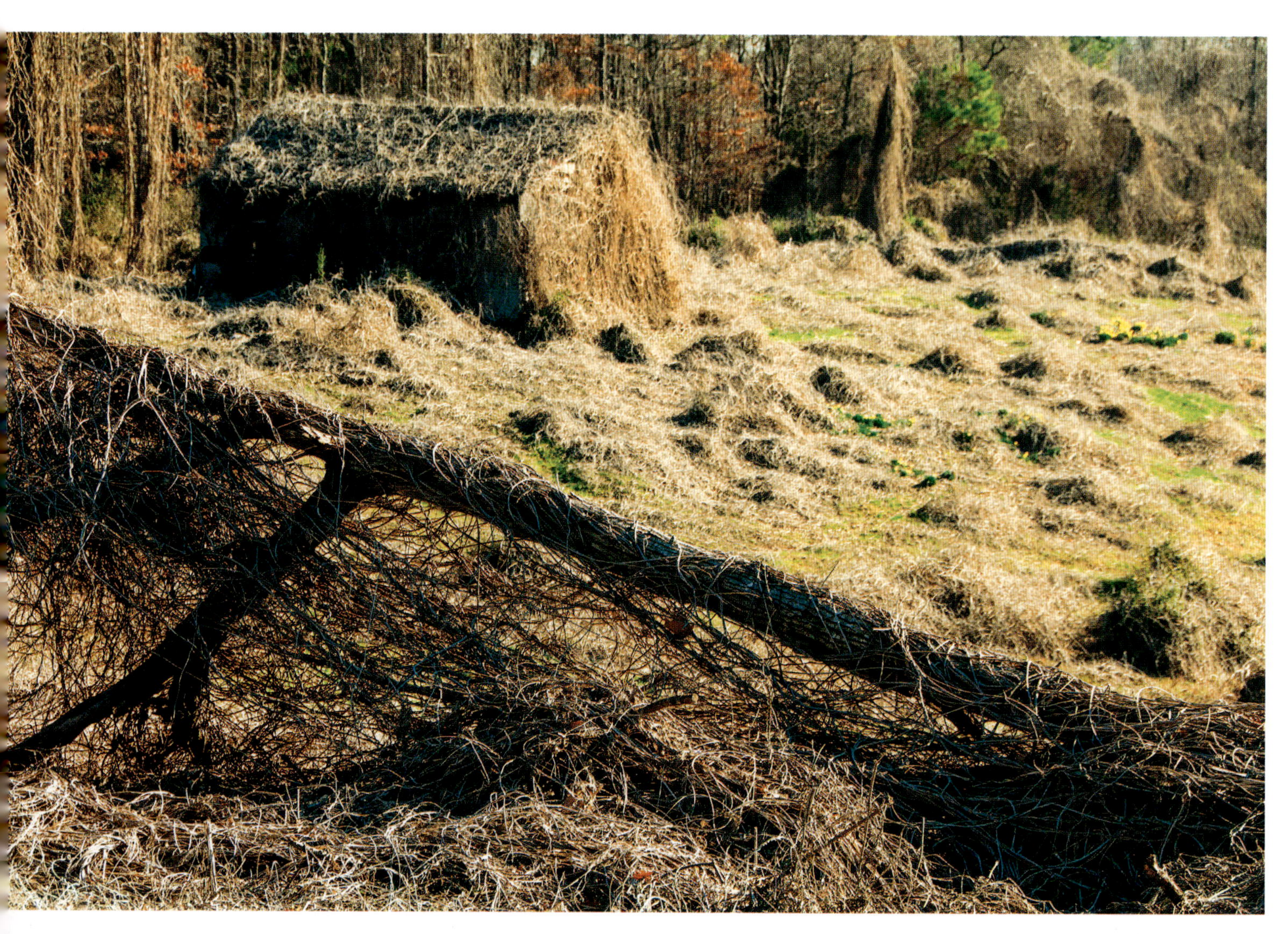

Opposite: Abandoned shack and field covered in kudzu, southern Atlanta

INTRODUCTION

The South is a place of corners.

In all the buckled, worn-out geography that drains the Appalachian Mountains to the Gulf and Atlantic coasts, there is little exposed rock left that can't hide behind a wall of kudzu or the deep bend of a river. If you hold out your hand to block the sun, a cliff at a mile's distance is about the width of three fingers, set well below tree line. A dense, green Tennessee forest cove might make ten thousand house-sized sandstone boulders invisible. Alabama gorges hide miles of steep rock, pulverized by time, and the collapsed remnants of limestone caves along a roaring creek. It's good climbing if you can find it, but you have to go down, not up.

The physical scale of Southern climbing is easy to wrap your head around. Most walls are one hundred to two hundred feet high, and you can find them damn near everywhere, once you know how to look. There is a familiarity and intimacy with the local climbing that is harder to feel in bigger mountain ranges. Southern climbers find their stone not on a remote peak but at the end of a road in the backwoods.

Owing to that, even the wildest landscape here seems entangled with the presence of man. Turning one corner reveals stunning and rare natural beauty; around the next, a junkyard. It's an ancient presence too. As you unpack your climbing gear under the dripline of a massive sandstone roof, you may find a spear point and realize the last human drama played out here at least a thousand years ago.

I began climbing in the South in the early 1990s, when a locals-only, word-of-mouth ethic still dominated. The scene was comfortably hermetic and fractured. But there was a problem. As was happening everywhere else in the country, forces were threatening to close off access to climbing areas, all while climbers were growing in number. Everything changed dramatically in the next couple of decades. Here in the South, a community self-assembled and offered a solution: private land ownership by local climbing organizations. The new ethic was one of long-term conservation and open access for everyone. At the same time, there was a shift in how climbers learned the ropes. In those days climbing knowledge was still mostly passed down through personal interactions in the outdoors. That mentoring was replaced by climbing gyms, with knowledge shared via guidebooks and the internet. Some knowledge was gained, while other knowledge and connections were lost.

This book is a collection of my photographs and stories of Southern rock climbing over the past few decades. They are not all-inclusive or exhaustive. Some are deliberately opaque. There might even be a tall tale or two. The sea change in climbing culture no doubt happened everywhere, but I think the way it happened here illuminates the relationship between culture and geography. I've lived and climbed in many places, but there is something unique about the South. Despite all the rapid change, the essential character of mystery and discovery in Southern climbing seems to be intact. That spirit is what I hope to share most of all. ◆

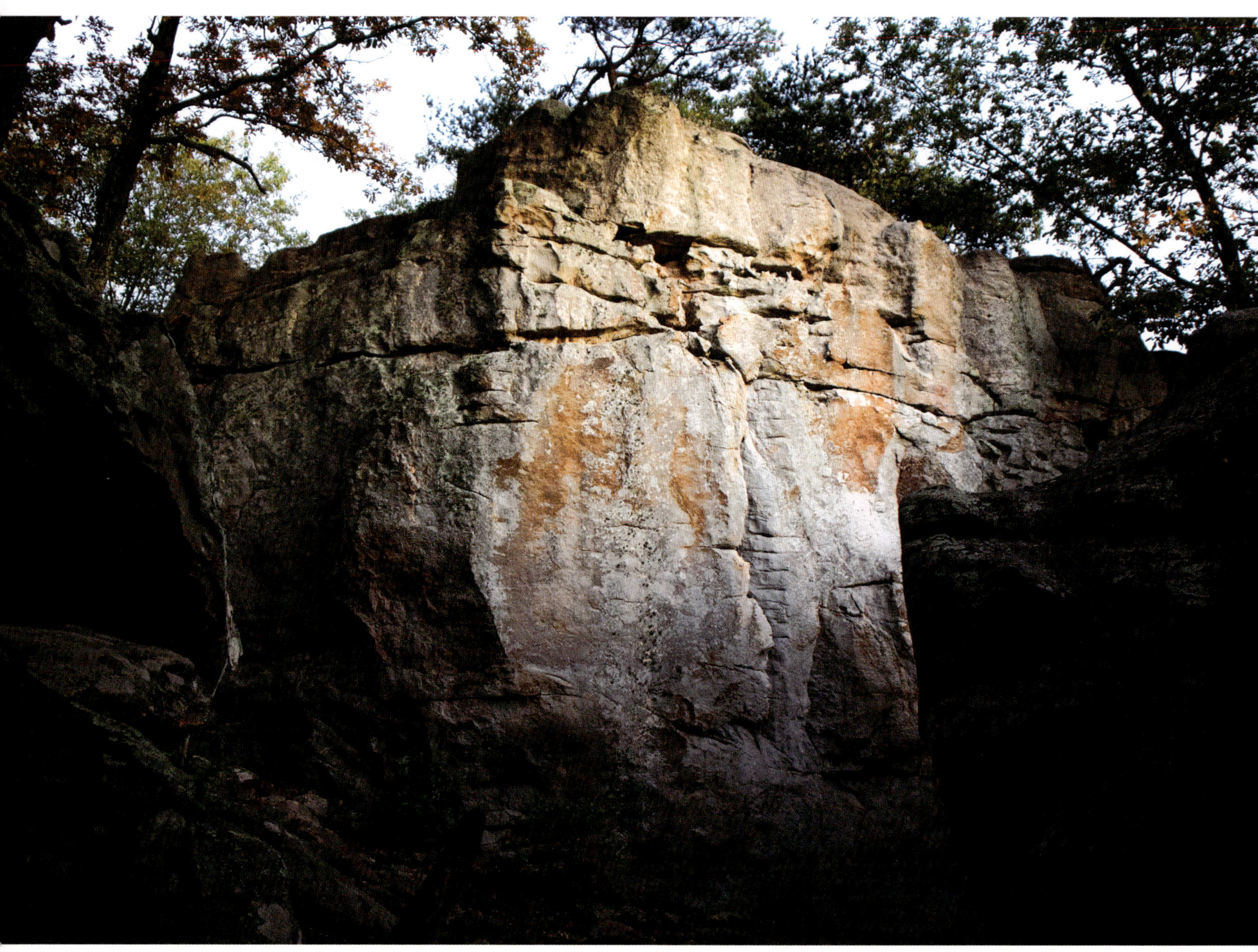

Early morning light on a wall at Sand Rock, Alabama

Opposite: Autumn along County Road 42, Oneonta, Alabama

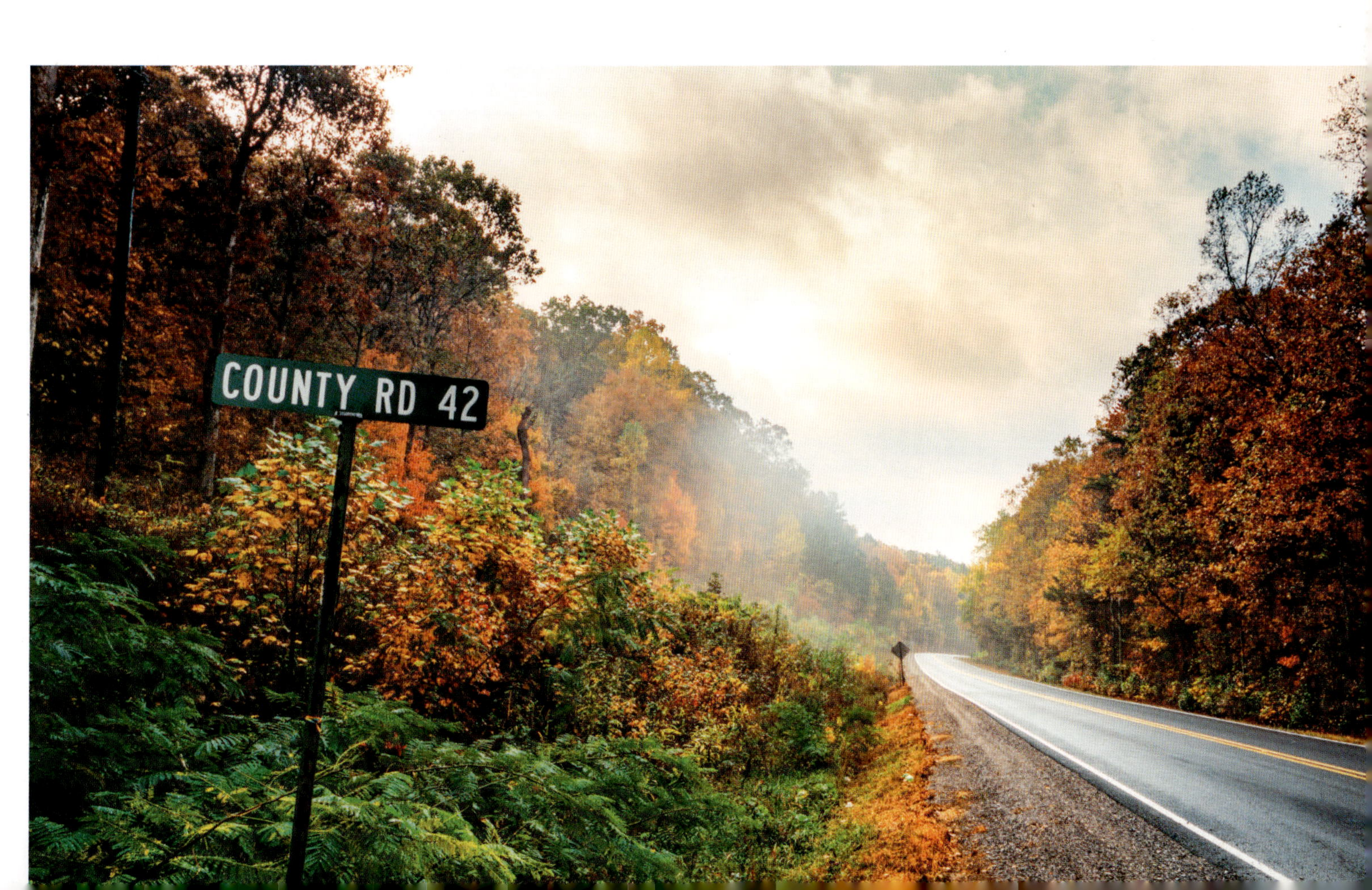
COUNTY RD 42

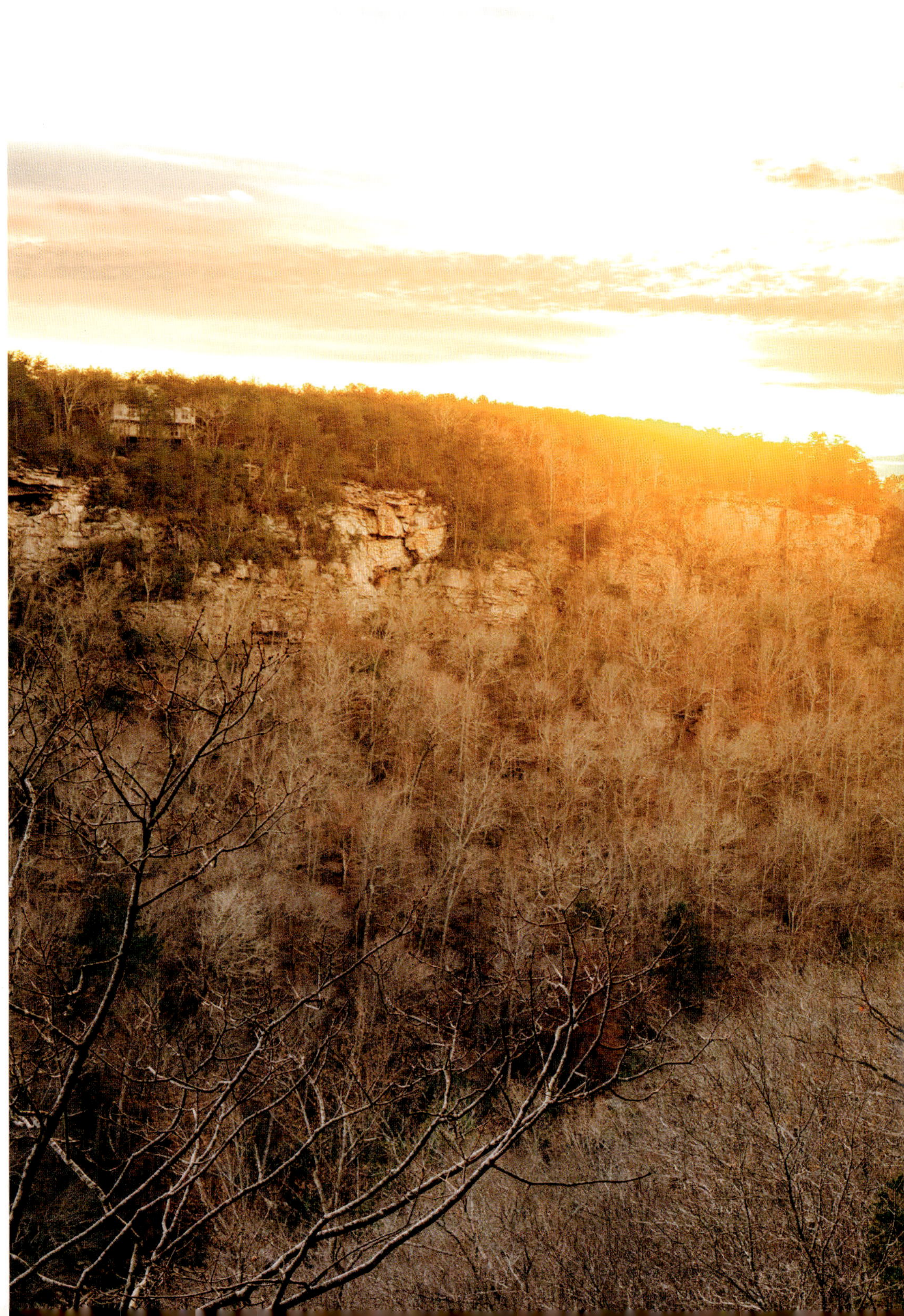

Jonathan Brandt on *Prodigal* (5.13d), Little River Canyon National Preserve, Alabama

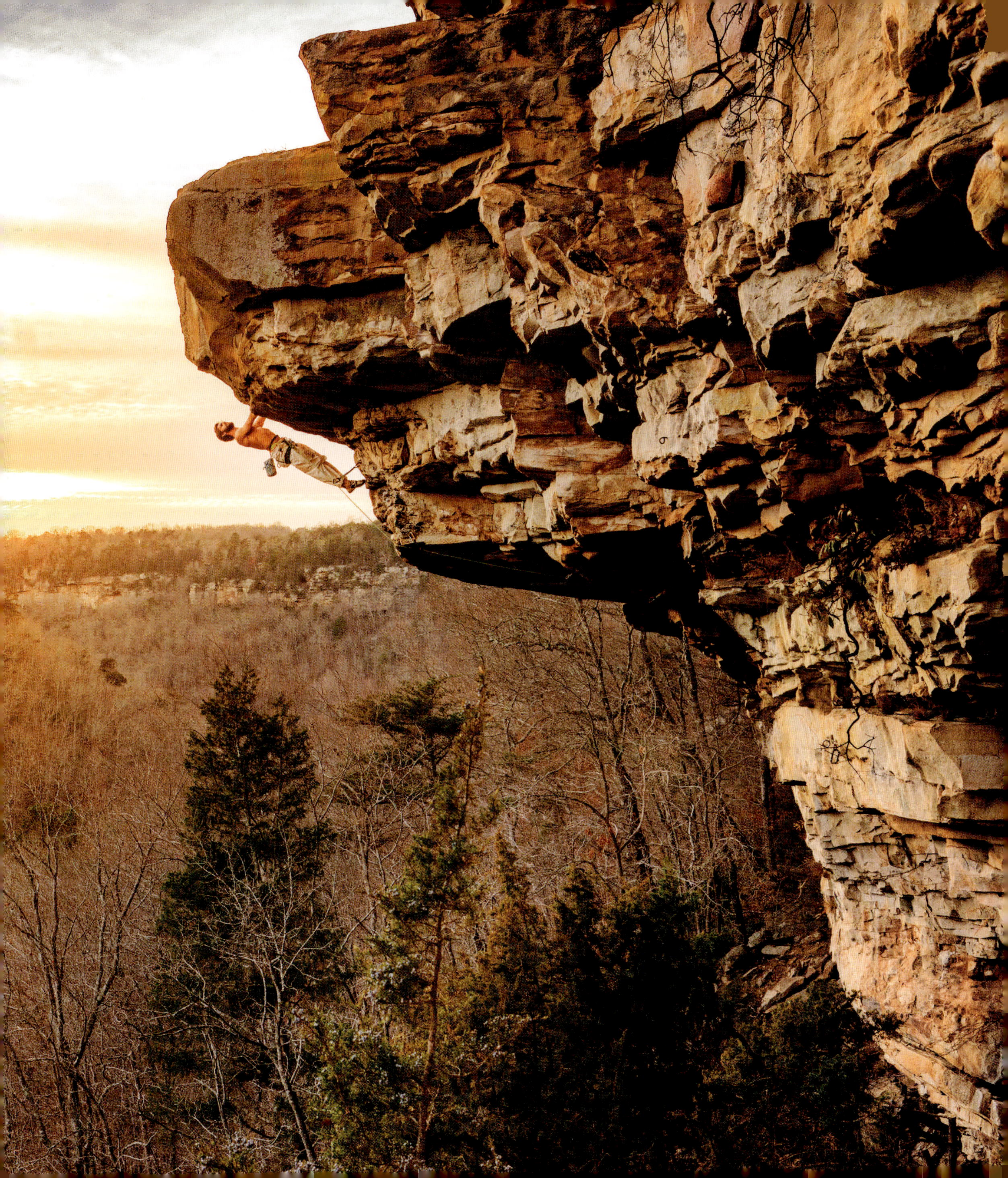

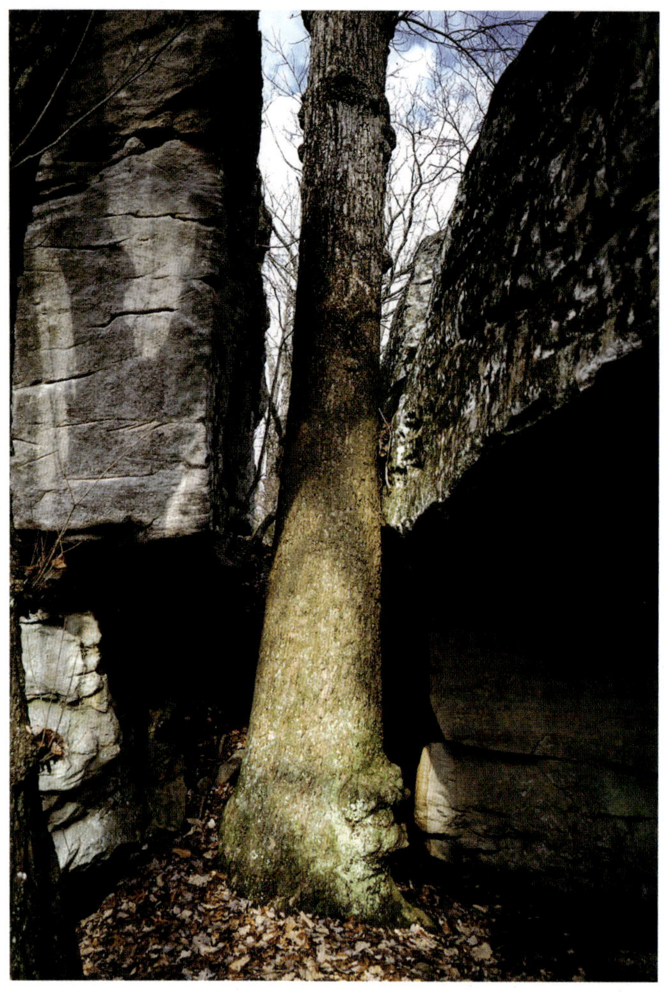

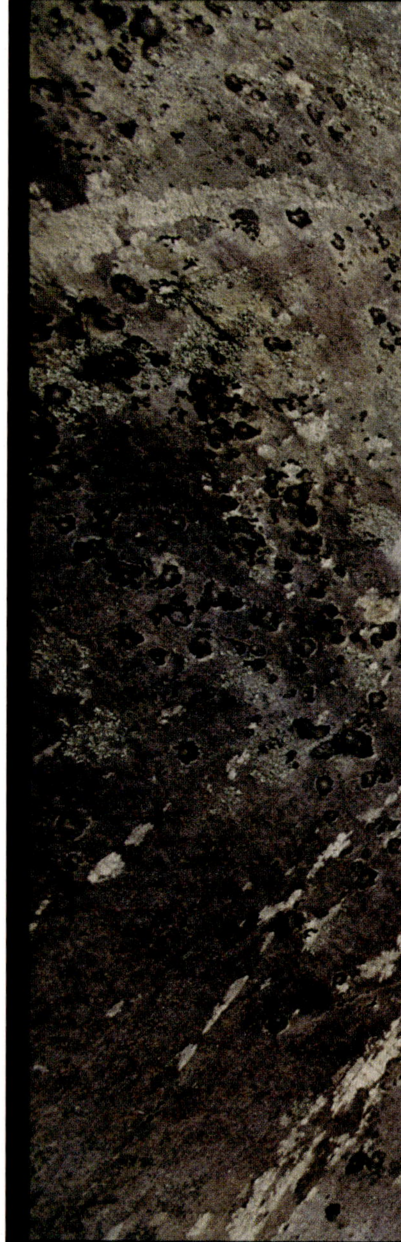

Corner, Zahnd
Wildlife Management
Area, Georgia

Anne Shields on the
first ascent of *Hearts
of Palm* (5.12c),
Jamestown, Alabama

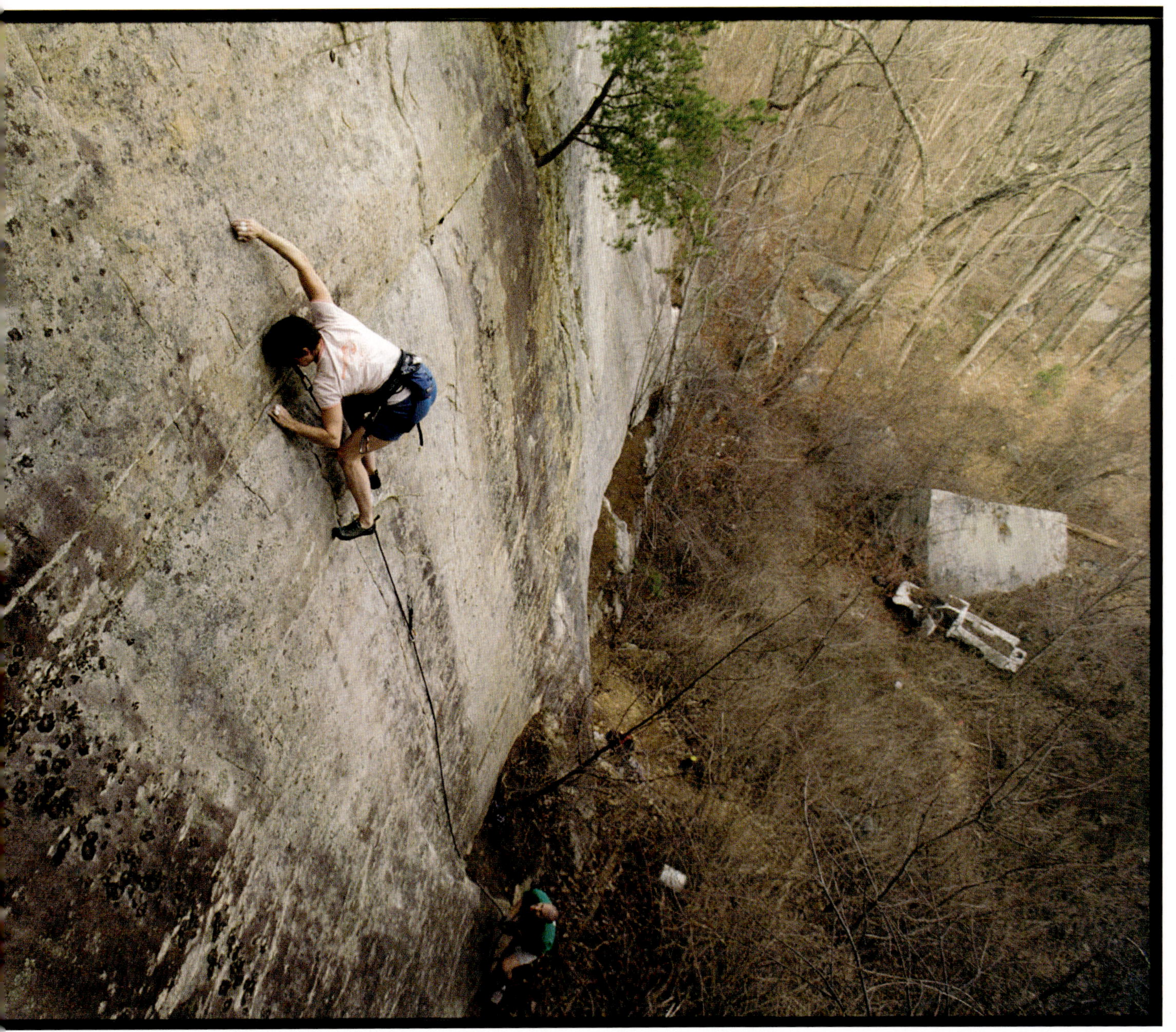

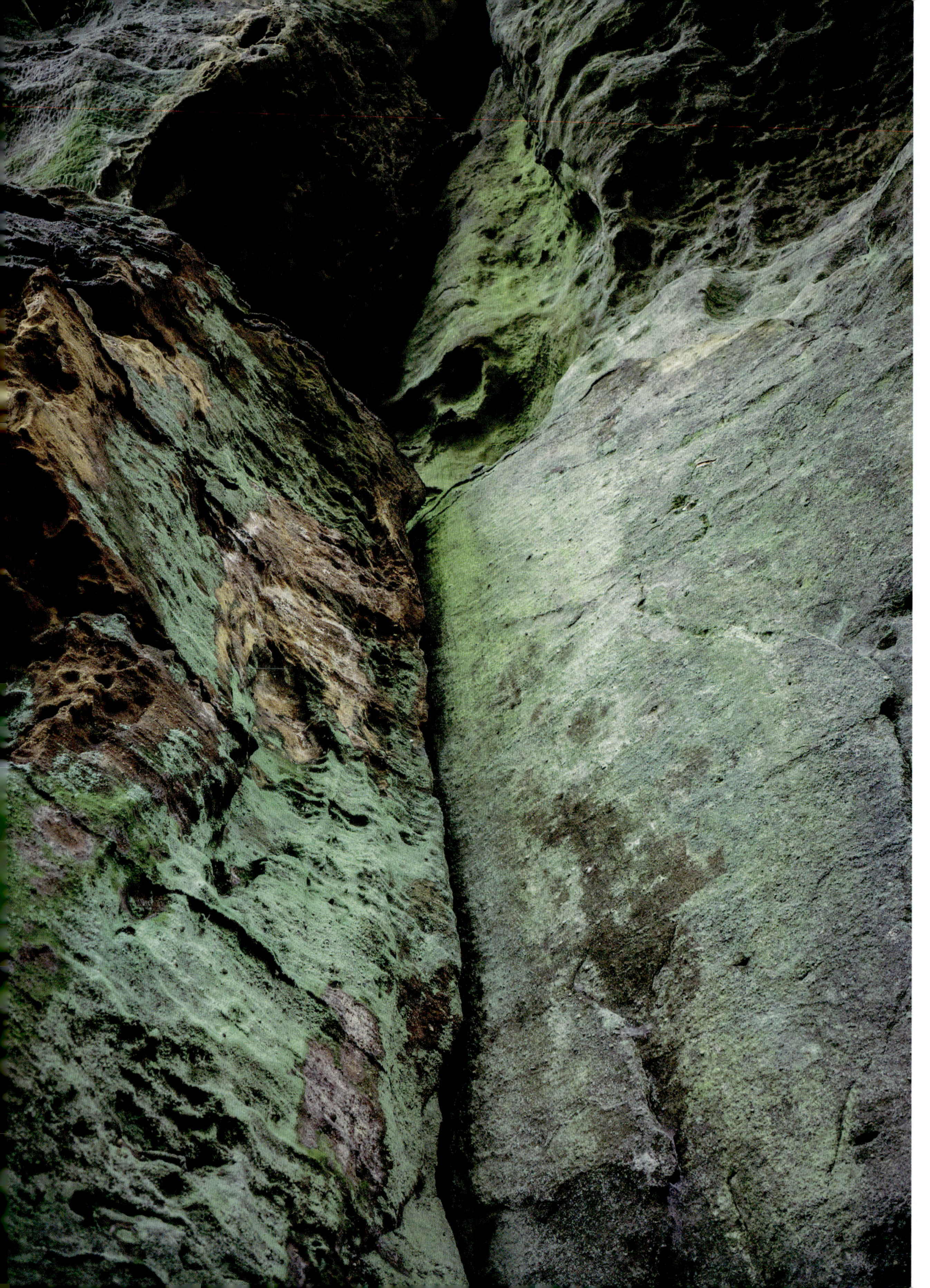

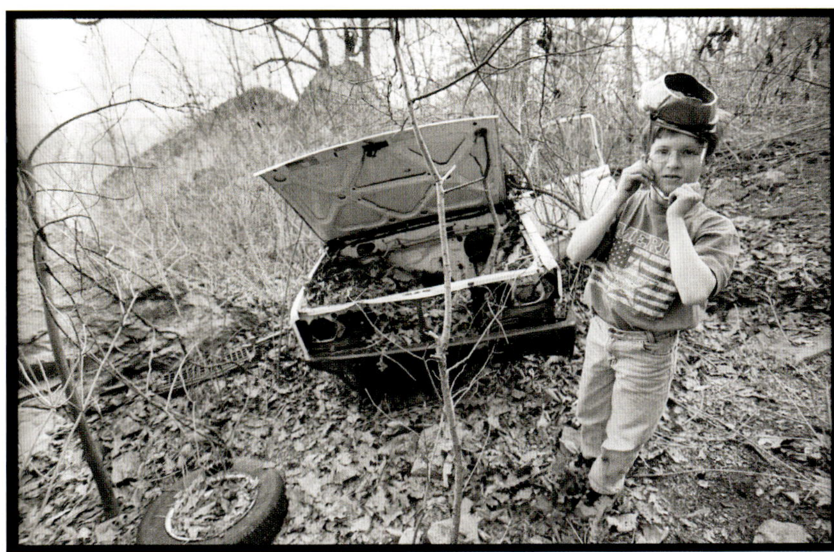

Ian Connell exploring a junked car at the base of the cliffs, Jamestown, Alabama

Corner, Zahnd Wildlife Management Area, Georgia

Opposite: Corner, Big South Fork National River and Recreation Area, Tennessee

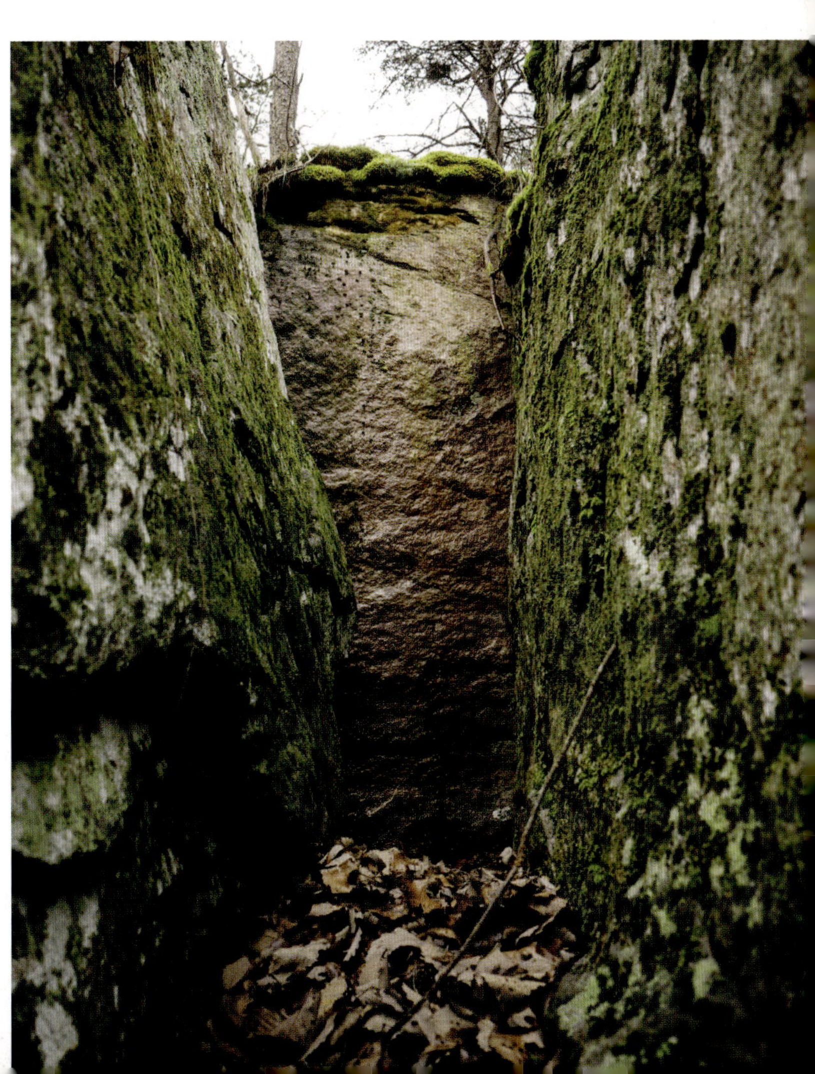

Greg Kottkamp on *Apes on Acid* (5.13d), Castle Rock, Tennessee

GO FOR IT, MAN!

The hike up to the Tennessee Wall gives you a lot of time to think as you wind steadily upward from the banks of the Tennessee River through a beautiful forest dotted with enormous boulders that have tumbled from above, slowly but occasionally violently shaping the river gorge. Only half a mile long but decidedly uphill, the walk is just hard enough to get you warmed up for the day ahead. It's a standard unit of measure for Southern climbing approaches (as in "Two T-Walls plus a stream crossing"), made a little harder by the fact that you've got a full climbing rack and maybe an extra rappel rope in your backpack. In January 1999, I was hauling that plus a camera kit, so I took my sweet time.

I plodded alone up the trail, contemplating the day ahead. The Chattanooga area is full of great climbing areas, but the Tennessee Wall is probably the most *important*, in the sense that spending time there is imperative for anyone looking to call themselves a Southern climber. Just like the approach, the climbs are also standards by which others are measured. Climbs like *Stone Wave* or *Finger Locking Good* are not only benchmarks of traditional Southern sandstone but also good training for destination climbing trips to the Utah desert or Yosemite. The sheer variety of routes at T-Wall means there is something for everyone, from classic moderates to some of the greatest free-climbable roofs in North America. No matter how hard you climb, you'd better have at least a dozen T-Wall ascents under your belt. After a couple of visits, I had my bona fides, which meant I either had to spend the day repeating routes in my comfort zone or step it up and try harder—or riskier—ones. I was in no rush to get ahead of myself, so I was set on repeating the moderates.

By bringing my camera along, I could always reason that I was there to take photos, not push myself on harder climbs. It may have been Harrison Shull who told me once, "You can either climb hard or take good photos, not both at the same time." In fact, he may have shared that the first time we met at the Tennessee Wall. He also reprimanded me for hanging on a single bolt to take photos of *Hands Across America* and for letting my dog wander leashless toward his sandwich while I did it. Shull was a legend of both photography and climbing of course, so I didn't believe a word of his warning, but later I decided he was entirely correct about all of it.

As the golden cliff line of the Tennessee Wall came into view, I was mostly thinking of the photographs I would take of a climber named Jerry Roberts, whom I'd met the night before in Atlanta. We'd sketched out plans to meet up here in the morning.

▶

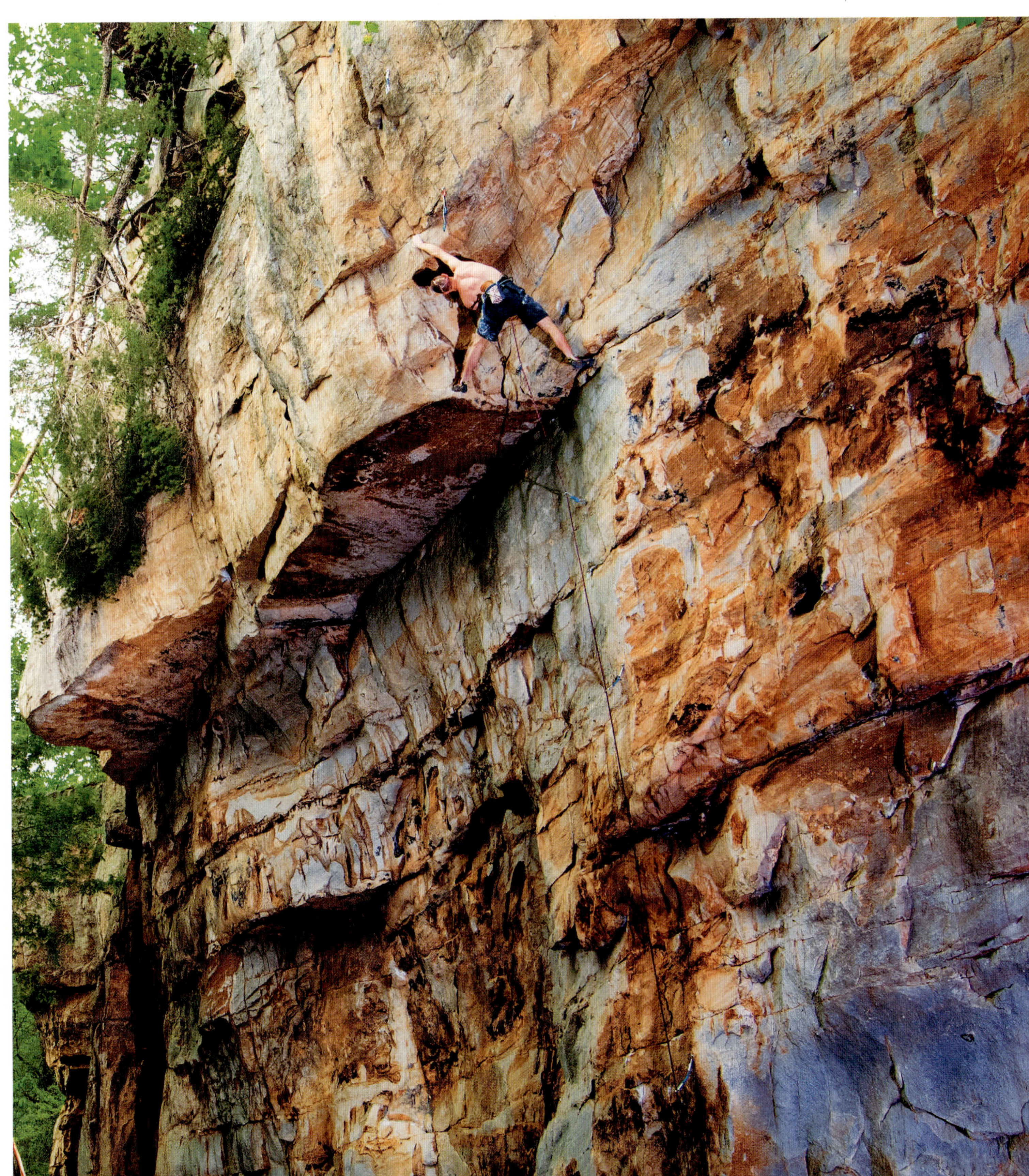

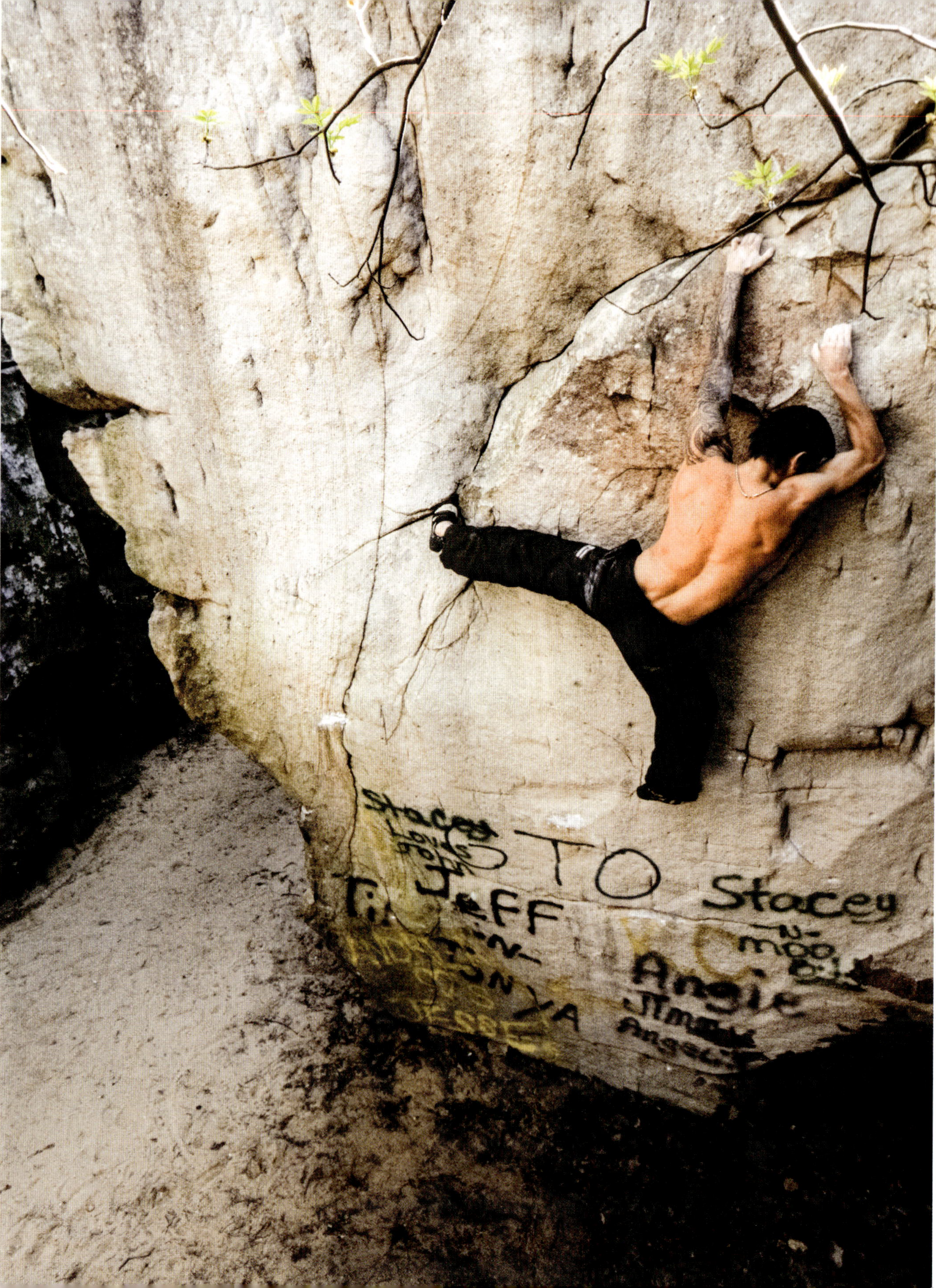
TO
Stacey
Angie

At the base of the cliff, I dropped my loaded pack below a wide crack and heard a commotion in the trees a hundred feet above. A fit bald dude in a muscle shirt was leaning out over the cliff from a tree limb. Loose pebbles and pine needles rained over the cliff edge from under his approach shoes. "Andrew?" he yelled down. "Be there in a sec!" He swung himself onto the rock, down-climbing a nearby line without a harness or rope, stopping here and there to traverse and inspect other features. A minute later he appeared at my side, dusting off his pants, and extended his hand with a cracked grin. "Hey man, I'm Jerry. Just warming up, checking out some climbs." He squinted up at *Golden Locks*, the 5.8 crack that he'd just free soloed down. It was the climb I had stopped under, thinking it would be a good one for me to start on.

"You've probably done this one a million times, right?" He gestured down the trail. "Ever done *Fly with the Falcon*?"

I looked over toward the line in question. Low, tiered roofs lead up to a dark, asterisk-shaped crux. If you make it past there, you're climbing a flaring, technical crack until the very end—only fifty feet long, but legendarily stout. The 5.11-rated climb was harder than anything I'd led on gear. I hesitated for a moment, and Jerry filled the silence. "Let's go do it! I'll give you all the beta."

Chris Sierzant on *GTO* (V7), Sand Rock, Alabama

After just a few tries, Jerry coached me up *The Falcon*. It was as burly as I expected, but somehow Jerry's presence and encouragement had defanged it for me psychologically. I redpointed it—climbed it from the ground up on gear without falling. From there he was focused on pushing me up ever-harder climbs. Time seemed to slow and expand at the same time, and I forgot all about taking photos. By the end of the day, we'd done a half dozen hard routes together. I'd even led *Mrs. Socrates*, a 5.12 testpiece I had no business on.

Then again, I probably had no business roping up all day with Jerry Roberts at all. A traveling hardman on the prowl for the latest climbing testpieces, he had just gotten back from Yosemite, where he had quietly climbed the second ascent of *Peace*, Ron Kauk's world-famous 5.13d face climb in Tuolumne Meadows. It wasn't in the news; he just mentioned it in passing. Many of the South's hardest routes have his name attached to them. Some are still undone projects, breadcrumbs for next generation of go-getters to follow.

No one was happier to hear about the completion of a Jerry Roberts project than Jerry himself. He loved sharing a new climbing discovery and wanted you to experience them first-hand. "Got a big-ass new untapped climbing area up here!" he would email me. "Come on!!" That was how it went with Jerry. When you were out climbing with him, you weren't watching, you were *doing*. In between, Jerry wanted to know all about my work, my life, and my goals, and he offered up stoke for all of them, encouraging me to get out of my comfort zone and "Go for it, man!" He scrubbed clean the moss that had been gathering on my life objectives and forced me to start rolling them stones *faster*.

Jerry died suddenly in 2020 after suffering a heart attack. It was a sad day for Southern climbing and the end of an era, but his spirit remains. Above all, Jerry was motivated by the future, the seemingly limitless potential of climbing on the Southern horizon. "I used to think I had seen it all around here and there was nothing else that would be really inspiring," he once wrote. "It's so nice to find, however, that the best is still to come." ◆

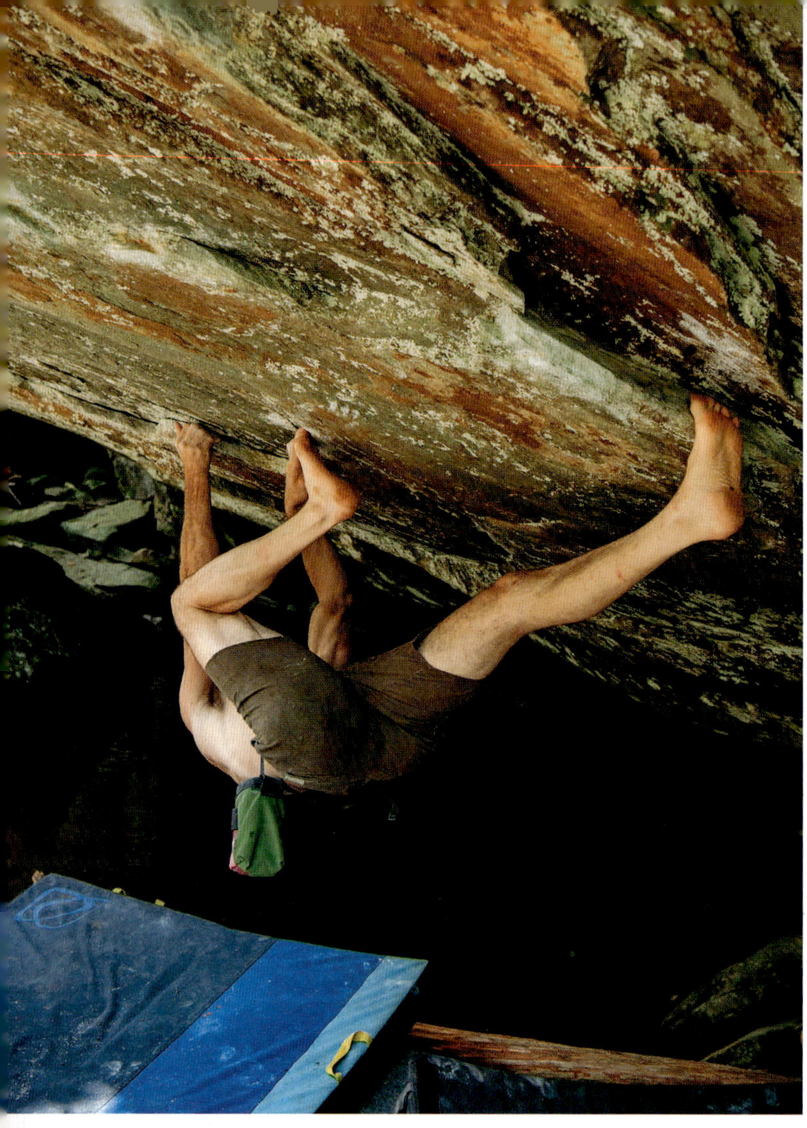

Joey Henson in the Linville Gorge, North Carolina

Rock formation at Zahnd Wildlife Management Area, Georgia

Opposite: Greg Kottkamp at Horse Pens 40 Ranch, Alabama

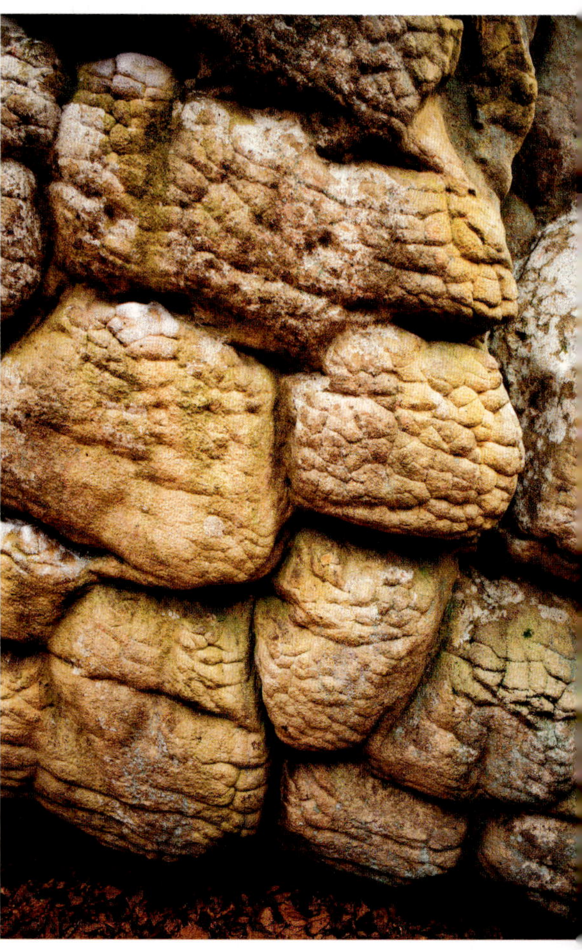

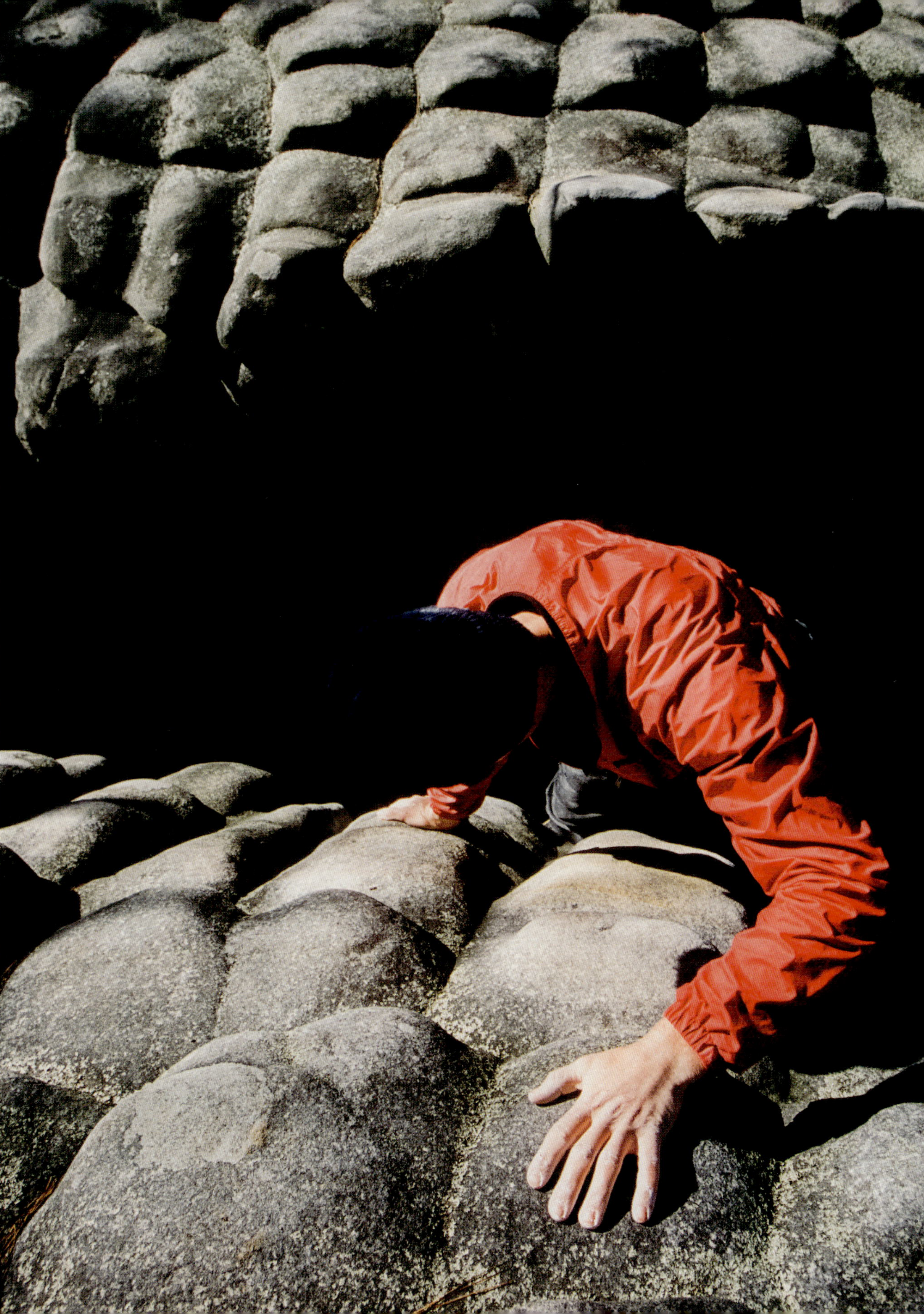

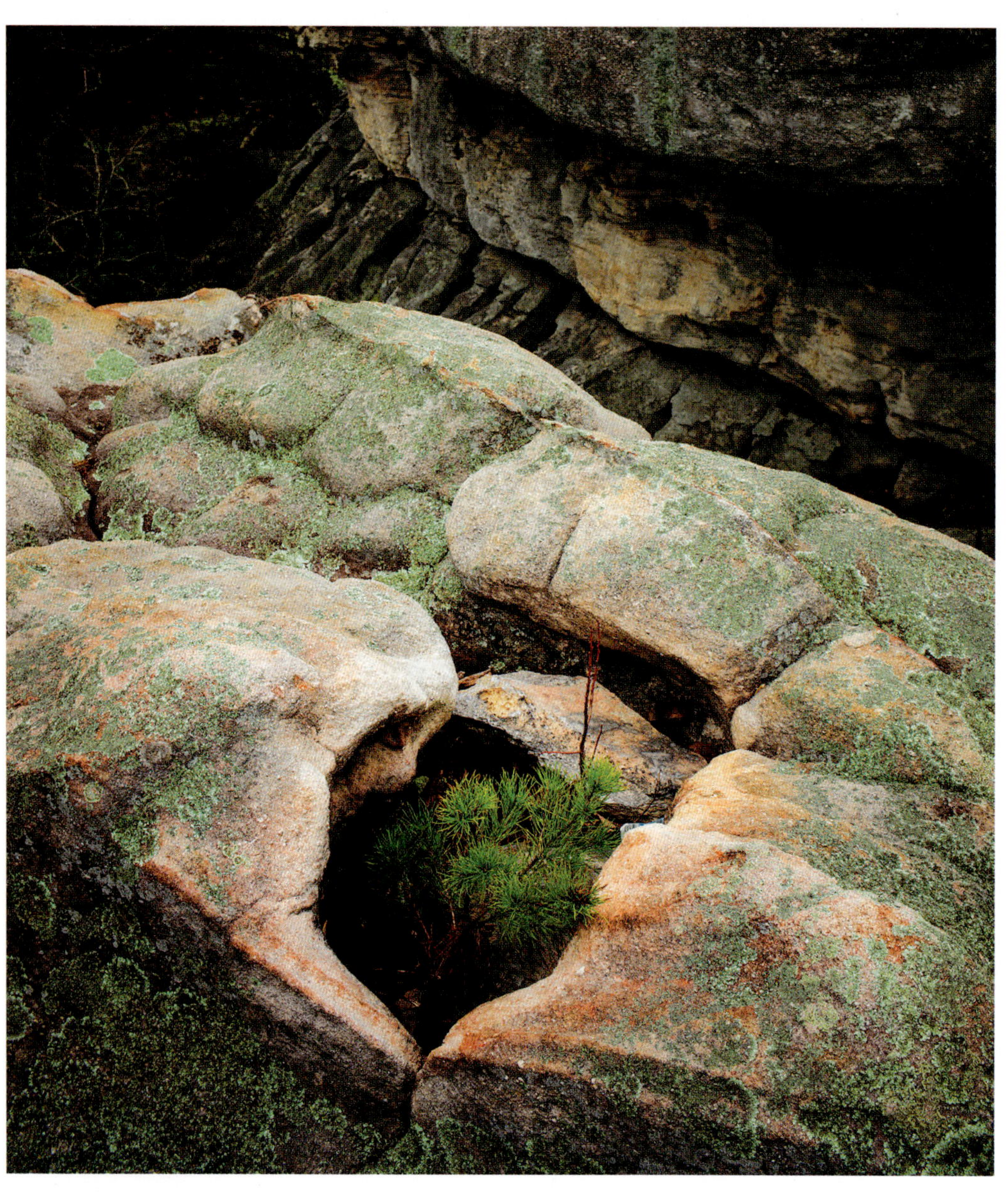

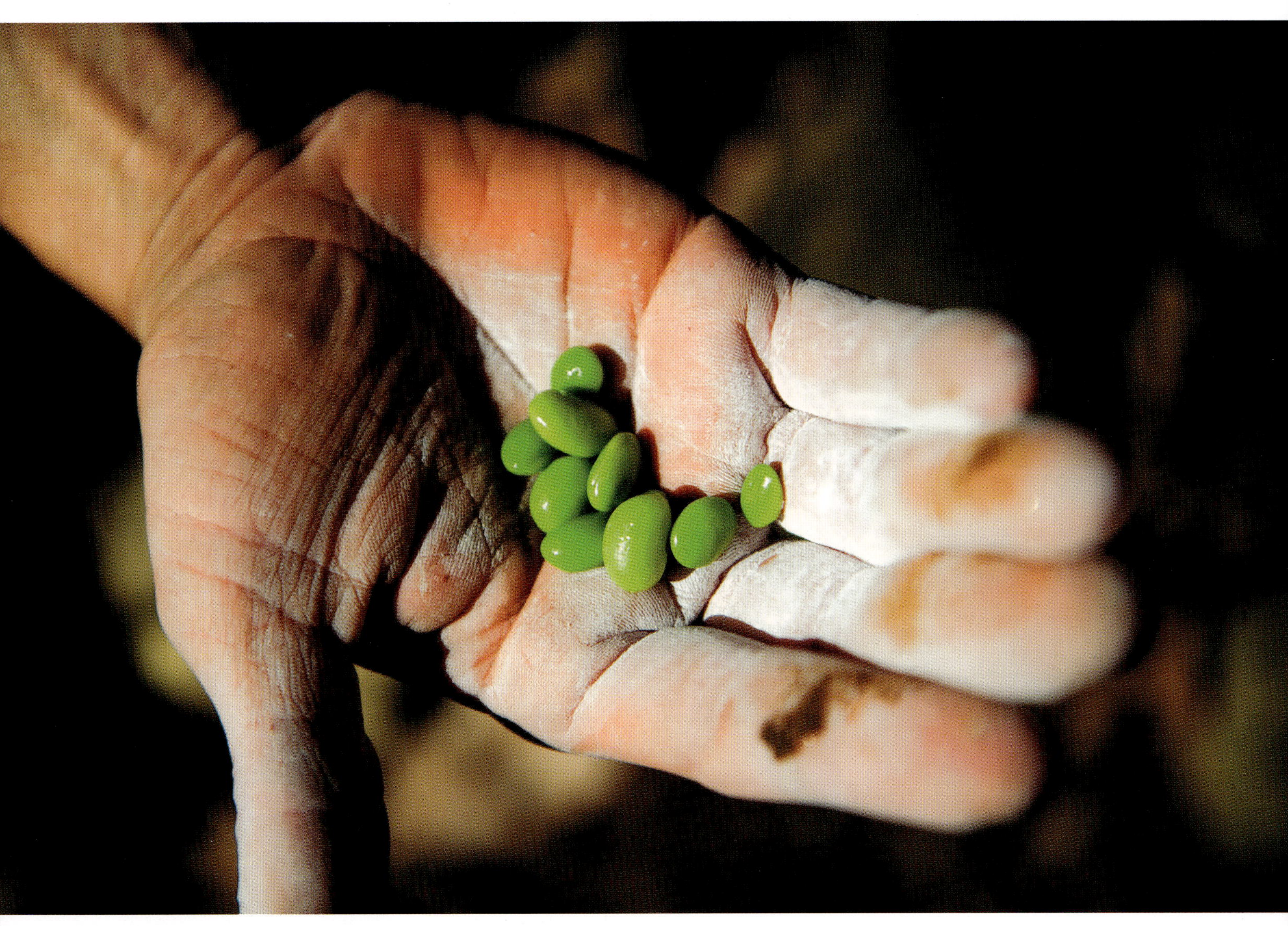

Opposite: Pine seedling in Zahnd Wildlife Management Area, Georgia

Greg Kottkamp holding edamame, Mount Yonah, Georgia

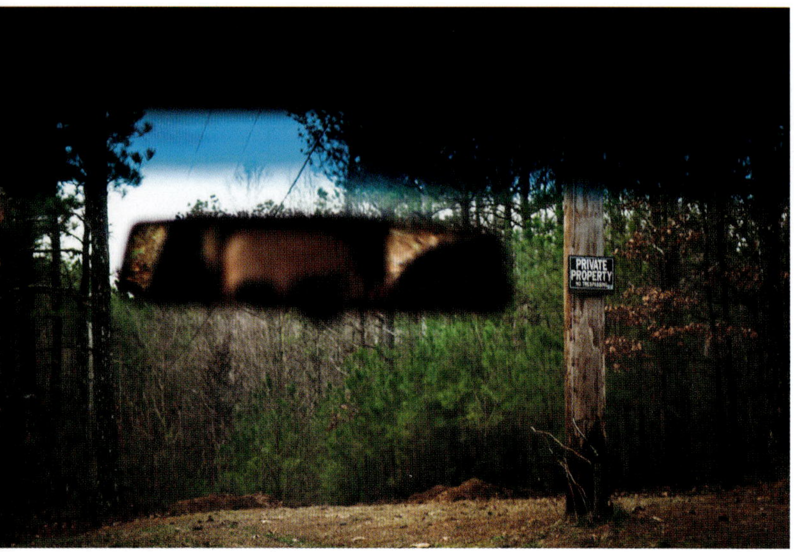

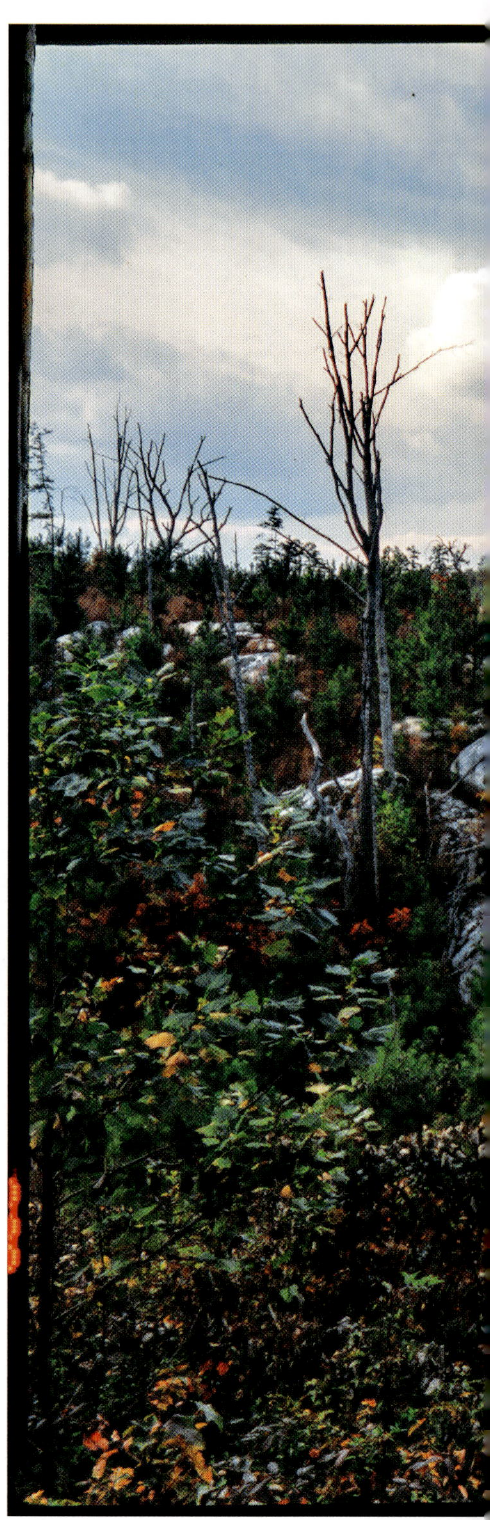

Josh Fowler in Alabama

Opposite: Clear-cut in Oneonta, Alabama

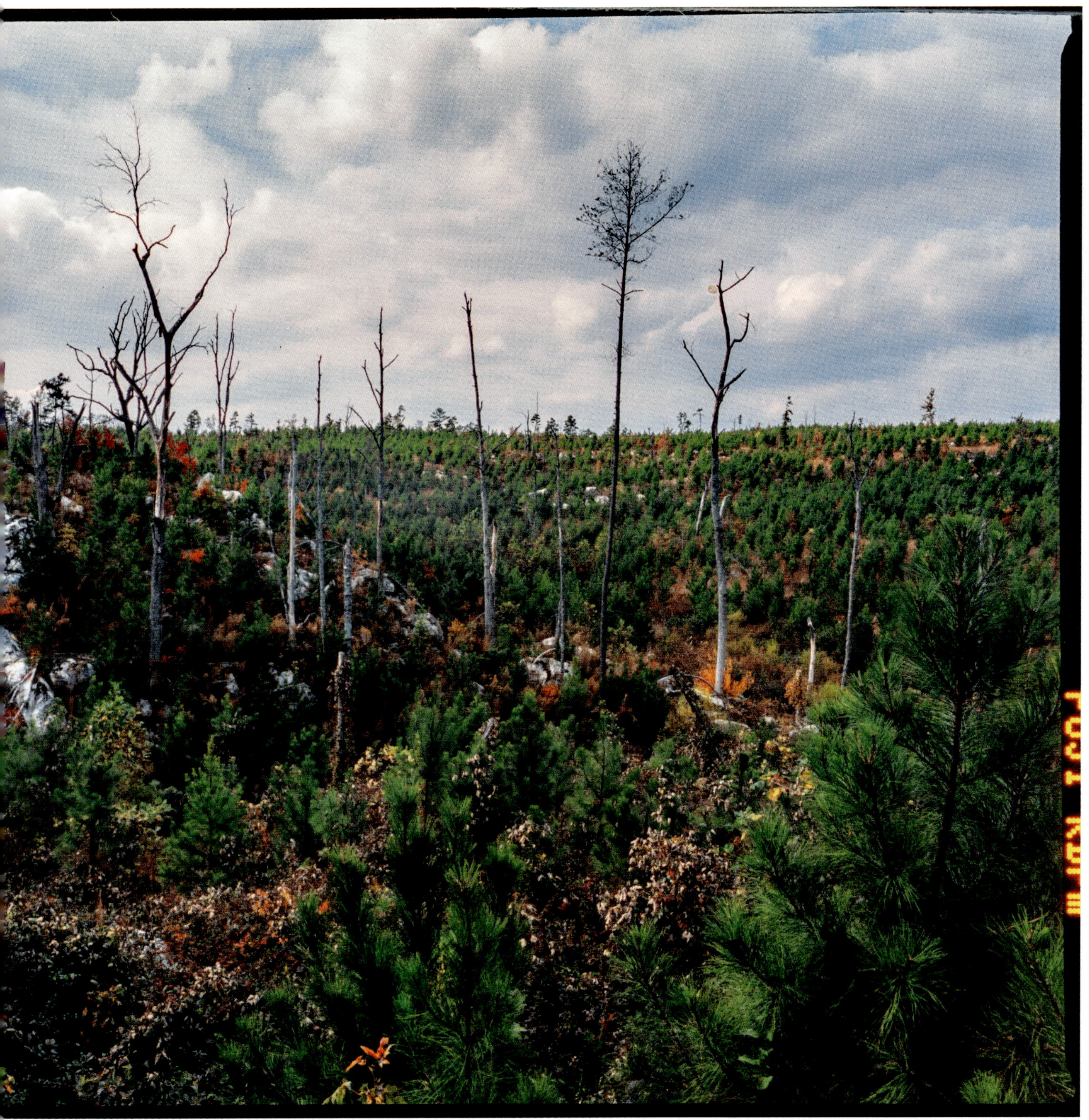

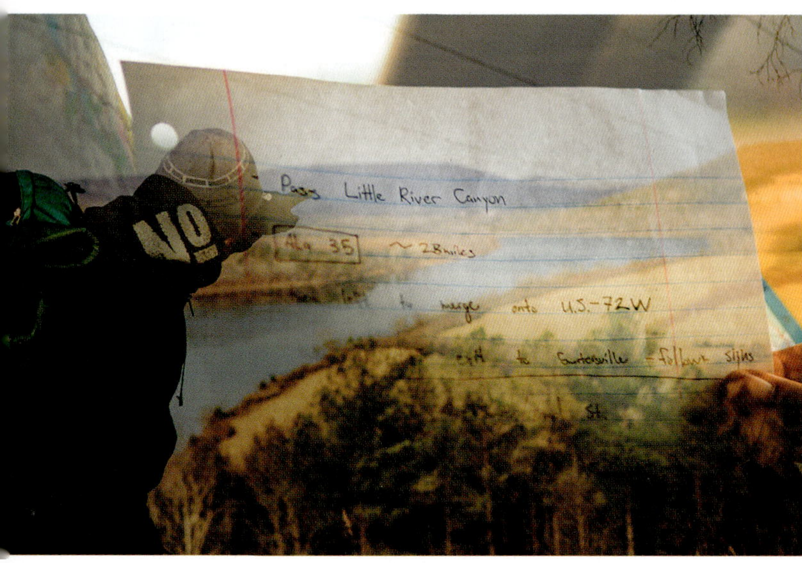

Greg Kottkamp on the hunt for unclimbed rock in Alabama

Josh Fowler and Greg Kottkamp in Alabama

Opposite: Steven Farmer and Anthony Meeks exploring the cliffs of Tennessee's Nickajack Lake by boat

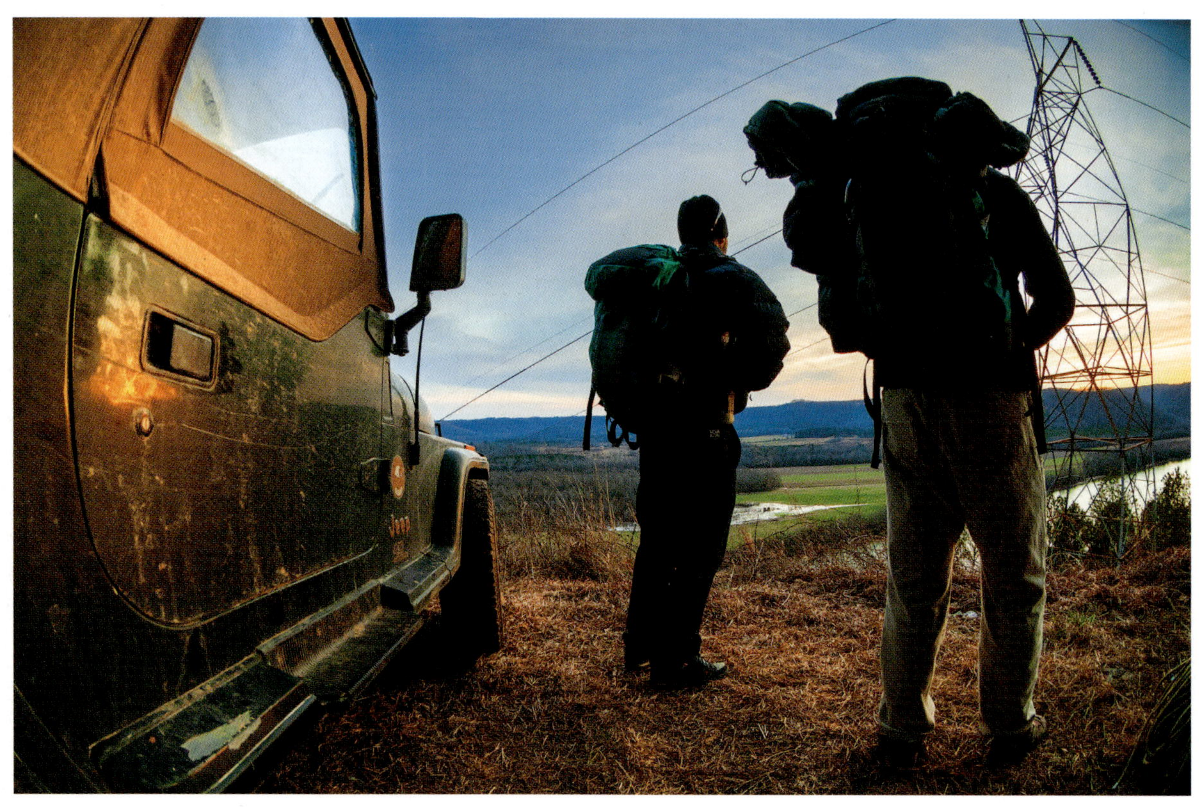

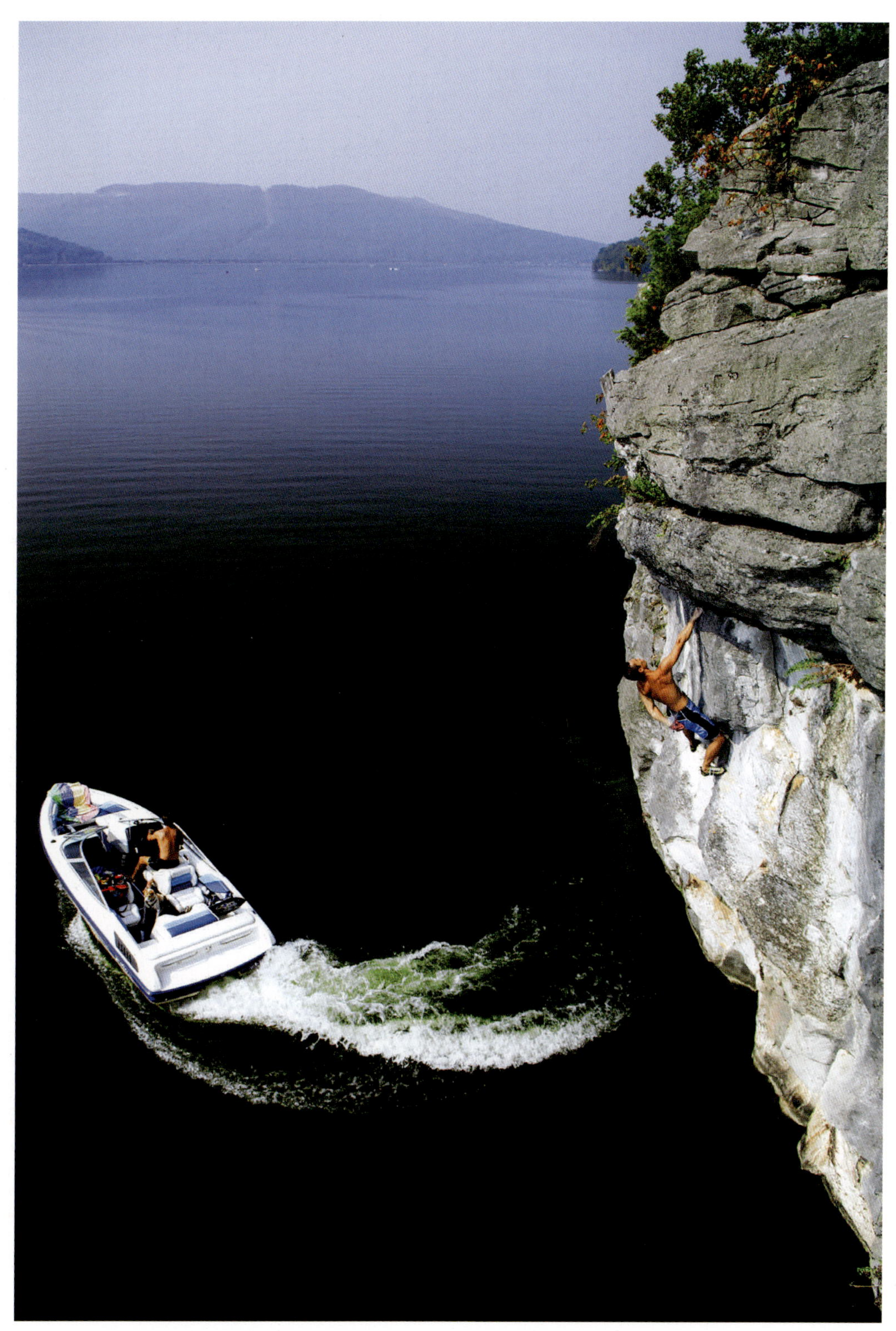

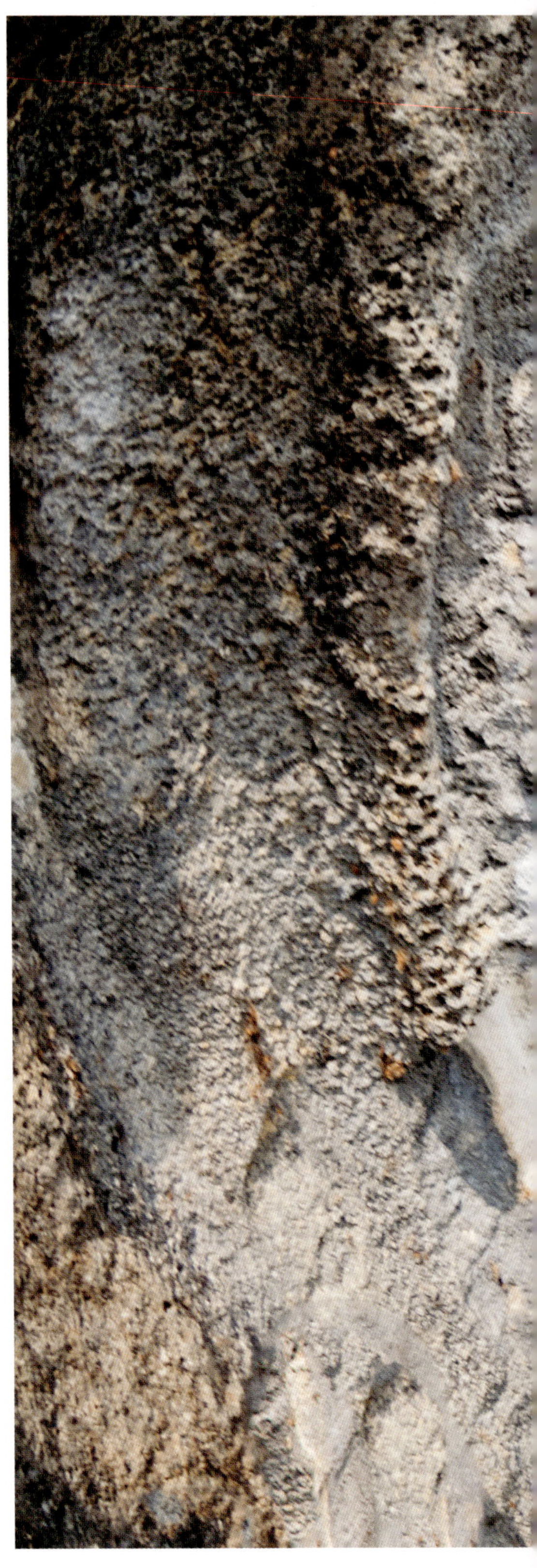

Anthony Meeks above
Nickajack Lake,
Tennessee

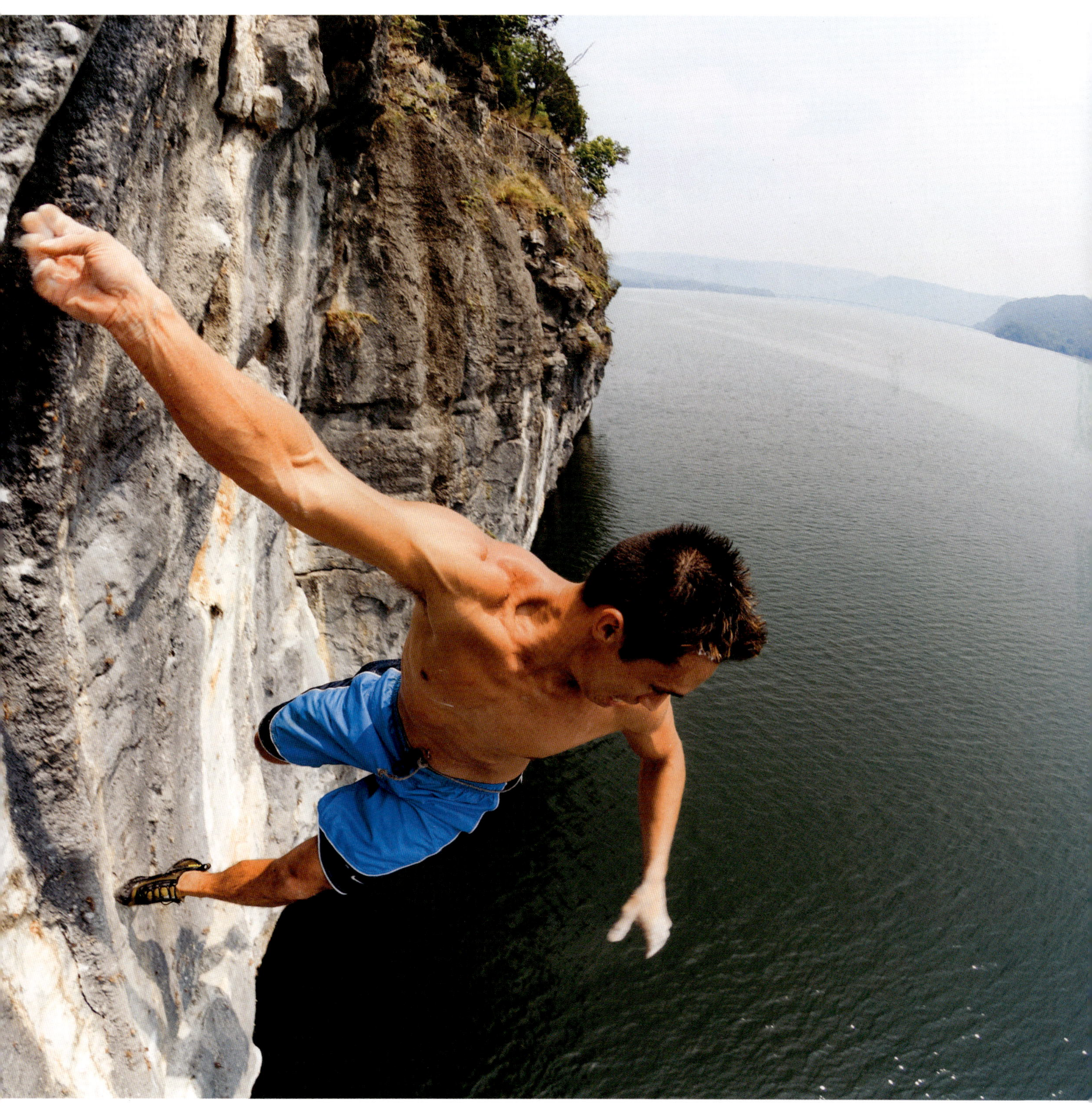

Winter at Georgia's Cloudland Canyon State Park

Opposite: Howard Shultz at Horse Pens 40 Ranch in Alabama

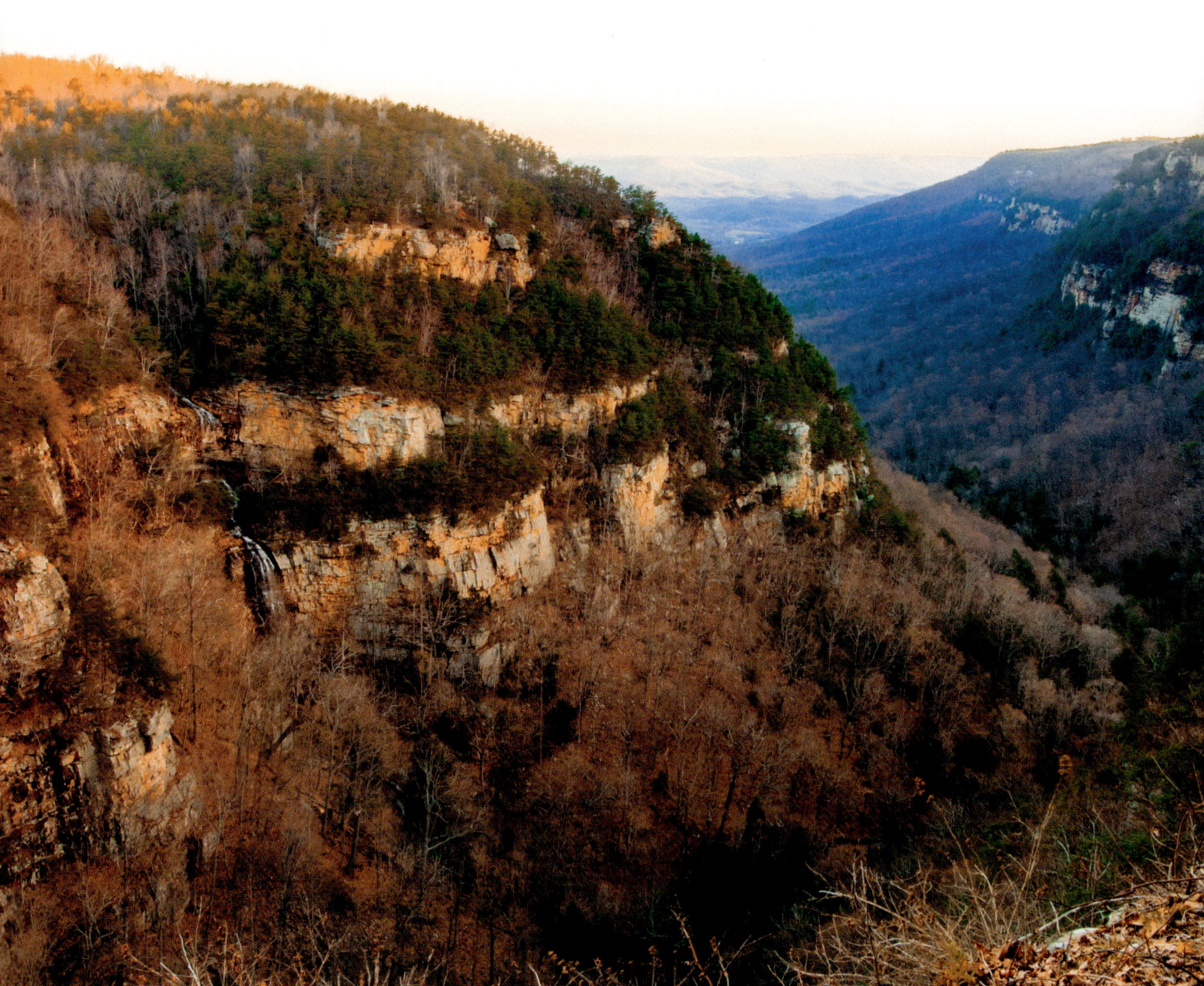

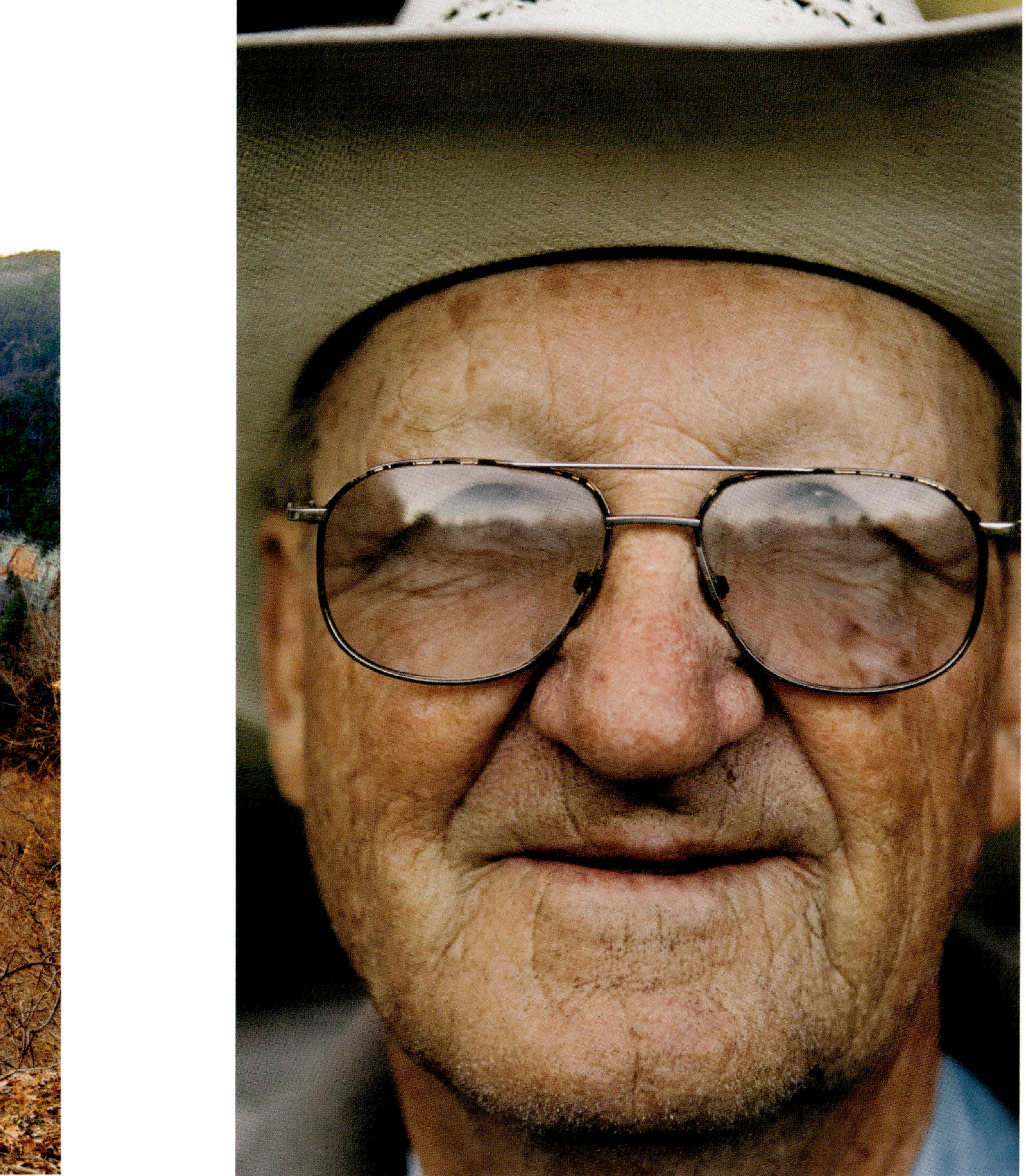

POTENTIAL ENERGY

When most people think of rock climbing, they envision a person scaling a sheer rock face using only their hands and feet, metal gear dangling from their waist harness. A rope tied to their harness trails down to a partner below—the belayer. If the climber falls, the rope will go taut, anchored to the rock at the highest point of "protection," where the climber has clipped the rope through a carabiner affixed to some kind of camming device or other metal gear wedged into a crack that can be removed later. That's traditional "free climbing." Pull on the gear to make upward progress, it's "aid climbing." Take away the rope and protection, it's "free soloing." Do it closer to the ground without any gear, it's "bouldering."

Traditional free climbing is the style most climbers strive for when tackling unclimbed walls in the modern era. A team starts from the ground and follows a natural path or "line" of cracks and features to use for both climbing and points of protection. After some number of attempts (the fewer the better), they finally climb the whole thing without falling, leaving no trace of their passing, and call it a "first ascent" in the best style. Often, difficult lines are pioneered as aid climbs, with the eventual goal of eliminating as much aid as possible until the line could be free climbed. American climbers of the 1960s and '70s were at the forefront of this style. In 1975, the trio of John Long, John Bachar, and Ron Kauk free-climbed the thousand-foot crack line *Astroman* in Yosemite Valley in California and helped popularize climbing as a hardcore pursuit that matched the social ethics of the time.

Opposite: Zack Pitts on *Hands Across America* (5.12c/d) Tennessee Wall, Tennessee

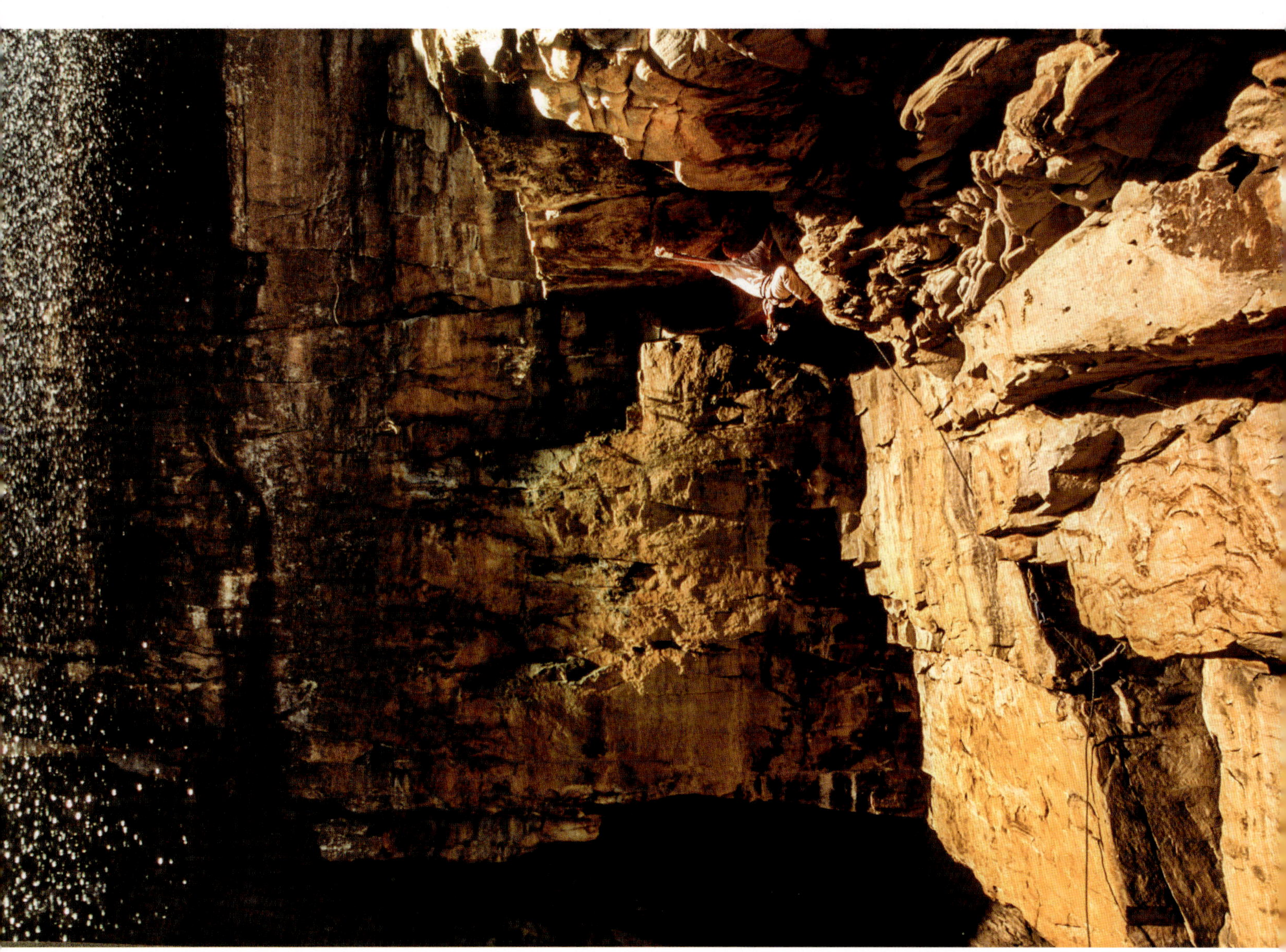

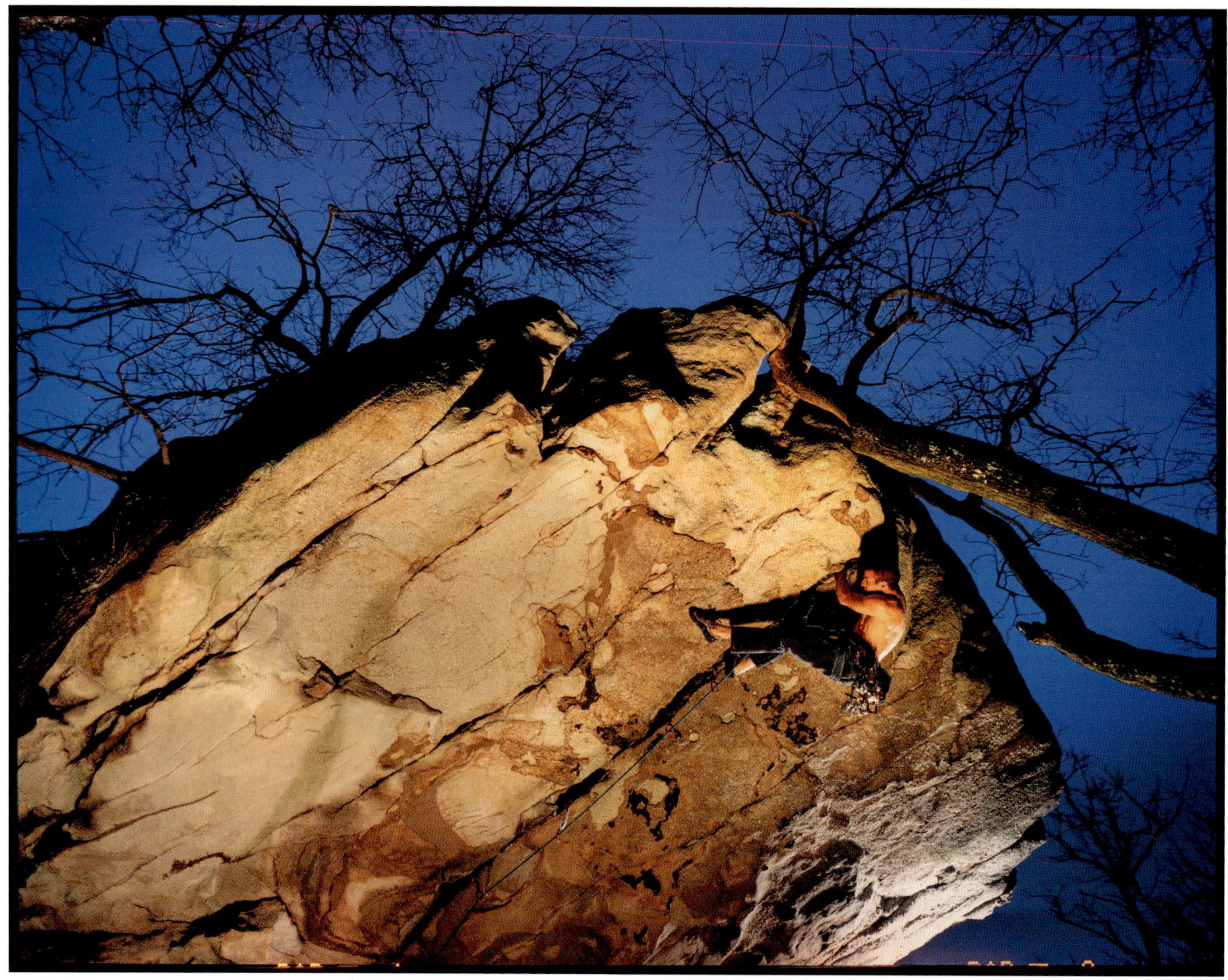

David Paulete on *Champagne Jam* (5.12d), Sand Rock, Alabama

The quest for free-climbing difficulty led climbers to steeper and steeper protectable lines, culminating in the ultimate challenge for the traditional free climber: the roof crack. The Yosemite roof crack *Separate Reality*, free climbed in 1978 by Ron Kauk, became recognized around the world as the icon of the new extreme, but it was on Southern sandstone that some of the biggest, baddest roof cracks were quietly being explored.

Granite of the kind found in Yosemite and the crags of other western mountain states is often split by climbable cracks, but they are rarely steeper than a few degrees off vertical—which is why *Separate Reality* is so cool. Limestone is awesomely steep, but it rarely forms naturally protectable crack features. The fine-grained and uniform sandstone formations of the Southwest are broken into canyons by the slow expansion of subterranean salt layers. Further eroded by the wind and clockwork freeze and thaw cycles, the resulting walls are split by parallel cracks of all sizes, and even arches and bridges, but the rock tends to be otherwise featureless and more brittle. In the South, the rock is just right.

The conglomerate-rich Pennsylvanian-age sandstone that dominates the Southern Appalachians is very hard and highly textured. Unlike out West, the underlying layers here are a mix of limestones and shale rock. In a temperate climate, those will erode quicker than the overlying sandstone. As the sandstone's Lego-like blocks are exposed, pushed up, and broken, the elements find a way underneath, hollowing out caves and voids. The resulting collapses are part of a dynamic weathering process, yielding this beautifully chaotic jumble of rock walls and ledges that are split by myriad cracks—*especially* roof cracks.

Roof crack climbing involves strange techniques and physical suffering to appall and delight climbers and non-climbers alike. "Under a roof," wrote former *Climbing* magazine editor and Southern rock connoisseur Jeff Achey, "you don't climb up or down. There is no change in potential energy. Yet it's some of the most physical type of climbing, moving your body upside-down along a natural line." Shielded from the elements, roof cracks are dark, dirty, and spider-filled. Even to the seasoned climber, it's a wild affair.

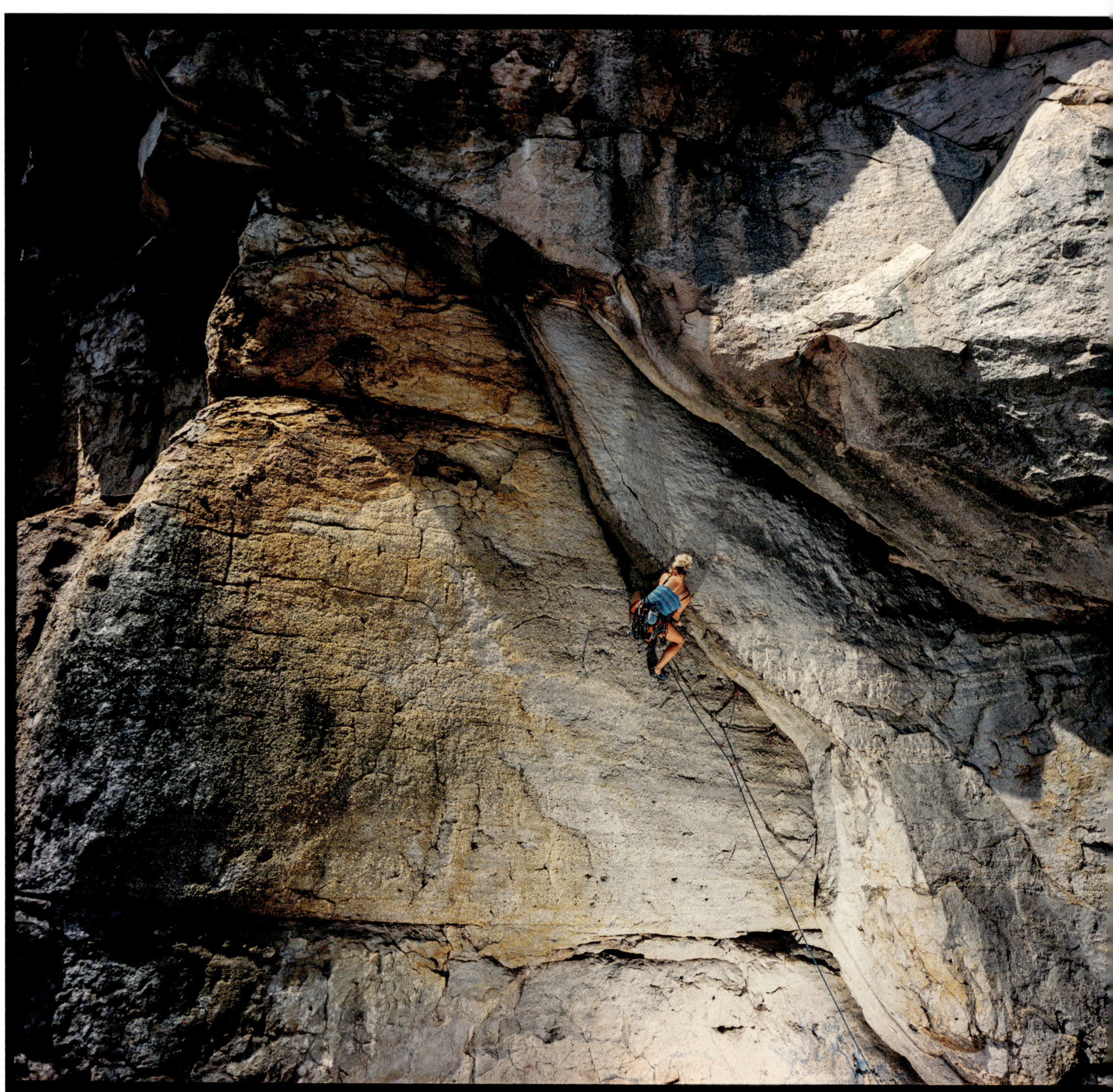

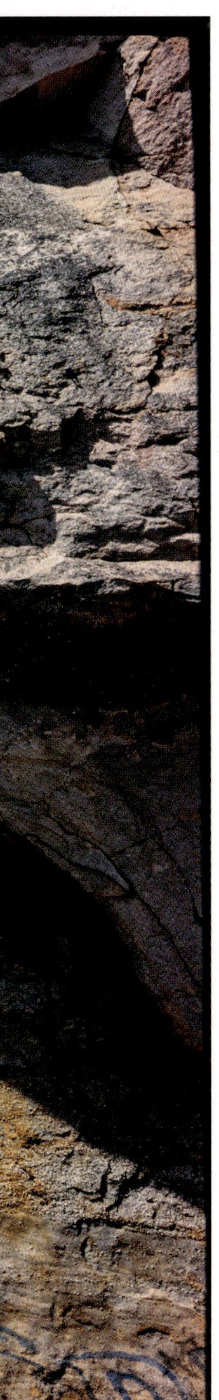

Jennifer Jenkins on *Sandburger* (5.10), Sand Rock, Alabama

A roof crack is sort of the mark of honor for a Southern cliff line. With nearly a dozen recorded roof crack climbs, it's no surprise that the Tennessee Wall is considered the "crown jewel" of Chattanooga climbing. Rob Robinson's Tennessee Wall "Triple Crown" of roof cracks—*Fists of Fury*, *Celestial Mechanics*, and *Hands Across America*, all rated 5.12c—have drawn countless traditional climbing masters, including most recently Kathy Karlo, who in 2018 and 2019 achieved a rare repeat of all three. Hidetaka Suzuki, Lynn Hill, and Tim Toula have all made their mark with first ascents or repeats of monster Southern roofs. These climbs make a deep impression.

Even a humble climbing area can be put on the map by a good roof crack. Sand Rock is a small, rough-and-tumble area in Alabama, much maligned by marauding four-wheelers and spray paint. Still, it's one of my favorites, with tons of great climbing—and then there's *Champagne Jam*. This iconic and brutal thirty-foot roof crack was first free-climbed in 1982 by Greg Collins, who said that the pebbles lodged in the crack rained down on his bare chest "like champagne bubbles." Some time later, during a quick tour through the area, western crack master Steve Petro swept through Sand Rock. He climbed the hand-eating fissure on his first go, and when no one wanted to follow, he down-climbed it back to the base without falling.

For all his prolific finds, Robinson is still haunted by what might have been right around the corner. "I've walked hundreds of miles of cliffs," he told me, "driven by the hope that, if I just keep walking, I might find an ultimate dihedral or a huge, perfectly formed roof crack or overhanging crack. *Keep hiking*. That was my modus operandi. That mother of all lines is just around the next corner."

I keep a list of these roof cracks, including rumors and unfinished lines: *Human Chew Toy, Fat Man in a Bathtub, Tennessee Tai Chi, Gilgamesh.* This last one may be one of the biggest confirmed roof cracks in the South at forty feet long, finally free-climbed in 2012 by Arno Ilgner. He remembers stumbling across it in the late 1990s with Glenn Ritter. "We were just walking along Daddy's Creek looking for new rock, and I particularly like roof cracks. So when we found that one, we didn't walk any further." It took Arno fifteen years to get back to it. "I had other projects, building a business, and well, to be honest, the climb is kind of intimidating! It's technically three pitches. The first pitch is a hundred feet of climbing, then the roof is forty feet long, then it's another thirty-foot pitch to get to the top." Arno worked the gaping roof crack move by move, pushing through fear and figuring out strange techniques for horizontal progress.

Routes like *Gilgamesh* are epic projects, requiring years of not only physical and technical training but also mental preparation. Arno's well-known book *The Rock Warrior's Way* focuses exactly on this type of journey of intelligent risk-taking, and alumni of his program include some of America's top climbers. *Gilgamesh* is a rare adventure that has all but disappeared in the last few decades.

The dominance of the roof crack as the pinnacle of free-climbing achievement began to fade with the widespread use of expansion bolts. These permanent pieces of protection had been used sparingly for emergencies or high-use anchors until the early 1980s, when European climbers began pioneering bolt-protected climbs on steep, blank limestone. Within a decade, climbers were bolt-protecting entire climbs as a matter of course. With bolts, you can climb almost anything safely, minimizing technical nutcraft and maximizing athleticism, and "sport climbing" changed the whole scene into something you might recognize in an indoor climbing gym. Today, the "state of the art" of free climbing is a blank wall—awesome climbing for sure, but visually somewhat sanitized. Over time, traditionally protected climbing fell out of fashion, and the remaining wild roof cracks of the South went unfinished and forgotten, their potential energy locked away for the next generation to rediscover. ◆

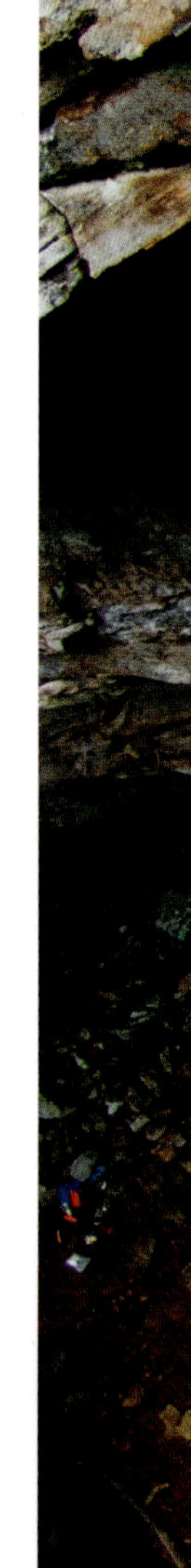

Anthony Meeks on *Wizzla* (5.13c), Chattanooga, Tennessee

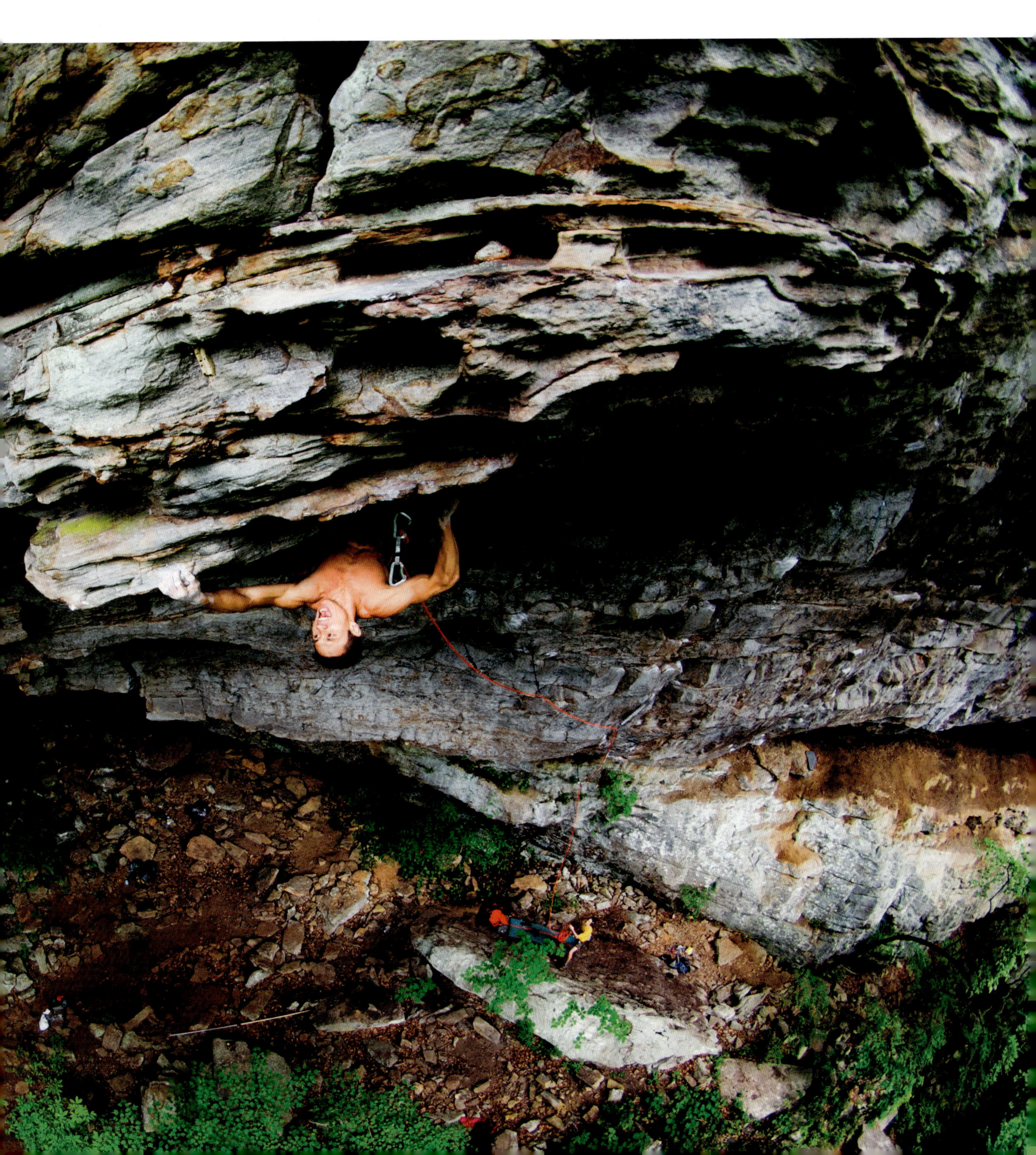

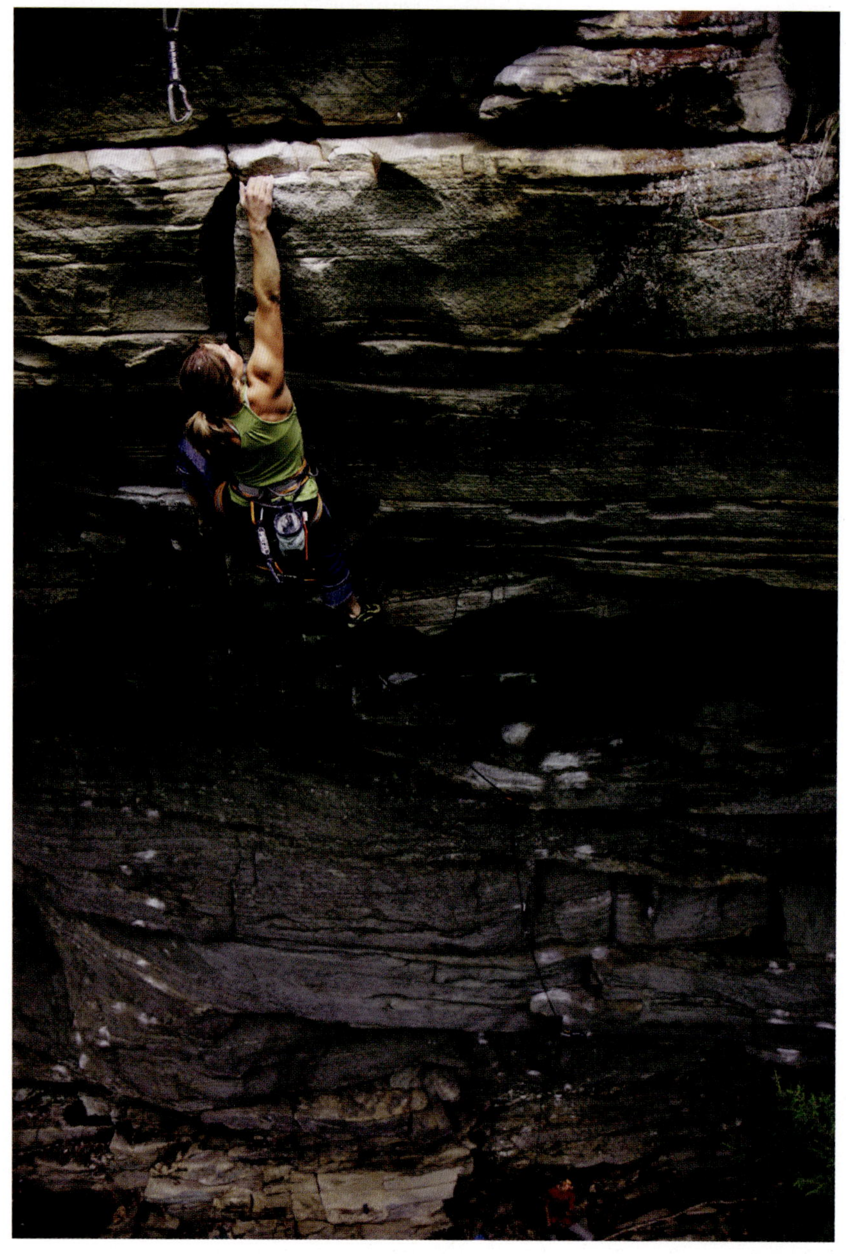

Whitney Boland on *Leakage* (5.12b), Deep Creek, Tennessee

Opposite: Katy Cook falls off *Bird Dog* (5.12) near Chattanooga, Tennessee

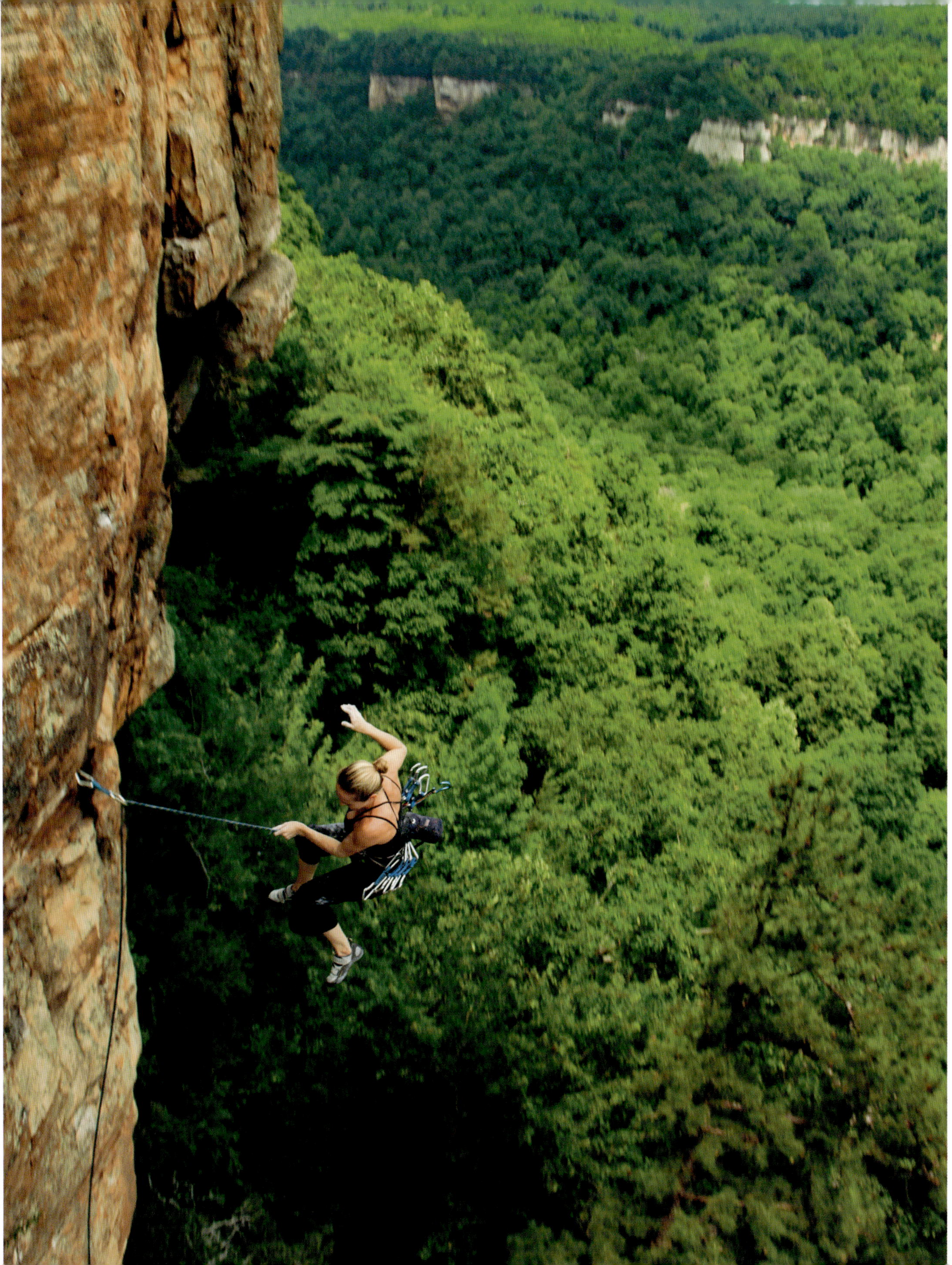

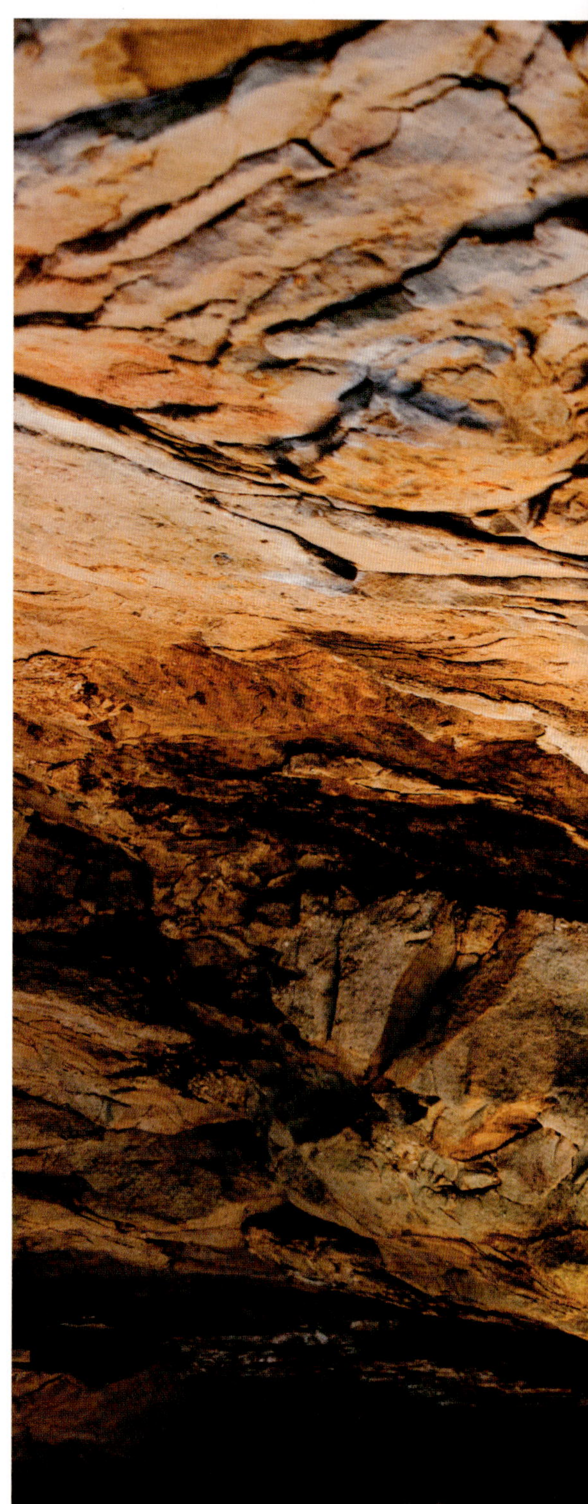

Rock shelter along the Rock Creek section of the Cumberland Trail in Tennessee

THE FIFTH ROOF

Everyone called him Big Wall Pete after the world-famous California wall master Pete Takeda. Our Big Wall Pete of the South, Pete Kovacevich was not as renowned, but he still had the bona fides to earn the nickname with some notable ascents under his belt, including a free ascent of the famed big wall free climb *Astroman*. Pete had just moved to Atlanta in the mid-1990s. Short and energetic with a Michigander accent and wit, he was an injection of energy and hilarity to the local gym scene. More importantly, he could "get out." His job designing aircraft interiors for wealthy jet-setters gave him a flexible schedule and some means to pursue weekday cragging. This made him a great partner for a freelance photographer.

Pete and I are about the same age, and we climbed about as hard in the gym, but Pete had that "real" climbing experience that I was hungry for. I use direct-aid techniques to get myself quickly up rock for photography, but I wanted to learn some more advanced techniques, like the kind you might use on a Yosemite multiday big wall adventure. I'd tried solo aid climbing before on some small walls like Allenbrook, a dusty, thirty-foot urban choss pile near Atlanta, but I needed Pete to coach me up some bigger lines.

We got out one Wednesday to Tennessee's Suck Creek Canyon, sans guidebook, and began scouting for just the right one to cut my teeth on. While walking the cliff line, we came to a section of steep wall with a wide crack system following one roof after another as far up as I could see.

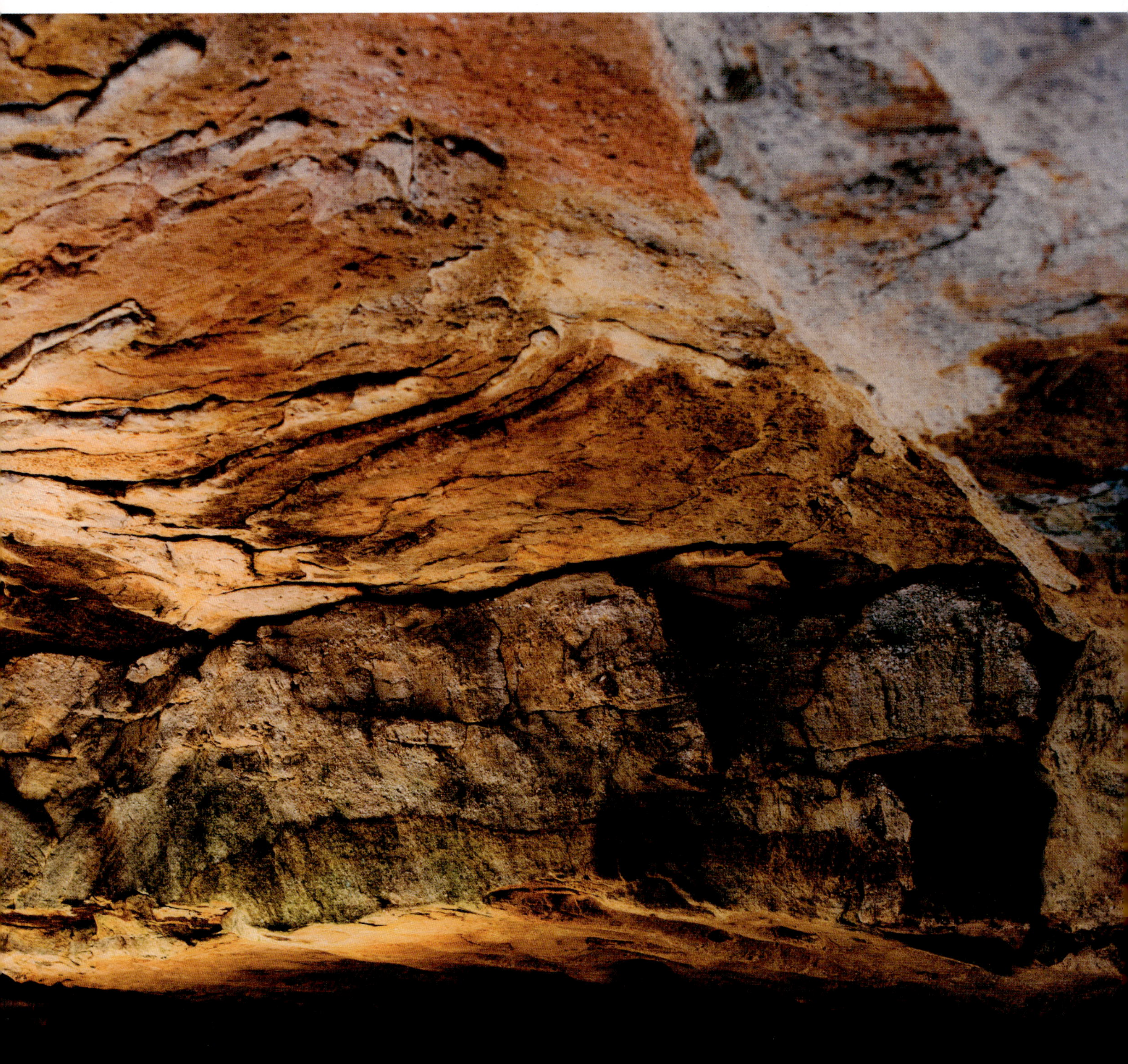

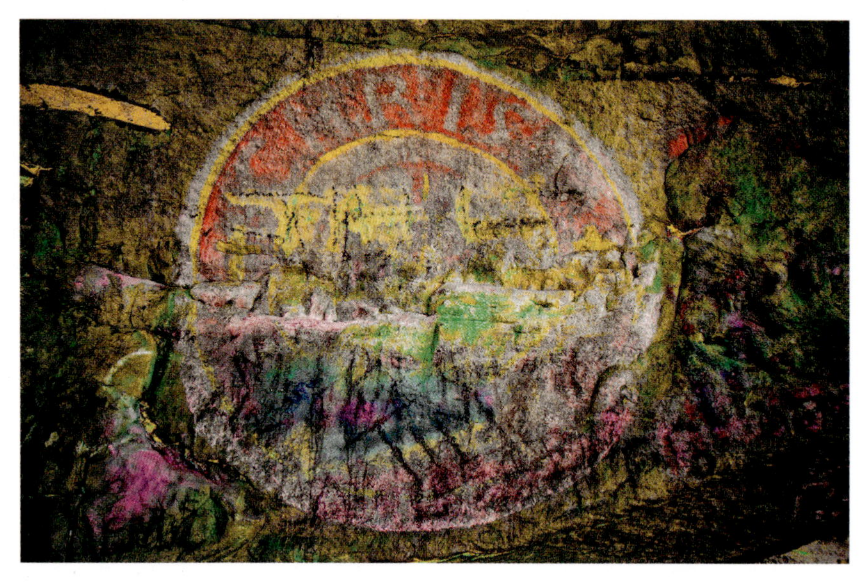

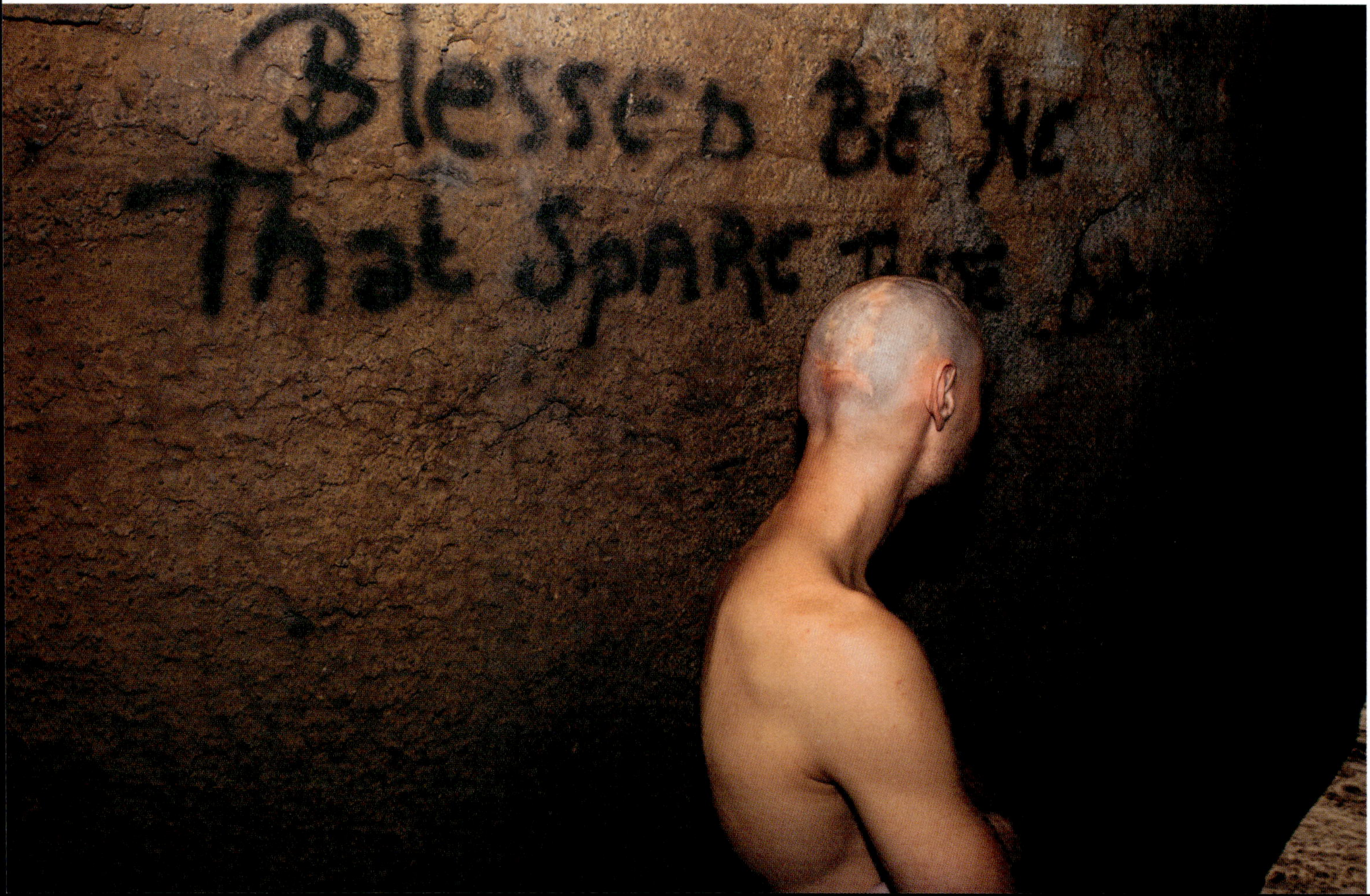

"Perfect. This one's for you, man!" Pete lit a cigarette and dropped his pack while I studied the line intently. It looked messy. It was at least a hundred feet high, and I couldn't see the top. I took a deep breath. "Alright, Pete," I said. "What do I do?"

Pete snarled at me, "Just take one step at a time, man! And stay in your aiders. *Don't start free climbing.*"

One step at a time. I could do that. I am the king of slow and methodical, and I had plenty of gear, still borrowed from a recent crack climbing trip to Utah's Indian Creek. I plugged a cam high into the rock, clipped my aiders to it, and stood up.

Slowly, I pulled roof after roof, the cracks gobbling up protection. Words of encouragement wafted up to me along with cigarette smoke, both getting fainter with distance. Two hours went by. I was well above the treetops now, and I'd lost sight of Pete. His stream of smoke and chatter had faded away. "Hey Pete! I'm out of cams!" I gave the rope a few tugs. Silence. *Was he asleep?* I looked up at what seemed to be the last roof: a dark, ominous slot.

There's something about moderate aid climbing that gets you real comfortable. You can't fall; you can only go up. Craning my neck, I could see the last fifteen feet after the roof seemed to be lower-angle rock. *Easy free climbing,* I thought. *Clear this last roof and it's smooth sailing.* I stood on a small ledge and placed my last cam to pull myself into the roof. It wasn't set very well in the crack, but I just needed it to help me reach over the lip. I searched blindly above the roof until my hand landed on a nice jug. I felt confident, casual even. "Hey Pete!" I yelled down. "I'm just gonna climb to the top from here!"

I grabbed the jug and crabbed my feet up, leaving my aiders behind. Pulling the last roof, I began free climbing—and immediately realized my mistake. I was in sneakers, for one thing, not climbing shoes. The rope suddenly felt heavy with drag, pulling me back down as I clawed about the lichen for purchase. All the gear I had placed in the last couple of hours was for the purpose of holding body weight, not a fall. I also had no chalk. Why would I? I was aid climbing. But here I'd made a move I couldn't reverse, and now I was committed to reaching the top.

Pete had disappeared below. All I could hear were his words echoing in my head. *Don't start free climbing.* The exposure seemed to scream it at me now. I moved robotically up the slabby rock, pulling the rope with me as hard as I could. Fifteen feet above the roof, I found a small gap in the sandstone. I fiddled in a small nut, wedging it as best I could into the horizontal crack. I clipped the rope to it and gave it a gentle tug to test it. The nut popped out and clanged down the face, disappearing under the roof. I felt a wave of nausea. If I fell here, I was looking at a thirty-foot flight into the void, *if* the tipped-out cam below the roof held.

I eyed the last moves before the safety of a tree trunk above as my vision pinched down to a dark tunnel. At the end of that tunnel I imagined Big Wall Pete, dragging on a cigarette and grinning back at me, nodding as if to say, *This one's for you, man.* I high-stepped, grabbed a dusty knob of sandstone, and lunged up toward the tree.

Years later, having long since sworn off aid climbing for fun, I returned to Suck Creek and found that line in the guidebook: a moderate 5.10 free climb with a "sinister, black roof slot" called *Five Roofs in Reverse.* ◆

Opposite: Graffiti in Laurel-Snow State Natural Area, Tennessee

Opposite: Greg Kottkamp at Sand Rock, Alabama

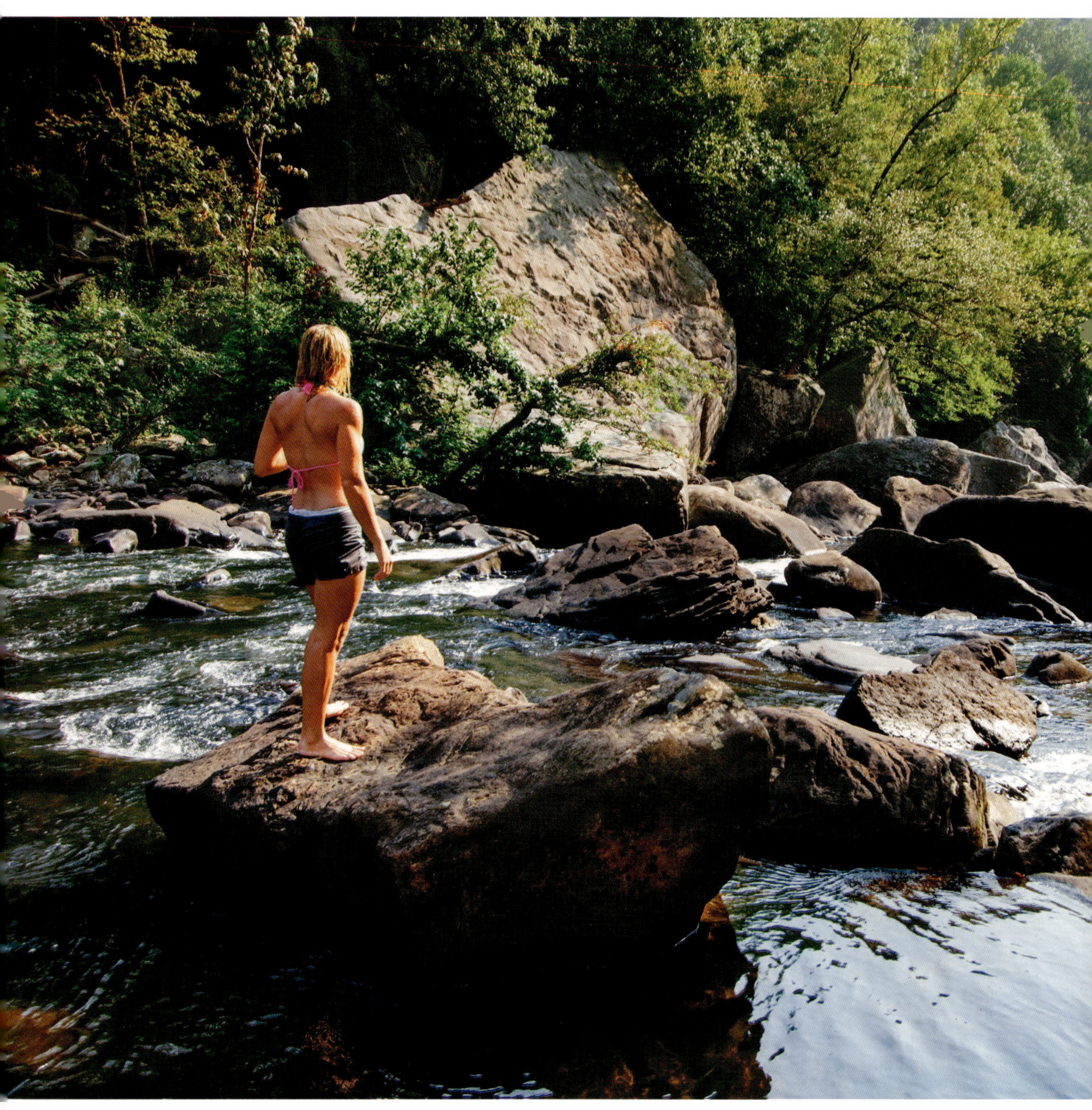

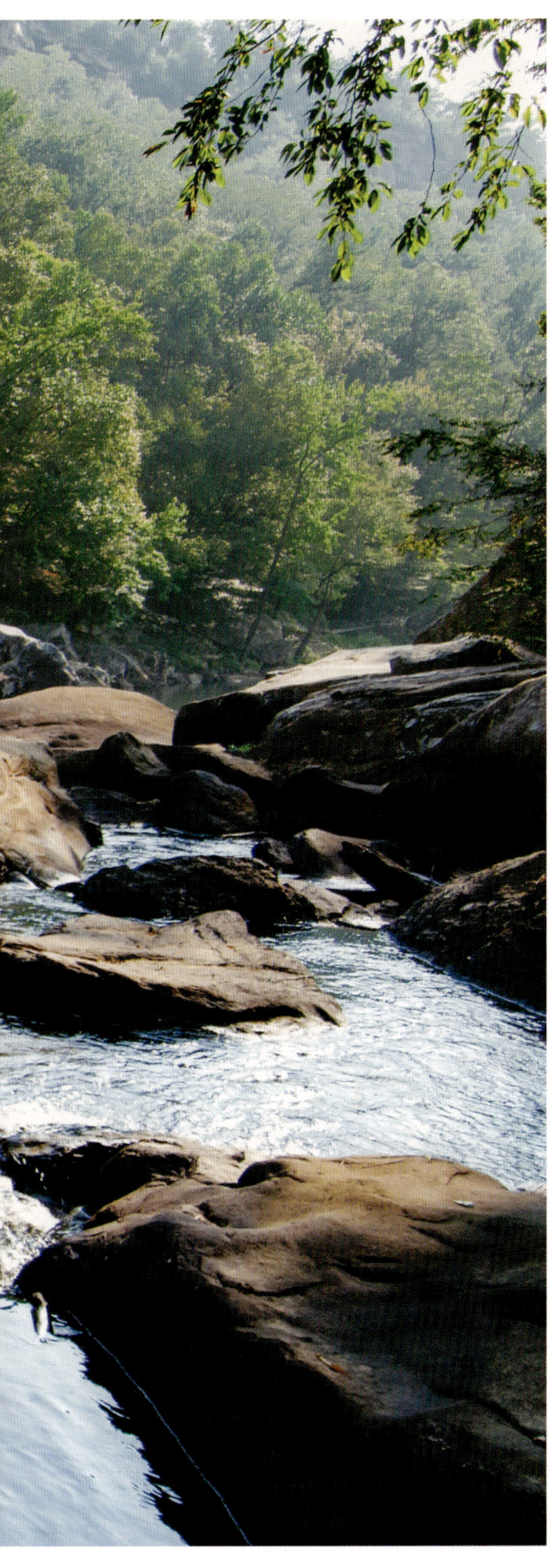

Jennifer Jenkins at Alabama's Little River Canyon National Preserve

PARADE OF FOOLS

Squashed between ancient parallel valleys that run south from the Cumberland Plateau like stacked shinbones, two forks of the Little River meet in the northeast corner of Alabama. From there, massive sandstone walls steer the river on both sides, gathering up cataracts that scour Little River Canyon for more than twenty-three miles to Weiss Lake. The result is one of the deepest, narrowest gashes east of the Rockies, filled with high-quality climbing and Class V rapids.

A well-maintained highway that winds along the rim of the canyon puts all of this tantalizingly close and easy to access, but you'd be surprised at how quickly civilization drops away only a few yards off the Alabama pavement. For an episode of the now-discontinued survival show *Man vs. Wild*, survivalist Bear Grylls was dropped into the canyon by helicopter, jumped down a cliff, shot the rapids in a Styrofoam junk raft, and killed a wild boar in hand-to-hand combat. The chopper scene was filmed on the clifftop backyard of a climber's retreat known as Split Rock, owned by some friends of mine, and as we stood there one evening, drinking beers and laughing about Gryll's antics, we still had to hand it to the guy. The canyon is indeed a wild place.

If you don't have a chopper handy, getting to the base of the hundred-foot sandstone walls of the canyon usually involves scrambling or rope work. There are few established hiking trails, save for what climbers and paddlers have worked out over the decades. It's isolated, and many climbers will tell you it has a "weird vibe." It's also mostly untrammeled and truly sublime. Being so close to Birmingham, Atlanta, and Chattanooga, the canyon is the perfect place for the weekend warrior to cut loose and do something drastic. Grylls was right to choose it for his boar-slaying escapades. The canyon tends to conceal things. It has been a hideout for vagabonds, a strategic safe zone for soldiers, a source of respite for lost souls, and—starting a few decades ago—a place for the region's hardest climbers to quietly test themselves at one of the most overlooked climbing destinations east of the Mississippi.

In 1799, Governor John Sevier of Tennessee wrote of the discovery of six skeletons in brass armor bearing the Welsh coat of arms, along with a series of caves and mortared stone walls built into the bluffs 325 feet above Little River. Local Native Americans in fact told Sevier that a mysterious tribe of men calling themselves "Welsh" built these walls long ago. These Welsh, they said, were later driven out of Alabama by the Cherokee and traveled north. There is a pervading local theory—half historical, half legend—that a Welsh prince named Madog ab Owain Gwynedd sailed to America in 1170, landing in Mobile Bay. Prince Madog (or "Mad Dog," as the locals are fond of calling him) and his crew then traveled up the river systems into northern Alabama, where they encountered rugged canyons and armed resistance to incursion. Perhaps these early outsiders fortified themselves here above Little River until, decimated, they traveled north, connecting the dots between a series of pre-Colombian building sites in Alabama, Tennessee, and Kentucky. What remained of them, as the story goes, was absorbed into various tribes, so illustrated in colorful seventeenth-century accounts of fair-skinned, "moon-eyed Indians" deep in the American frontier who spoke a peculiar European-like language.

Today the Welsh Caves are off-limits, but most of the artifacts have been stolen or kicked in over the years, and there's better rock downriver, as climbers have known for years. Despite the construction of the southern half of the Scenic Highway in the 1950s along the most scenic parts of the canyon, or May's Gulf as it was called then, there hadn't been much tourist activity in the area until recently. Technical climbing in the canyon dates back to the '60s and '70s, including a few forays by the influential John Gill and Henry Barber, but the rock—stacks of blocky sandstone in various stages of disintegration—did not lend itself to traditional protection. It wasn't until the sport-climbing revolution hit the South in the '80s that climbers understood the potential of the miles of steep rock above Little River.

Named a national preserve in 1992, Little River Canyon is the southernmost terminus for migrating sport climbers traveling south in the fall, following warmer temperatures. As Birmingham climber Adam Henry puts it, "These climbers get pissed off at the New, and then it's too cold to climb at the Red, and then they get tired of the Obed and end up here." But by then, the numbers usually dwindle to a diehard few.

Climbing was mostly off the radar before the canyon went federal. The park was busy dealing with bigger issues like search and rescues or the occasional automobile salvage. With high-angle rope skills, knowledge of the terrain, and plenty of free time on their hands, climbers could be useful to have around in that respect.

In the early 1980s, the landowner of a nearby popular sport-climbing outpost called Yellow Bluff abruptly closed it to climbing, a move many people attributed to unwanted attention from a magazine article about the area. After that, the drive to explore and develop new routes in the canyon became more intense.

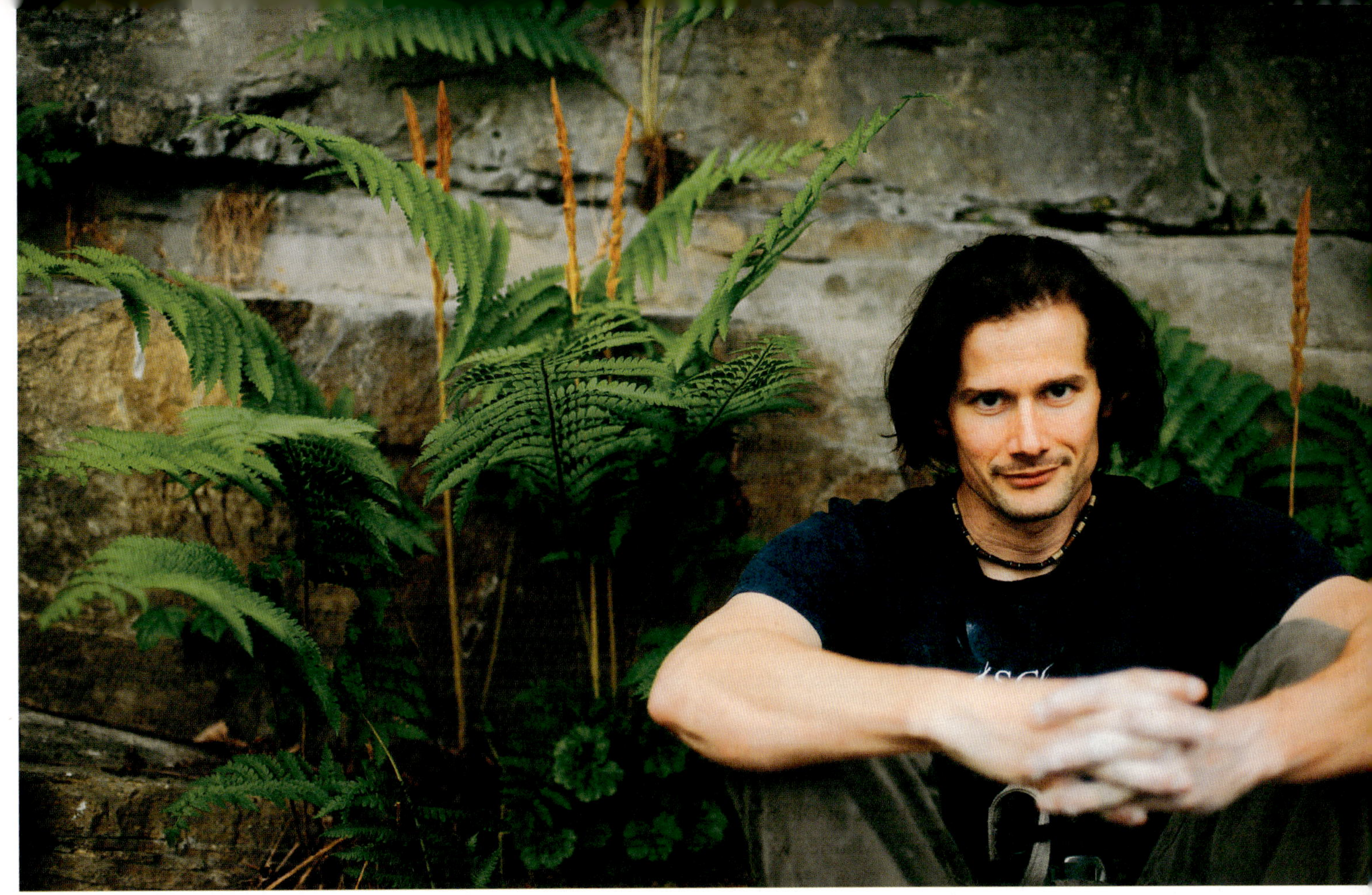

Paul Morley at
Yellow Bluff, Alabama

Intense scenes attract intense characters. Stories from those days seem to be more about high-speed car wrecks, hard liquor, and nude free solos than first ascents. Maurice Reed, one of the main canyon developers, was one such character. A photo taken by fellow canyon heavy Mark Cole in the late 1980s shows Maurice with a rattlesnake, one he caught with his bare hands, around his neck. "He was one of those guys you'd look at and you just knew he was crazy," says longtime canyon climber Adam Henry. "He had a bushy fireman's mustache and tights. He always wanted to have his feet above him. He was a wild climber. The early developers were larger than life."

Chris Sierzant on *Hooligans* (5.13), Little River Canyon National Preserve

The canyon's Unshackled Wall was one area where locals pushed the envelope of what was possible—and acceptable—on Southern sandstone. Named after a popular religious radio program that Birmingham climbers would listen to on the drive over, the colorful walls have some of the most compact and beautiful rock here. Prolific East Coast route developer Porter Jarrard found the crag in the late 1980s and subsequently put up its first route, *Exploding Boy* (5.11b).

Adam spent a lot of time at Unshackled Wall around this crowd in his early climbing days, and from the names of the routes down there you can see that he came up in some fine Southern traditions. "*Hot Taaka* (5.11b) was Maurice's favorite 'value brand' vodka," says Adam. "They would go down there and get shitfaced all the time."

He recalls, "There used to be a bottle of Old Spice underneath *Movie Star* (5.12b). Every time Maurice would try that route, he would splash some on him. Even after it was empty, we would act like we were splashing cologne on us. It became part of the route."

Doug Reed had left the area's eponymous route *Unshackled* as a project, and one of Adam's partners, Jake Slaney, had his eye on it. "I asked him if maybe he would sell the project to us for $20," remembers Adam, "and Doug said, 'I don't know, maybe $250 would be sufficient.' Neither of us had any money, so we left the route alone. That was back in the day when we used to respect each other's routes and such."

Unshackled Wall held other mysteries for a young climber that left a strong impression. "You go out into the woods there and find these big crystals," says Dave. "Everybody takes them now, but we always resisted that urge. They look like kryptonite. Adam is superstitious about it." He continues, "Come to think of it, he's superstitious about everything. I've been climbing with him where he'll put his rope bag down and a big spider will jump out or the wind will blow a weird way, and he'll just pack up and leave." Adam confirms he steers clear of Unshackled these days, though it's probably more that he's climbed everything there already.

With no rules and enough steep rock for everyone, the canyon was the perfect place to seek more creative paths to hard free climbing. Jeff Gruenberg contributed the powerful testpiece *Area of Doubt* (5.13a), a line of slots and pockets on a steep, white wall at Unshackled. The route was fabricated with a drill-enhanced slot at the crux. "There was not that much thought at the time," says Gruenberg. "The route was devoid of holds, and the line needed to be climbed. At the time it was an "area of no doubt." I do have mixed emotions, about robbing the future and all that. On the other hand, pin scars and bolts are fabrications as well." This was the early 1990s, well into the sport climbing revolution, and the fully artificial experience of climbing gyms were in their infancy. Was this an embrace of what climbing might someday become? I pressed Jeff, but he shrugged it off, "Who knows what the future might be?"

This creative experimentation enjoyed in the isolation of Little River Canyon finally culminated in the *Teflon Route* incident. In 1992, upstream at a wall called the Crazy House, Cole developed a new hard route with the intent of installing a bolt-on modular hold in a blank roof. Maurice Reed was adamantly against it.

Adam recalls the standoff: "Maurice said enough was enough and that he would kill Mark if he did it. Mark was then pissed off that Maurice had taken such a hard stand. That was the only time anyone ever heard Mark Cole say a curse word. He was a good Christian." Adam continues, "It was maybe a year or two later that Mark took the hold off and chiseled it instead. At the time that was the thing they were doing at Smith Rock, and in Squamish where those guys had made an outdoor gym of sorts, but at the canyon it just stopped after *Teflon*."

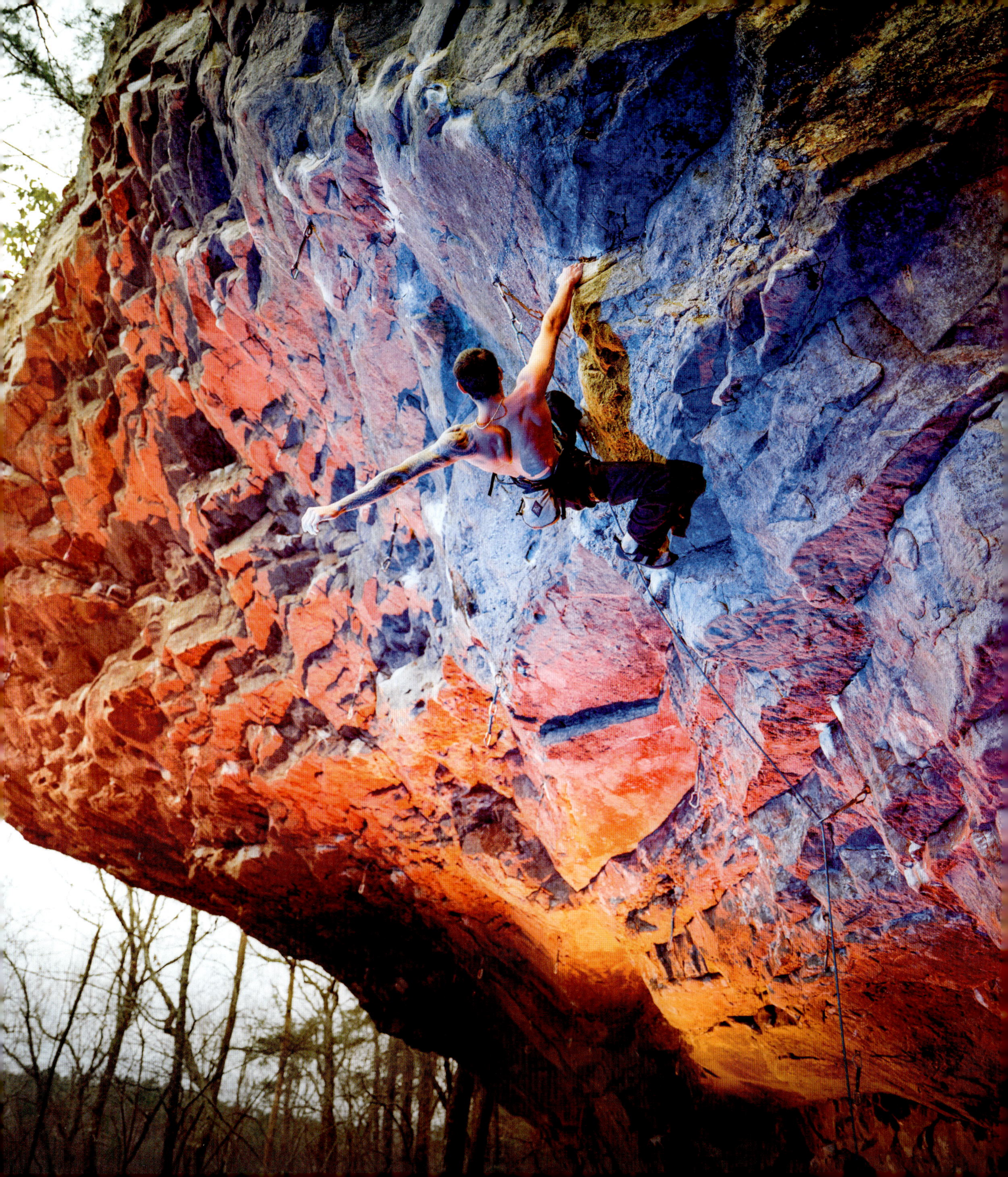

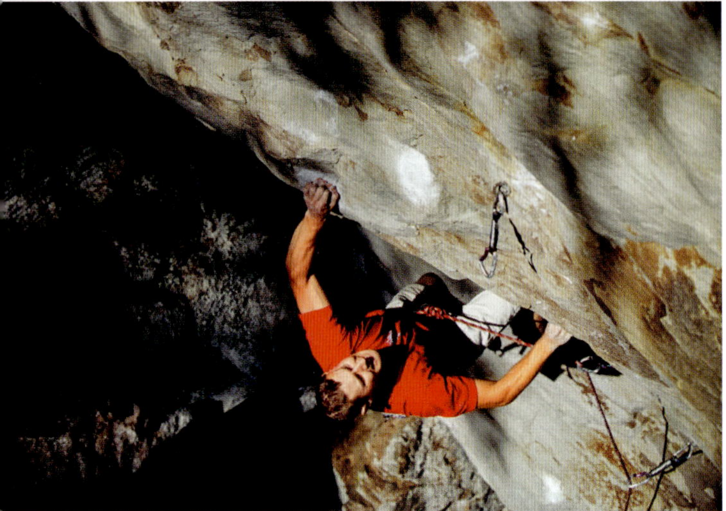

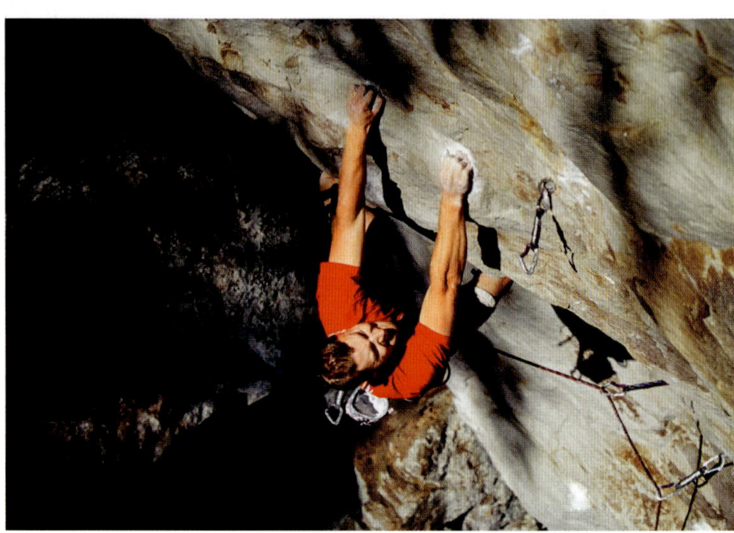

Greg Kottkamp figuring out the sequence on *Back in the Day* (5.13d) in Little River Canyon National Preserve

Teflon Route remains an unfinished project, abandoned due to a (naturally) broken hold. Like much of the area's history and folklore, the significance of this era is open to interpretation. "I give Mark Cole 100 percent credit for making sport climbing what it is today in the Deep South," says Adam. "Were his tactics always the best? No, but it was a time and a way of doing things that I think has to be appreciated, even though it's something that I would never want to see happen again in the canyon."

Rather than relying on outsiders to draw the boundaries of what was acceptable, climbers decided among themselves what was best, and that tradition was passed on. It seems to have worked out. Cole in particular was a mentor to many of the younger climbers then. "Mark had a whole group of youngsters that he would bring to the canyon," says Dave. "He taught 'em how to climb, and he taught 'em well."

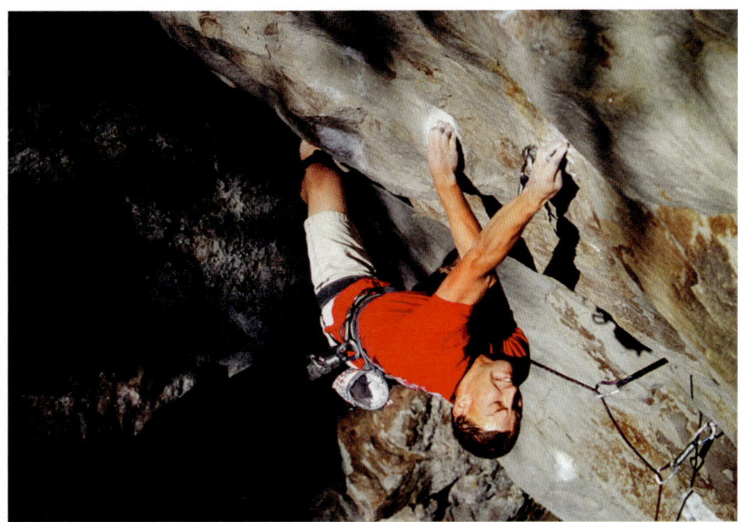

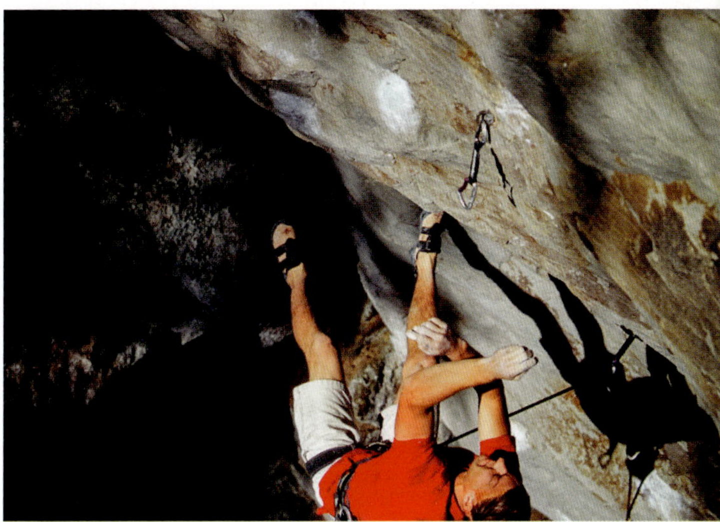

Such unorthodox apprenticeship—all but vanished with the rise of today's gym scene—left a legacy of strong climbers with a deep respect and awe for local traditions, but word was spreading by the early 1990s. "People were coming from all over to climb there," remembered Jake Slaney in an interview. "There would be twenty or thirty regulars there on the weekend climbing at different crags, putting up routes, exploring for new cliffs." It was the crag's golden age of development, and everyone wanted a piece of it.

"One time Maurice was up there bolting a climb," says Dave, "and I was walking by with a bunch of Atlanta climbers, and Maurice muttered that it was 'a parade of fools.' That's what he named the route. I was probably leading everyone around pointing out routes like a big dog, but we really *were* a parade of fools."

Occasionally an outsider on the hunt for a Southern test-piece would leave with a mouthful of humble pie. In the same year as the *Teflon Route* incident, French climber Alain Ghersen came to town. Fresh from speed solos in the Alps, he had just ripped up the New River Gorge in West Virginia, quickly repeating Doug Reed's benchmark 5.13 *Quinsana Plus*, among others, and made his way down south to Alabama's Little River Canyon. Ghersen had his sights on *Masquerade*, one of Gruenberg's new-wave creations thought to be 5.14 at the time.

"He drove in from the New, and everybody was down at the *Jungle Gym*," says Adam. "This guy comes walking around the corner and everyone's head turned. You could tell he was the outsider for sure. It was like a scene from a surf movie."

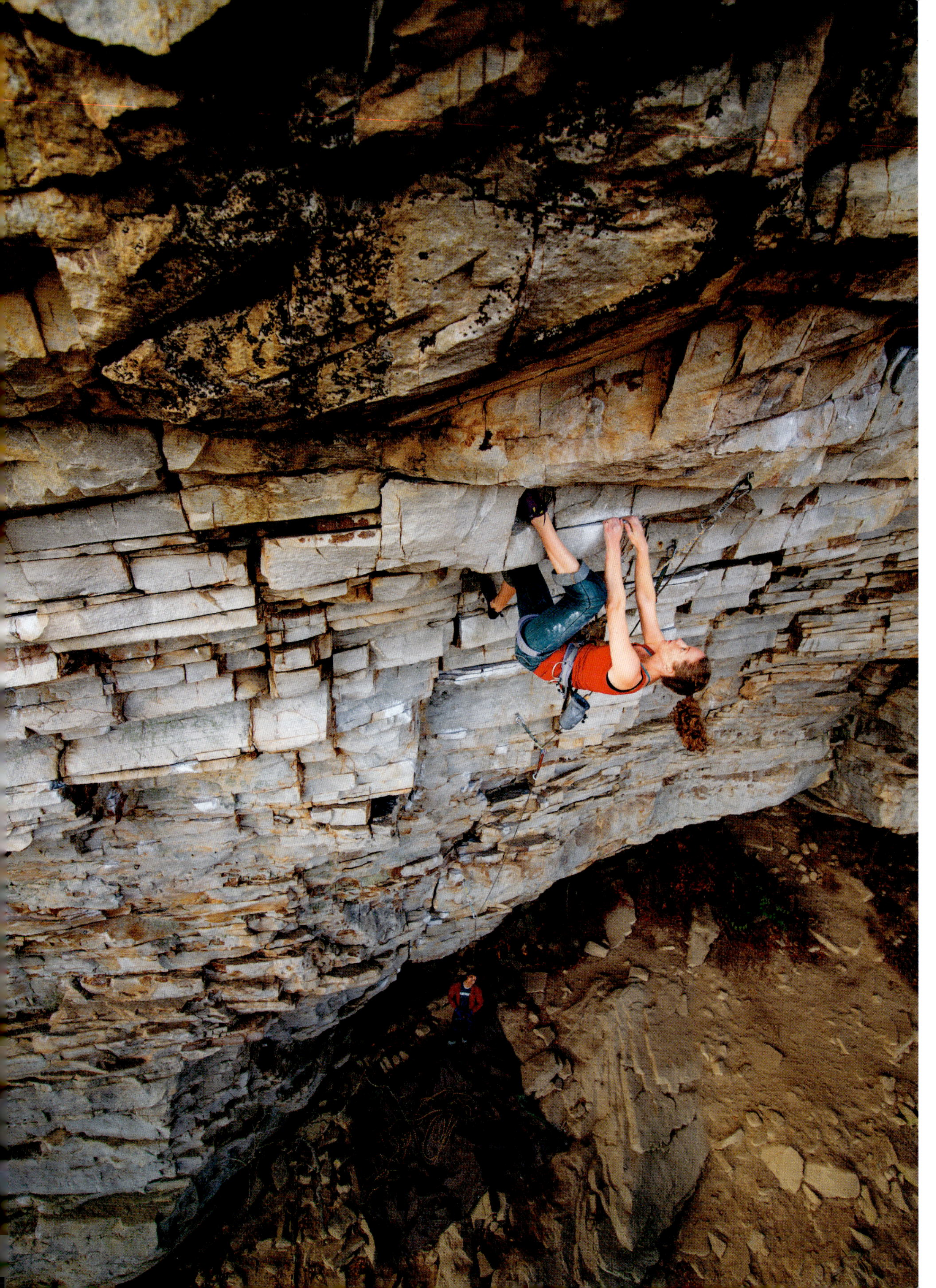

Dave was there too. "I remember he was with a hot French girl and walking around asking in his French accent, 'Ouere ees *le Masquerade*?' and I remember we were all laughing like, 'Oh, right, you're just going to go hop on *Masquerade*.' Nobody ever climbed it! It was one of the hardest routes around, and it was over there by itself. There were routes like that that were just *hot* back then."

Masquerade—which now goes at a consensus of mid-5.13—heads steeply out of one of the larger cave features in the canyon on striking sculpted blue-and-black sandstone. It's steep enough to create horrific rope drag, forcing a leader to use more technical double-rope techniques to try it safely. Notoriously difficult to figure out without the help of local knowledge, it requires all the tricks a Southern climber learns over the years and then some. Adam smiles about what happened next. "Ghersen's bail carabiner is still on it. He spent maybe a day and a half there. After that, he left town. If you ask Jeff about that, he'll get a wry look on his face and tell you, 'It was an adventure.'"

Things change. Over a decade later, another famous Frenchman encountered a more open Southern scene. Tony Lamiche swept into town in December 2006 with colorful clothes and a huge smile from that year's Triple Crown, a long-running annual bouldering competition. This time the outsider was welcomed wholeheartedly, and in a single day of climbing, Lamiche established a new baseline for Southern bouldering with first ascents of nearly a half dozen unclimbed lines, including *The Shield*, which is now one of the most celebrated hard boulders in America, up there with Yosemite's *Midnight Lightning* or Hueco's *Slashface*. Suddenly it seemed like the South was wide open. The old canyon hardmen would have hardly believed that bouldering would put Southern climbing on the map. ◆

Annie Graefe on *Iron Mike* (5.12a), Little River Canyon National Preserve

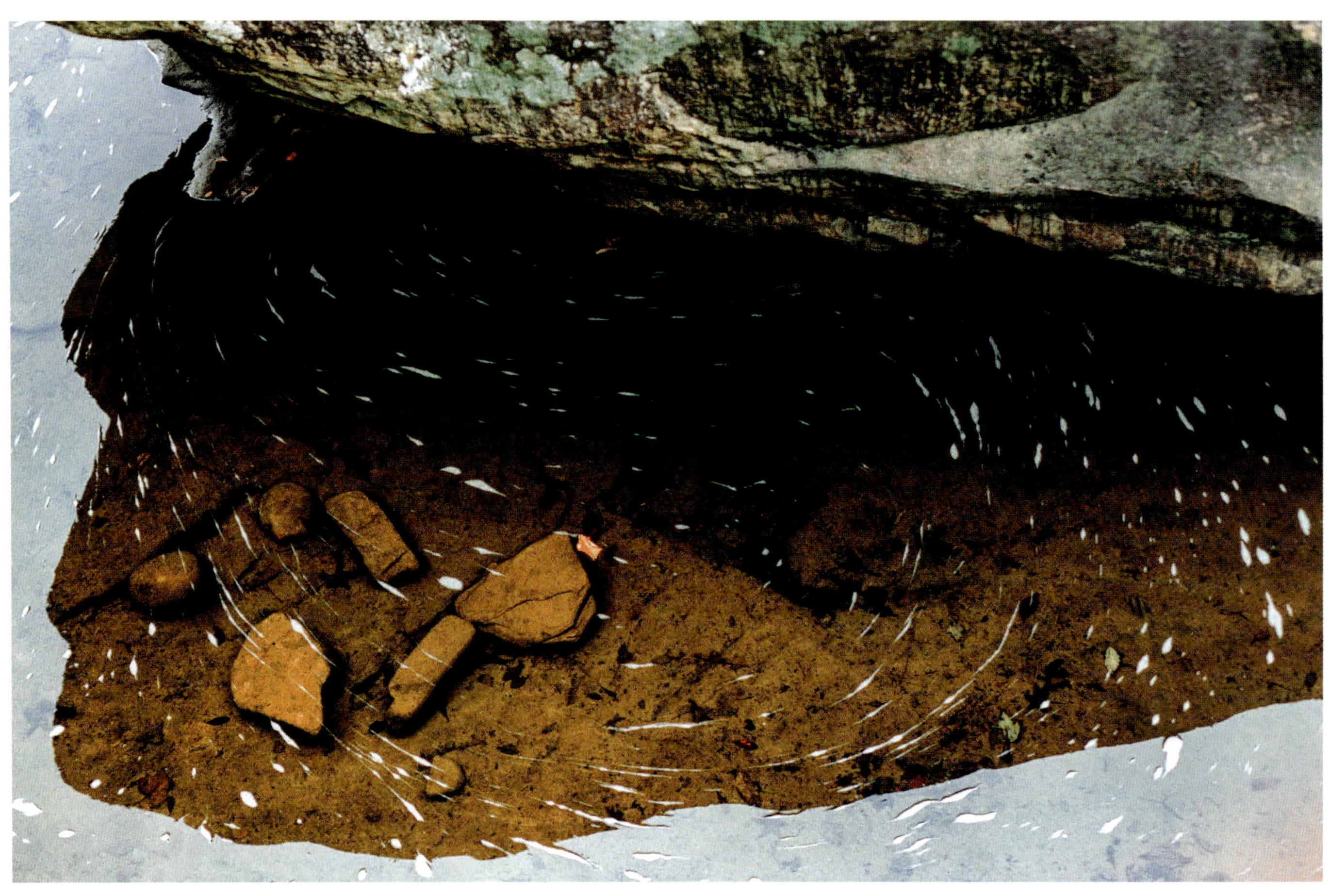

An eddy in Alabama's Little River Canyon National Preserve

Opposite: James Pullum holding a natural quartz crystal near Little River Canyon's Unshackled Wall

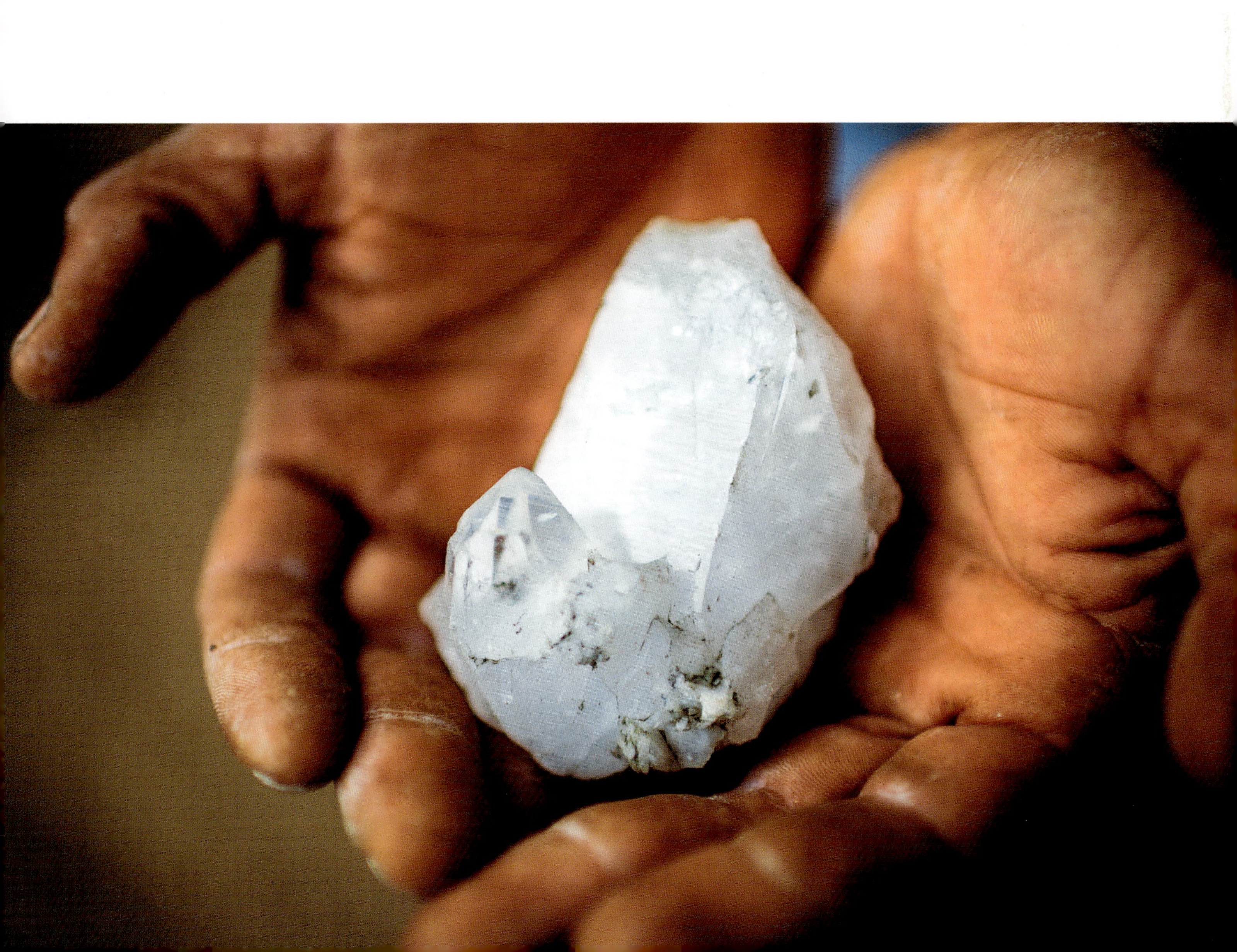

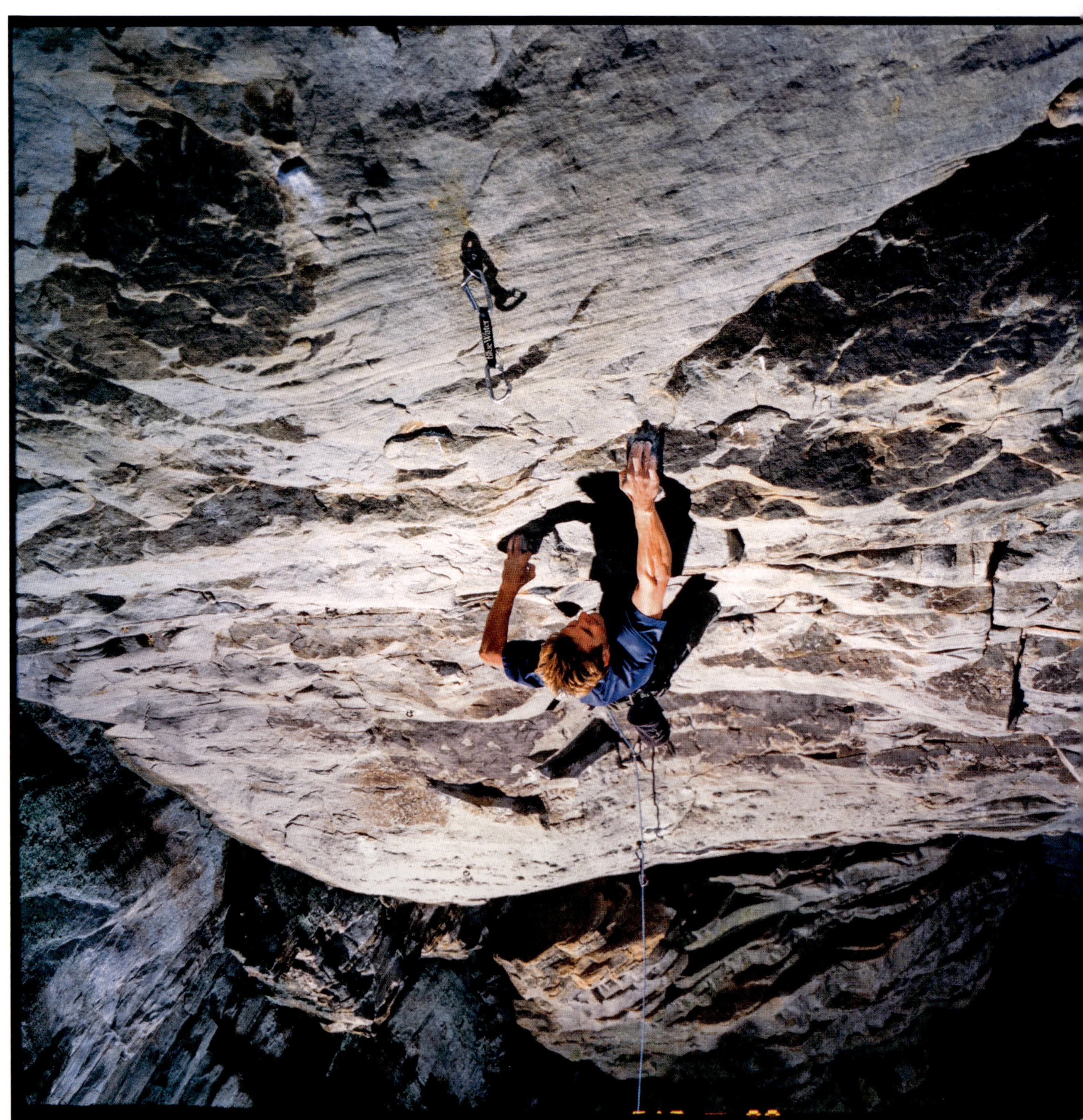

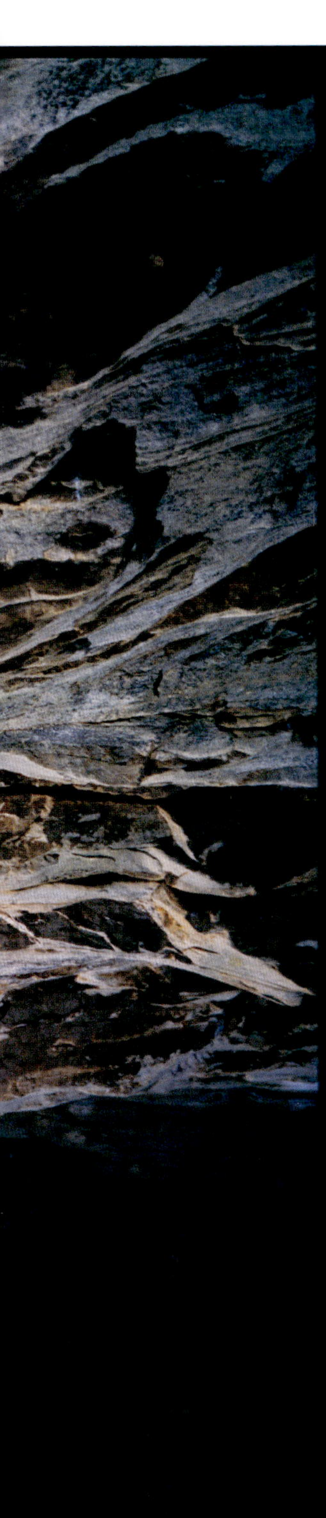

Opposite: Mihai Popa on *Area of Doubt* (5.13a), Little River Canyon National Preserve, Alabama

Adam Henry at his home in Alabama

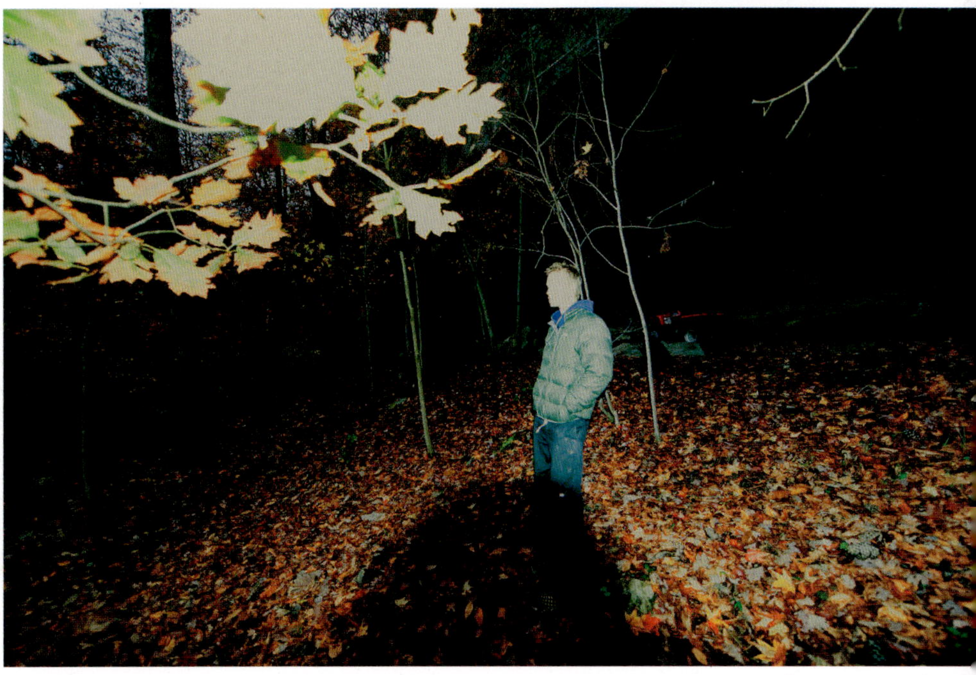

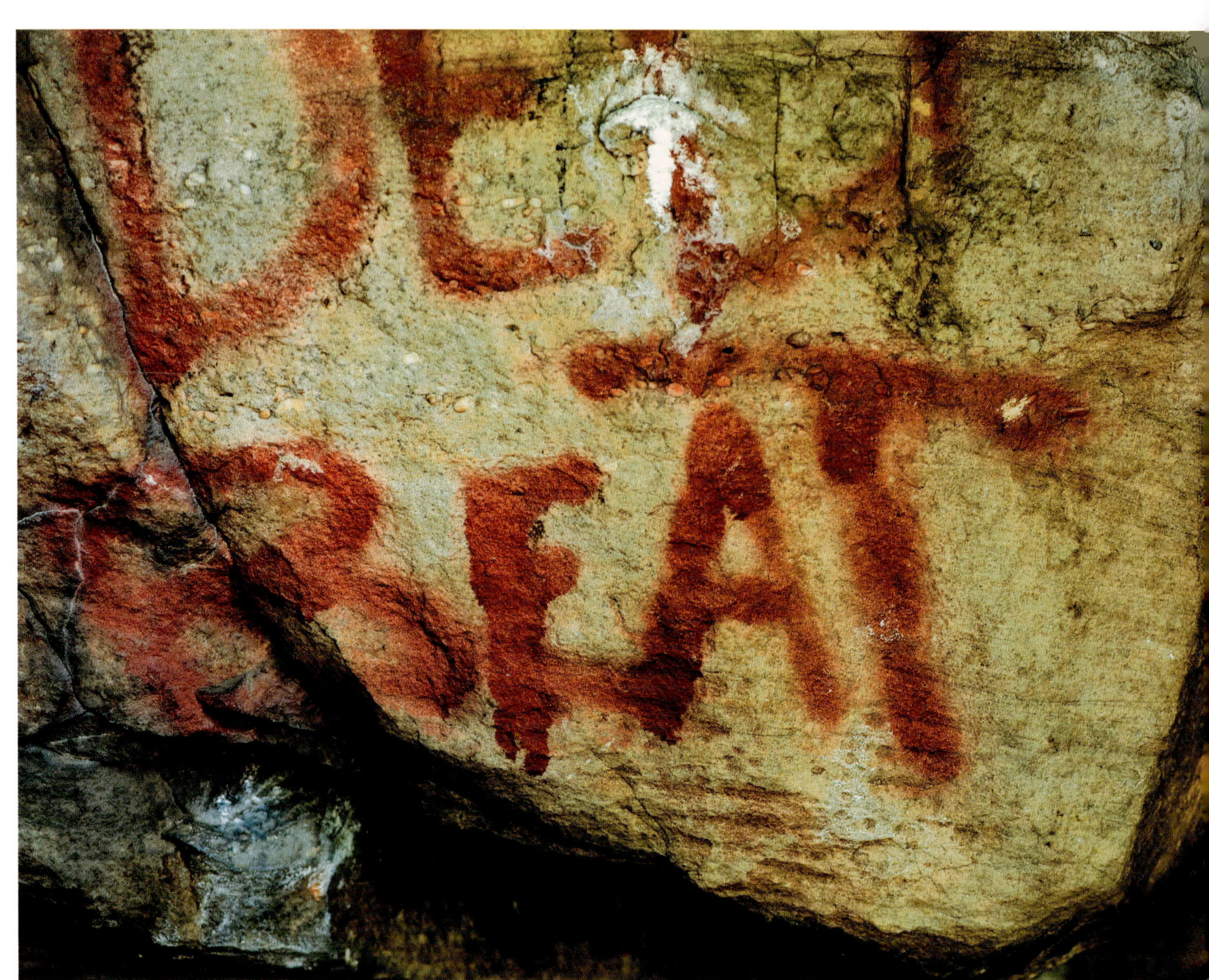
REAT

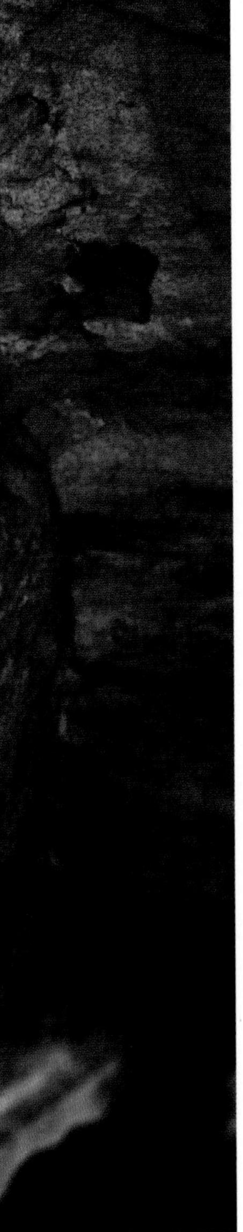

Graffiti in Laurel-Snow State Natural Area, Tennessee

BETTER GIT ON

Anthony Meeks, Greg Kottkamp, and Adam Henry stood in a clearing, squinting at a chest-clutching line of orange sandstone walls. Sweaty and laden with climbing gear, they were careful to look for timber rattlers, wasp nests, and deer ticks as they burrowed through thick mountain laurel. Now between them and all that stone was a boy.

"Y'all better git on before Bob gets here," he said. Not more than thirteen, he stood with a small firearm next to a camo-painted ATV.

Two younger boys on another ATV nodded and squinted back down a rough trail. There was an interval of silence. The boys, all of them armed, seemed nervous.

The climbers knew they were well within their rights to access the cliffs down this path, but there was a game to be played. "It was obvious," Adam later recounted, "that we didn't want any part of Bob—whoever that was—so we got outta there quick."

As the three climbers turned to go, the kids started up their ATVs. The youngest hurled a final salvo, "And don't y'all come back!" and they disappeared in a cloud of dust. ◆

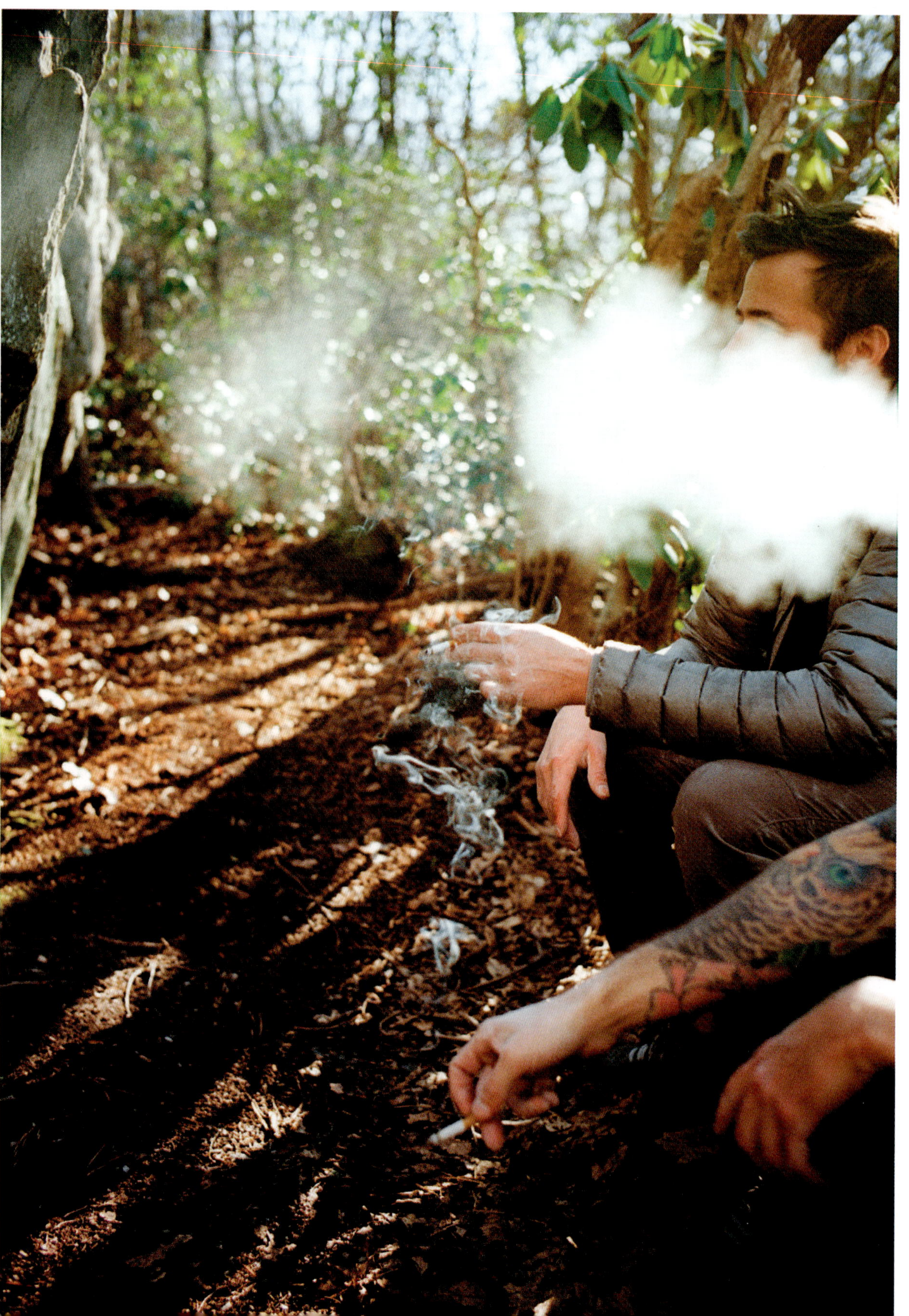

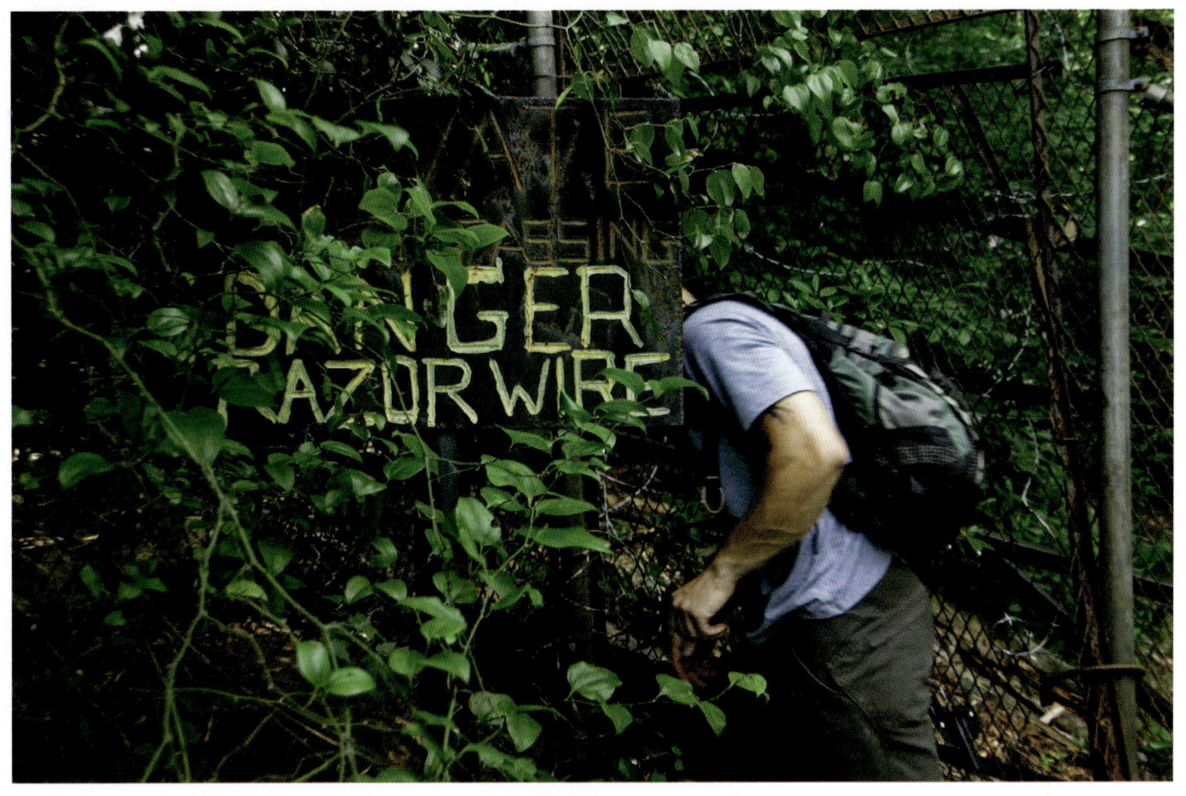

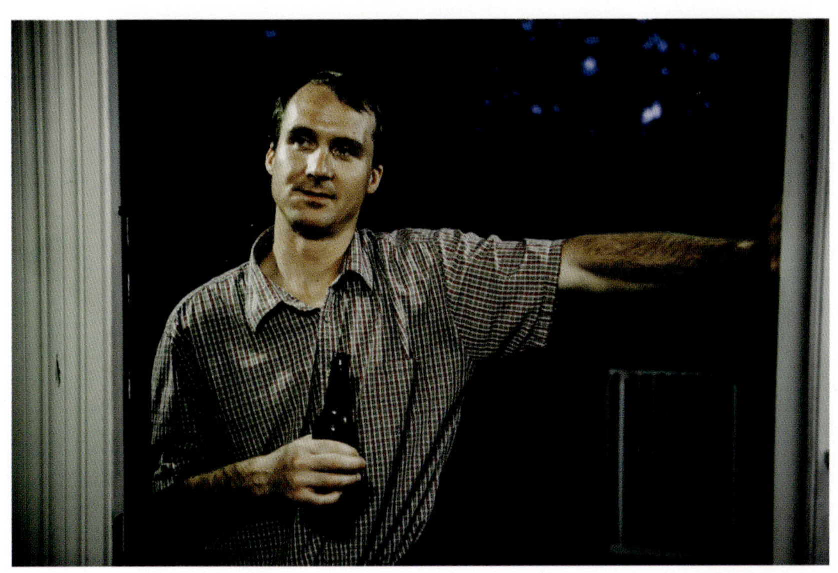

Opposite: Will Dorinsky and fellow climbers at Moore's Wall in North Carolina

David Paulete exploring near Atlanta

Justin Eiseman in Chattanooga

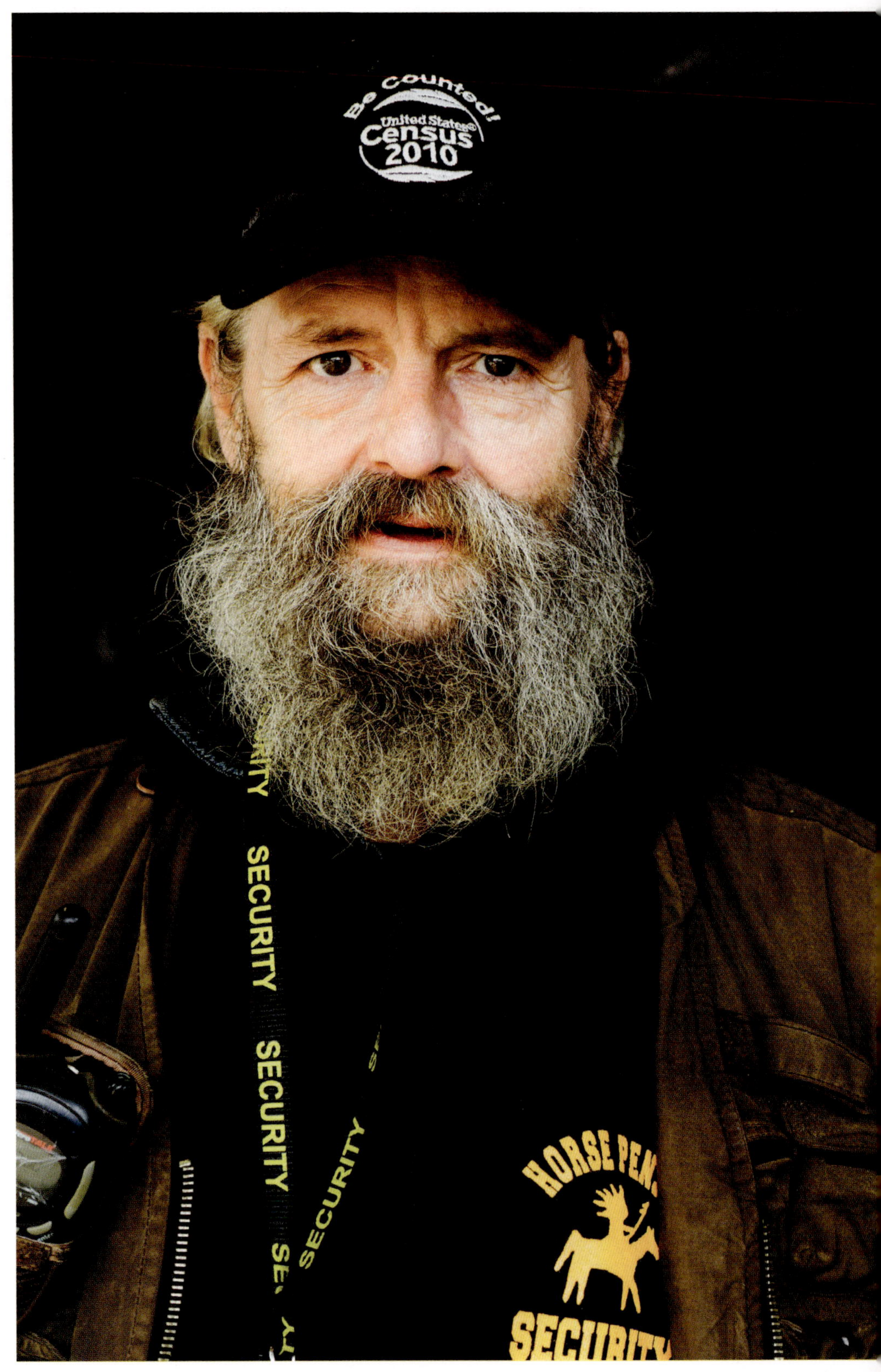

Ronnie and Greg, the security detail at Horse Pens 40 Ranch, Alabama

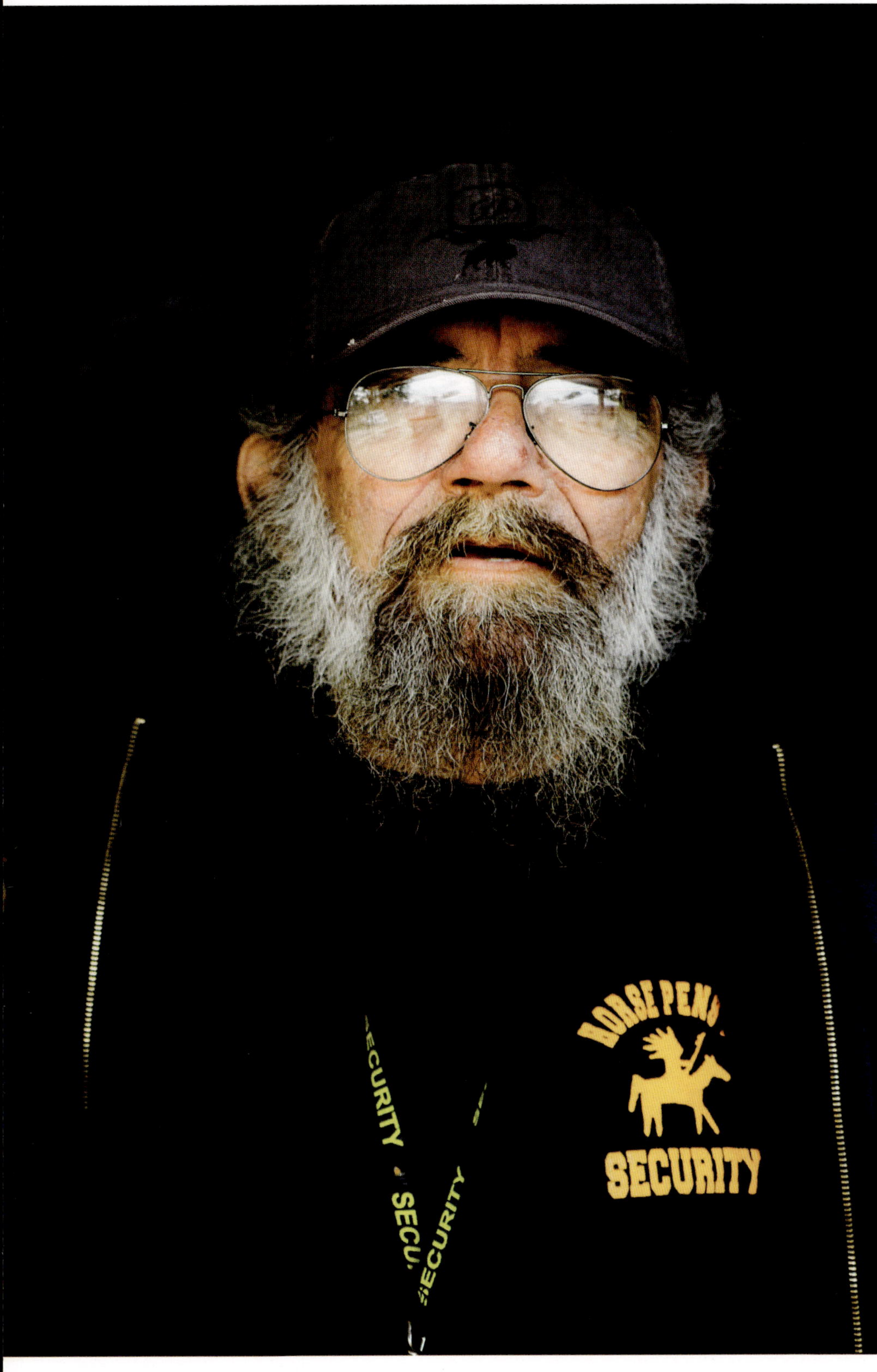
HORSE PENS
SECURITY
SECURITY
SECURITY

LITZ PROBLEMS

In 2008, climber and national park ranger Rob Turan asked me to collaborate with him on a story about Tennessee climber James Litz. He would write it, I would shoot it, and we'd split the fee. "Well Rob," I said, "you can write about him, but how do I photograph a ghost?"

Rob—who passed away in 2024—was a walking guidebook for Middle Tennessee and a great writer. He had been a ranger at the Obed Wild and Scenic River as well as at other major climbing areas like Chattanooga's Sunset Park and Kentucky's Red River Gorge. Unlike the mysterious James Litz, Rob was an open book, his enthusiasm always on display in person and in writing. He loved bridging the gap between the state and the vagabond climbing world, and in doing so he would steer young climbers right while also convincing state and national parks to embrace climbing as a legitimate activity. He did it so well because he was the real deal in both worlds.

"I did love being the climbing ranger at Sunset," he told me. "People who didn't know me saw my name tag and would say, 'Hey, you're the guy who put up *Spawn* at Obed. Best route ever! Can I shake your hand?'"

Then, as now, James was quietly establishing some of the hardest climbs in the country, operating on the periphery of the scene, both geographically and in terms of skill—his lines are rarely repeated, but instead simply tried, looked at, or merely talked about. James's routes are too remote, the holds are too small, and the moves are too hard; just another "unrepeated Litz problem." These were scattered all around the South. Legend has it few had ever met or talked to the guy. His climbs spoke for themselves.

But Rob knew him well. Fifteen years before, Rob was the climbing-obsessed ranger at the Obed Wild and Scenic River, a spectacular gorge in middle Tennessee's Cumberland Plateau. Bob Cormany, Craig Stannard, and others had explored the area's boulders and walls many years before the Obed's designation in the national park system in '76, and Rob had found himself the benevolent keeper of the climbs, keeping tabs on new ascents and acting as ambassador to traveling climbers looking for a challenge. In 1996, a scrawny 125-pound James walked into the park office and introduced himself. Rob had already heard of him—he was the kid who just climbed *Whatsherface*, which at 5.13 was the hardest route in the park at the time. James needed a challenge, so Rob took him to one of his favorite testing grounds, the nearby Lilly Boulders.

That day James climbed Rob's personal unclimbed project, *The Turansformer Traverse*, which he graded V9, and suddenly the possibilities of the Lilly Boulders were wide open.

Over the next few years, mostly exploring the boulders on his own, James left a legacy of extreme climbs at both Obed and Lilly Boulders. Despite its status as a national park, this was a very rural area, and access to the climbs in those days was only possible by the generosity of the locals. Dogs roamed the area freely, often in packs of fifty or more at a time by James's estimation, and interactions with them and their owners occasionally went south quickly. James was in high school then.

"I had a hard time dragging anyone over there," he told me. Once he started college, bouldering was a better choice for solo trips on a flexible schedule. At Lilly he pushed the standards into V10 territory with *Litz Blitz, Mean Squeeze,* and *Johnson City*. Every few years, as other climbers caught up and repeated his climbs, James would return to up the ante. As a result, today Lilly has a remarkably high concentration of extreme boulder problems, culminating in Litz testpieces like *Testify* (V12), *Tilted World* (V13), and *Chinese Arithmetic* (V13). He did the same at other Southern boulder fields and beyond.

I had just been investigating one of James's higher-profile first ascents, a boulder problem in a far corner of Idaho at Castle Rocks State Park. I spent a week there with my friend Josh Fowler filming scenes for our first climbing film, *A Fine Line,* centered on attempts to repeat this Litz problem. The problem starts on the extreme lower right of Castle Rocks' Taco Cave, follows a spiraling arc of Twix bar–sized grips, climbs horizontally to the leftmost lip of the cave, and exits on a powerful twenty-foot V10 face climb called *Out of Africa*. James had called that particular geometry *Warpath*. At V14, it was one of the hardest unrepeated boulder problems in the country. A video of the climb appeared online, but other than that, James didn't have much to say about it. The climb was the statement—it was up to others to decipher it.

Despite the collective efforts of pro climbers Dave Graham, Jimmy Webb, and Daniel Woods, no one could do *Warpath* in its entirety on camera, and we left with only fragments of footage: a few frustrating attempts, standing around in the cold like penguins, and exploring strange granite formations in a blizzard. Daniel repeated *Warpath* off-camera, so the best I could do was film a reenactment of this now-repeated Litz problem. It was a fiction, a ghost story.

The conundrum of our film led us out of Idaho, then to Colorado, and inevitably right back to the South. Later I tried the single-move Litz problem *God Module* at Horse Pens 40 for myself. Finally, Rob called me and connected us. I was fortunate to photograph James at his old stomping grounds, the Lilly Boulders, as well as in Dayton, Tennessee. Rob's article in *Urban Climber* offered a great glimpse of the legend. Far from elusive, James was gracious with his time and full of great stories. Before he disappeared again, he left me with a final thought: "Privacy is more important than fame." ◆

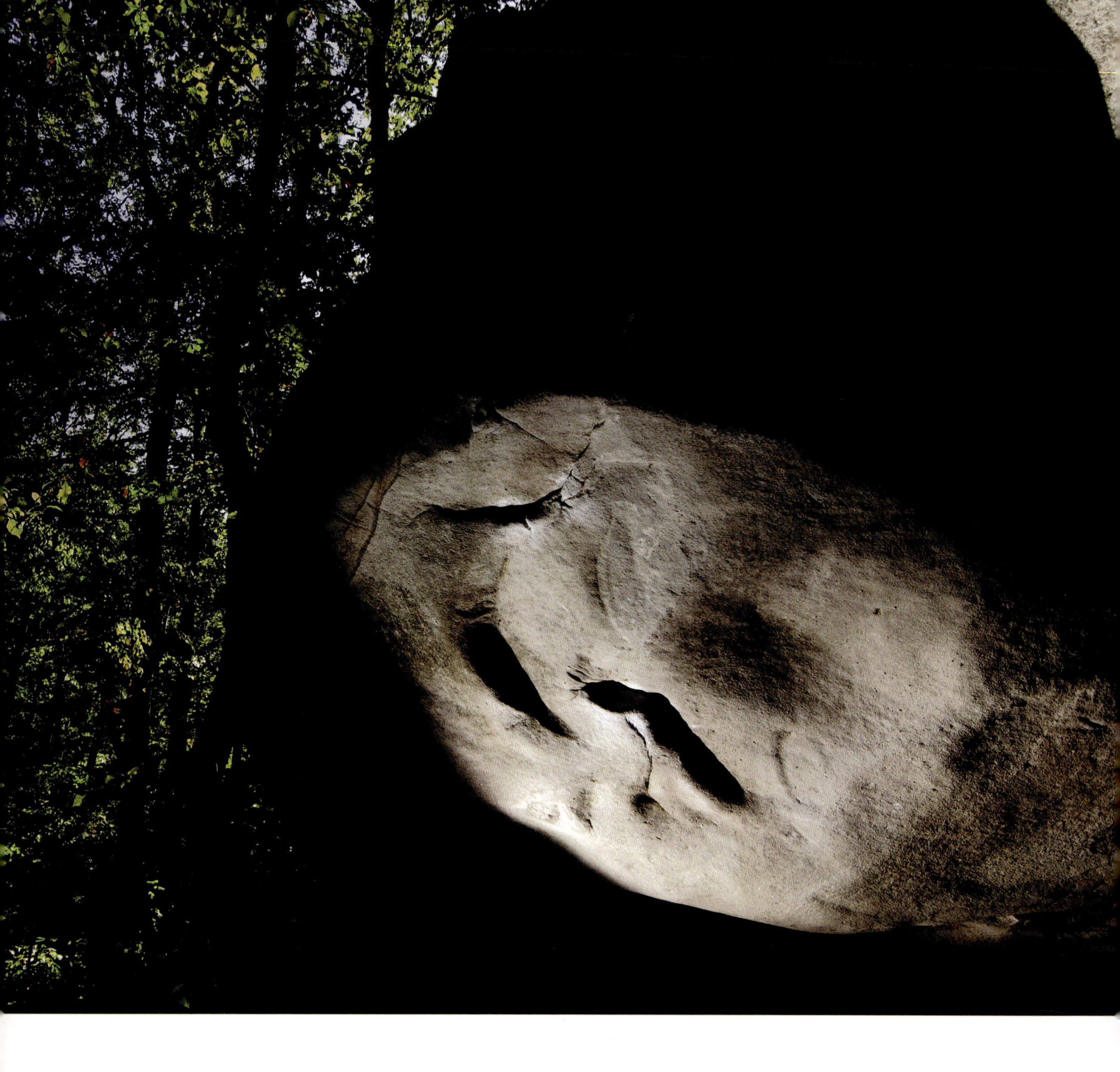

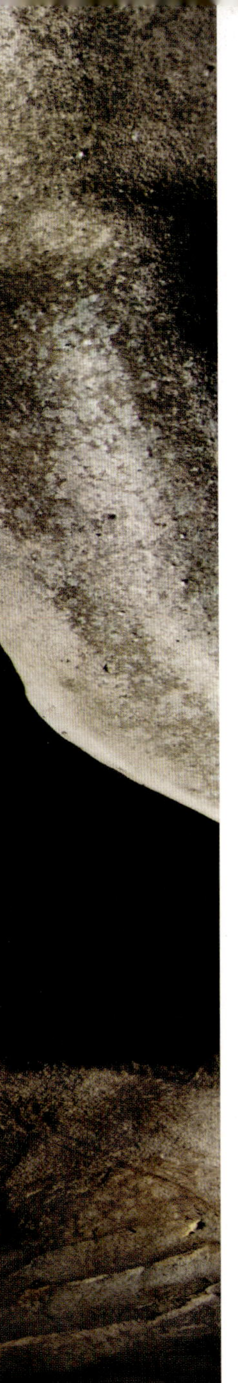

God Module (V11), Horse Pens 40 Ranch, Alabama

Light on sandstone at Horse Pens 40 Ranch

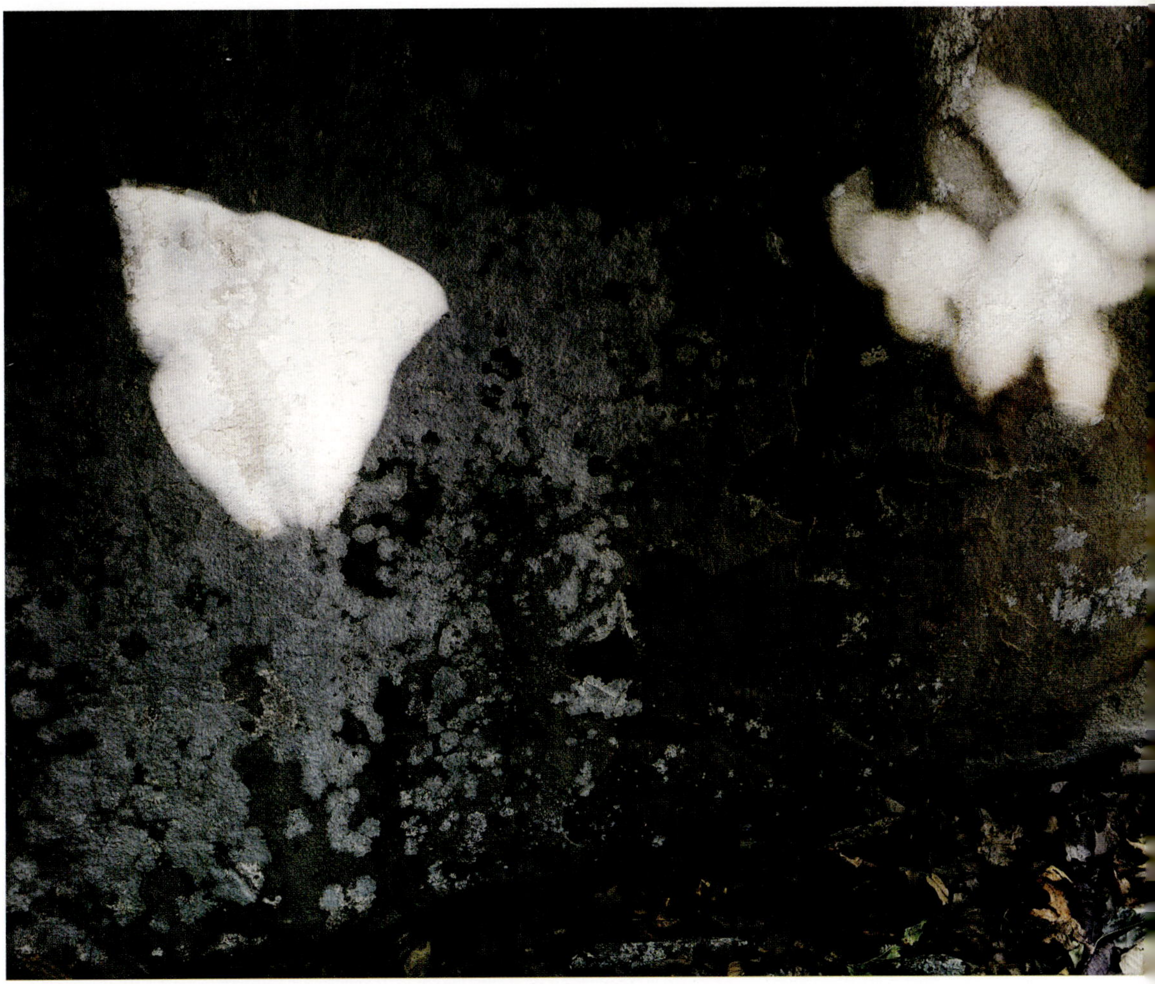

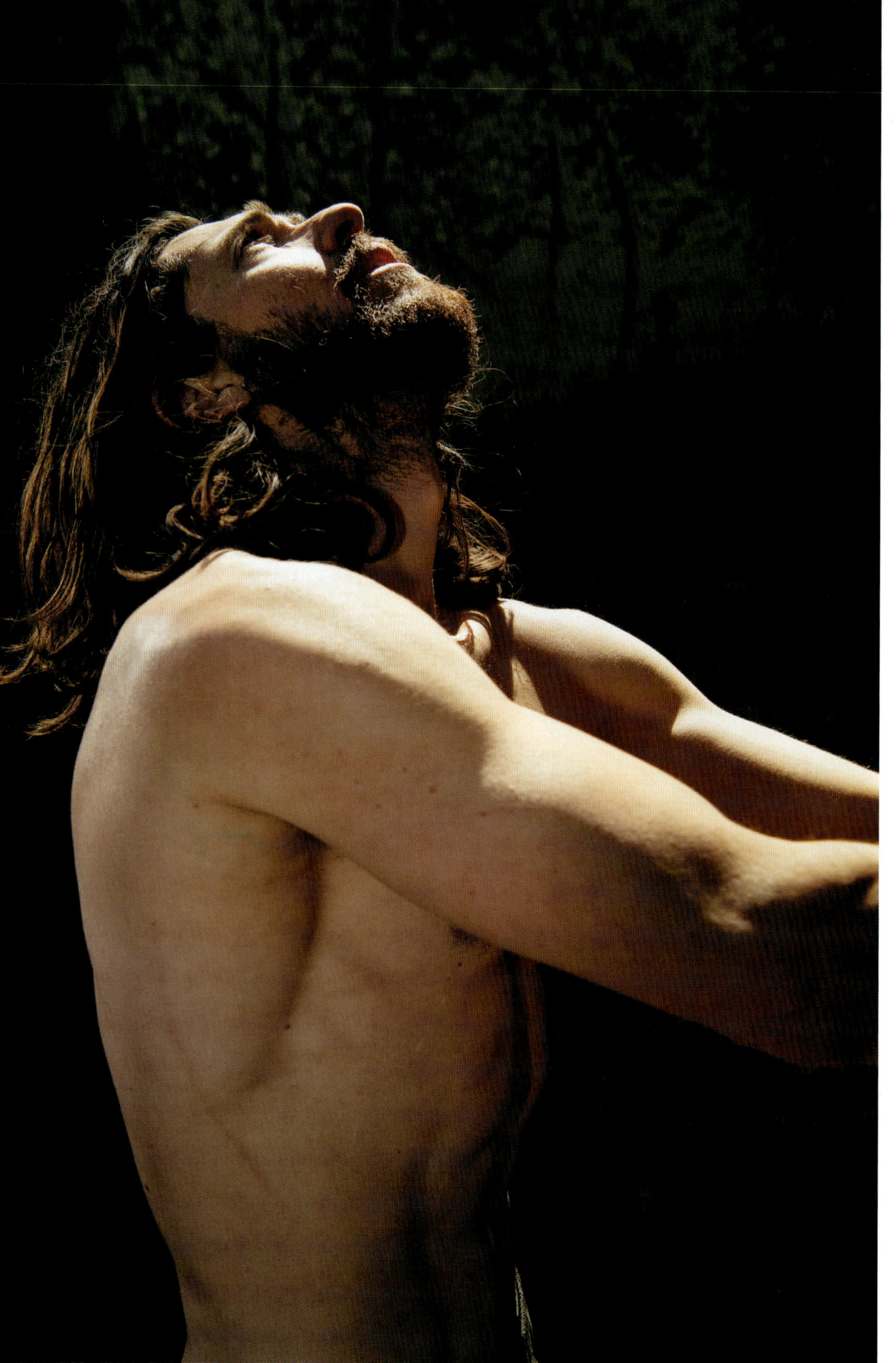

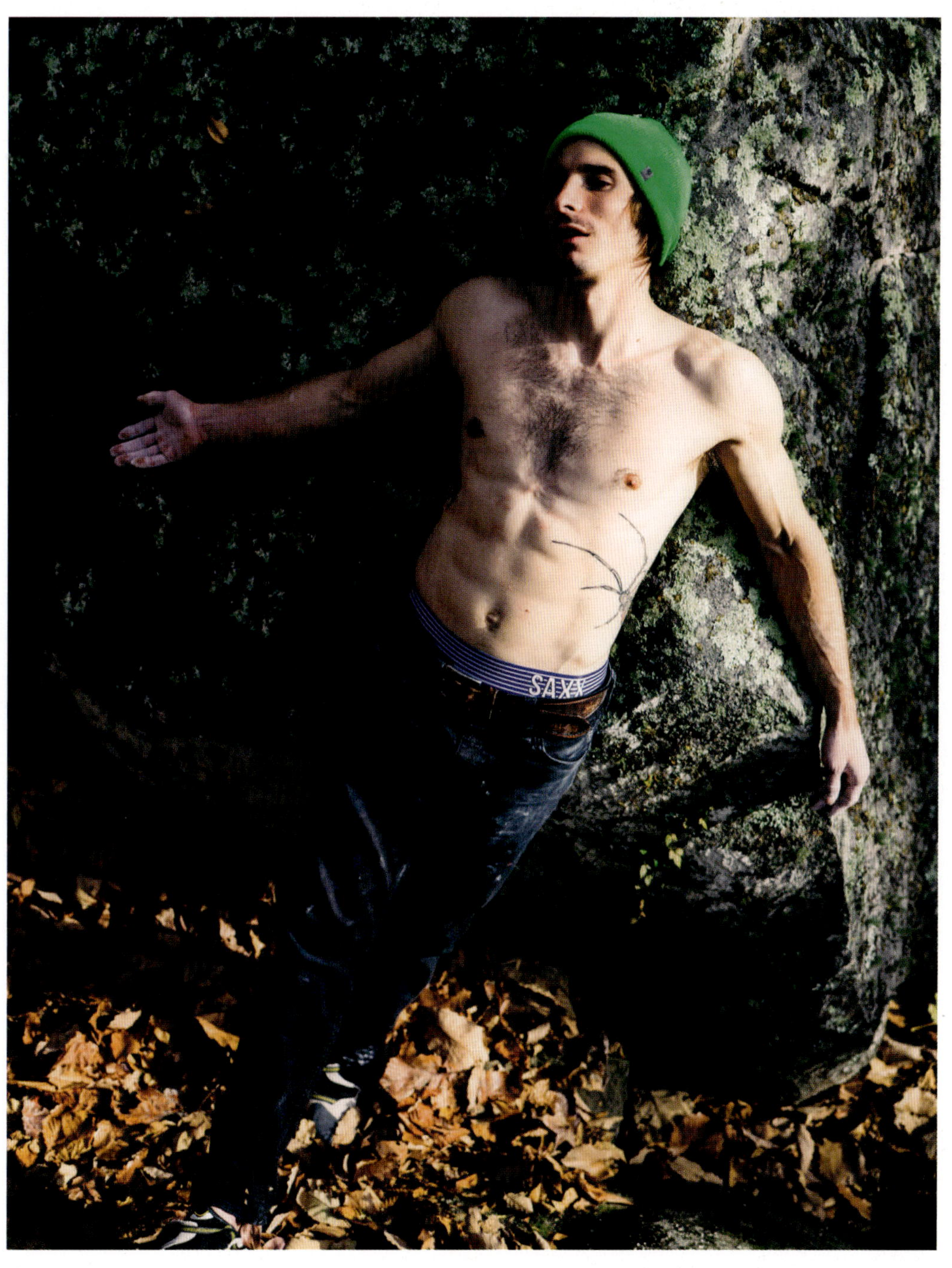

Opposite:
Issac Caldiero at
Stone Fort, Tennessee

Daniel Woods at Horse
Pens 40 Ranch, Alabama

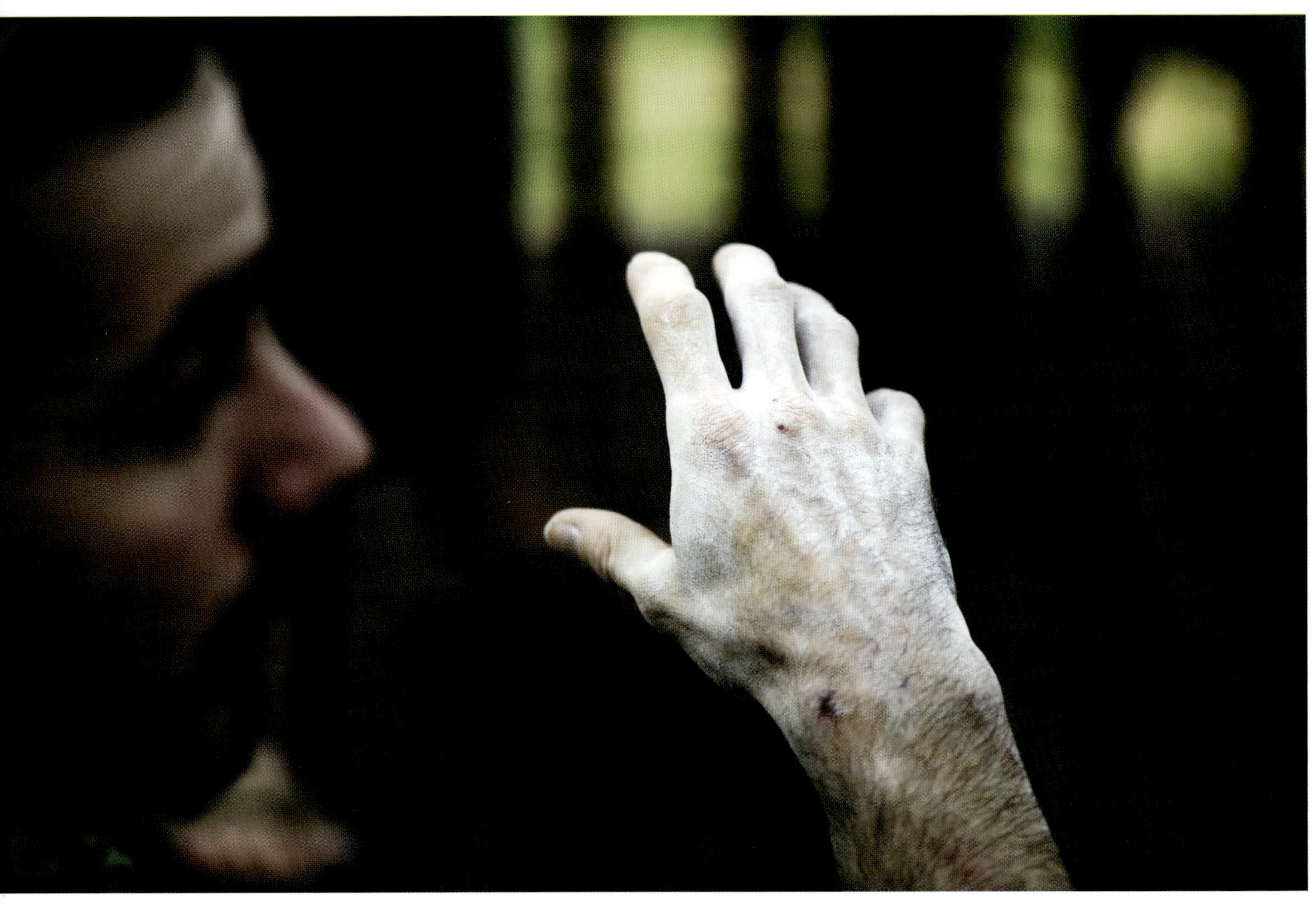

Ronnie Jenkins at
Stone Fort, Tennessee

Opposite, top:
Tony Lamiche on the
first ascent of *New
Sensations* (V11),
Stone Fort

Opposite, bottom:
Paul Robinson at
Stone Fort

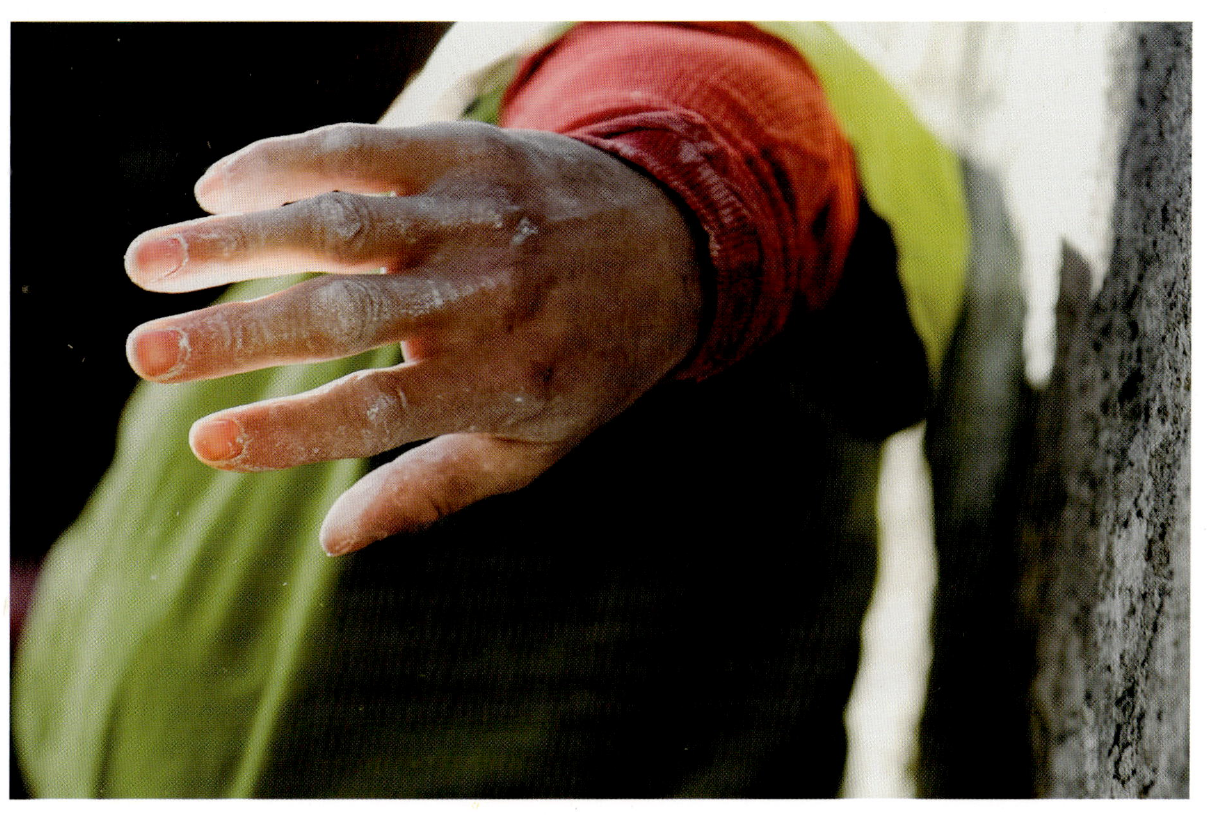

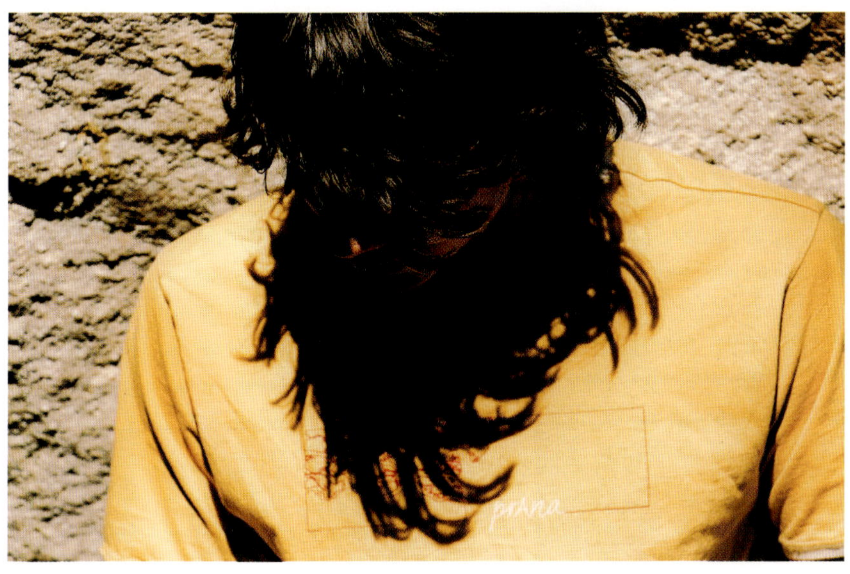
prAna

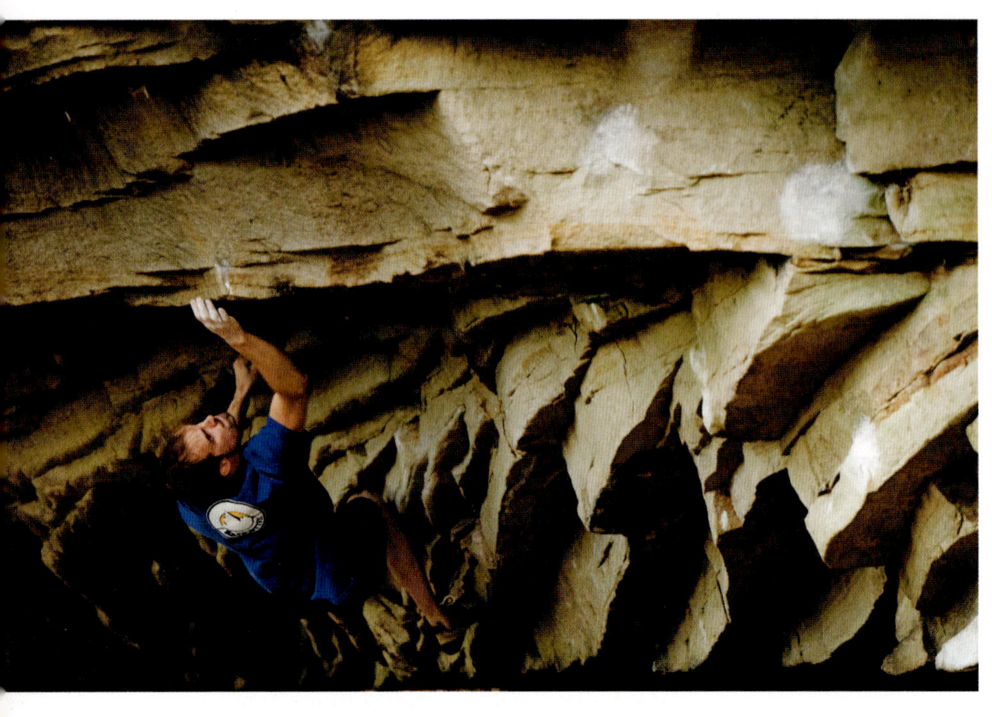

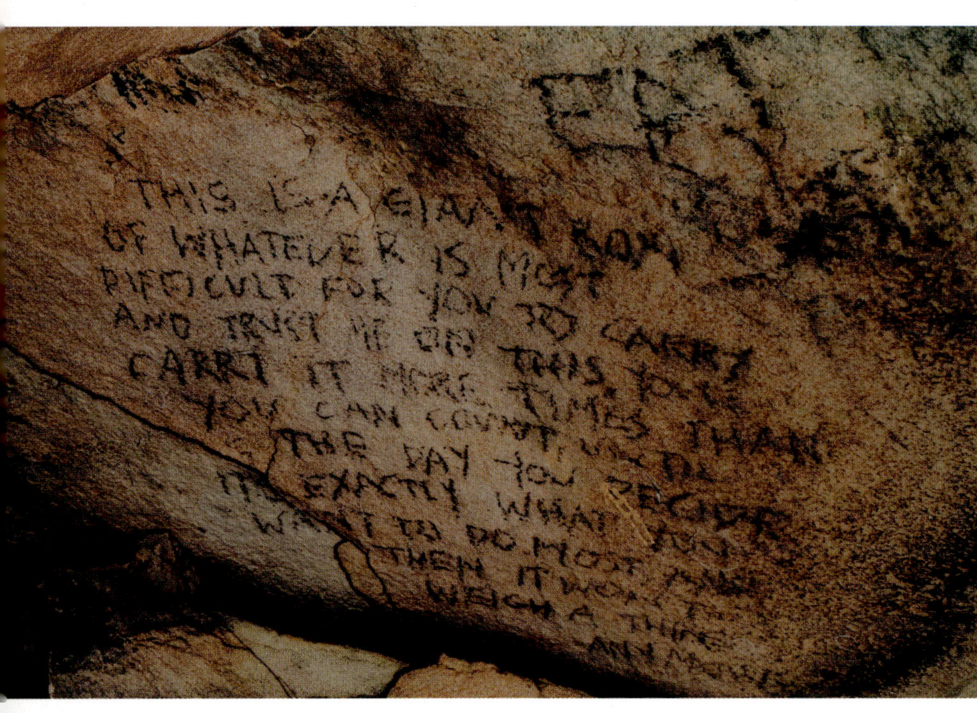
THIS IS A GIANT BOX
OF WHATEVER IS MOST
DIFFICULT FOR YOU TO CARRY
AND TRUST ME ON THIS
CARRY IT MORE TIMES
YOU CAN COUNT TIMES THAN
THE DAY YOU DECIDE
EXACTLY WHAT
WANT TO DO MOST
THEN IT WON'T
WEIGH A THING
ANY MORE

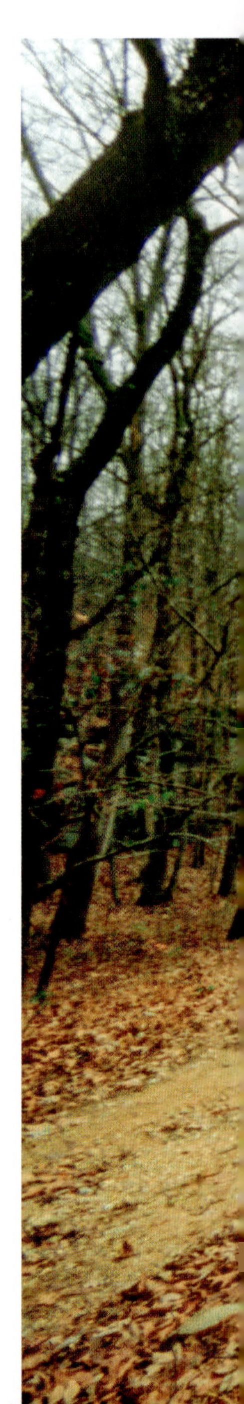

Opposite: James Litz on *Chinese Arithmetic* (V13), Lilly Boulders, Tennessee

Opposite: Graffiti near Chattanooga, Tennessee

Andrew Traylor (left) and Steven Jeffery, Horse Pens 40 Ranch, Alabama

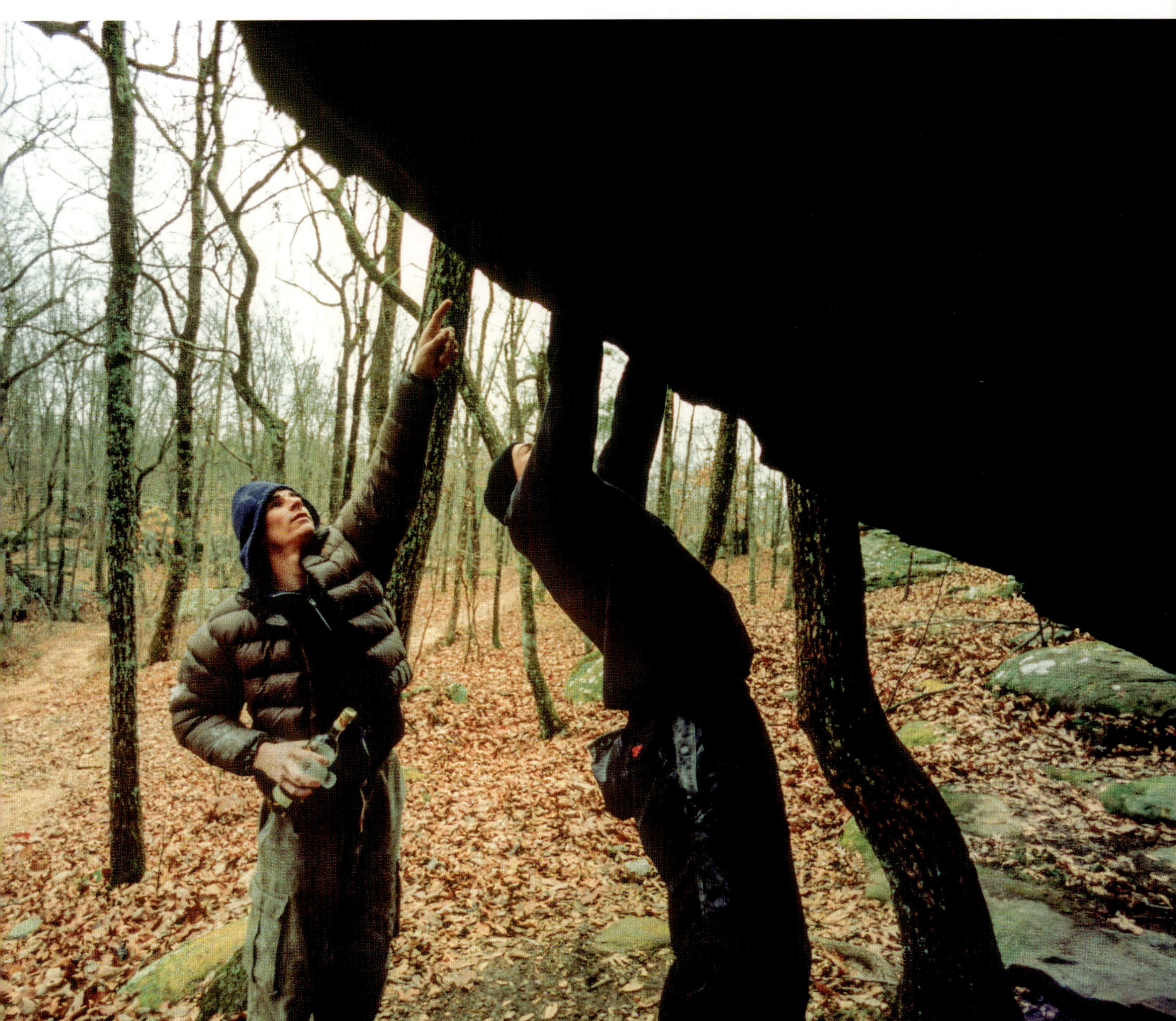

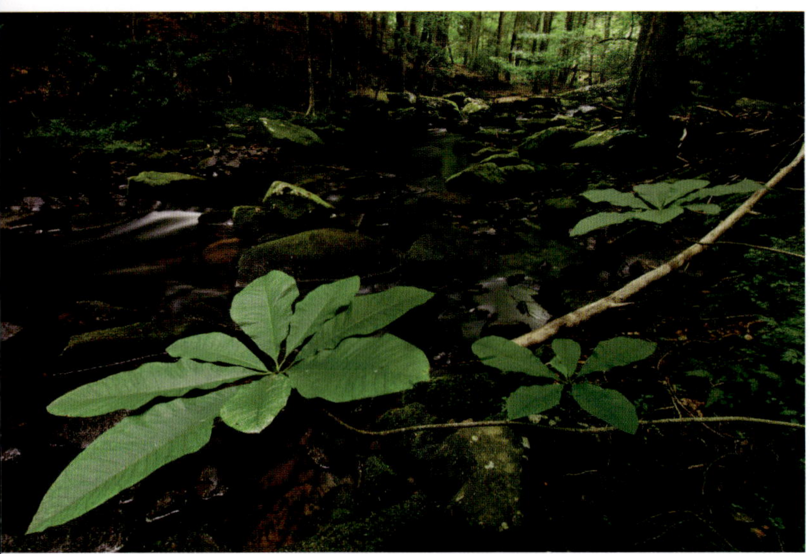

HIDE-AND-SEEK

Southern rock is so plentiful and high quality that anyone with a little time on their hands can revel in their own secret area. For climbers who have traveled enough to know how rare it is, there is an irresistible urge to share the miracle of Southern climbing with the world. Usually, those two impulses are at odds, but sometimes, they are embodied by the same people.

On a map, start at Atlanta, Georgia, and trace a route to Boone, North Carolina. Then go up to Lexington, Kentucky, on down to Birmingham, Alabama, and then back to Atlanta. This heart-shaped region, along with Chattanooga, contains more climbable rock than any other metropolitan area in the United States.

Opposite: Magnolia over Fiery Gizzard Creek, Foster Falls Small Wild Area, Tennessee

Reels Cove, Tennessee

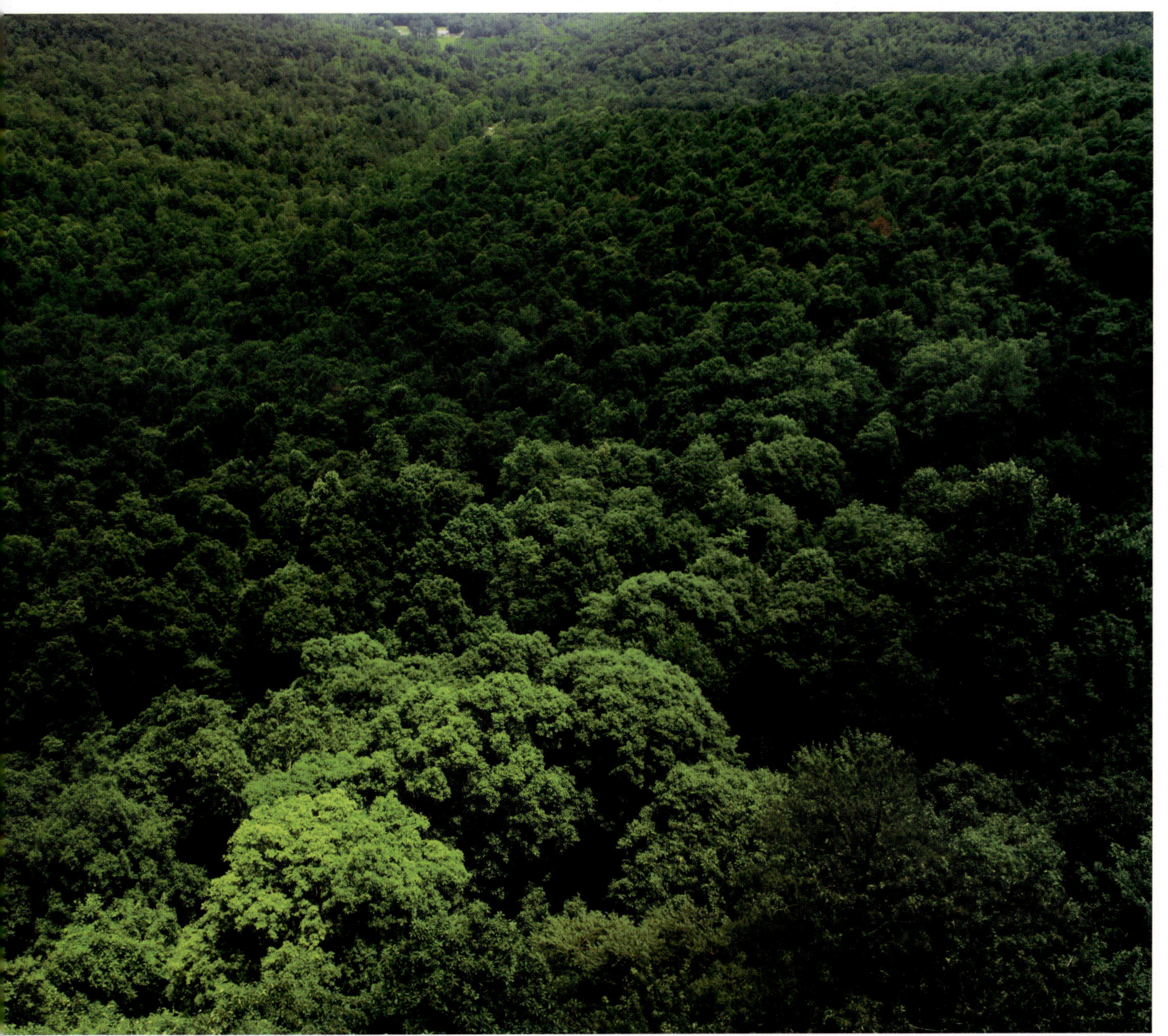

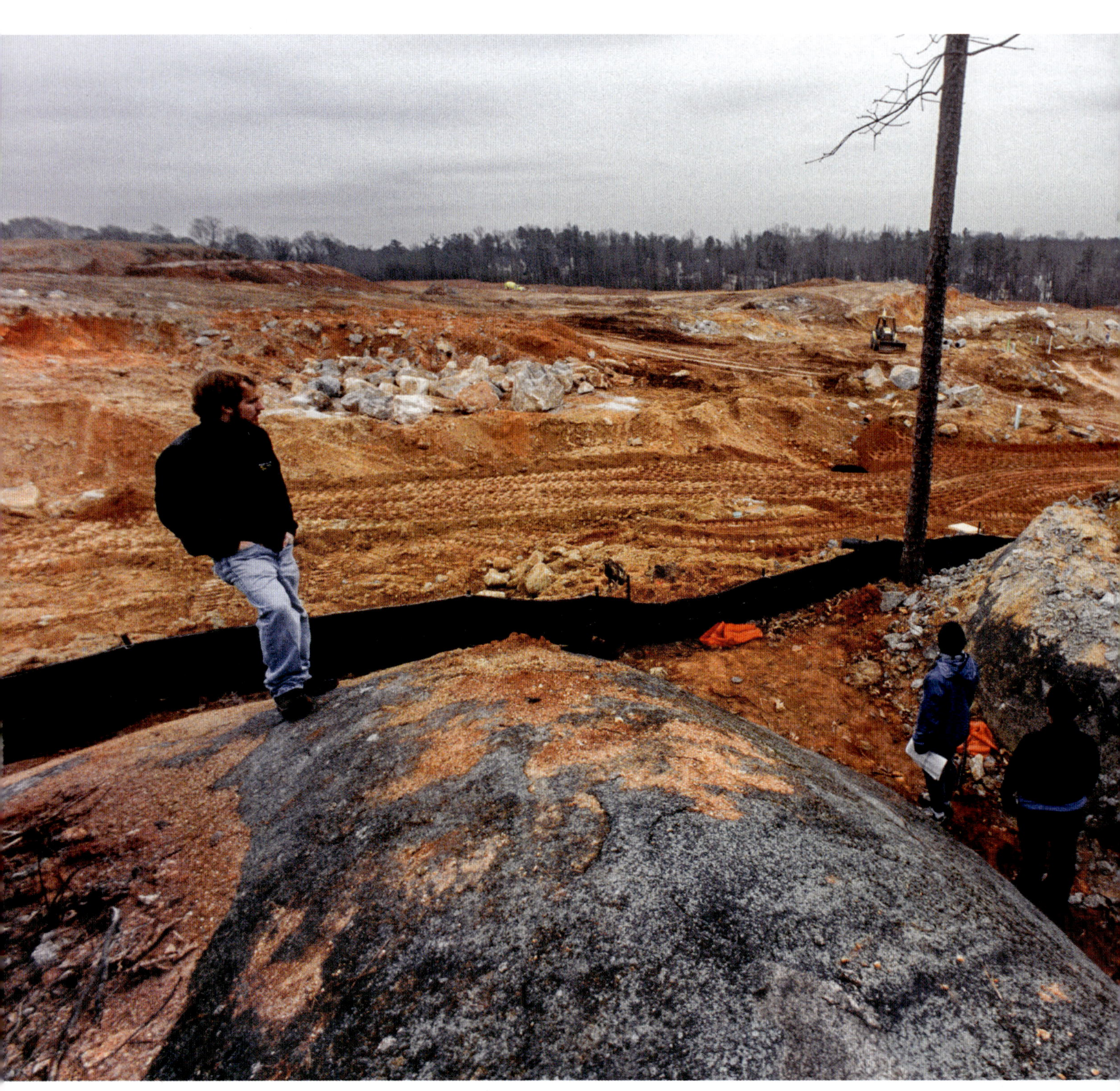

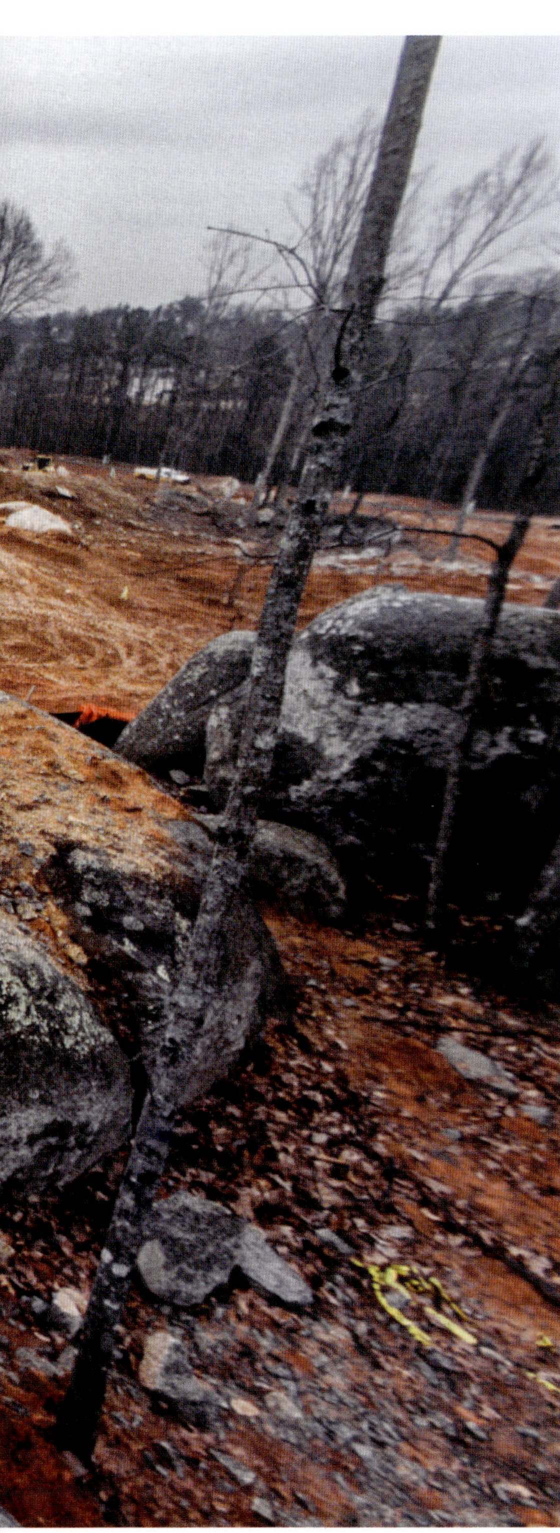

Development underway at Boat Rock in southwestern Atlanta

Much of it remains unexplored for climbing owing to lack of permission. Overlaying property lines reveal a patchwork of land ownership. Most of this climbing is on private land, with some state and federal management mixed in. Around the 1970s and '80s, to the average Southern landowner, climbers were at best trespassers on par with four-wheelers and deer poachers. Access was held by a select few and shared by word of mouth. If you were lucky, you had a face-to-face conversation with a guy in a truck, traded him a twelve-pack of Bud Light, and he'd let you and your friends do your thing on his cliffs. Eventually, someone would screw it up by wandering in unannounced on a Sunday or—God forbid—publishing a picture of that fellow's back forty in a magazine, and next time he'd return with a shotgun.

Encroaching urban development added its own pressure to boulder fields and cliff lines, some of which were physically disappearing. In 2001, a developer's heavy equipment moved into a mile-long stretch of granite-studded forest known as Boat Rock, the crown jewel of Atlanta's bouldering scene. When it was over, half the rock was blasted into driveway gravel.

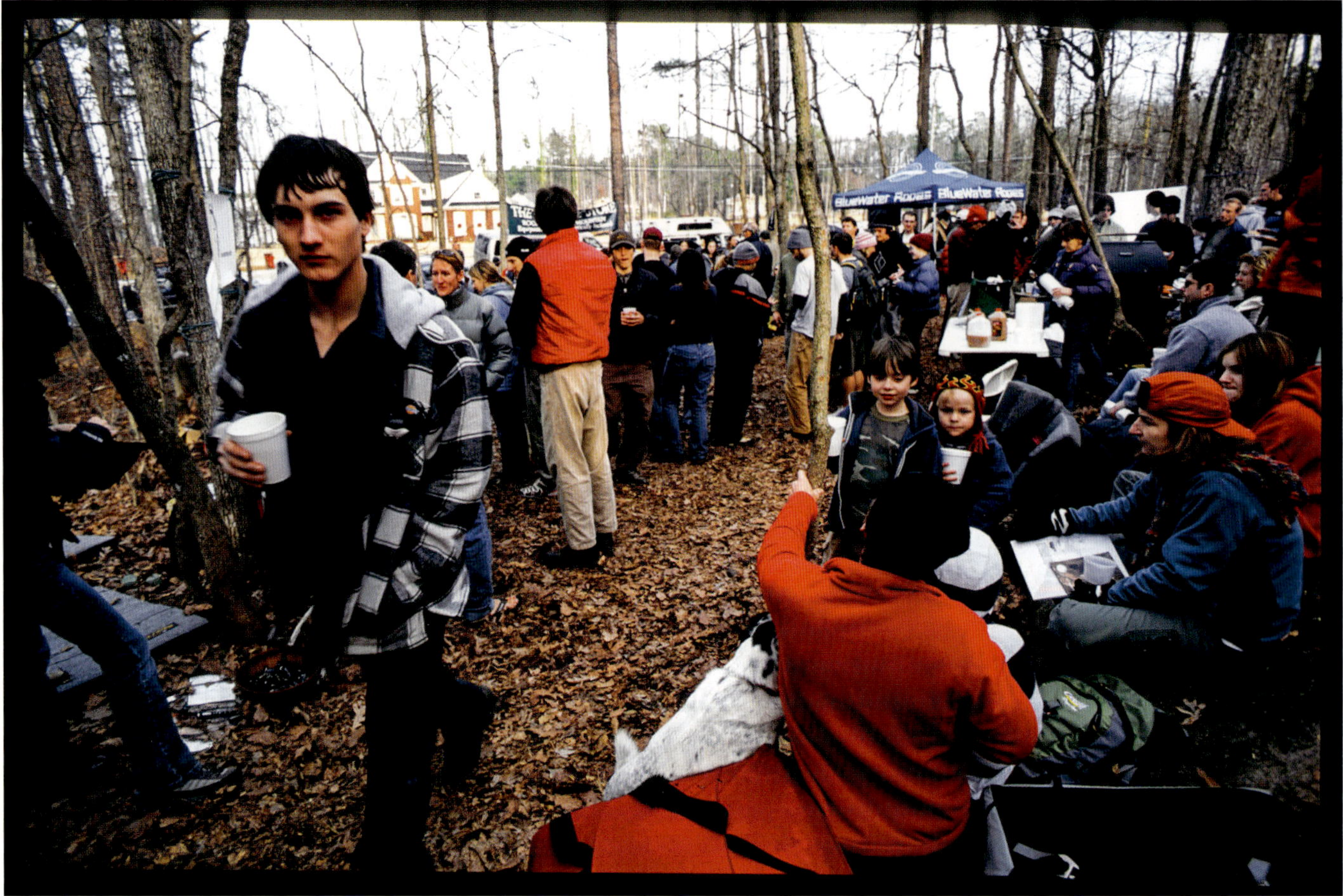

A decade earlier the local climbers had come together as the Southeastern Climbers Coalition (SCC), focused on slideshows, competitions, and some trail building. Suddenly, they had their cause: raise money to buy the remaining five acres and preserve it as a park. That January, the SCC put together the best event they knew how to pull off well: a clean-up and competition at Boat Rock. The bulldozers were rumbling in the background while the locals climbed and shared a huge pot of chili. The SCC had about $1,000 in the bank, but that Boat Rock episode was the spark, when community enthusiasm for access burned and spread across the South. In five years, they raised $130,000, enough to purchase the remaining land and designate it a public park, boulders and all.

Opposite: The 2005 Boat Rock Climbing Competition in Atlanta

Southeastern Climbers Coalition meeting at Split Rock, Little River Canyon National Preserve, Alabama

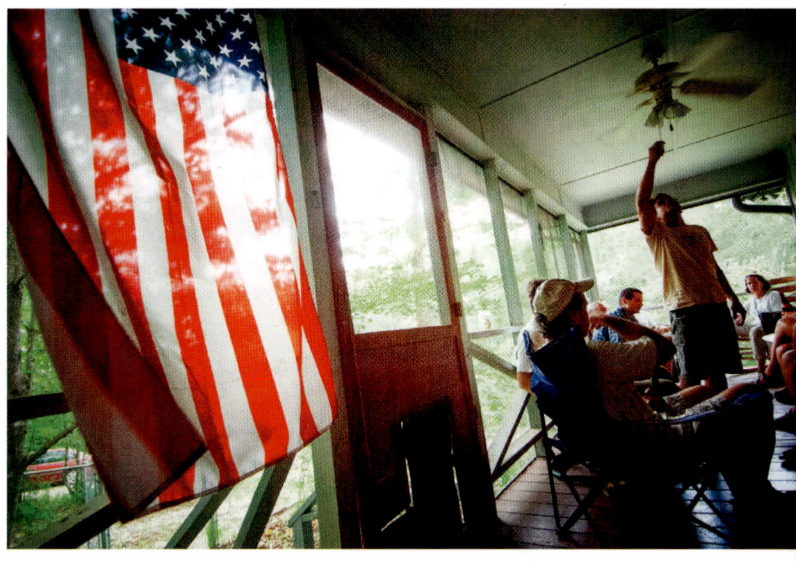

Land studded with giant boulders and stone bluffs was striking to look at but didn't generate much revenue for the typical farmer or developer. A few years before, North Carolina climbers held a climbing competition at the Hound Ears Club, a mountainside country club in Boone. The hope was to raise money for Howard's Knob, a beloved climbing area threatened by development. Southern climbers were hitting on a solid strategy: convince these landowners to sell or lease their property to a nonprofit that would in turn steward the land. Climbers would be low-impact, conservation-forward, and help keep the off-road vehicles and riffraff out. The SCC and the neighboring Carolina Climbers Coalition used loans to buy access deeds or even whole crags and raised money to pay them off with events like that first one, only bigger. The Hound Ears event in Boone eventually joined forces with two other events in Alabama and Chattanooga to become the annual Triple Crown Bouldering Series, a massive three-month-long festival that became the primary fundraising tool for climbing access. Howard's Knob was never saved, but the next twenty years was a remarkable time of organization and expansion by climbers in the South.

This turning point in Southern climbing was the subject of my 2009 film, *Heart of Stone*, which I directed with Josh Fowler. Atlanta climber Brad McLeod was the cofounder and treasurer of the SCC in those days—and the key, really, to the whole Boat Rock deal. A former Navy SEAL, compact and bursting with energy, Brad is one of the most downright *cheerful* people I've ever met, a quintessential happy warrior.

▶

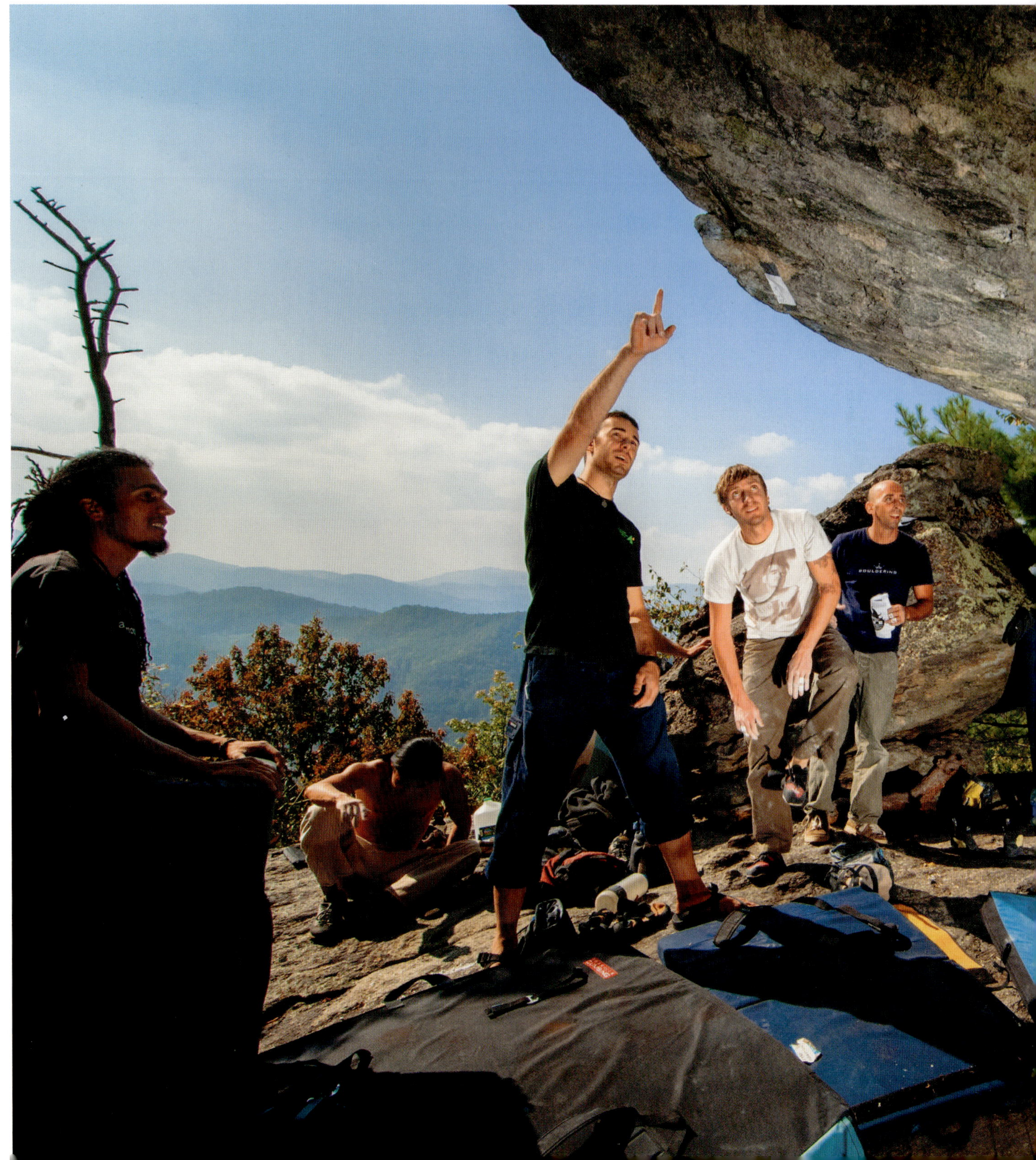
BOULDERING

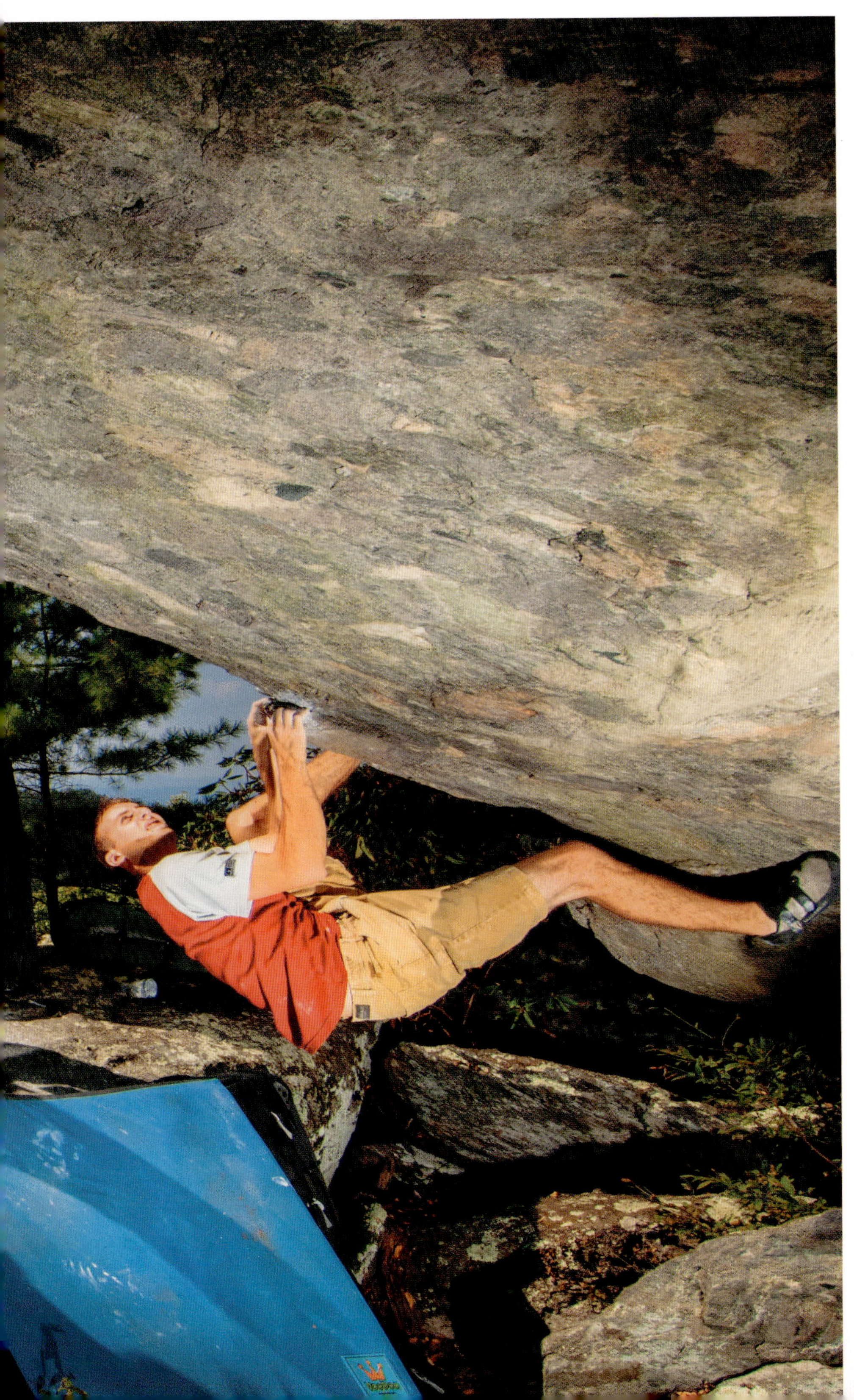

The 2005 Hound Ears Bouldering Competition in Boone, North Carolina

Josh Edwards (left) and John Maldonado at Stone Fort, Tennessee

We followed Brad around for months, documenting the SCC's acquisition work as it happened. In one scene Josh captured, we've pulled off the side of a back road outside of Steele, Alabama, to view a mile-long cliff line surrounded by farm fields and forest. It's a crisp autumn day. A perfectly metaphorical barbed wire fence separates us from the area. Climbers had been accessing the walls of Steele clandestinely, dropping in from the top until the mid-1980s after one of the clifftop landowners got sick of climbers traipsing through his tomato fields and began aggressively policing the area.

"Makes you wanna go climbing on a day like this!" Brad's cell phone rings. It's Deborah, a local realtor. He hangs up after a short conversation. "She'll be here in just a few minutes." Suddenly, after twenty-five years, Steele was in play.

In the next scene, we are walking through a sunny patch of woods on a rough trail of pines, young hardwoods, and exposed sandstone. Brad looks up at an overhanging wall of rock, easily a hundred feet high, while holding a stack of papers detailing property lines and potential access points.

Cut to an open field. Brad and Deborah look down at the maps together. Tomatoes dot the dry dirt at their feet.

Finally, we see Brad standing next to a shed. Leaning against a truck opposite him is a big man in jeans and muddy work boots, Deborah at his side. Brad makes his case to the landowner from a respectful distance. An environmental engineer by trade, he's in his element having face-to-face conversations with ordinary folks about the minutiae of land boundaries and harvesting cycles.

There's a pause as the landowner leans harder against his truck and looks off at the cliffs. He declares, "Maybe it'll work out. Like ah' say, I'm not knockin' it, but if ya like climbin' rocks," and then he pauses. The agent laughs, and the tension breaks.

"Well, if we do get it," says Brad, "you'll know that someone's smiling and enjoying this land. I'll assure you that."

"It's pretty up there, I can tell you that," the landowner replies. He reminisces about how he and his brothers cared for the property, begrudgingly logging it by hand here and there to afford the cost. He picks a dry stalk of grass and motions toward the proposed access trail. "But right up here on yonder way, nothin' was cut. Just got too rough for us, an' I was tired of totin' my saw." He gives Brad a serious look and continues, "We just didn't come in here and wreck the land or nothin'."

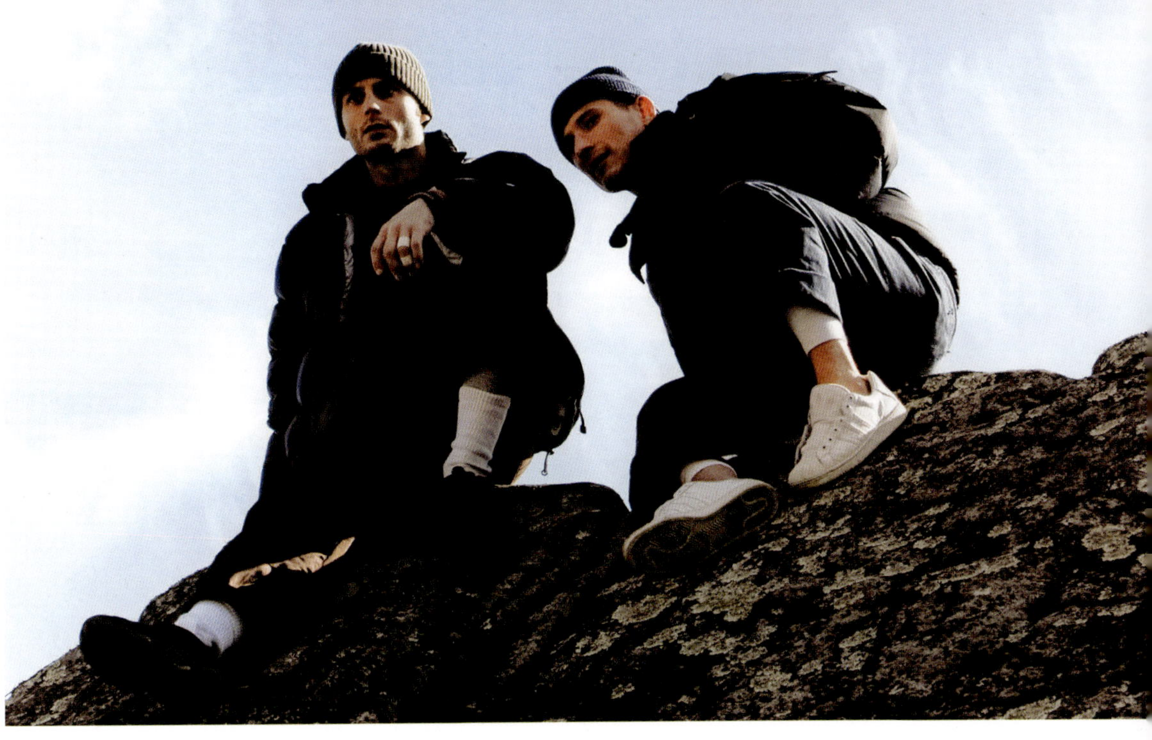

"Mm-hm," Brad replies as he nods off camera.

For years, climbers had simply assumed the owner of the clifftop tomato fields controlled access to the entire cliff. As it turned out, this landowner—one of several who leased the fields for farming—held property at the base of the rock walls. The SCC would purchase a parcel from him that would give them permanent legal access to the climbing walls without ever having to set foot on top of the cliff. There would be a parking lot and pit toilets courtesy of the American Alpine Club and the Access Fund.

The landowner picks at the stalk in silence, lost in thought. "Well, we better get on outta here," he concludes. They all shake hands. And that was how Steele was opened.

Years later, Brad remembers the excitement of it. "I love to think back on that whole scene. It will always be one of the best times of my life," he says. "It was like a treasure hunt, digging through tax records at the county courthouse and finding something like that. It's the most unsexy part of climbing, but we were making history. It was like the Southern version of pioneering Yosemite big walls."

The strategies the SCC used to gain access to crags like Steele helped other climbing organizations around the country learn how to approach their own big walls. In Southern California or the Front Range, the market may not bear buying a mile of cliff line like in rural Alabama, but there were treasures out there. You just had to go to the courthouse and dig through the tax maps to find those leftover, undesirable bits of land—"the bones," as Brad calls them—that can give you access to the rock.

"Then you have the treasure map," says Brad, "but you need the *people* to make it happen. People like Bob Cormany. When I first moved here from California, I was going all over the place looking for the gymnastic overhanging climbing that the South is known for. One day Bob showed me around Boat Rock in Atlanta. I got thoroughly spanked on the blank granite there, and maybe didn't appreciate it that much. But he sat me on the back of his truck afterwards and opened my eyes to what that area was about, and why it was so special to him. That was the tipping point for me." ◆

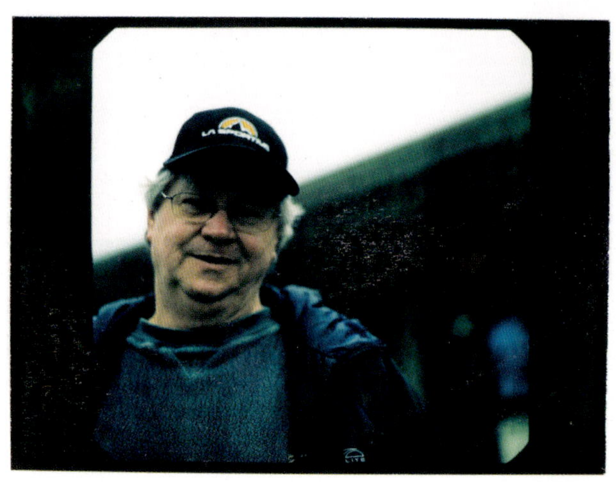

Portraits from the Triple Crown Bouldering Series, left page, clockwise from upper left: Norm Pitts, Eric Pittman, Ronnie Jenkins, and Jimmy Webb

Right page, clockwise from upper left: Brion Voges, Whitney Boland, Lee Means, Conrad Anker, and Pat Goodman

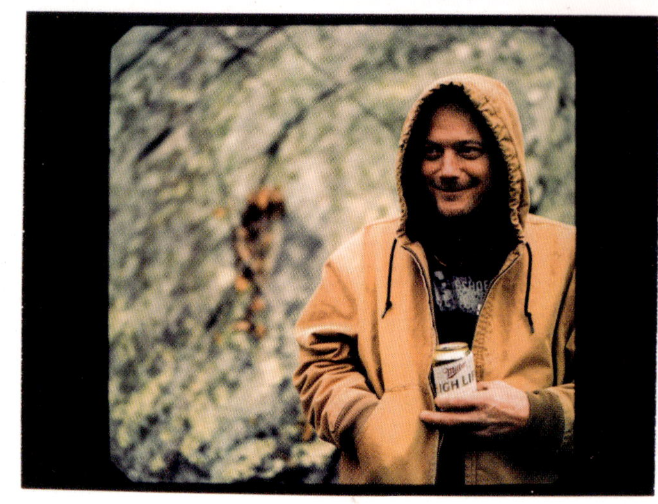

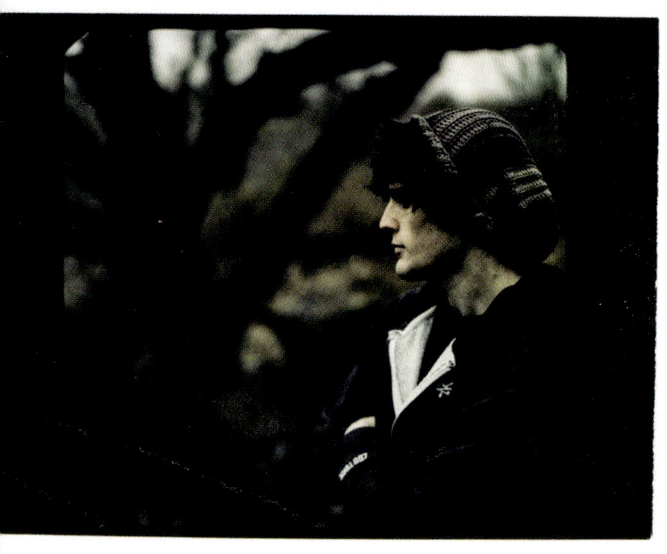

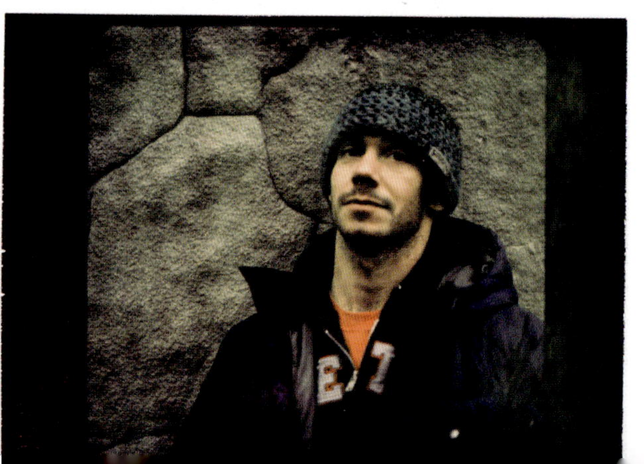

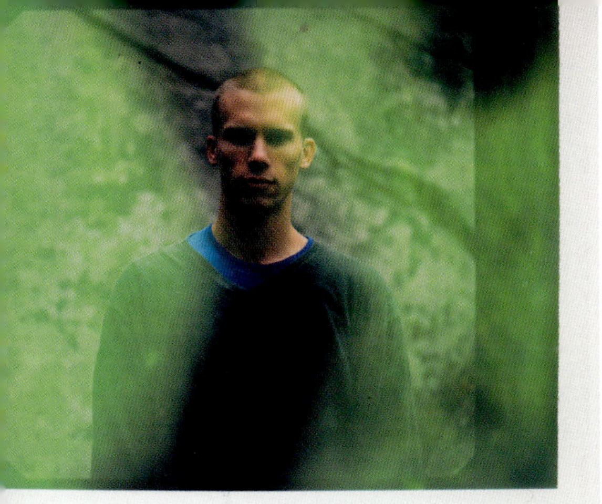

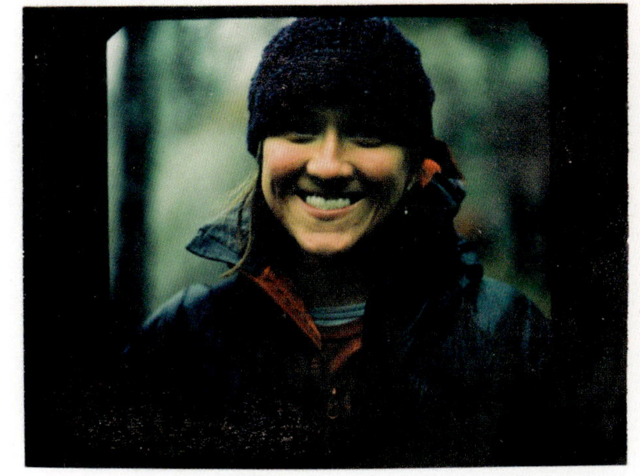

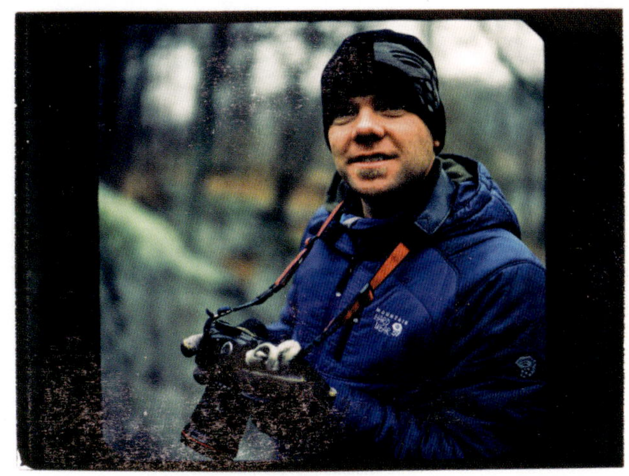

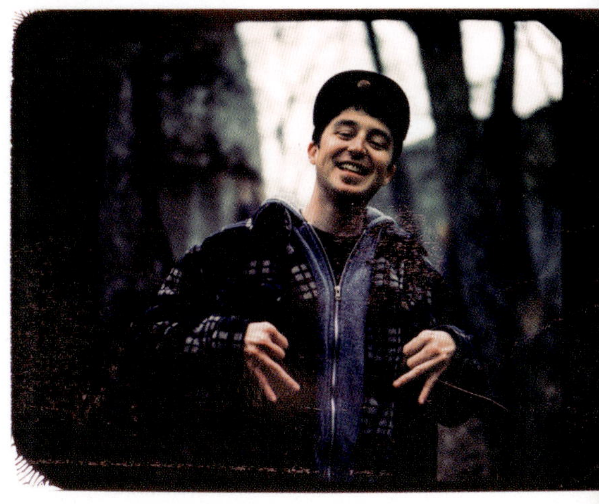

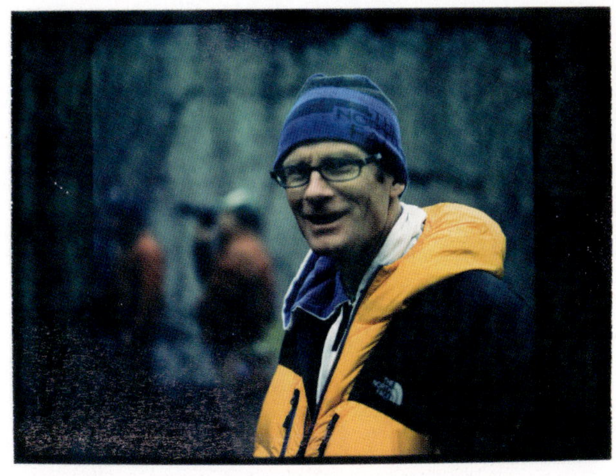

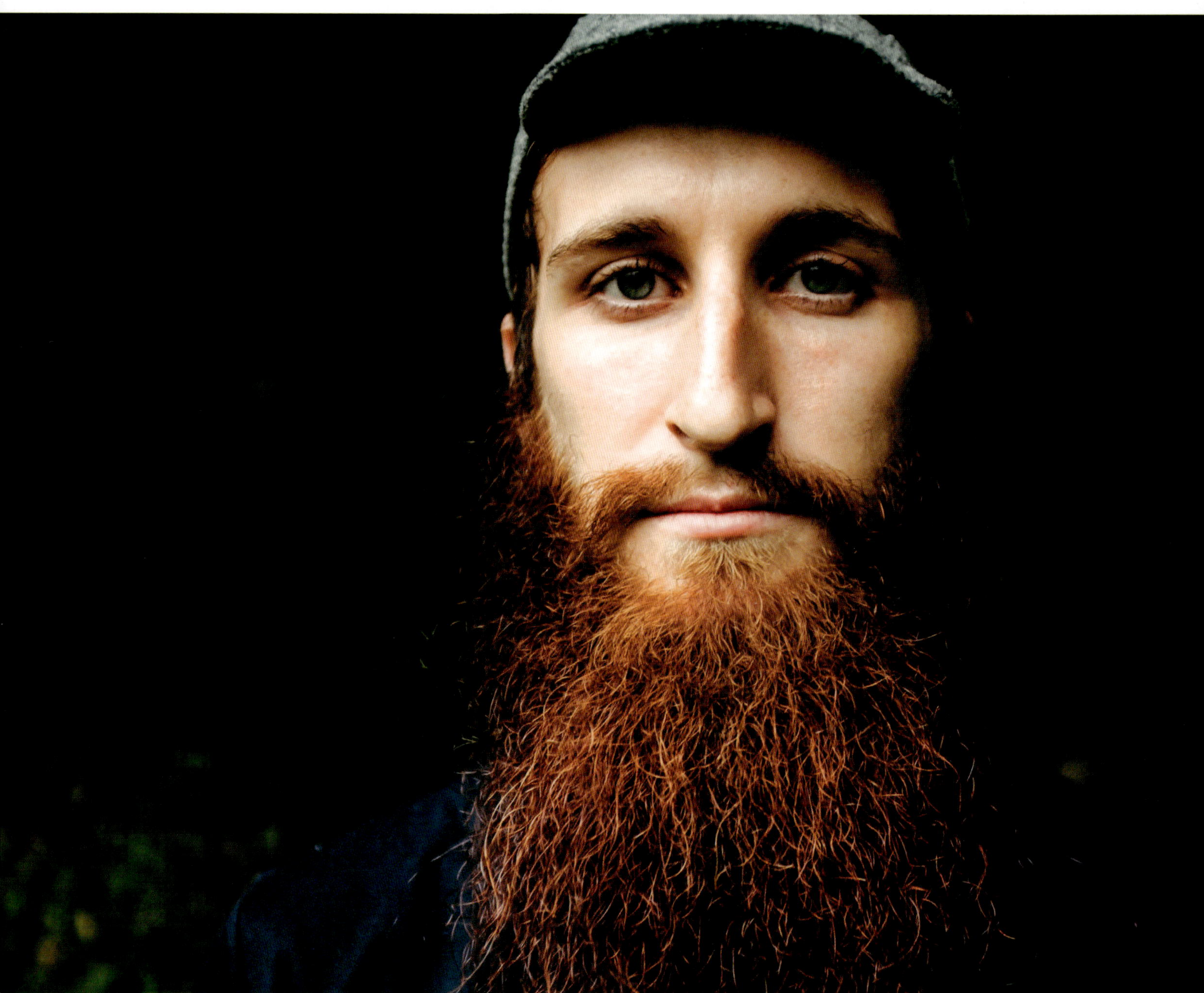

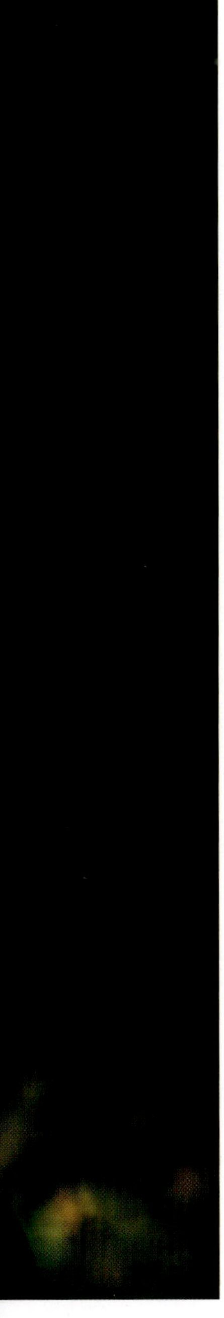

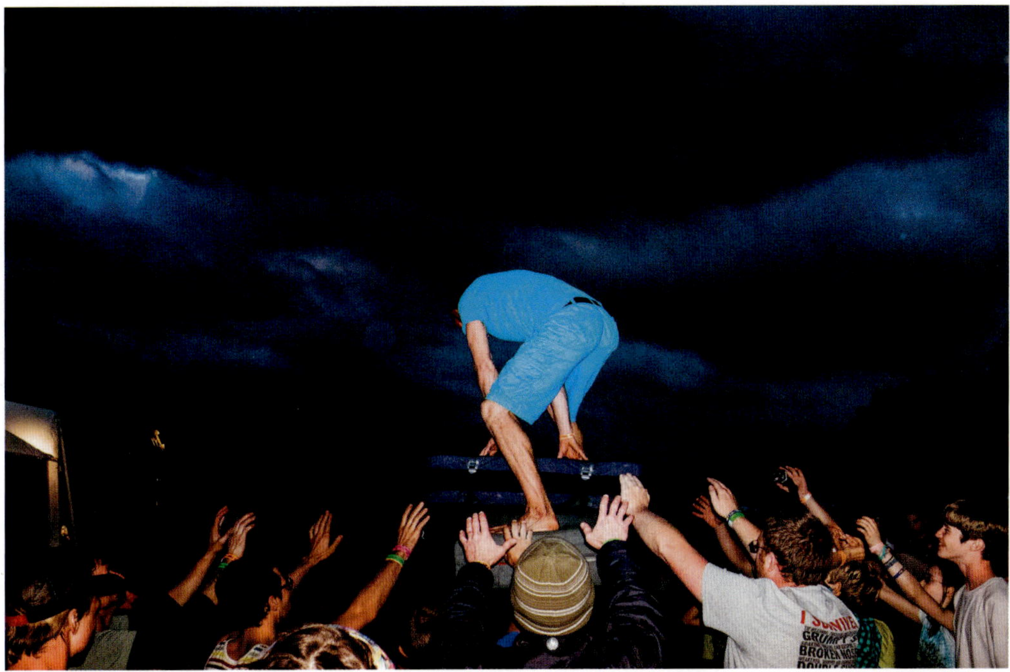

Opposite: Mitch Vernon at Grandfather Campground, near Boone, North Carolina

Crash pad surfing at Stone Fort during the 2014 Triple Crown

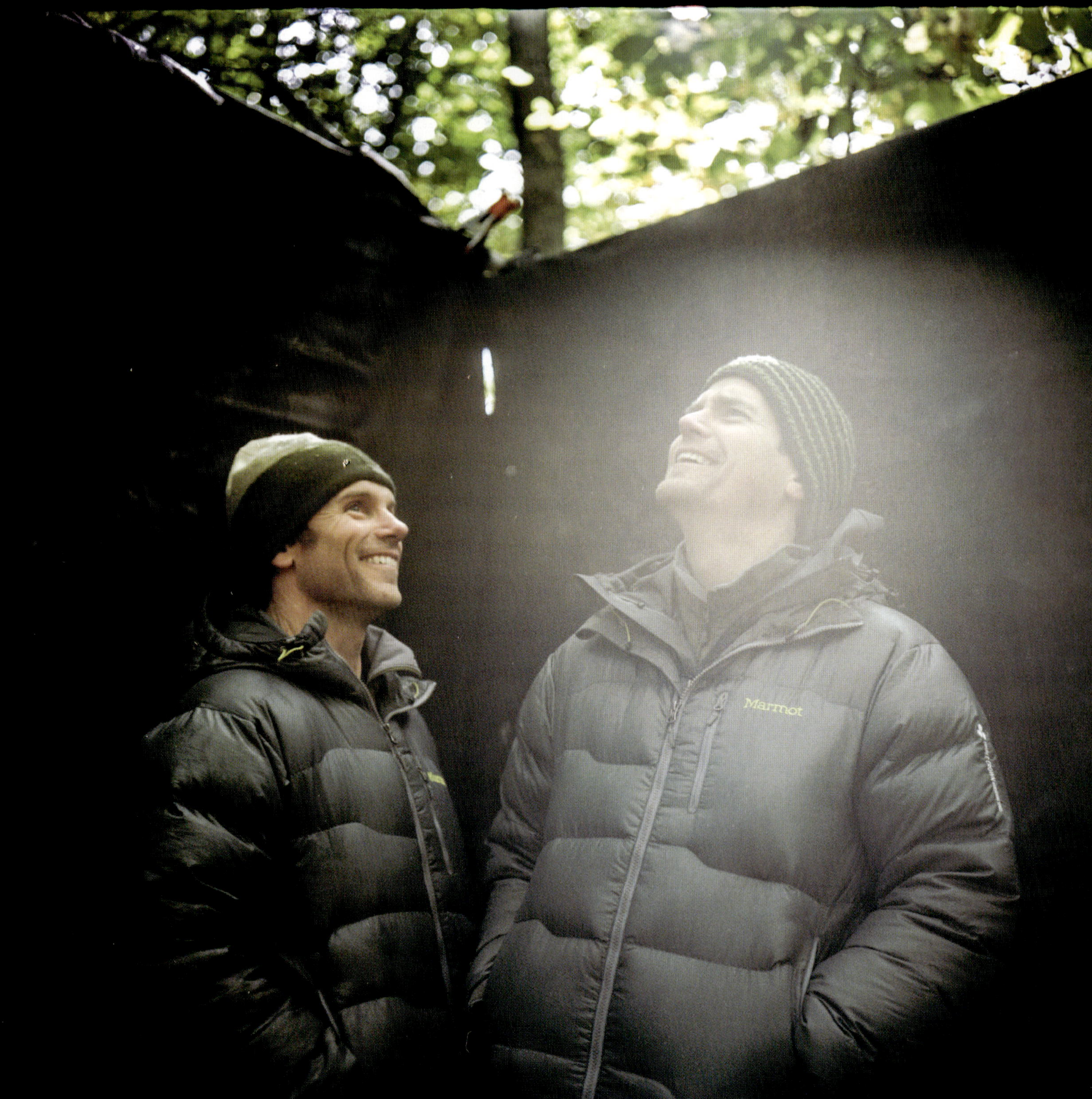
Marmot

Opposite: Chad Wykle and Jim Horton, founders of the Triple Crown Bouldering Series, at Hound Ears, North Carolina

Hands of boulderers at the 2003 Stone Fort Bouldering Competition

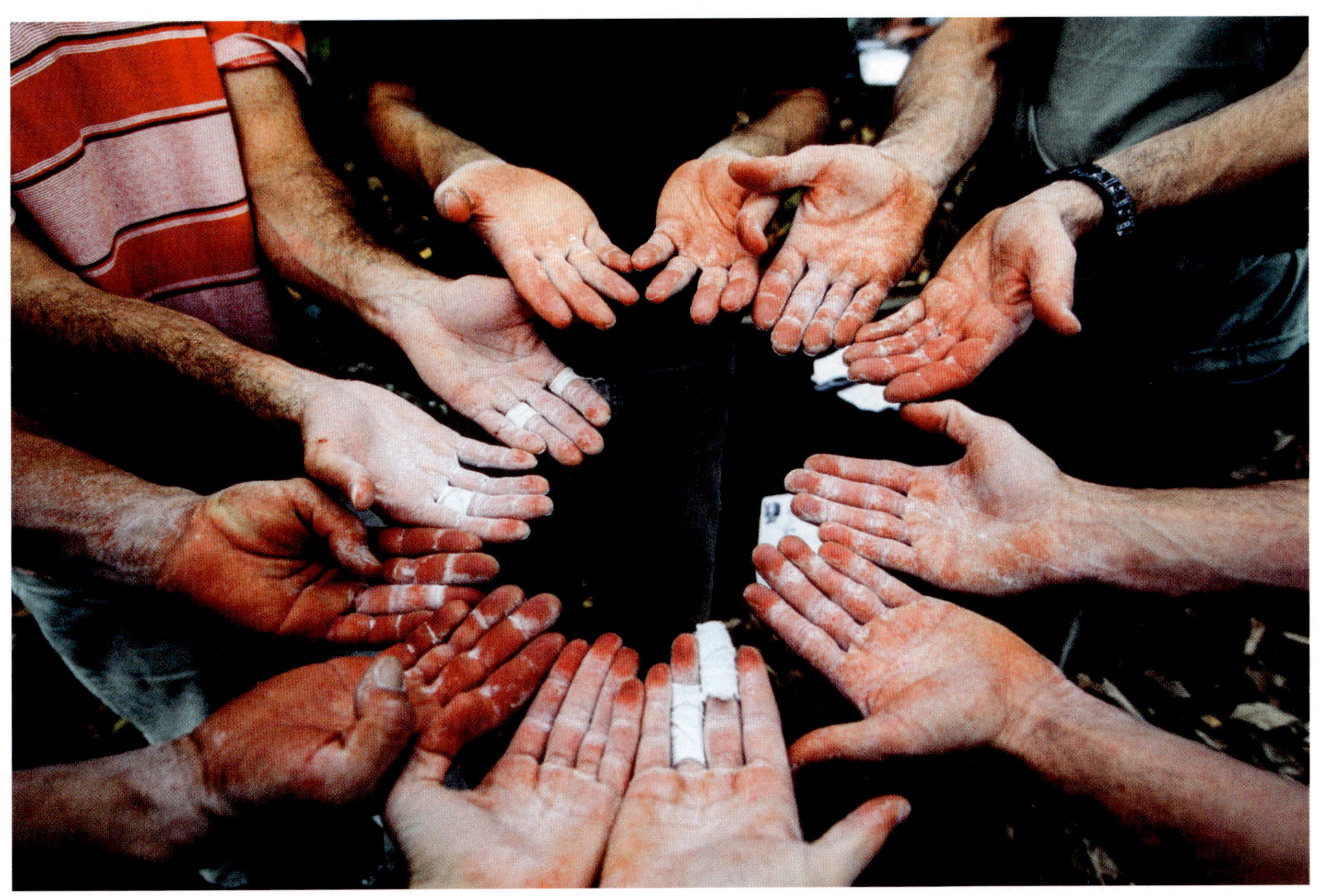

Sandstone textures,
Stone Fort, Tennessee

UNCOMMON FRUIT

The first time I made the trip to Boone, I got good and lost. I had no idea which route to take or where I might stay along the way. I just knew where I was headed: the Hound Ears Club. The posh gated community on a ridge line between Grandfather Mountain and Boone was rumored to have great climbing. I planned to meet up with my friend Christian Olsen from Florida, who'd gotten wind of a little bouldering event at Hound Ears organized by some local climbers.

It takes about an hour to escape the metro Atlanta gravity well. Once you get to the South Carolina border, the route bifurcates like branches on a tree through the Blue Ridge Escarpment leading into the Southern Appalachians. You can veer north, following the Chattahoochee River, then on past Tallulah Gorge and into the Nantahala National Forest. Or you can wait a bit longer and make your move at Clemson, through Panther Gap and onto Asheville, or take the next branch past Travelers Rest toward Pisgah National Forest. In between are sub-branches leading through Highlands, Cashiers, and Brevard. Eventually these back-road tendrils come back to Route 221 past Linville Gorge and lead onto the main branch of Highway 105 past Grandfather Mountain. In the days before GPS navigation, you would ask three different climbers and get a half dozen directions, all with important geographical and spiritual power spots to hit along the way.

It was the most beautiful autumn day, and somewhere in that back-road jumble, I took a detour following a sign for "Apples," then another detour for "Pottery." I ended up with some preserves and a couple of face jugs, folk art vessels depicting misshapen faces that have their roots in African ceramic art—a complicated and mysterious tradition still very much alive in the Southern Appalachians.

At the second annual Hound Ears Bouldering Competition, Christian and I climbed all day on granite so sharp that to this day I can still feel the fiery indents on my fingertips. I got to know the organizer, Jim Horton, who introduced me to his buddy Joey Henson. Through Joey I met his artist neighbor, Kim Fuelling, and her husband, Paul. We met Scott Temple, who invited us to stay in his teepee camp where he and his wife were living full time in the woods outside Boone. We shared apple butter and climbing stories around a campfire. Climbing wove them together like the homespun quilts displayed on those back-road porches.

Jessa Goebel is part of that fabric. She grew up in nearby Greensboro and started in her teens as an indoor competition climber, traveling the country. By the time I met her at Hound Ears in 1998, she was looking for something deeper to access in climbing but was unsure how to make it happen. "I thought it was one extreme or the other," she told Chris Kalous on his *Enormocast* podcast. "Either work your ass off and only go climbing on the weekends, or you're the typical Valley dirtbag, like digging-in-the-trash-can stuff." She found a middle way in Boone climber Pat Goodman, who lived a relatively stable life with a day job and still traveled and climbed at the highest level. "He lived in a house. He had a car. I had no idea that was possible."

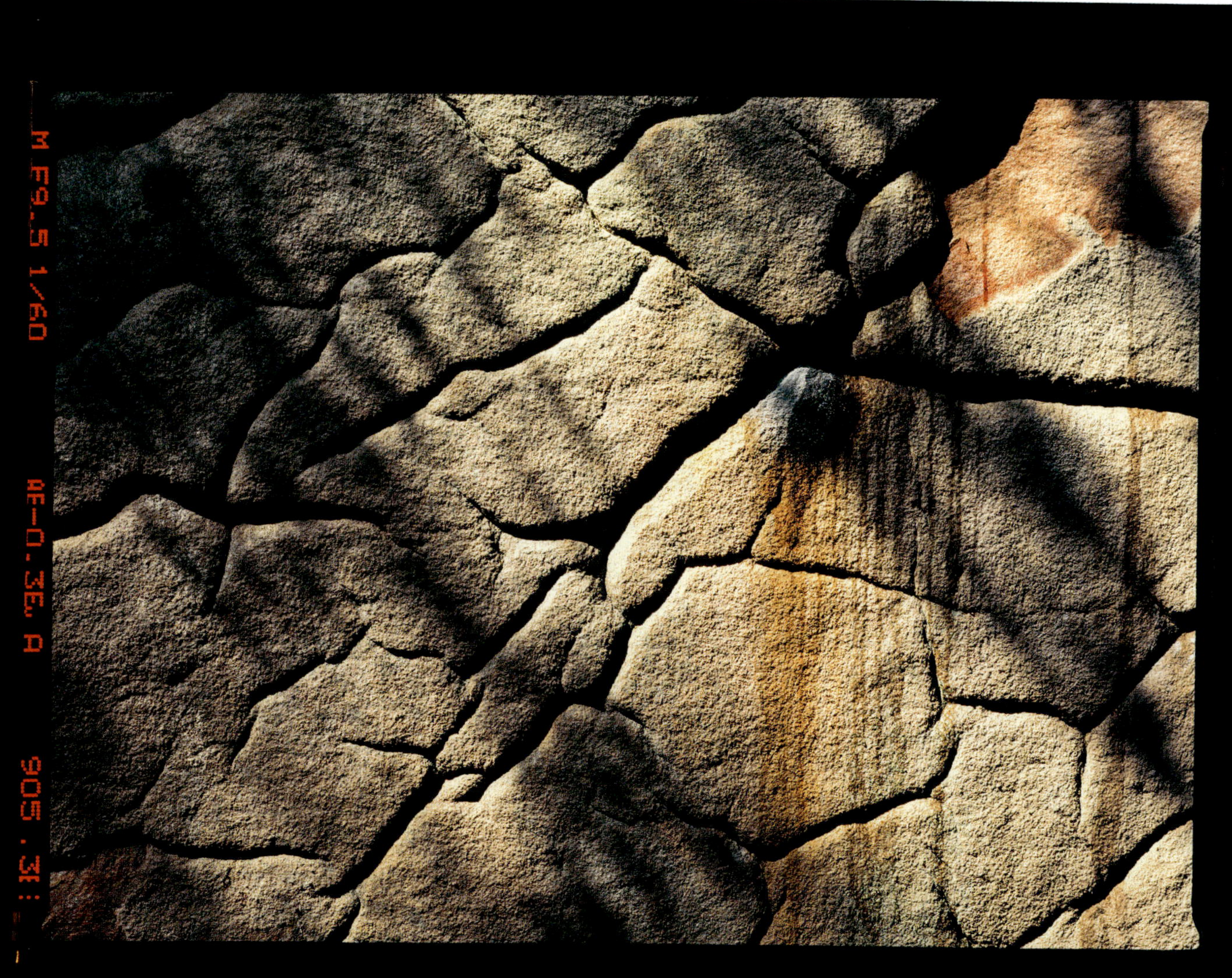

Portraits from the Triple Crown Bouldering Series, clockwise from upper left: Daniel Woods, Charlie Fowler, Paul Morley and Anthony Love, Kurt Smith, Rebecca Wykle and Katherine Farmer, Wills Young, unknown crash pad jumper, and Bob Cormany

Pat also showed Jessa what was possible in traditional climbing. "I'd always thought that was a thing of the past, what the old dudes do," she told Chris. "But Pat came into the picture and gave that side of climbing a new definition. He was climbing the super cool, futuristic, edgy lines. He was doing the badass sport climbs, but on gear. I had no idea that was even an option." Over time, Jessa left competition climbing altogether and began establishing herself as climber in all disciplines, from hard bouldering to traditional routes, and establishing new routes on Canadian big walls with Pat. I reconnected with her at Hound Ears a decade after we first met, where Josh Fowler and I were working on *Heart of Stone*. Jessa had been there volunteering for days, and we asked her why she was doing that instead of out climbing some hard new route or dominating the competition. She laughed humbly and said, "I feel like I owe the climbing community something."

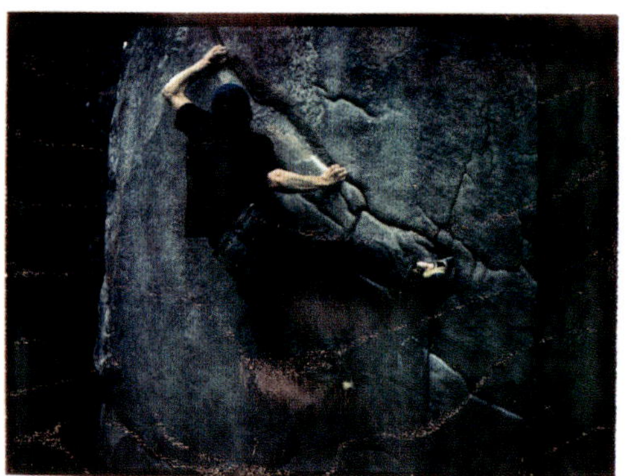

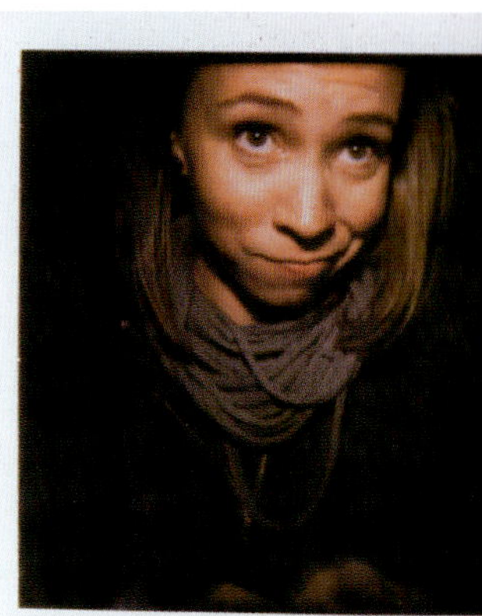

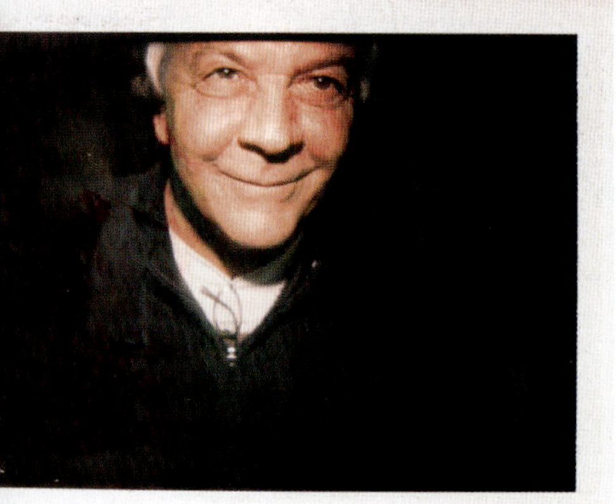

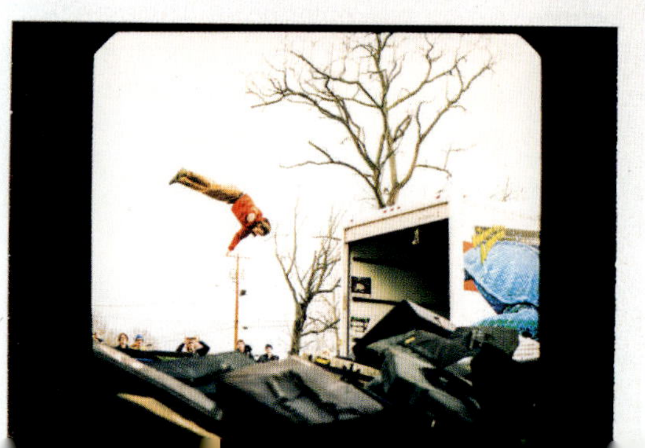

I was learning that Southern climbers follow an unspoken rule that you spend just as much—or more—time and effort volunteering for trail work and community events as you do climbing. If you placed in the top three at Hound Ears, the next year you're putting on a volunteer T-shirt and helping judge for this year's competition. To an outsider from Colorado, California, or Utah, where the volume and size of climbable rock dwarfs anything in the South, this strong volunteer ethic may seem like a lot of work, but it makes practical sense in a place where constant grassroots organizing is the key to accessing climbing areas that are mostly on private land. This ethic has power beyond that though.

A few years ago I photographed a story for *Smithsonian* magazine about a little loblolly pine farm in North Carolina that was growing Bianchetto truffles. A Nigerian microbiologist at a local university named Omoanghe Isikhuemhen, who goes by Dr. Omon, devised a way to stimulate the growth of these truffles—golden, strangely aromatic, and fabulously expensive—under these ordinary pines. In the gourmet food world, this was a big deal. It's the only place in America where Bianchettos have been grown successfully. Dr. Omon's formula is a closely guarded secret, and it seemed like its origins were just as mysterious to him. "It came to me in a dream," he says.

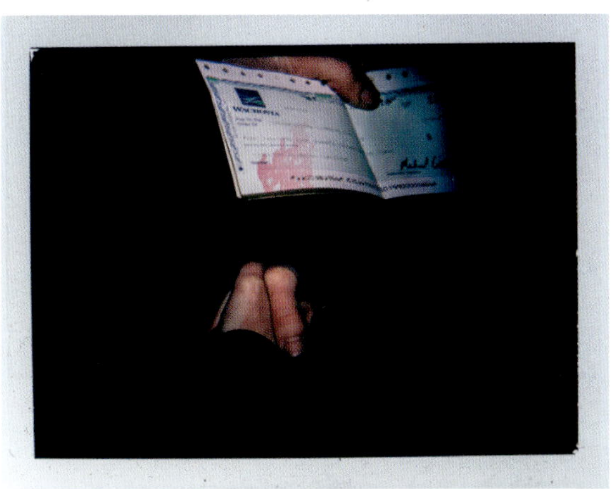

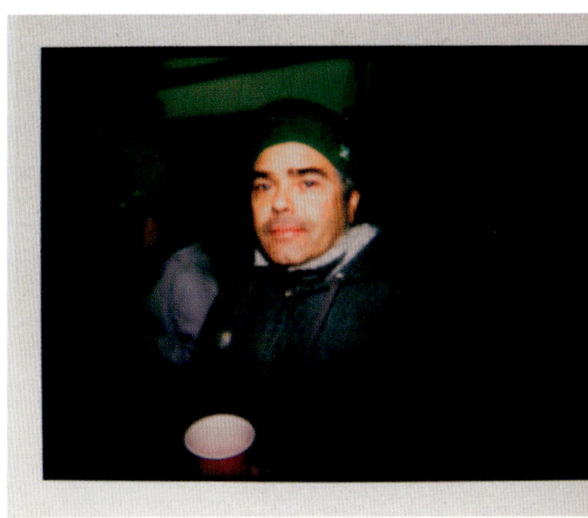

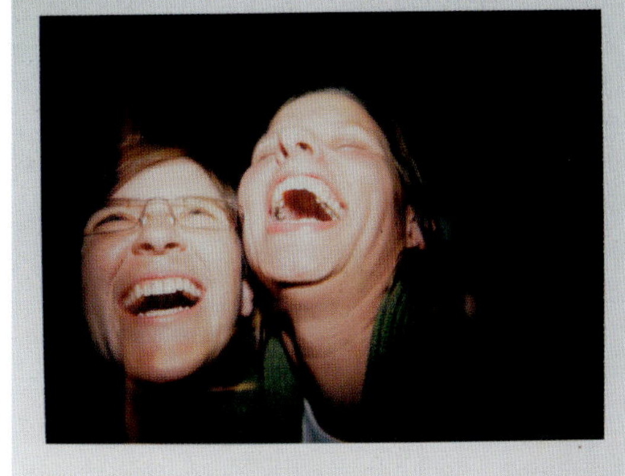

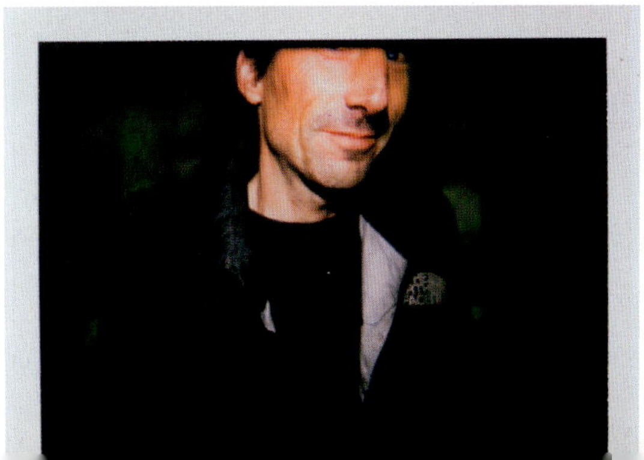

Kasia Pietras at Horse Pens 40 Ranch, Alabama

The truffles are the fruiting bodies of a type of mycorrhizal fungus that spreads throughout the soil underneath the trees. The thin, wispy tendrils of these fungi entangle themselves with the tree roots and increase their ability to absorb nutrients from the soil. In exchange, the fungi get carbon from the trees. The network—popularly called the "wood wide web"—hoards and organizes collective resources. In times of stress it can redistribute them to struggling trees, even those of other species.

"When all the participants' roles are considered," writes naturalist David Yih, "the network as a whole emerges as a kind of higher-order organism in its own right, fitter than the sum of its parts." This powerful underground ecosystem felt like an apt metaphor for the local climbing community. Like the stand of humble pine linked together by Dr. Omon's miracle formula, it's powered by a current of organized energy that not only increases its resilience but also produces something uncommon and beautiful.

World champion climber Kai Lightner famously began his journey by ascending a flagpole at age six in Fayetteville, North Carolina. A passing climber gave Lightner's distraught mother the address of the local climbing gym. Top boulderer Jimmy Webb grew up on a farm outside Knoxville, Tennessee, where he says "I always had my mom or dad freaking the hell out because I was way up in some tree." A climbing coach got him out onto the rock of the Obed Wild and Scenic River. Now Kai and Jimmy travel and live far from home, but like Pat and Jessa, they are still quintessentially Southern climbers—it's how they were raised.

I caught up with Jessa recently. These days, she lives in Fayetteville, West Virginia, spitting distance from the New River Gorge. For the last decade she climbed full time, working for Five Ten and Petzl, self-funding expeditions, and quietly climbing hard routes in her beautiful backyard. She's out of the industry now and focused on her own business crafting metalwork for private commission. The New River Gorge is now a national park, and the influx of tourism hasn't been all that great for the climbing scene. There's more traffic on the rock, but fewer people stick around. "This place used to attract a certain type of climber, you know, people that really, really like to climb," she said. "They weren't here to climb certain *grades*. They were here to climb certain *routes*. Now you have a lot of climbers who will visit, tick off everything they can, and then leave."

"So why do you still want to make it work *here*, not in Boulder or Salt Lake?" I ask.

"Well," she responded. There was a pause on the line. "These little Southern towns are not easy places to live and climb. There's not much work, the weather's weird, the climbing season is short, but the *culture* is what keeps me here. It's all the weird, intricate, nuanced culture of Appalachia. When I lived in Boone, I could tell whether you were from Blowing Rock or Banner Elk just by the differences in your accent, and those are all within a twenty-mile radius. That's the way it is around here."

Above all remains the ethic of involvement, something she thinks about as she encounters younger climbers looking for the same mentorship that helped her thrive twenty-five years ago. "It's not enough for them to just go to the gym and then give money to the organizations and call it good," she says. "I tell them that you gotta get your hands dirty. I realize I've been climbing for longer than some of these kids have been alive, and now the roles have changed. Now they come to me, like 'I wanna go climbing with you, I need you to show me how to place gear!' It's funny how it comes full circle." ◆

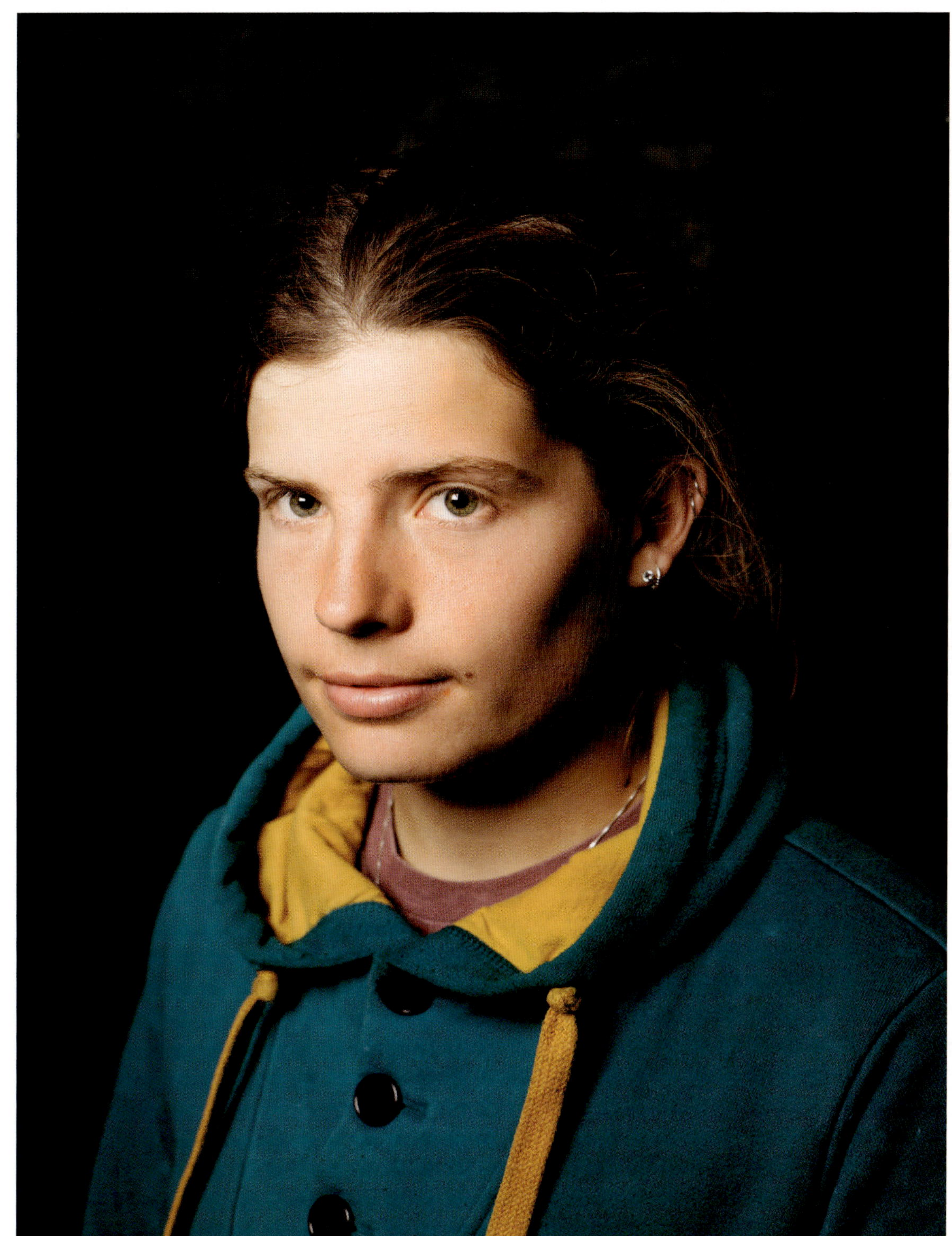

John Dorough at Stone Fort, Tennessee

Opposite: Samantha Levy on *Flat and Sassy* (5.10c/d), Deep Creek, Tennessee

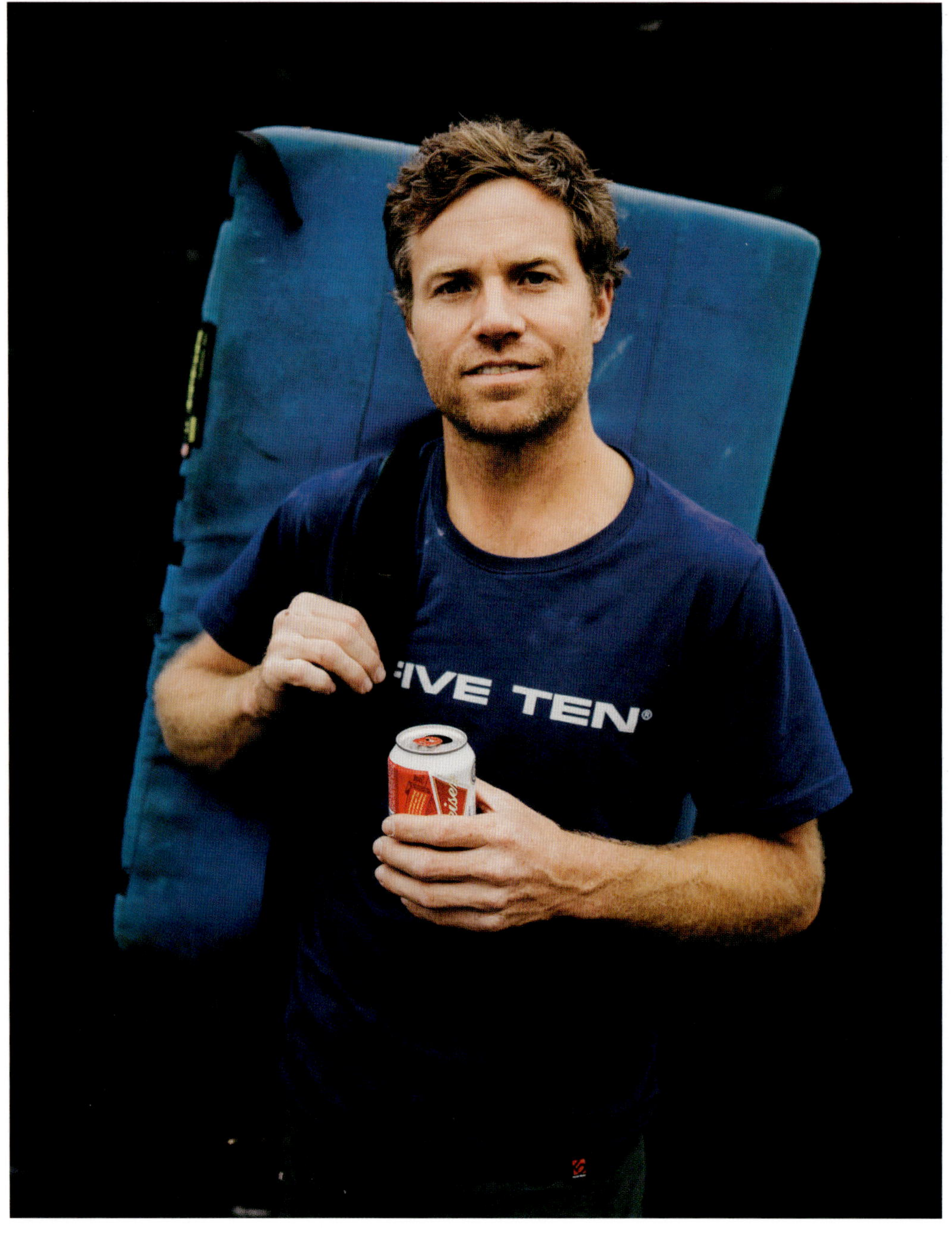

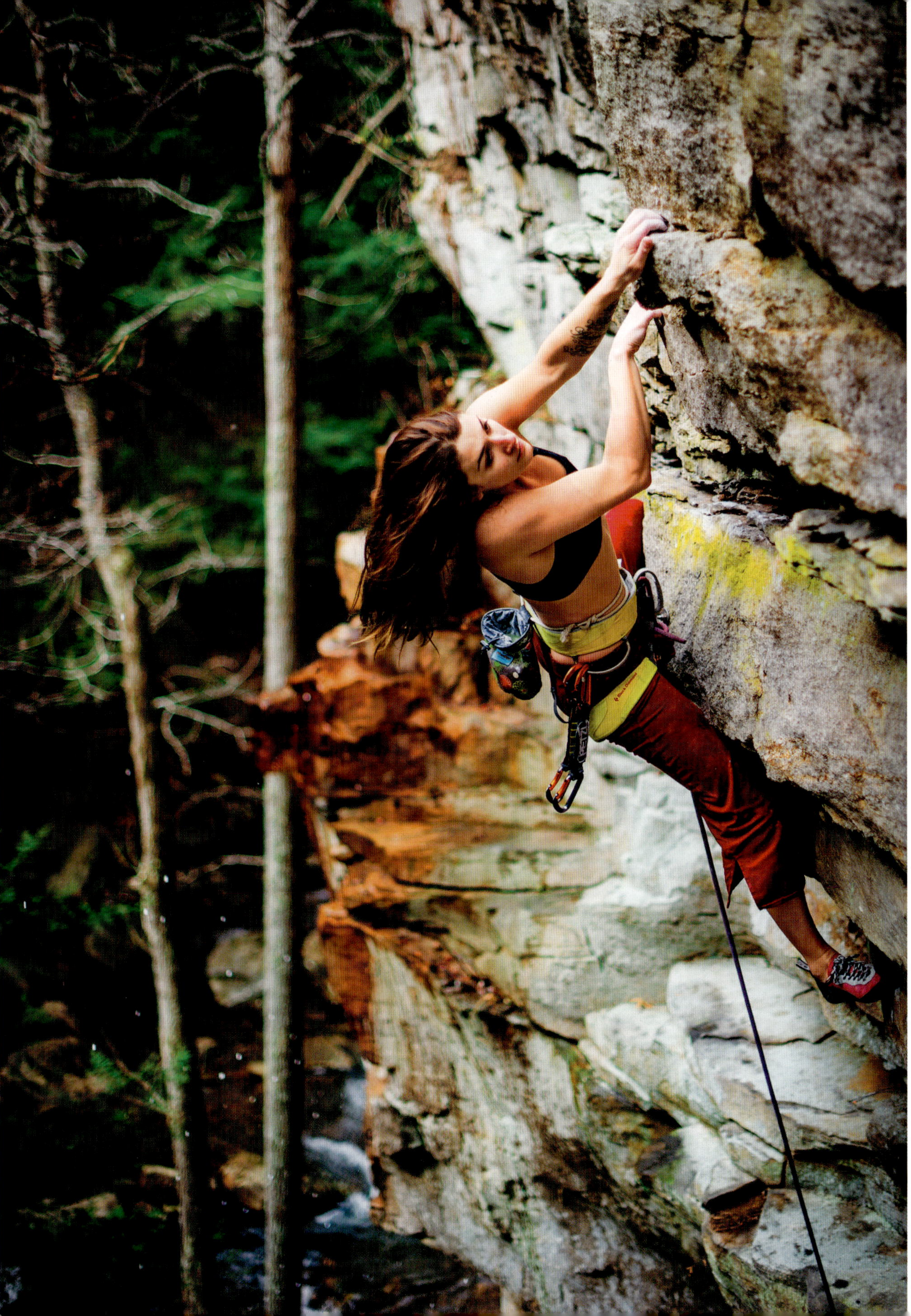

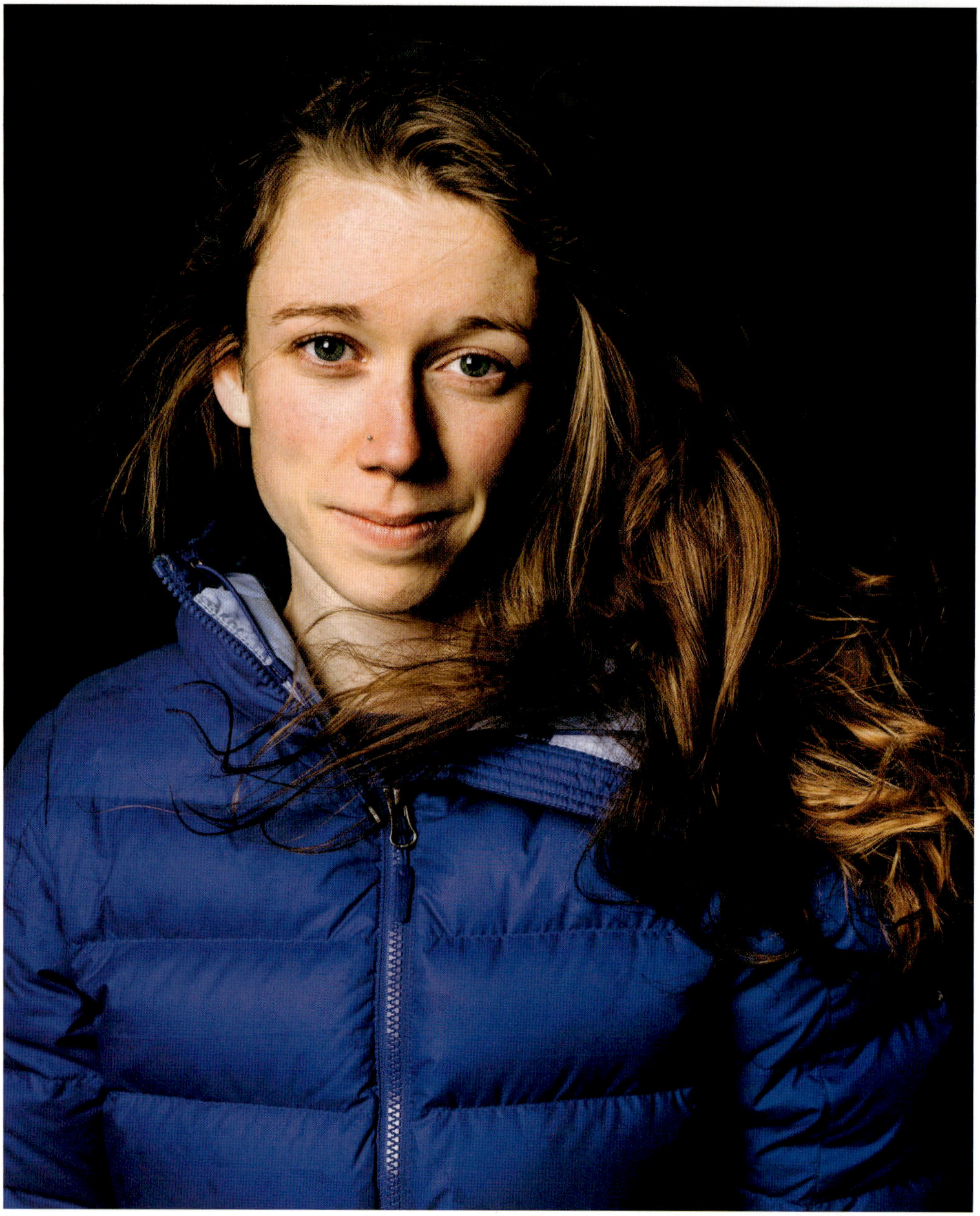

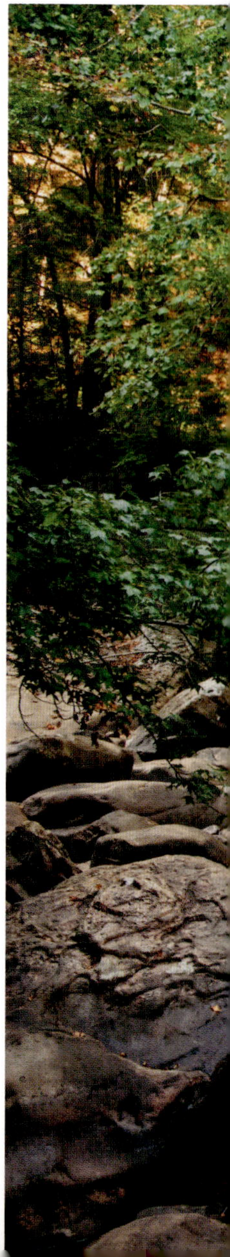

Opposite: Kaitlyn Honnold at Horse Pens 40 Ranch, Alabama

Left to right: Lisa Rands, Chad Wykle, Ronnie Jenkins, and Wills Young at Laurel-Snow State Natural Area, Tennessee

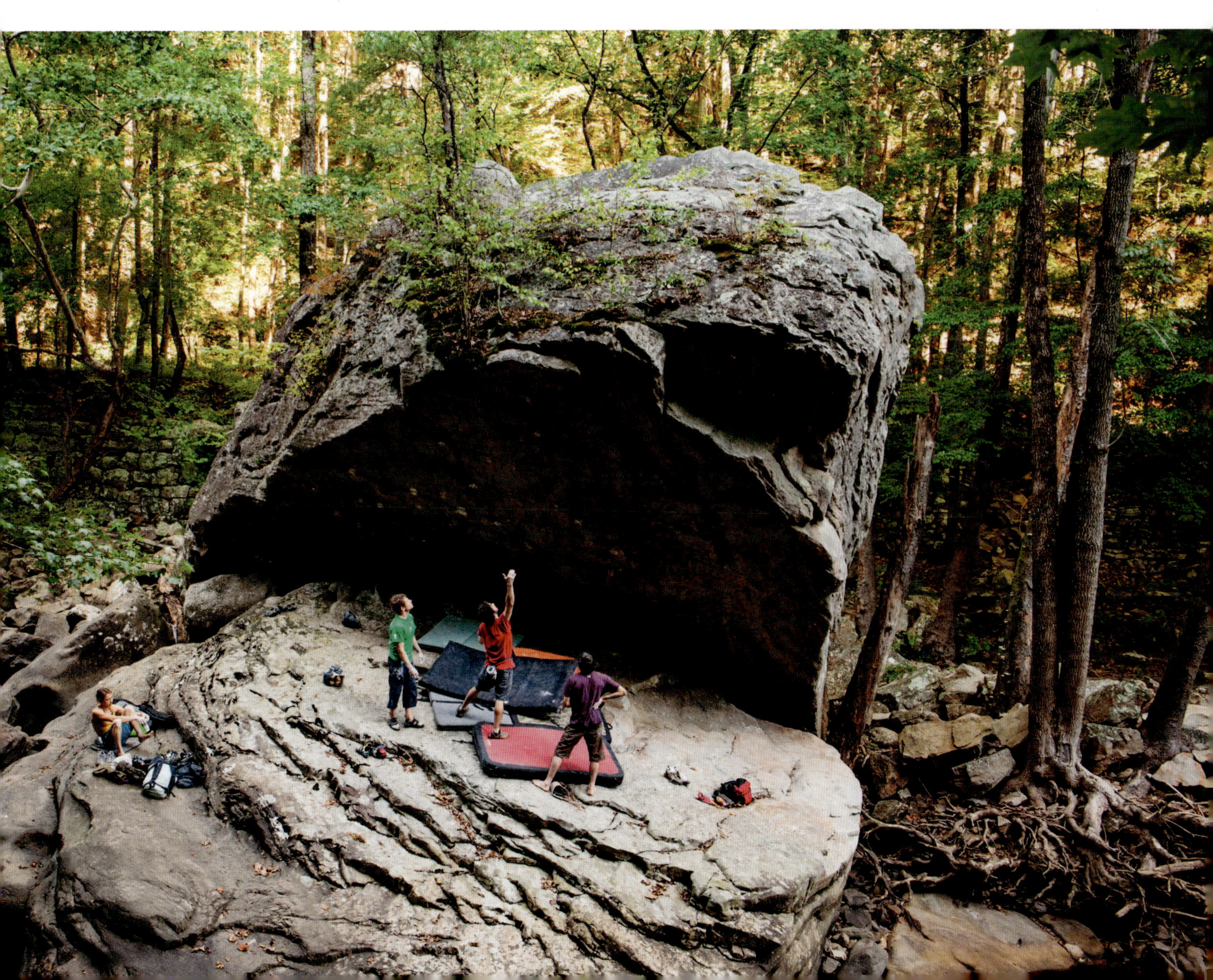

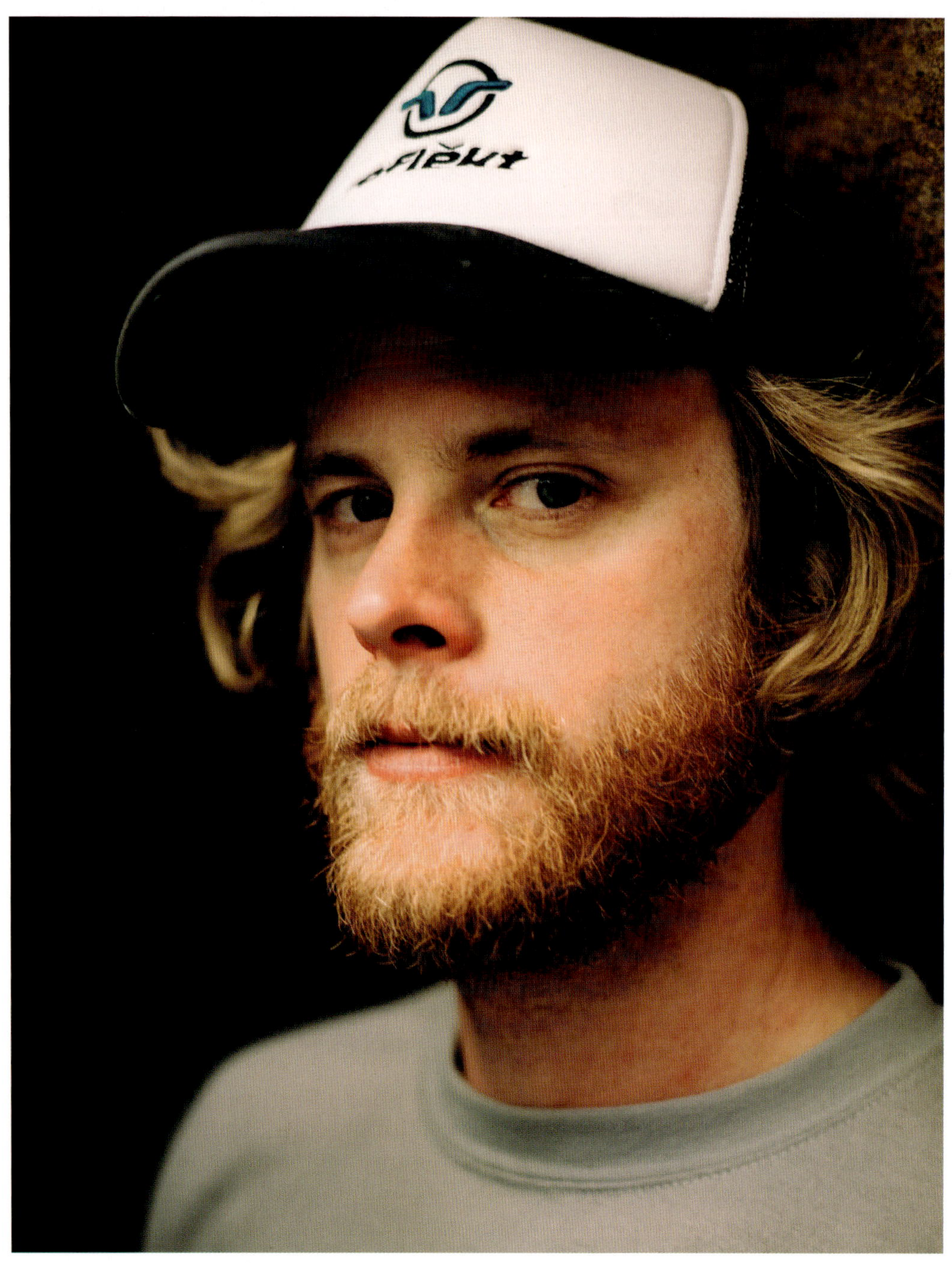

Wes Napier at Stone Fort, Tennessee

Opposite: Kayla Hendrickson at Rumbling Bald, North Carolina

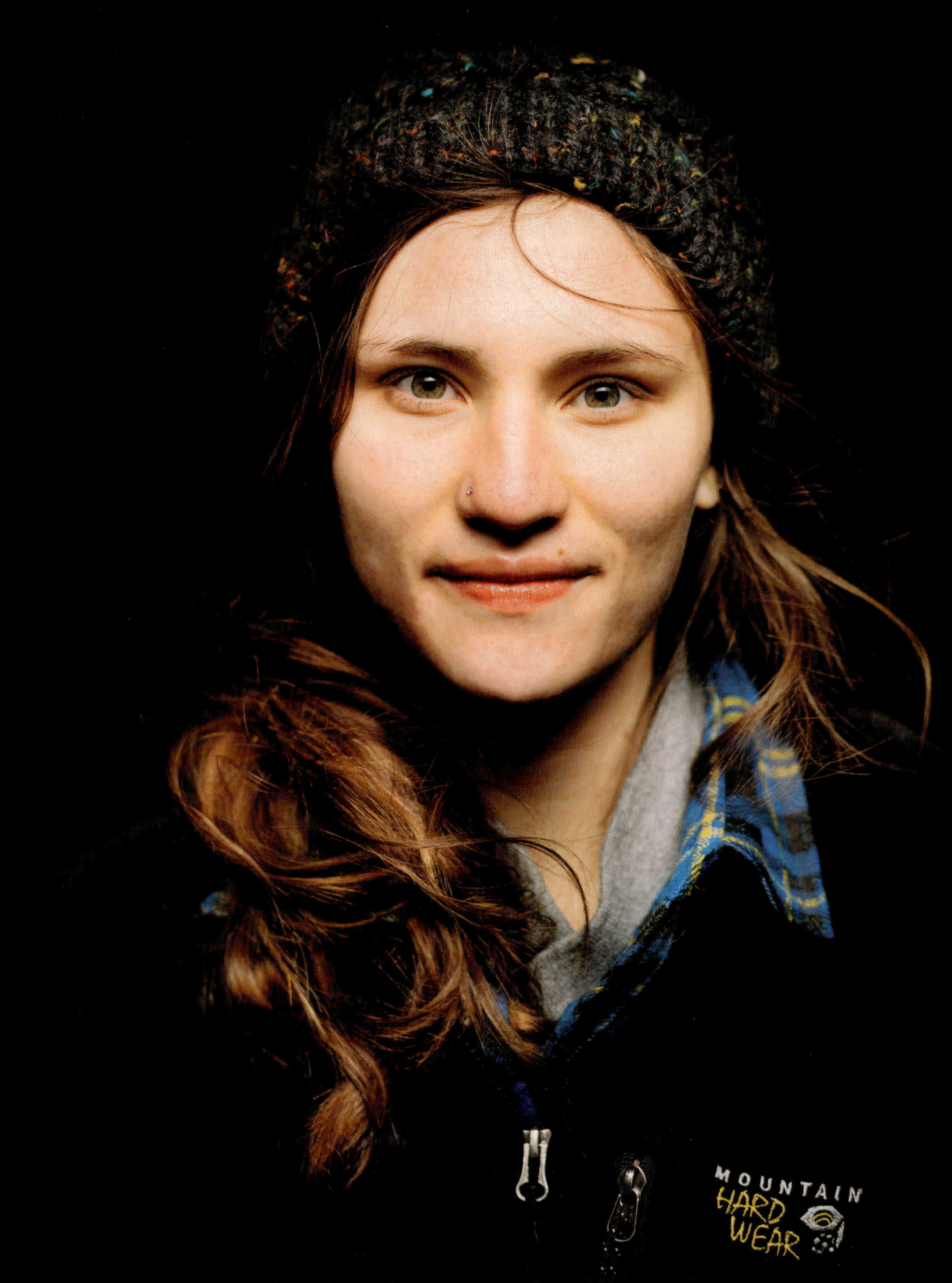
MOUNTAIN
HARD
WEAR

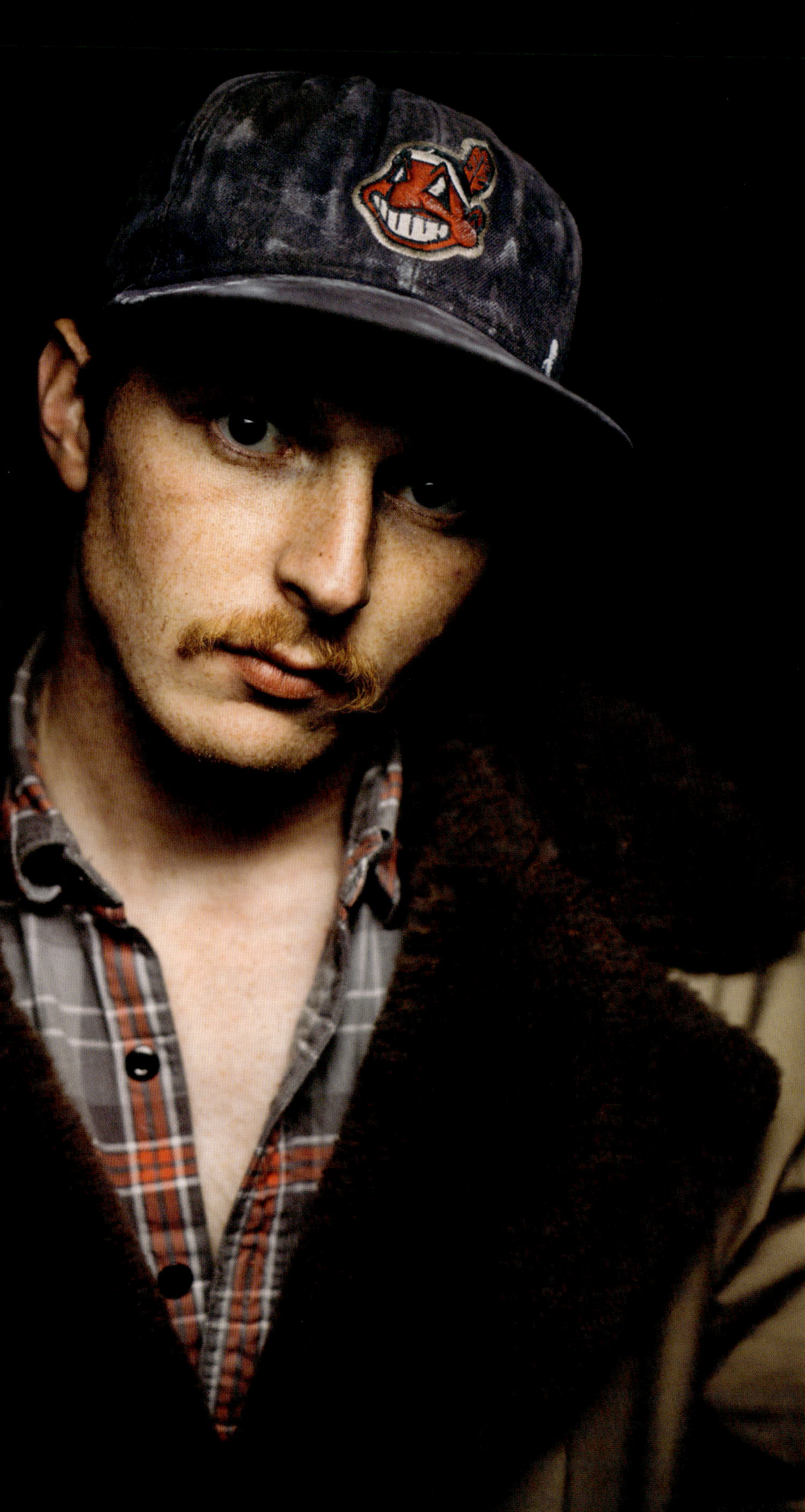

Opposite: Robert Snow at Rumbling Bald, North Carolina

Anthony Meeks sailing off a 5.14 project near Chattanooga, Tennessee

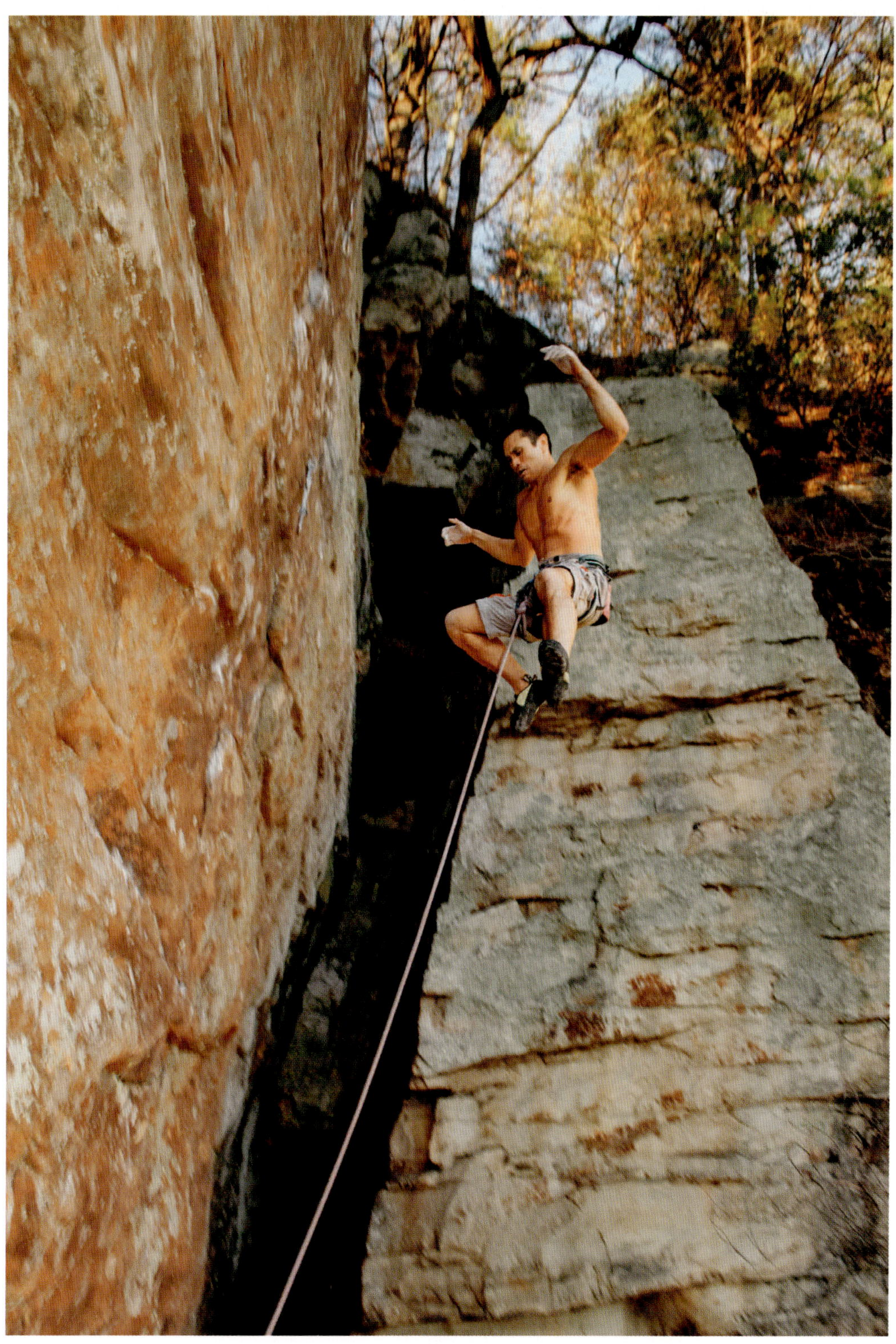

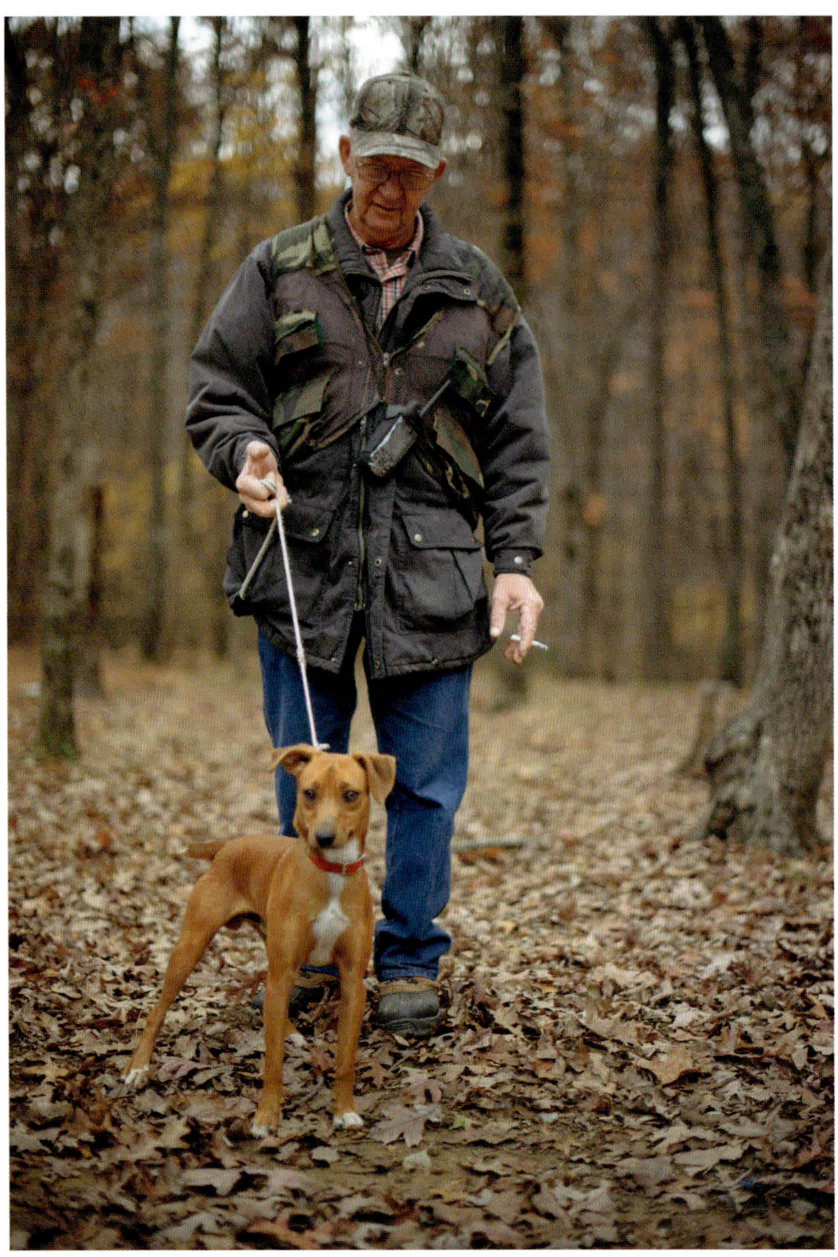

Out for a walk at Pigeon Mountain, Georgia

Opposite: Nathan Joseph at Rocktown, Georgia

Opposite: Oak tree at Horse Pens 40 Ranch, Alabama

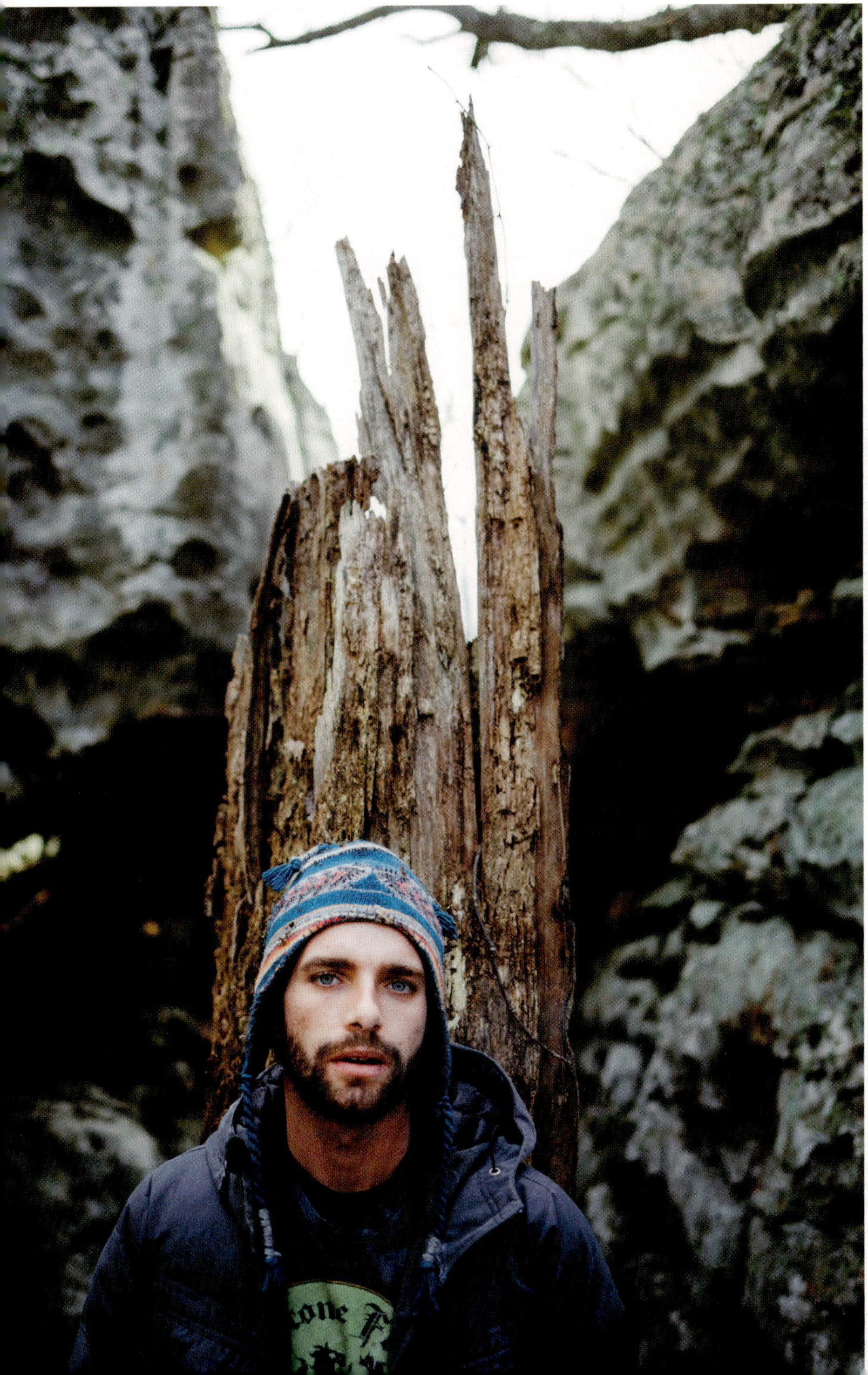

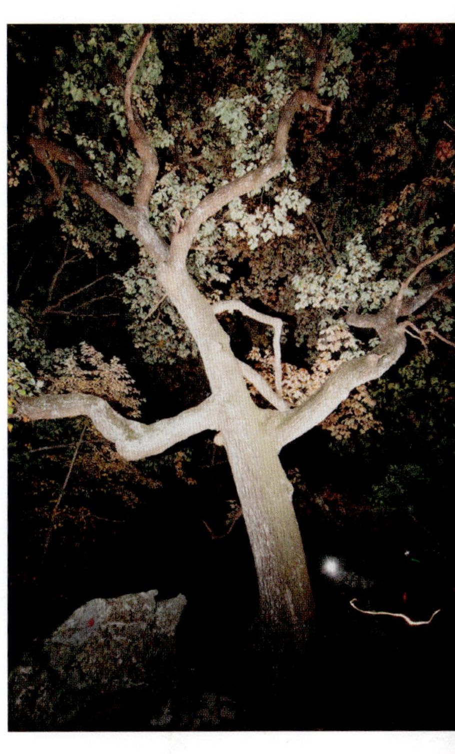

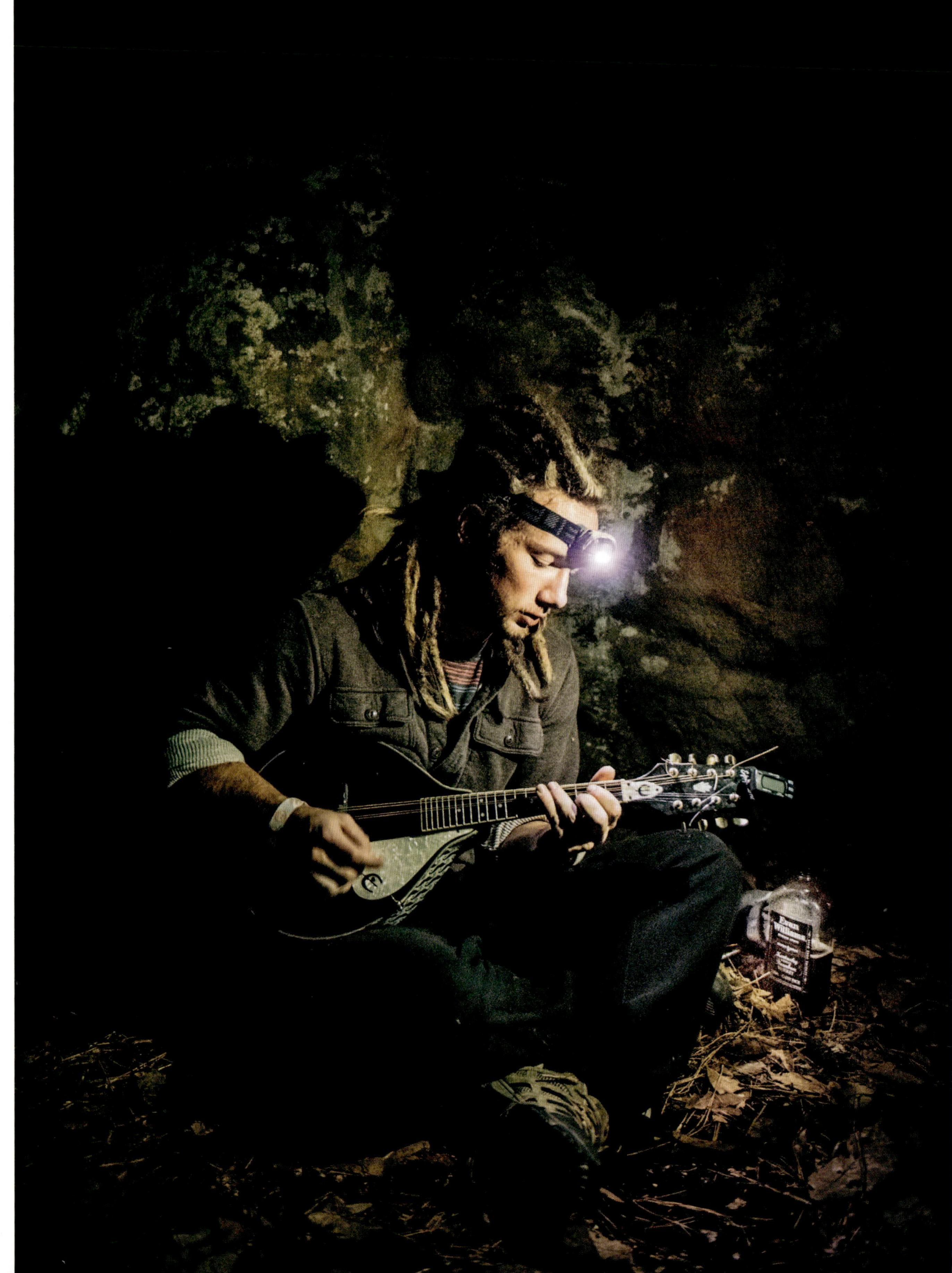

Opposite: Michael Ackerman playing the mandolin at Horse Pens 40 Ranch, Alabama

Rachel Meyers at Hound Ears, North Carolina

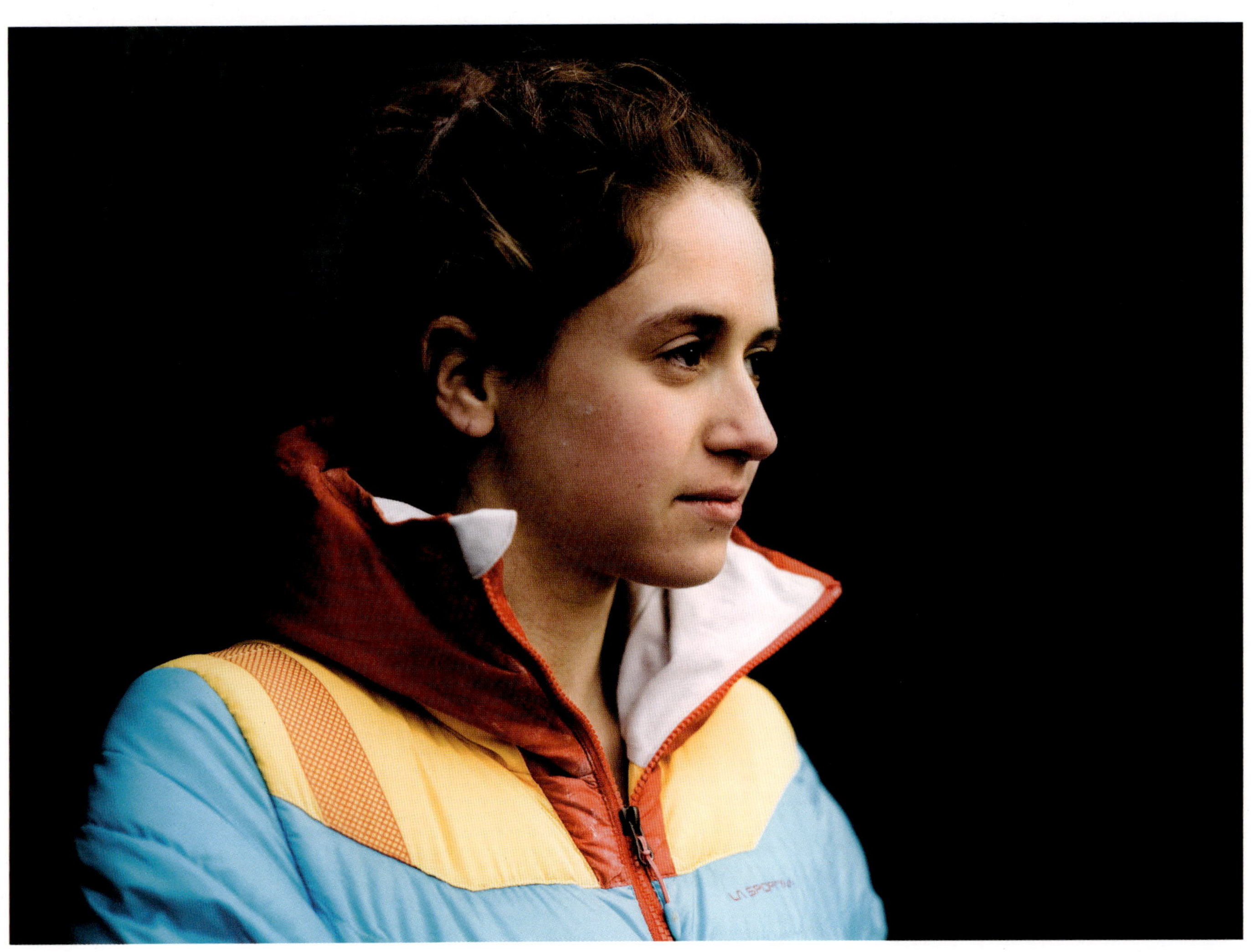

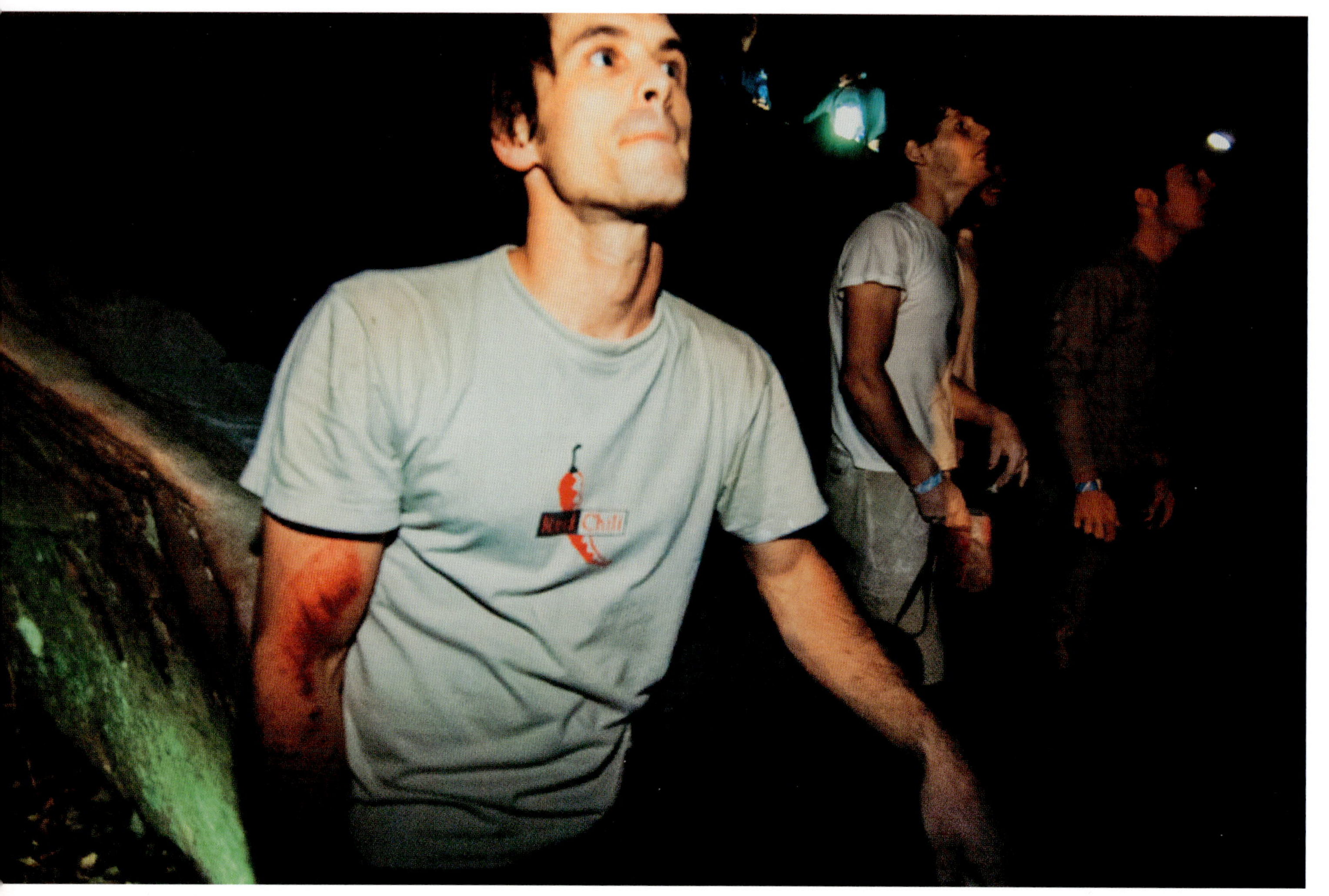

Zack Pitts at a night bouldering session at Horse Pens 40 Ranch, Alabama

Opposite: Taylor McNeill (left) and Cooper Lambla in the Linville Gorge, North Carolina

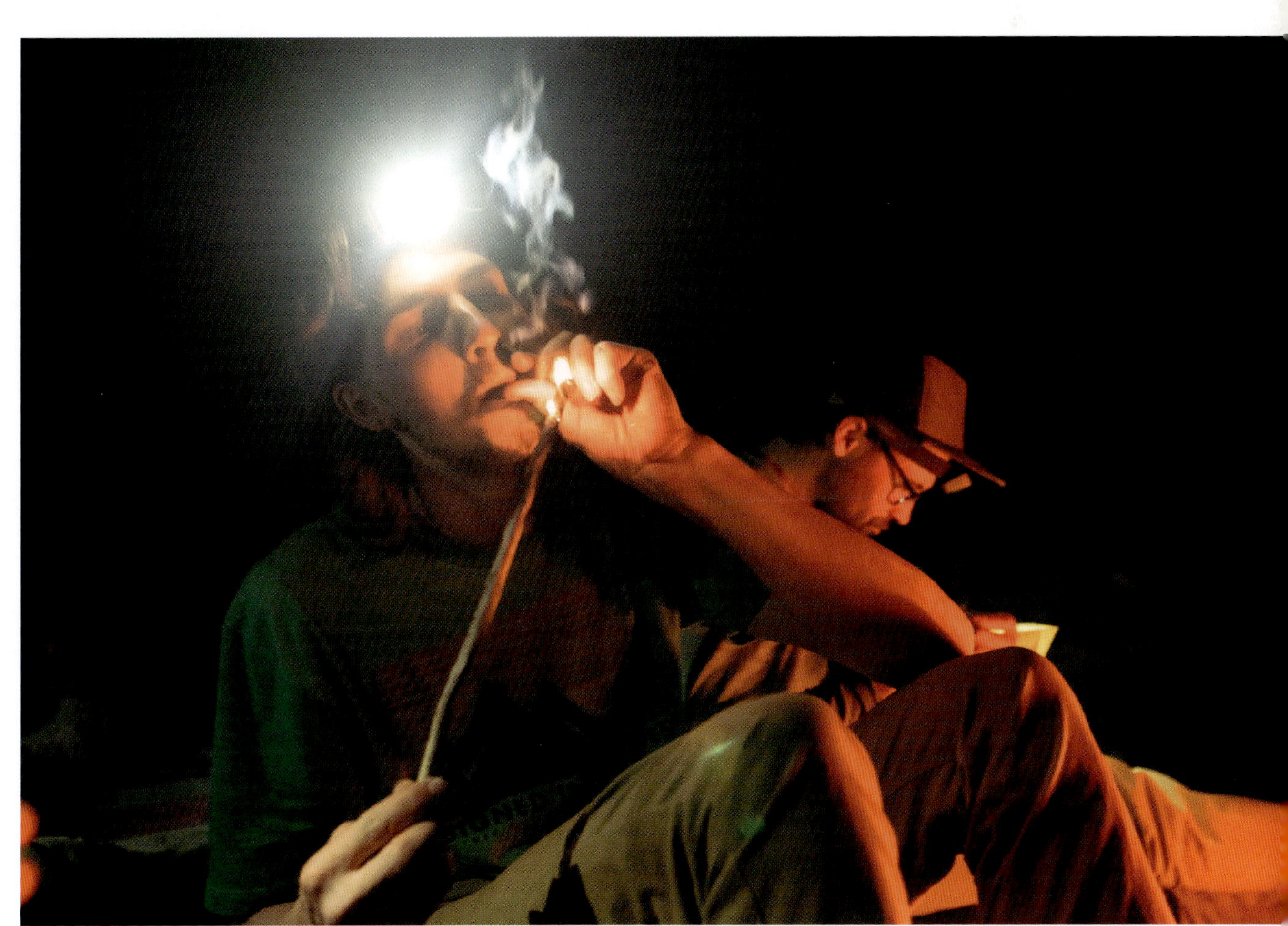

THE PERMANENCE OF EPOXY

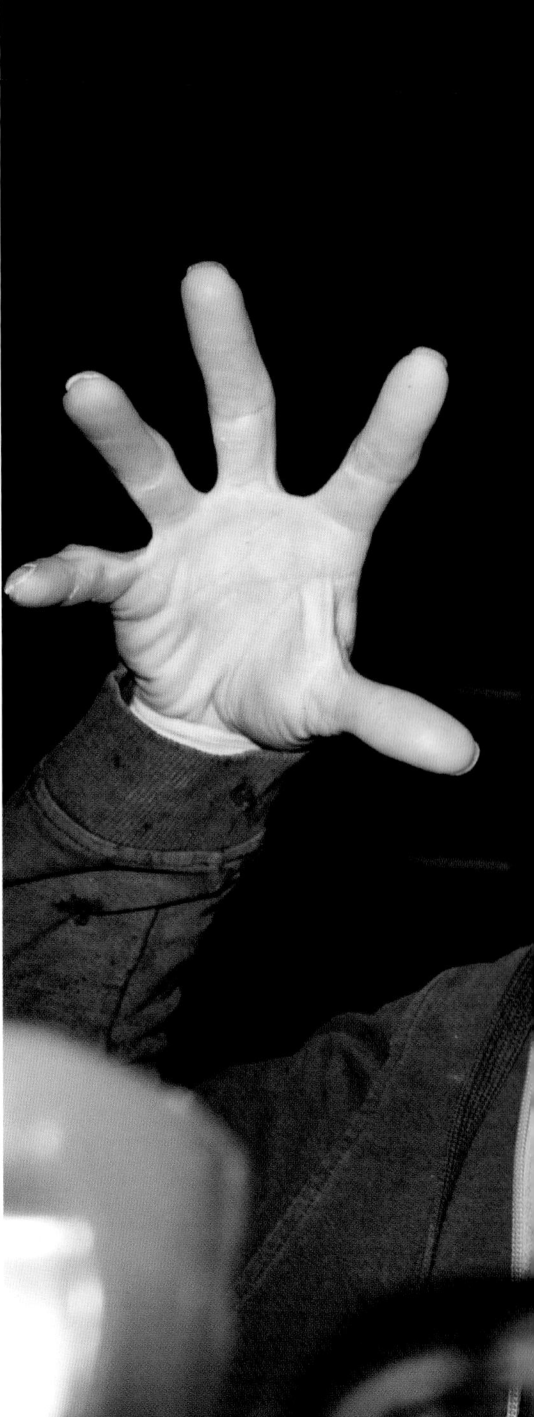

In the 1980s, about the same time bolt-protected sport climbing was eclipsing traditions in the mountains, something equally radical was happening in the cities. In places where there were enough climbers to make a community but not enough climbing close by, it was natural to fancy the occasional manmade structure to practice climbing. Around this time, almost all at once and everywhere around the world, climbers began gluing rocks and wood to hard surfaces, particularly overhanging bridges and tunnels, to make their own climbing walls. In the South, where climbers generally live far away from mountain environments, glue-ups were suddenly everywhere.

Revisiting the glue-ups of the South, you are transported back to the way climbing was at that time. Jeff Coke takes me down to the Pump Tunnel, a glue-up he created over several years in the late 1980s in a Chapel Hill underpass. A contractor for the town at the time, he was breaking cinderblocks apart in a nearby parking lot and gluing bits and pieces onto the wall. Often he would glue them up in patterns that mimicked popular climbs he and his buddies were puzzling out on North Carolina cliffs. Then he began bringing home souvenir rocks from climbing trips all over the South and out West to glue up as reminders of places he'd been. Thirty years later, stories of the Southern climbing experience are literally set in stone on those concrete walls.

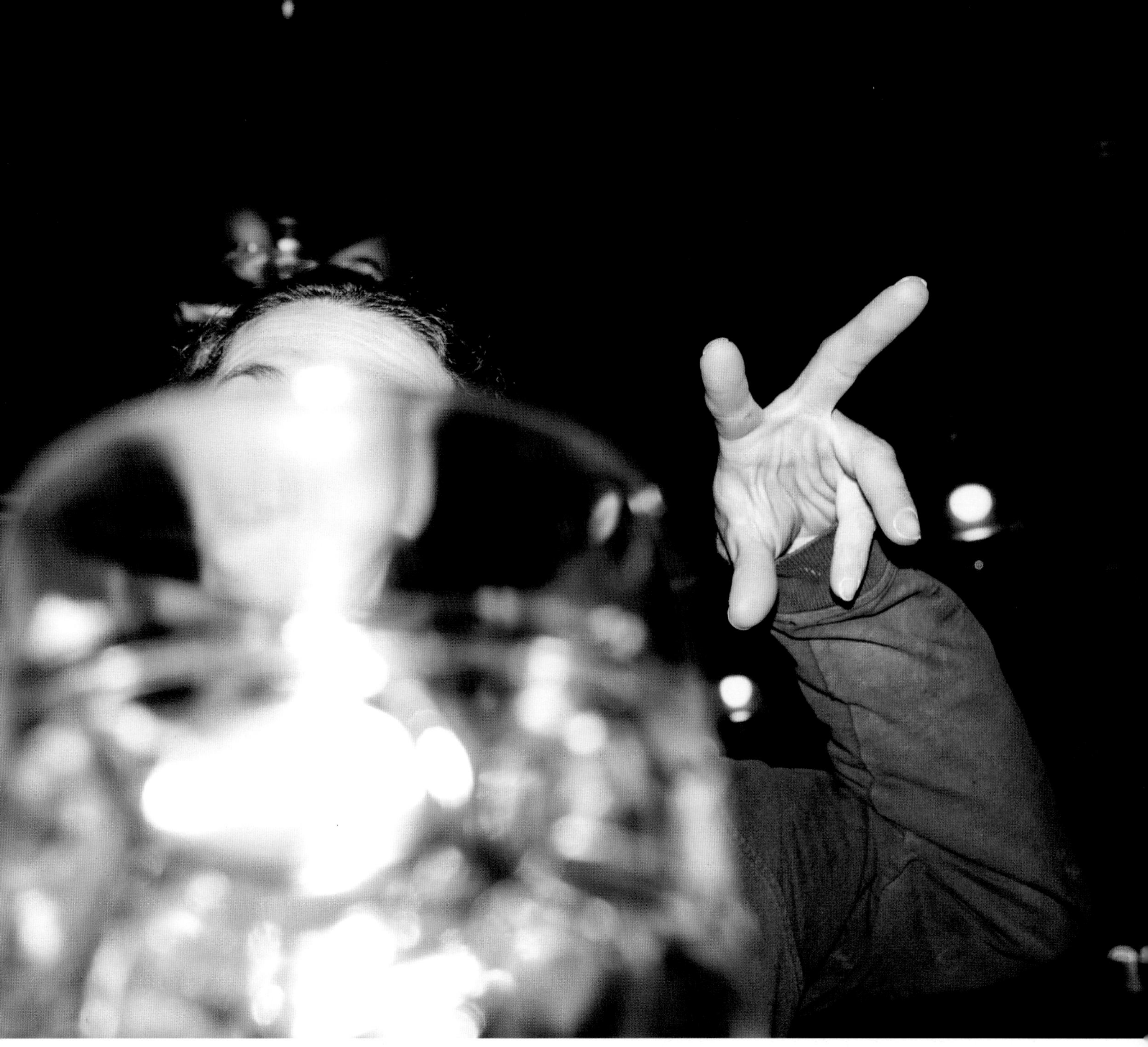

Isaac Caldiero
in Chattanooga,
Tennessee

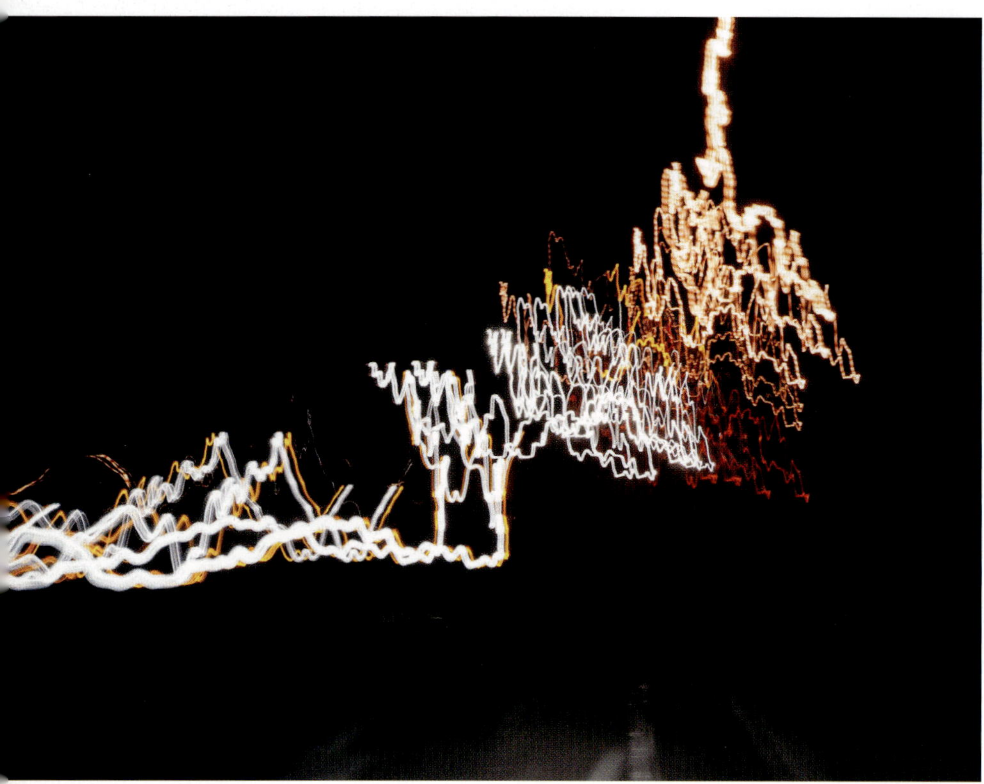

Trail of headlights on Interstate 75 north of Atlanta

Opposite: Nico Brown slacklining in Jim Horton's attic, North Wilkesboro, North Carolina

The routes in a climbing gym are changed often enough to satisfy short attention spans and offer infinite training possibilities. The routes and individual rocks in the Pump Tunnel, however, are exactly as they were when Jeff glued them up, with the addition of several layers of spray paint. Jeff and others would set routes to mimic important outdoor climbs. Jeff's friend John Provetero did the same in another overpass in Raleigh dubbed the Beta Center. Places like the Pump Tunnel and Beta Center are like a museum of what climbing was like in the 1980s in North Carolina. To know how each rock got there is to know the history of North Carolina rock climbing.

"I'm kind of a stone collector," Jeff cackles, and he shows me a large egg-shaped piece of smooth brown sandstone spotted with white. "This rock was from the ledge at the top of the first pitch of *Dark Shadows*, a classic 5.8 in Red Rocks. The whole ledge looked like this; it's got leopard spots all over it. It looks like something out of a Doctor Seuss book."

He pulls out another hunk of rock resembling a piece of German chocolate cake. "I got this at the base of a limestone cliff just outside of Vegas. Pretty nice climbing. Saw a nest of golden eagles on the side of the cliff."

"I know I'm not supposed to pick up rocks in a national monument and put them in my pocket." He grins at me. "But don't tell anybody!"

The glue-up era was short-lived, but it opened a Pandora's box for climbing. Urban climbers experimenting with epoxy and stone quickly figured out how to mix the glues with sand; then they began shaping artificial rocks with plastic resins and molds, and the artificial climbing hold was born. The first indoor training facilities began popping up in the late 1980s. Chapel Hill's own climbing gym in the town's community center was built in 1988 by a lot of the same glue-up regulars like Lee Munsen and Bill Webster, an administrative assistant at Chapel Hill Parks and Recreation. The local competition

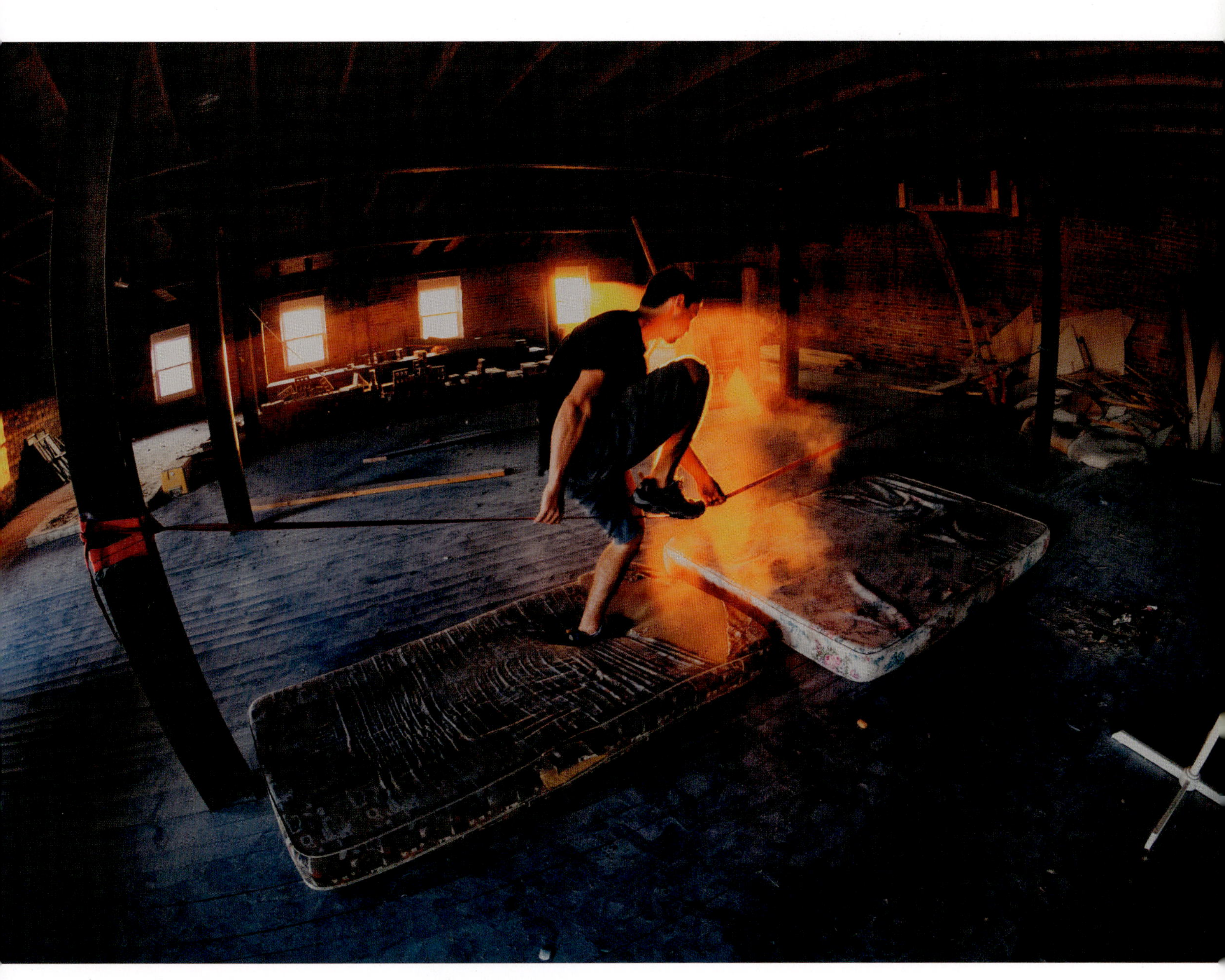

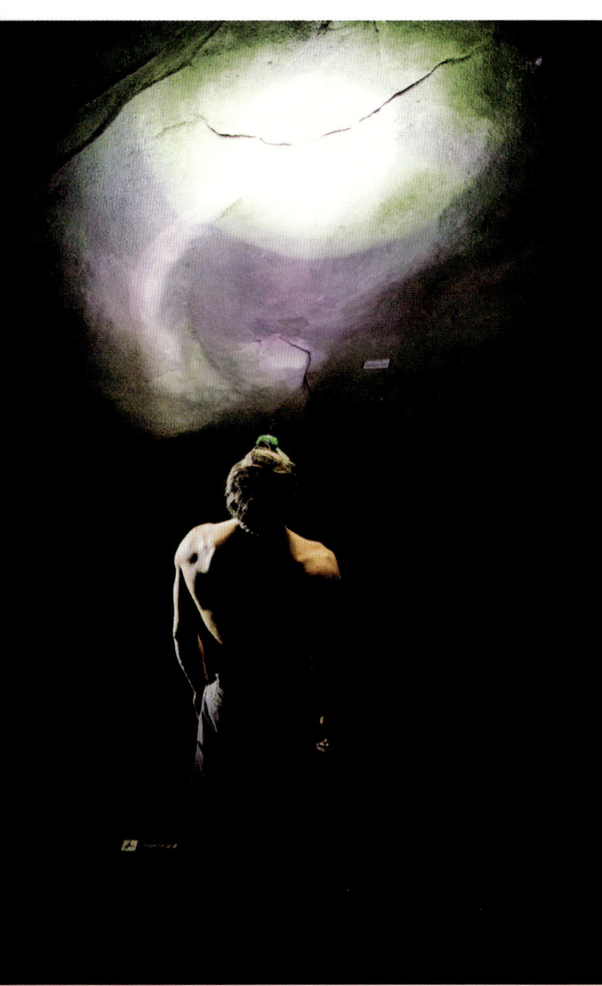

Nathan Joseph staring down *God Module* (V11) at Horse Pens 40 Ranch, Alabama

Kai Lightner at Central Rock Gym in Watertown, Massachusetts

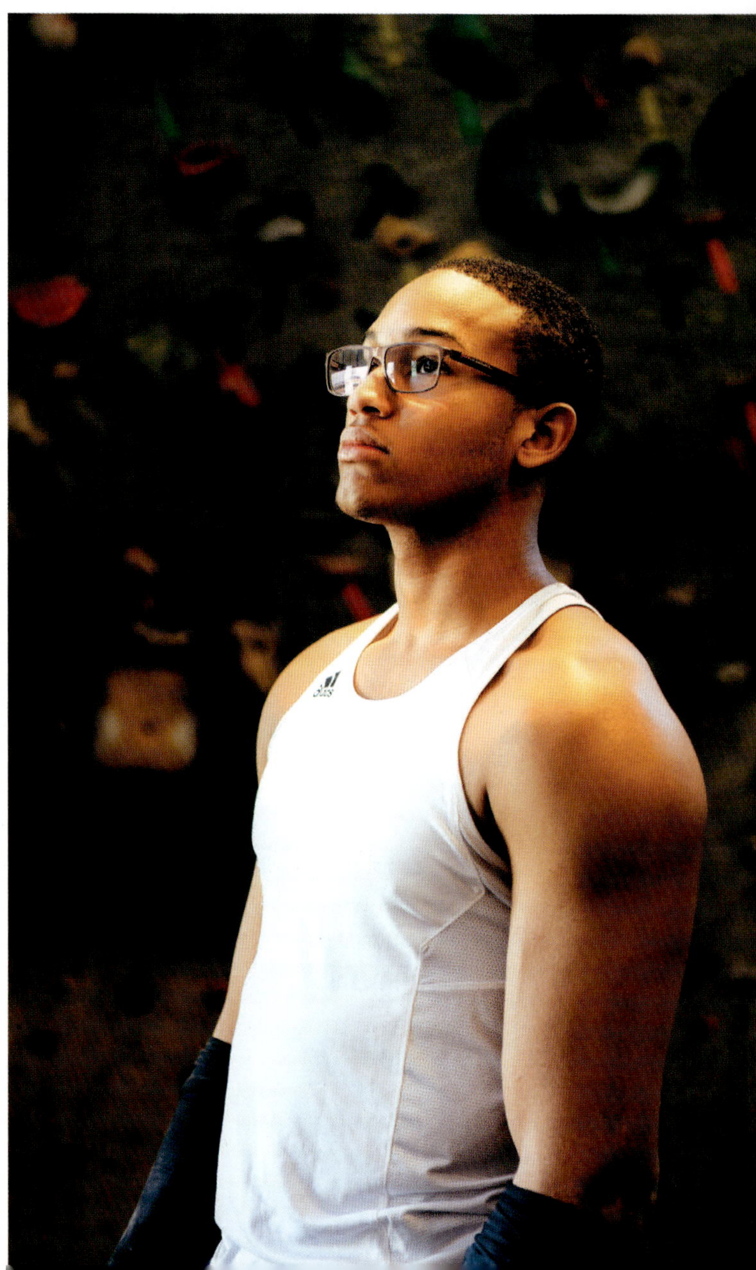

they held there every year (now called Bill Webster's Rock the Hill) is still the longest-running indoor climbing competition in the country, and Jeff's own crushed-rock footholds are still on the wall.

It took only a few years for commercial climbing gyms to proliferate, and today you can climb all day in immense air-conditioned caverns alongside a yoga studio and juice bar. Glue-ups were not only records of local climbing history, they were also the foundation of what climbing would eventually become. "Going to the Pump Tunnel is like visiting Paris and seeing Roman ruins," Brian laughs, sweeping his hands for dramatic effect. "There was a whole civilization here, and modern climbing was built on top of it."

By way of demonstration, and definitely illegally, Jeff mixes up a batch of PC-7 epoxy. Brushing down a few square inches of the underpass, he applies the tarry mix to the surface. He rips off a length of duct tape and applies it to a broken handlebar of cinderblock. He squeezes the block against the epoxy, pressing the tape against the wall on either side with both hands and keeping pressure on the rock with his lips, as if christening it with a kiss. In a day, the epoxy will set, and he'll remove the tape.

"I wanted to go to school for architecture, but they passed my grades back across the table and said *nuh uh*," he laughs, "so I ended up doing landscape design instead." He runs a finger over the slick spray paint coating an old rock. I ask him if he thinks what he created down here is art. He shakes his head. "I think maybe people come down here and see the graffiti and the holds and think it's some kind of a sculptural thing."

He laughs, "I did sometimes take a little bit of artistic liberty with the holds. Things for people to look at and go, 'Oh my God, it's a fried egg!' Or 'It's a penis!' But no," he shakes his head, "it's not art. I always looked at it as a device for training for outdoor climbing." He smiles up at the concrete arch, lost in memory.

I think I understood. To have impact, art has to transform the ordinary and established into something radical and transcendent. Art takes ideas and makes them physical, but in climbing, there is a certain blasphemy in that. The 1980s experimentations with chisel and epoxy sometimes crept on to natural surfaces: a curse of the glue-up era.

Climbing is the opposite of art. Traditional free climbing, practiced almost religiously in North Carolina, is as ephemeral an act as there can be. You follow the route the rock dictates, and you alter nothing in the process.

The best part of climbing is what disappears, and that's why we chase it. Staring at that underpass, jonesing for the mountains, what are you obsessing over? A glob of sand and epoxy and the arc of colorful plastic resin freshly arranged on a wall? Collecting photographic mementos in a book for posterity? Or the fading memory of a line of dark fissures guarding a thousand-foot wall of granite, a sudden storm, and the pounding inside your head that made you turn your back on a shining summit? ◆

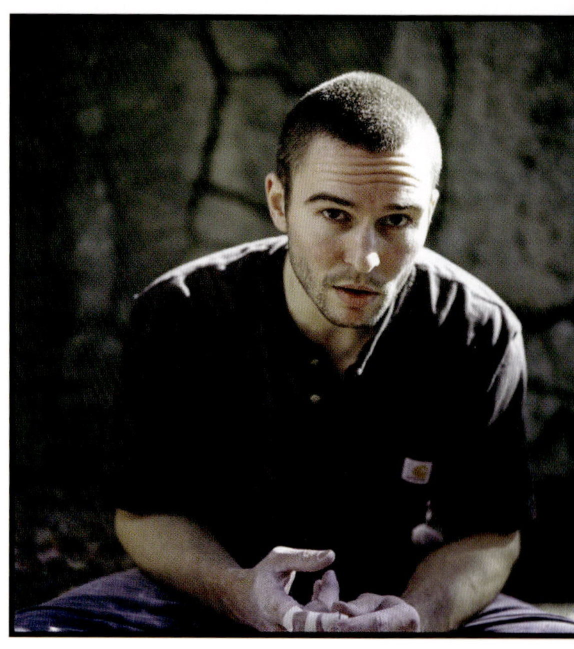

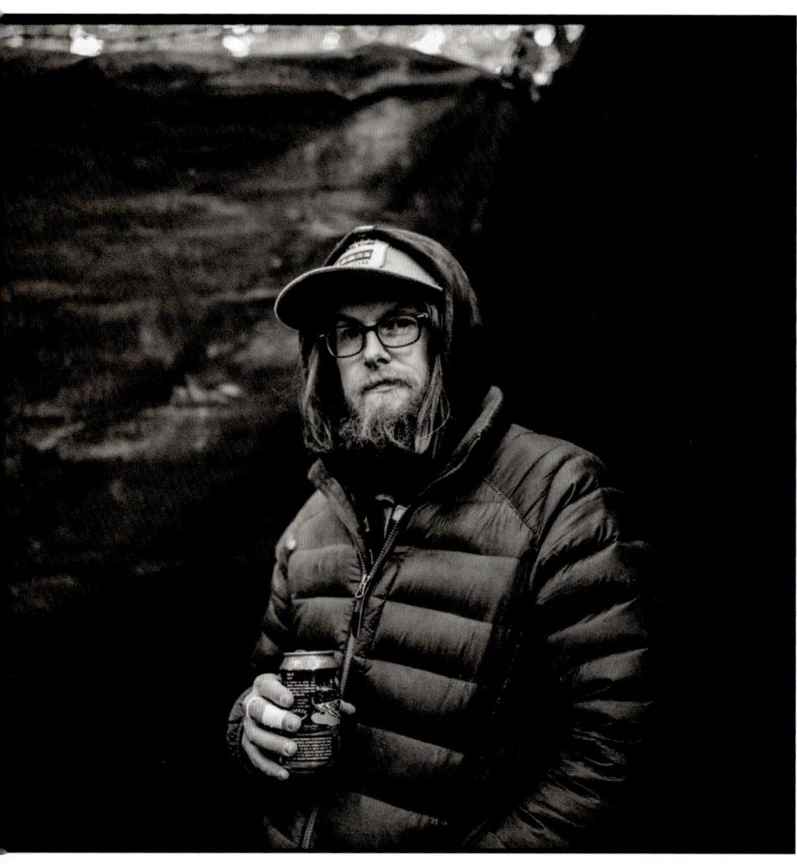

Geordan Green,
Boone, North Carolina

Jeremy Walton,
Stone Fort, Tennessee

Opposite: Amanda Maze,
Stone Fort

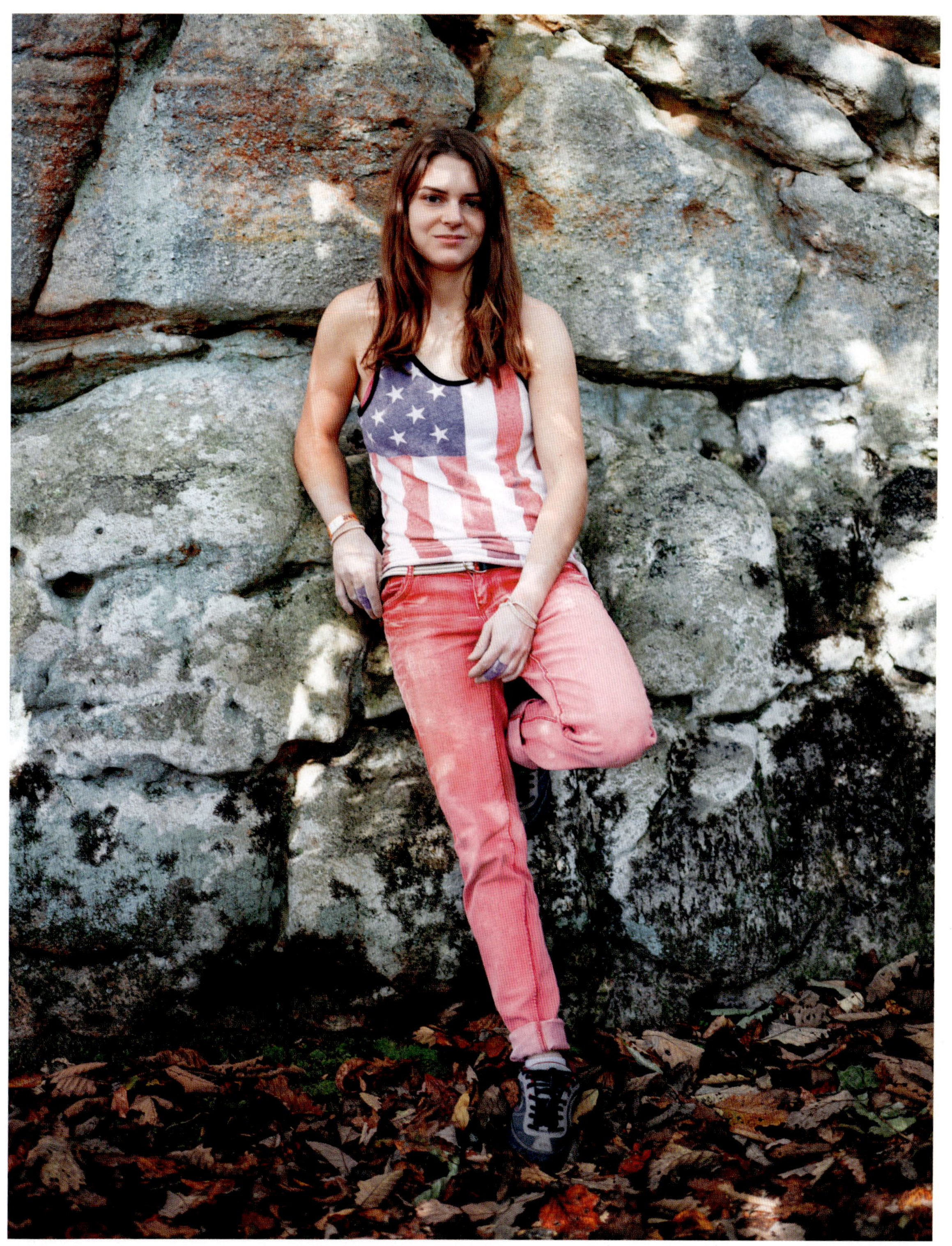

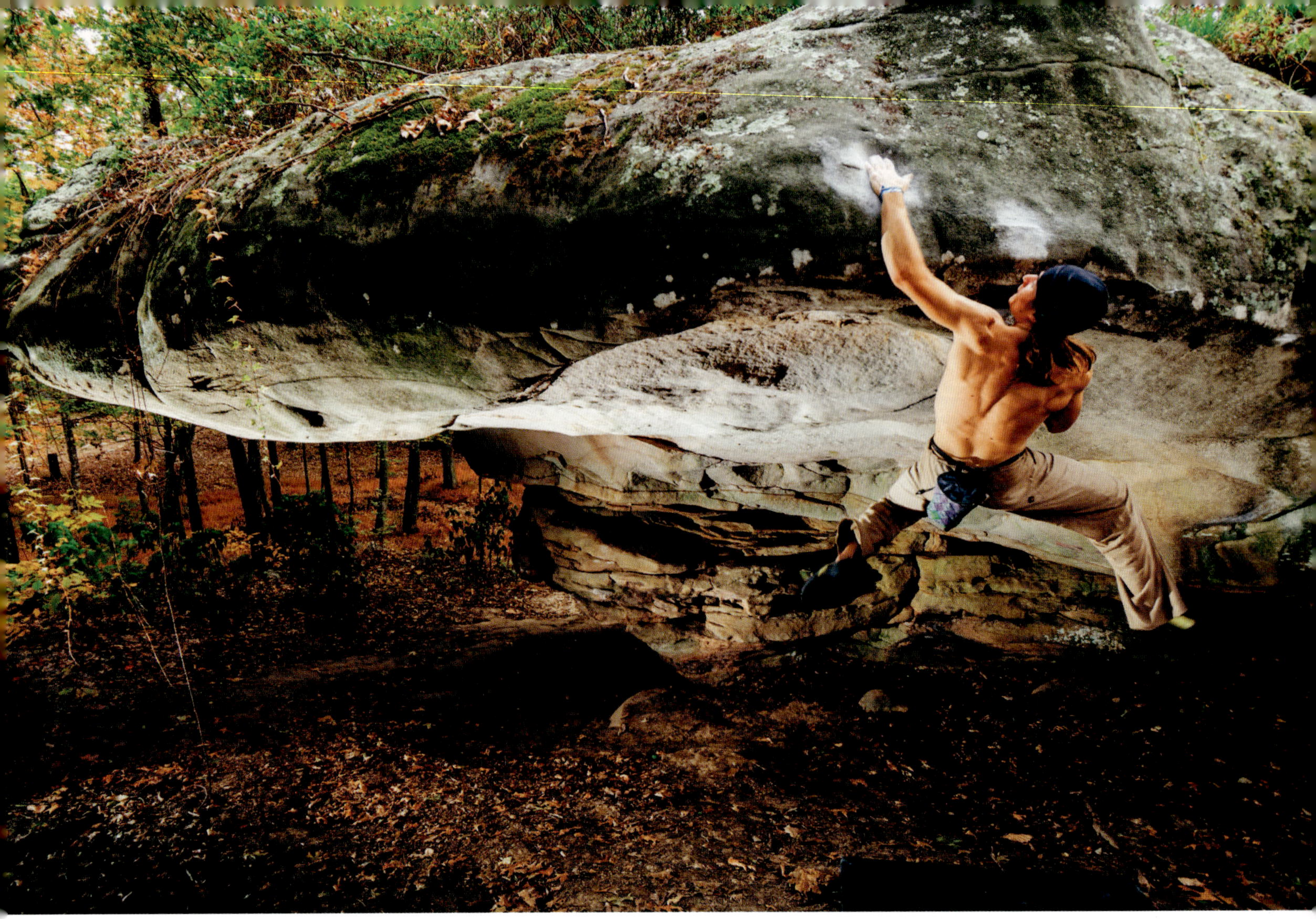

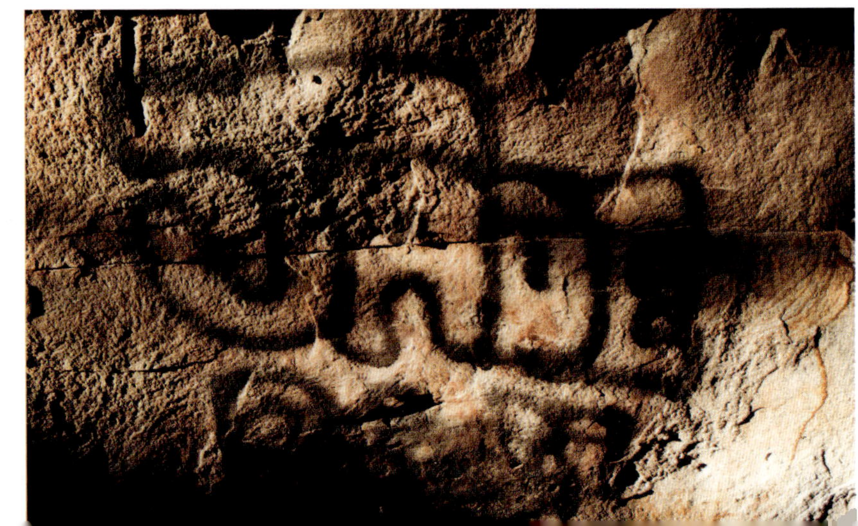

SPARE THESE STONES

Given our geography—the actual, mixed one of great trees and of fields littered with Styrofoam, of still-awesome mountains and of valleys dense with tract houses—is it possible for art to be more than lies?

–Robert Adams, *Beauty in Photography: Essays in Defense of Traditional Values*

Ethan Pringle on *Stingray* (V9), Horse Pens 40, Alabama

Graffiti at Fort Payne, Alabama

As a child growing up in southwestern Ohio, I remember the moment our wilderness disappeared. The woods just beyond our backyard were a fort-building haunt for me and my siblings, but one day we came home to find our neighbors had cleared it. Once it was gone, I realized how pathetically small our landscape of adventure really was: just a copse of junk trees no bigger than our living room.

With a few exceptions, the mixed geography of Southern climbing is very much a backyard wilderness. Every forest here has been cleared at least once. Mining pits, old fence lines, and logging roads are a constant reminder that even the deepest of coves have not escaped violation. Even the rock itself, if not blasted for gravel, bears the mutilation of man. Graffiti is about as common on these rocks as on the underpasses of Los Angeles. Some do battle with it with acid wash and wire brushes, but most just accept it and learn to climb on it. Some popular climbs are even named after the tags that were on the rock during the first ascent, like *Fuc Yo* at Hound Ears and *GTO* at Sand Rock.

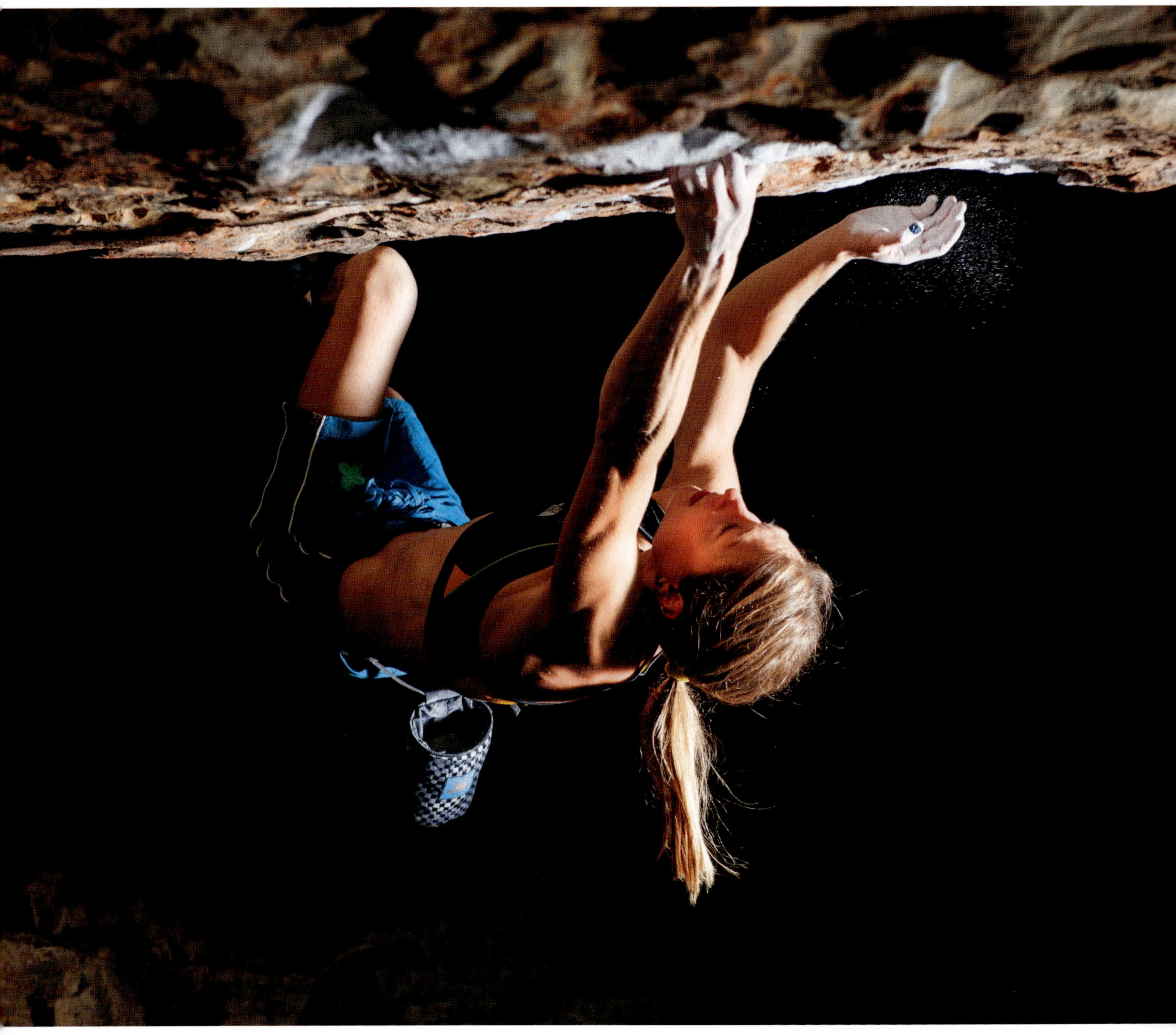

Protective of the secrets of his own sarcophagus, William Shakespeare wrote a tongue-in-cheek warning to would-be vandals that was used as his epitaph:

> *Good friend for Jesus' sake forbeare,*
> *To dig the dust enclosed here.*
> *Blessed be the man that spares these stones,*
> *And cursed be he that moves my bones.*

It seemed fitting to turn a corner at Sand Rock—a beat-out Alabama crag under constant siege from over-bolting, four-wheelers, and graffiti—and encounter a line from Shakespeare's final work, misquoted in dripping black spray paint on delicate sandstone: "Blessed be he that spare these stones." Eventually, the spray paint disappeared. The ghosts of Sand Rock rest, and the climbing carries on. As I study photographs I've taken here over the decades, I realize it's a cycle I have embraced since I was young. Like photographer Robert Adams, I tend to avoid depictions of pristine landscapes.

Sand Rock would become a kind of photographic laboratory. When not building forts as a kid, I was skateboarding and studying the pages of *Thrasher* magazine, which were filled with fisheye lenses on Hasselblad cameras, high-speed strobes, and colored gels. The aesthetic fit perfectly with those gritty urban environments, and I had the sense it would work well here, too, especially at Sand Rock. It was easy to rig camera and light placements in the maze of its pinnacles and boulders, and what's more, the close proximity of everything kept things cool and dark, meaning I didn't have to overpower the sun with my artificial light. The graffiti was a plus too.

Lisa Rands on *Vapor Lock* (V11), Laurel-Snow State Natural Area, Tennessee

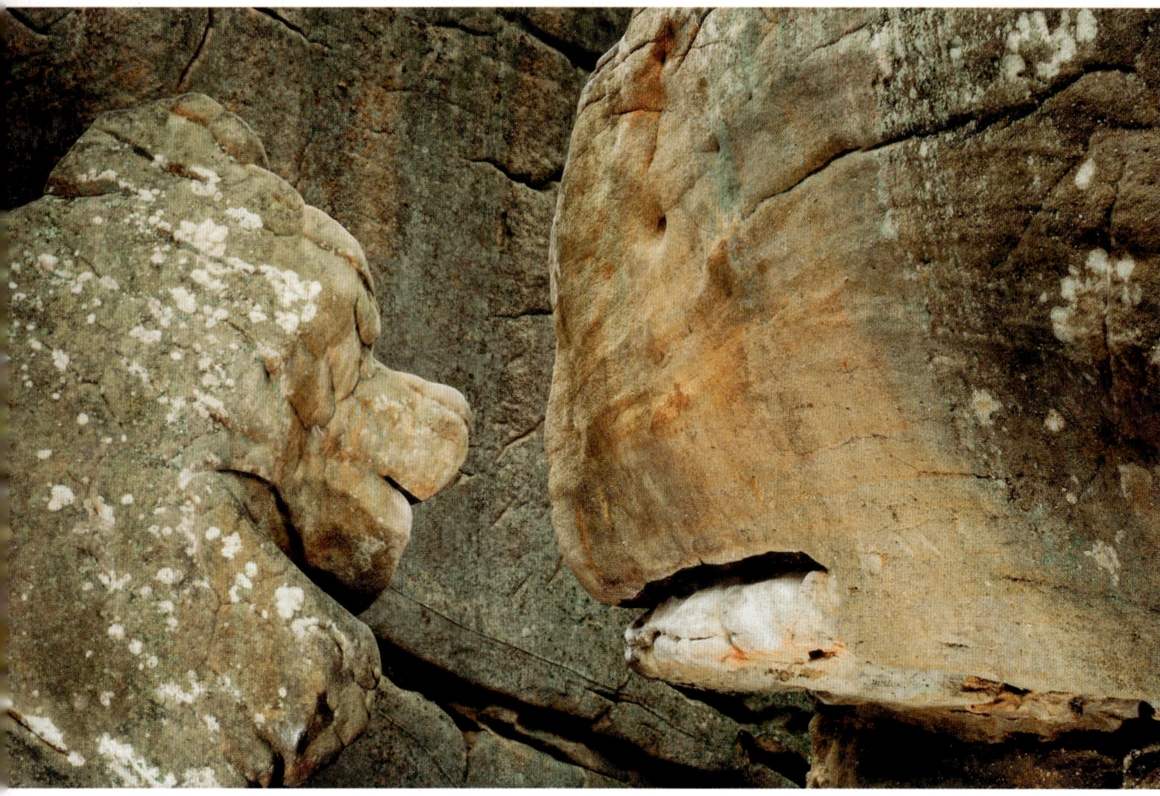

Boulders at Horse Pens 40 Ranch, Alabama

Opposite: Michael Adair on the B-Minor Boulder, Sand Rock, Alabama

This was in the early 2000s, and at that time, mainstream climbing magazines were emphatically not publishing anything but natural-light photography, and generally on 35 mm film or digital cameras. In conversation with editors, it was clear: photographers should adhere to the illusion of the climber caught in action in the pristine landscape. In between my "normal" work, I was shooting with artificial light and weird film formats in other locations around the South. There were a few other photographers working with alternative techniques at that time too—Keith Ladzinski and Tim Kemple, to name a couple—and we shared intel. It was the fringe magazines that began taking a chance on this "lit" climbing photography: *Hooked* (actually more of a fishing-oriented magazine) first published several of my early efforts, then *Urban Climber* and finally *Climbing* and *Rock & Ice*. A few years later, *Rock & Ice* editor David Clifford would tell me, "I never did see your lighting techniques applied to climbing prior to you doing so. You not only pioneered it for action-style climbing but also did it well, and on a format that is much trickier than digital."

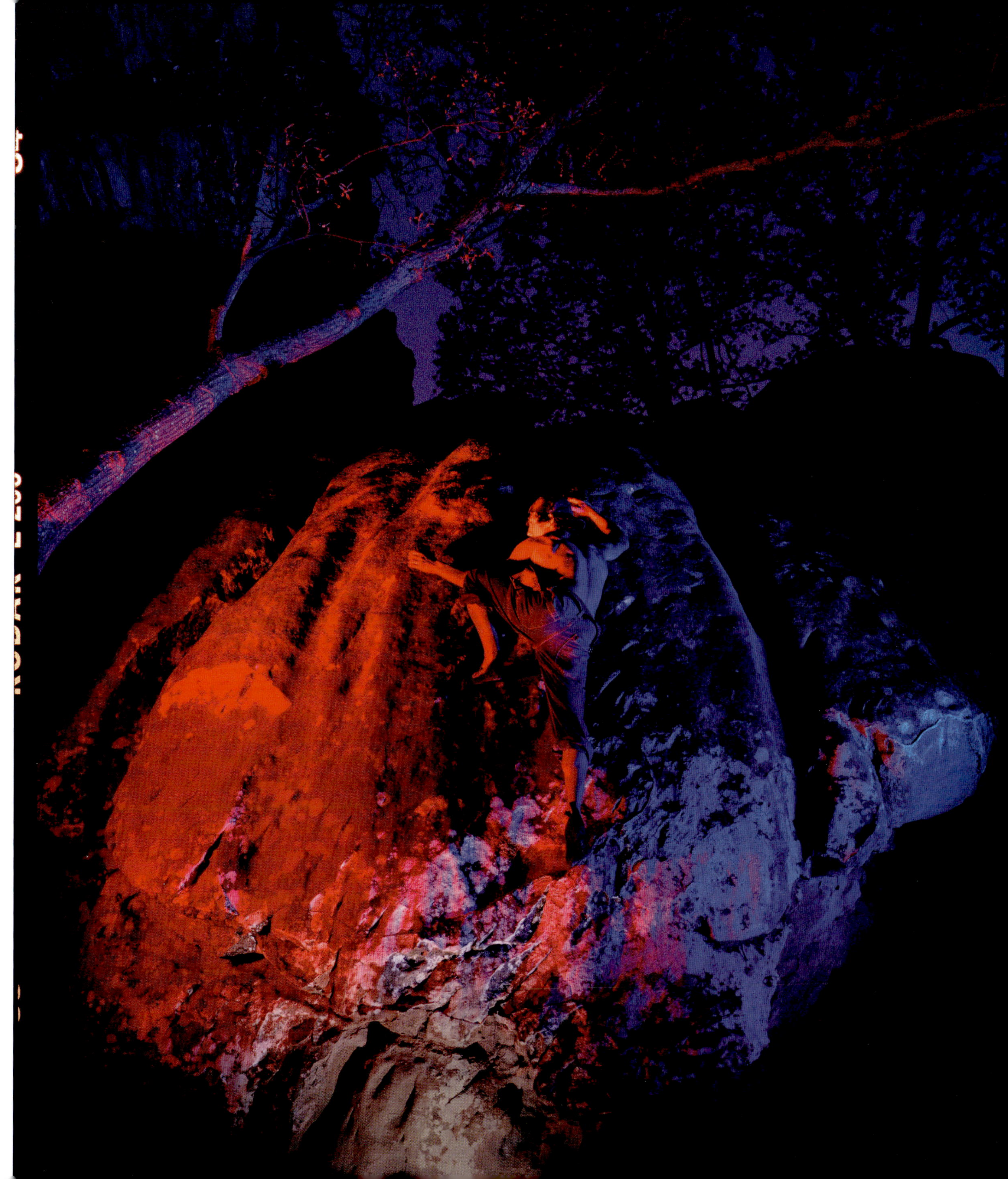

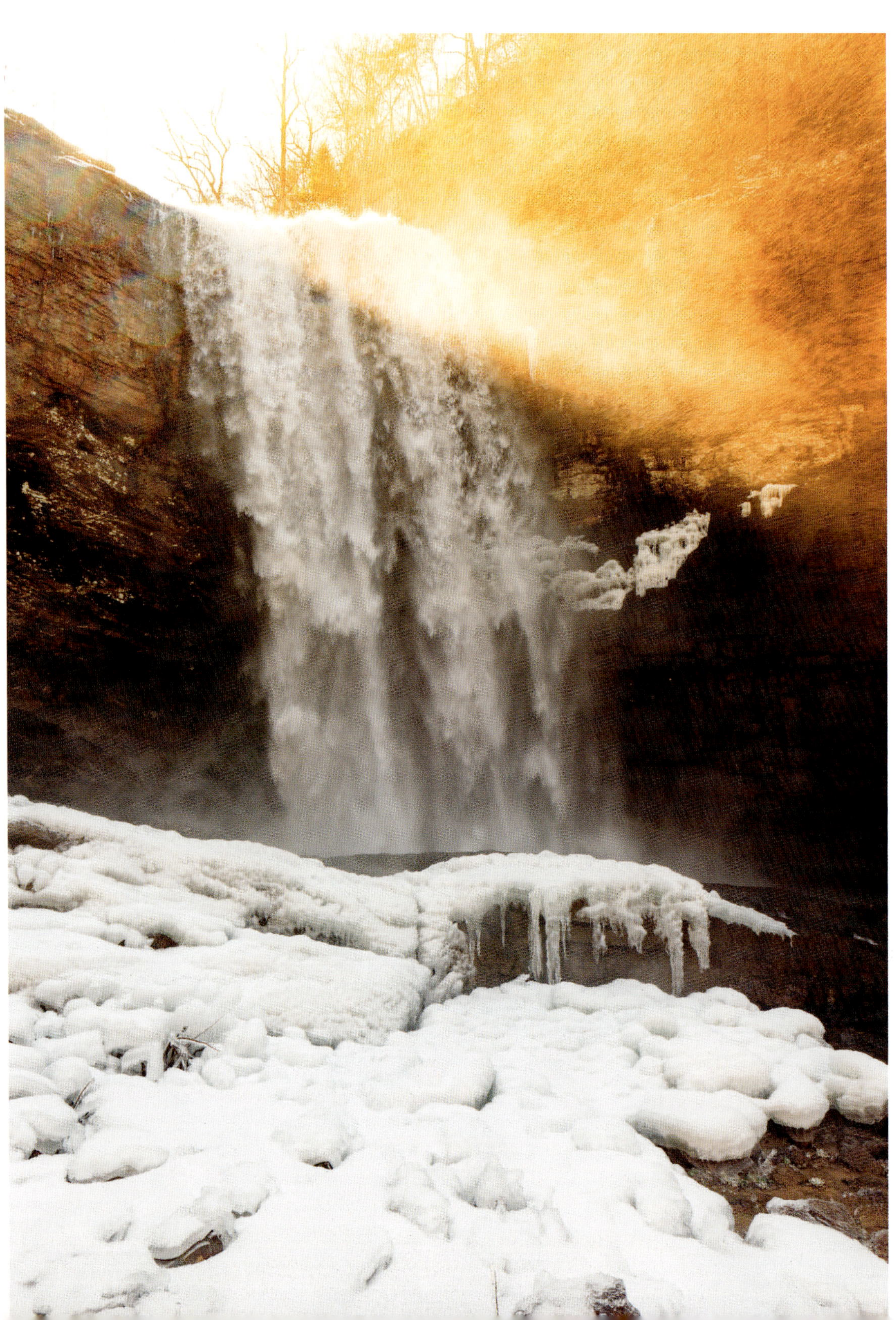

Winter at Lula Falls, Lookout Mountain, Tennessee

Opposite: Greg Kottkamp on *Dreamscape* (5.11), Sand Rock, Alabama

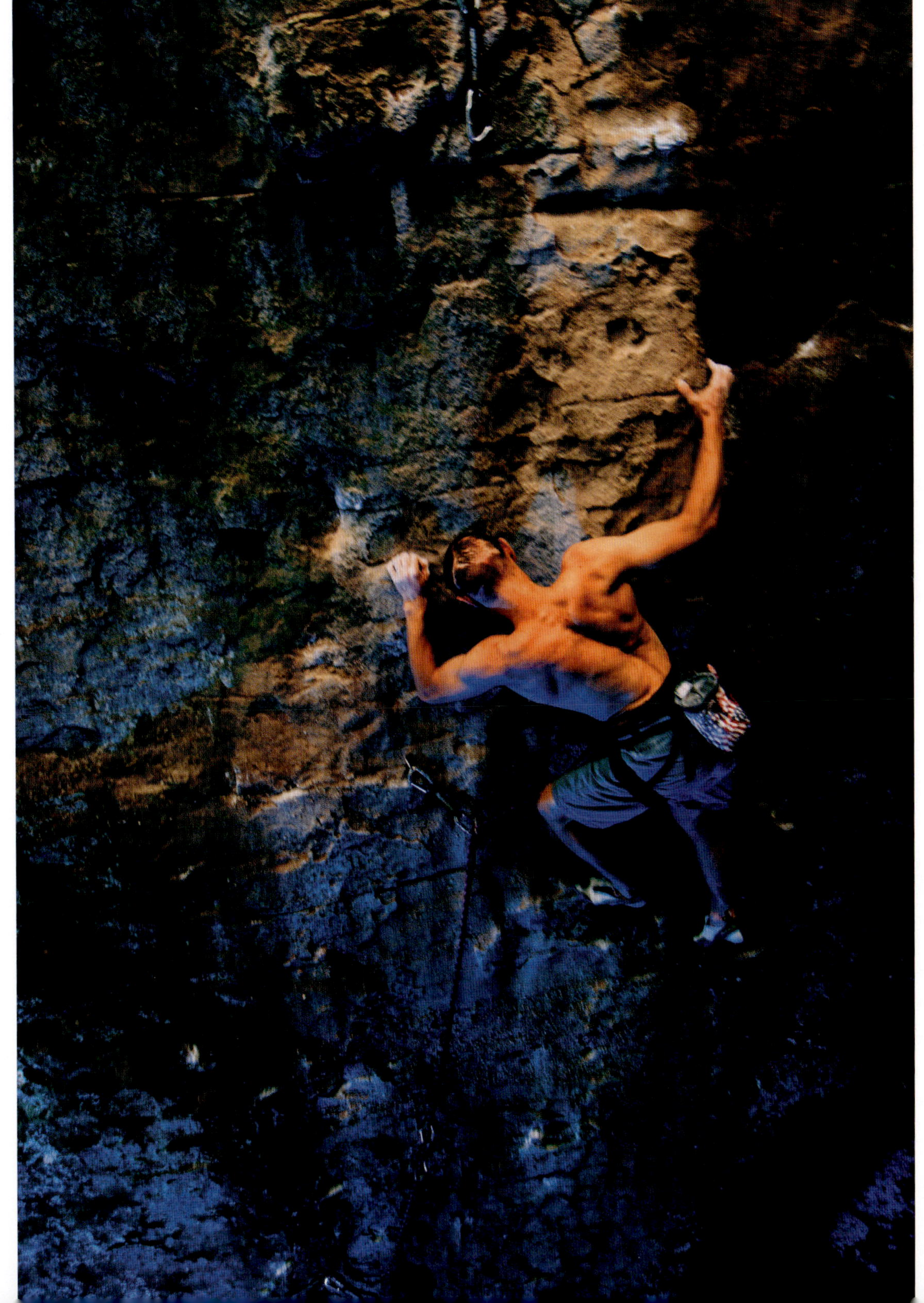

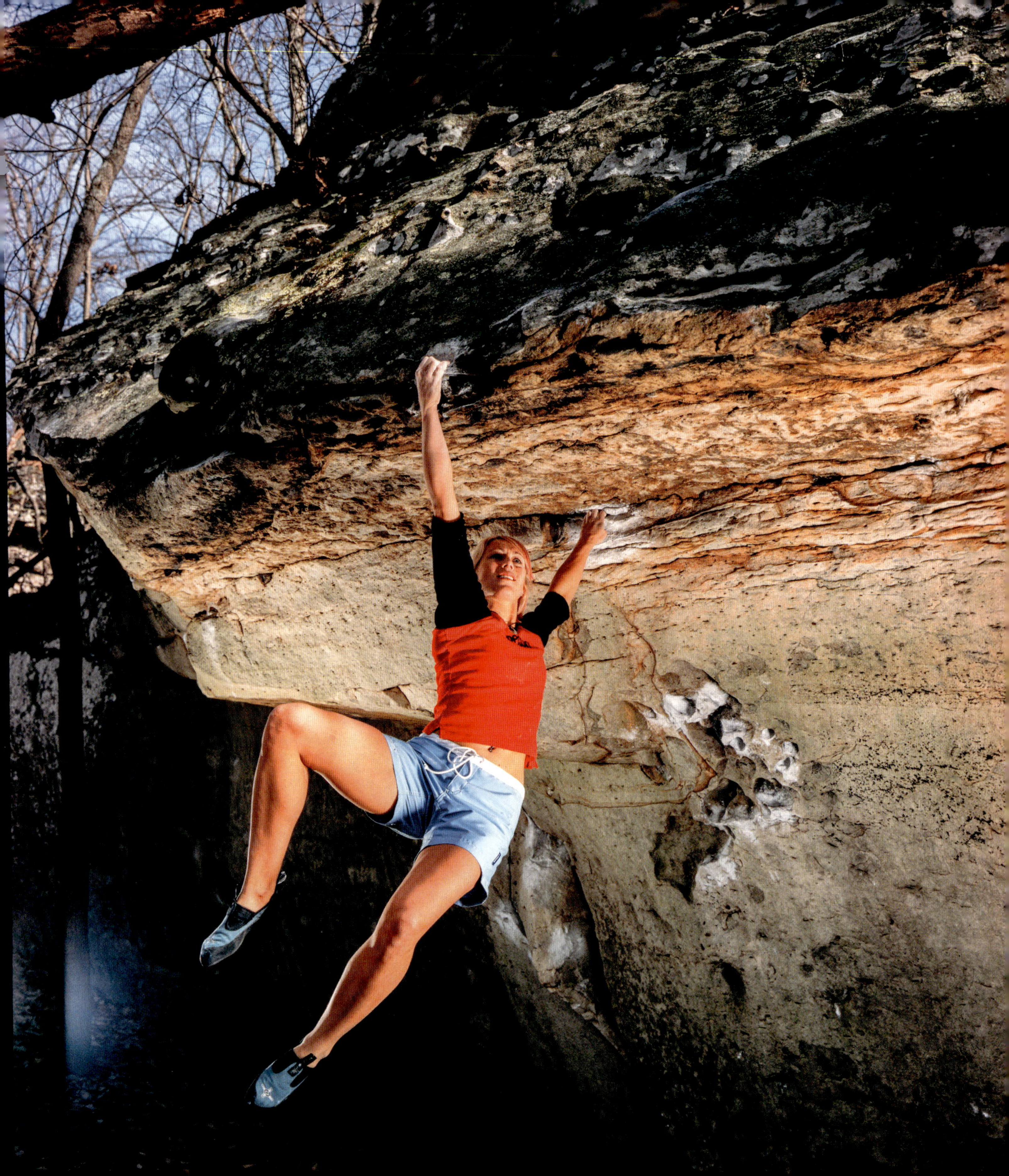

The look flourished for about a decade, probably to excess, and now climbing photography is back to a healthy balance of lighting styles. Breaking the mold a little bit gave us a way to illuminate more humble Southern geographies that may otherwise have been overlooked as mundane. In retrospect, a lot of these experiments were probably about more than just my subjects. It was emphatically *not* detached reportage; my own ideas and enthusiasms were very obviously part of the photographs. I think they also told a deeper story about our little backyard wilderness.

"Landscape pictures," Robert Adams declares, "can offer us, I think, three verities—geography, autobiography, and metaphor. Geography is, if taken alone, sometimes boring; autobiography is frequently trivial; and metaphor can be dubious. But taken together . . . the three kinds of representation strengthen each other and reinforce what we all work to keep intact—an affection for life."

The subculture of climbing in the South is deeply entwined with the ruined landscape. There is metaphorical power in emphasizing that vital connection rather than minimizing it. ◆

Jennifer Jenkins on *Tunnel Vision* (V6) at Rocktown, Georgia

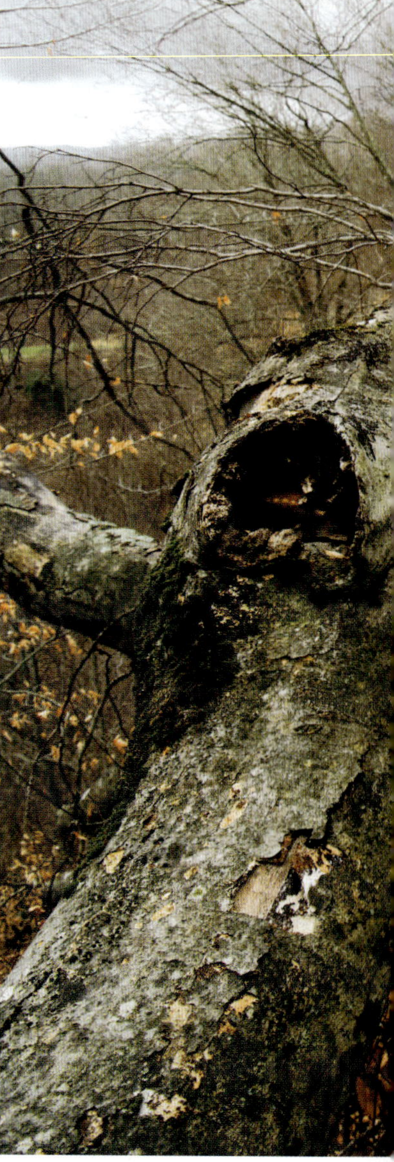

Remains of an exploded tree in Mabel, North Carolina

DEAD ENDS

From: Andrew Kornylak
To: Jeff Jackson
Date: Nov 7, 2005
Subject: Re: Alabama

Hi Jeff.
I am currently working on the Triple Crown feature but I'd like to revisit the "Southern Legends" idea we were discussing a while back and see if it is still a viable article for Rock and Ice. See below for examples of what I'm thinking.
Cheers —Andrew

Synopsis: *Southern Legends* is a collection of tall tales about Southeastern climbing. Most of them are expanded versions of stories and short notes in Rob Robinson and Chris Watford's entertaining guidebook, *The Deep South Climber's Companion.* Each story would be accompanied by a photograph or two, recreating the legend in a creative way.

1. *Flying Frog* (5.10), Tallulah Gorge, Georgia
BACKGROUND: It wasn't until the 1970s that climbers began exploring the awesome walls of north Georgia's Tallulah Gorge for free-climbing potential. Sometime around 1976, Shannon Stegg was in the gorge with Rich Gottlieb working on the first pitch of a thin, single-pitch crack line main wall. Fresh off a climbing trip to France, Stegg was holding forth about the natural free-climbing ability and body awareness of French climbers. Without warning and

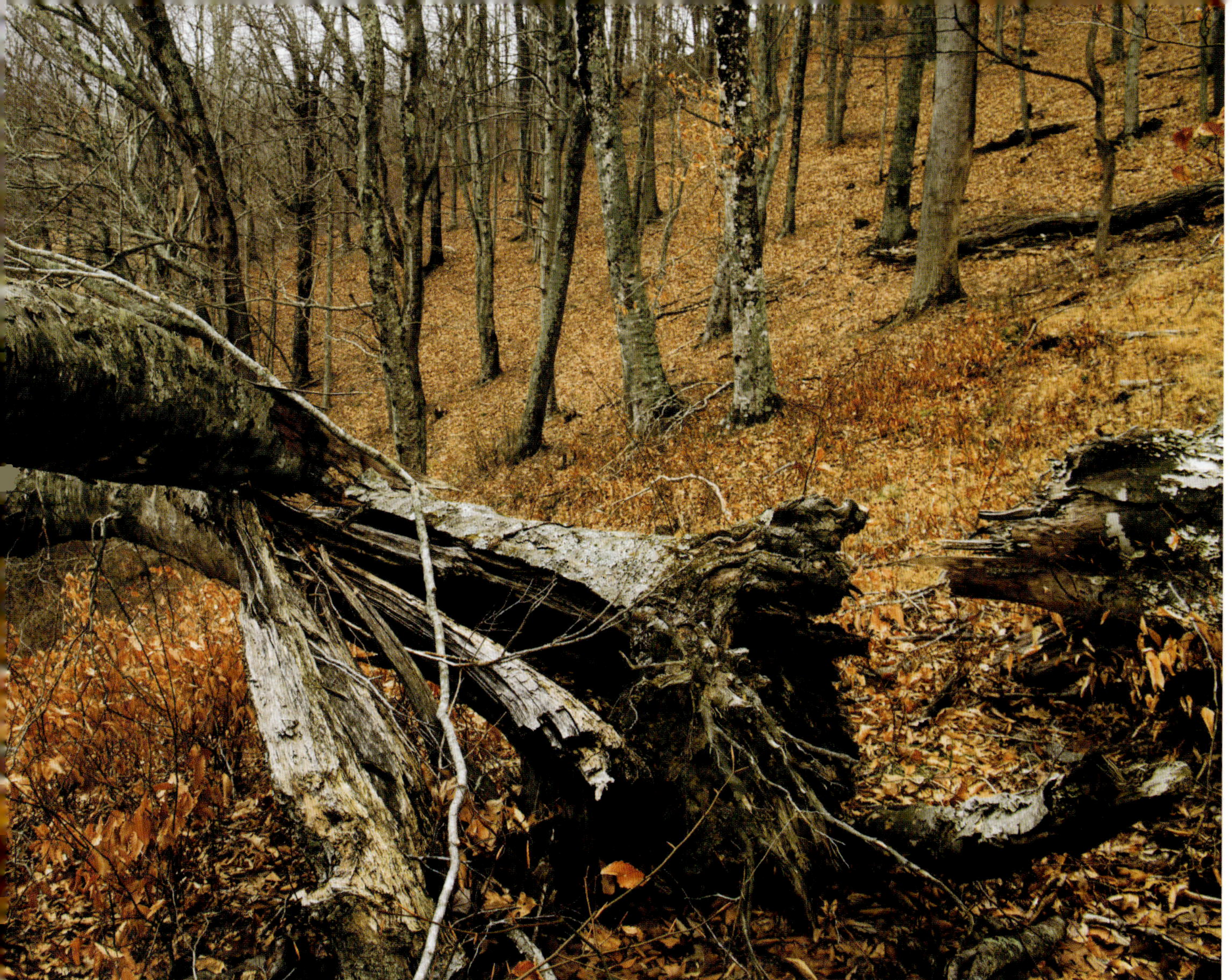

with scant protection under him, Stegg peeled off the top of the climb. Instinctively, he leapt from the wall, spun 180 degrees in midair and grabbed a high tree branch on the way down. Executing a perfect gymnastic salto around the branch, he dismounted to land with both feet on the ground. The pair eventually finished the line and named it *Flying Frog* after Stegg's Francophilic escapade.

PHOTO 1: A heady, dizzying shot from high on the first pitch of *Flying Frog*, the camera focused on a climber dangerously far above his last piece of protection, leaning away from the rock and looking down at the trees far below.

PHOTO 2: Full-body portrait of big, burly Shannon Stegg in his front yard, a plug of tobacco in his mouth. His daughter Chelsea hides behind him clutching wildflowers and glaring at the camera. In Stegg's hand is a single flower.

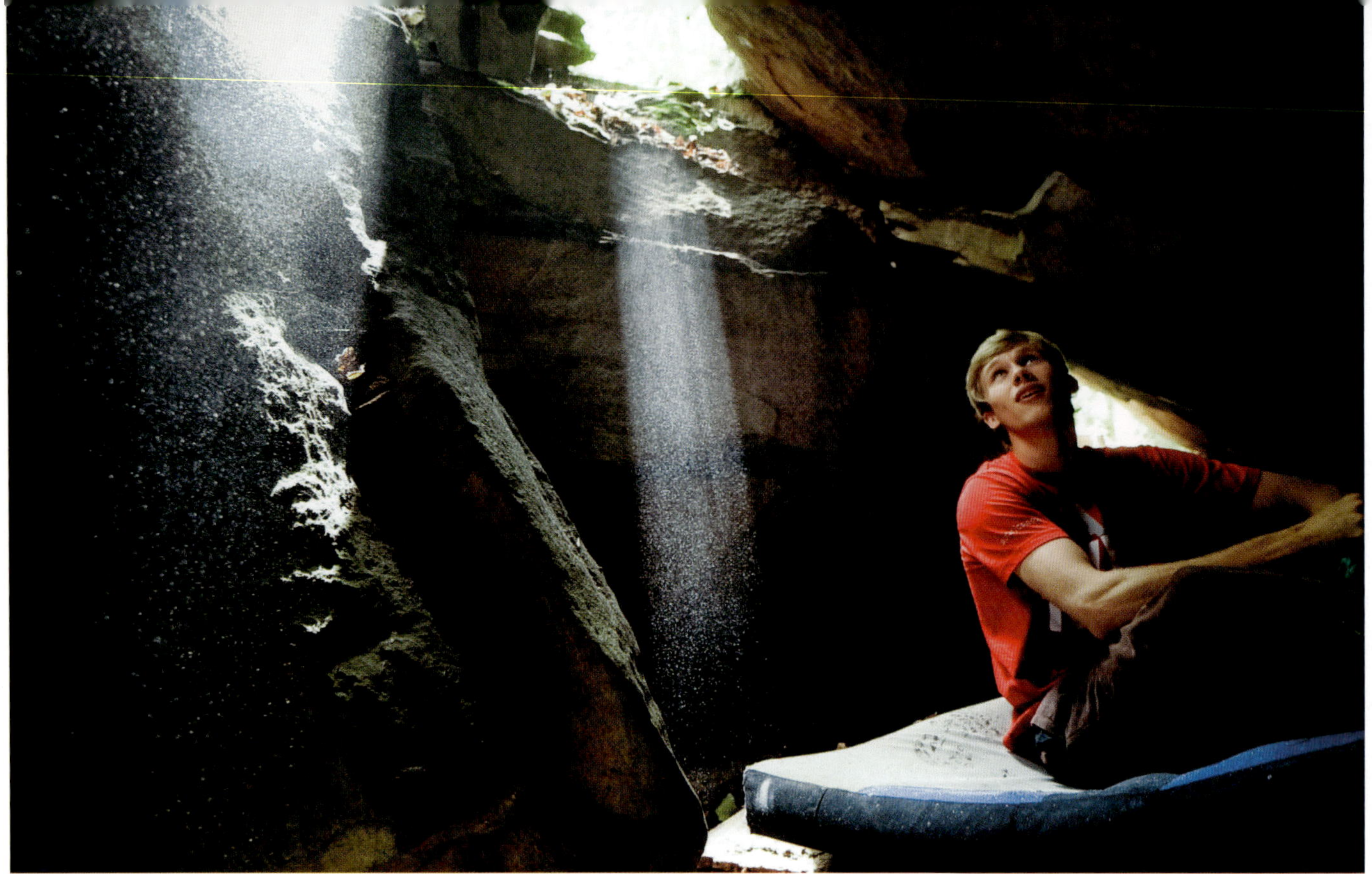

Brion Voges at Stone Fort, Tennessee

Opposite: Paul Fuelling at Hound Ears, North Carolina

2. *The Zipper* (5.12), Chattahoochee River, Atlanta, Georgia

BACKGROUND: In 1979, Dempsey Medford, Jeff Scully, Tracy Rodgers, and Richard Hauert found this scrappy little twenty-foot roof crack nestled in the woods down by the river. Scully had just returned from climbing out West, armed with an early prototype set of Ray Jardine's Friends, a new type of active camming device for protecting crack climbs. Using these, he aided out the crack easily. Medford then stepped it up and attempted to aid the crack with traditional stoppers and hexes. Nearing the lip, he popped a piece, then another and another, until he was left dangling a few feet above the ground, at which point Rodgers calmly reached out to offer him a cigarette. Years later, the crack was freed at 5.12 by Philip Fisher and Robyn Erbesfield-Raboutou. I hear there are other versions of this story that involve broken limbs.

PHOTO 1: I think this would be a great shot with Chris Sierzant, a strong local climber who has been wanting to boulder (free solo) the route. The shot would look fully modern, with artificial lighting.

PHOTO 2: A close-up shot of a climber (Rodgers) hunched over on a nearby rock watching the scene unfold. Smoke rises from a half-smoked cigarette in one hand. A pack of cigarettes is folded under his T-shirt sleeve.

3. *Mega Death* (5.10), Lost Wall, Georgia

BACKGROUND: In the late 1980s, this climb was first ascended by Tom Woodruff and Steve Ritchie. During the ascent, huge blocks fell from the crack, landing on the tips of Tom's toes. Apparently his climbing shoes—La Sportiva Megas—were a size too big, and though they were lopped off guillotine style, his toes were intact! The pile of rubble still marks the base of the climb.

PHOTO 1: A shot from above of a wide-eyed climber in 1980s climbing garb dislodging rubble from a ledge and shouting "ROCK!" down to his partner.

PHOTO 2: A close-up photo of the tips of a pair of climbing shoes sticking out from under a large block, wicked-witch style.

4. *The Standard Route* (5.6), Dead Man's Rock, Sand Rock, Alabama

BACKGROUND: Now known simply as "The Pinnacle." Legend has it that, around the turn of the twentieth century, there was a rumor that there was gold stashed on top of this pinnacle, easily seen from the village below but hard to get to. Two enterprising brothers got it in their heads to get that gold and headed for the hills. After much effort, they got to the top of the seventy-foot tower of rock. One brother died trying to get back down; the other died of starvation. The location of the gold remains a mystery.

PHOTO 1: Two young men in period outfits (overalls, no shoes, the elder brother with a newsboy hat) and perhaps a short length of rope, fearfully scrambling up the pinnacle at dusk, lit dramatically with a subtle golden glow emanating from the top of the pinnacle. ◆

From: Jeff Jackson
To: Andrew Kornylak
Date: Nov 15, 2005
Subject: RE: Alabama

Andrew,
I'm still interested in the idea. I'd like to see more Southeast coverage. Get me and Cliffy some photos to look at and we'll make something happen.
Jefe

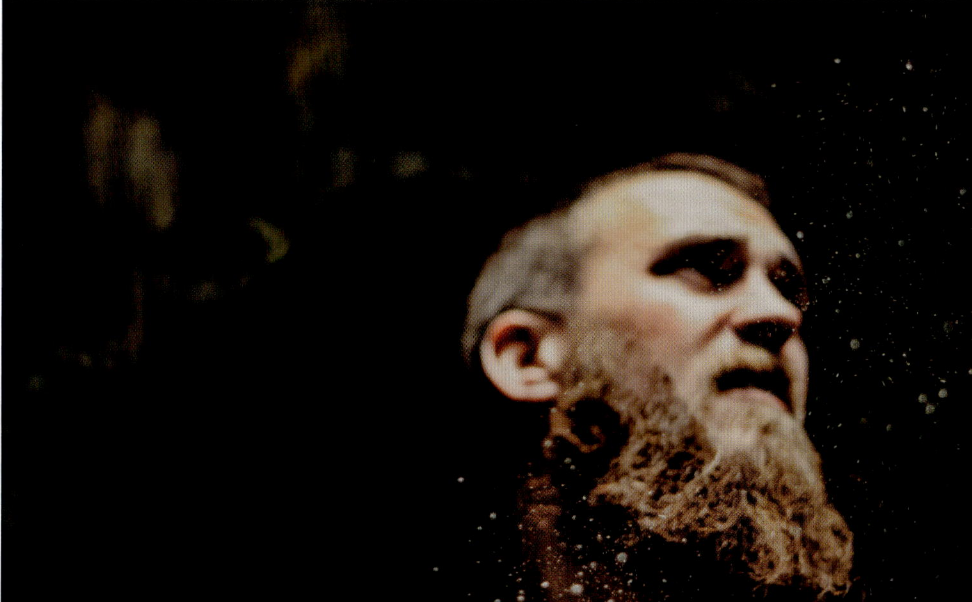

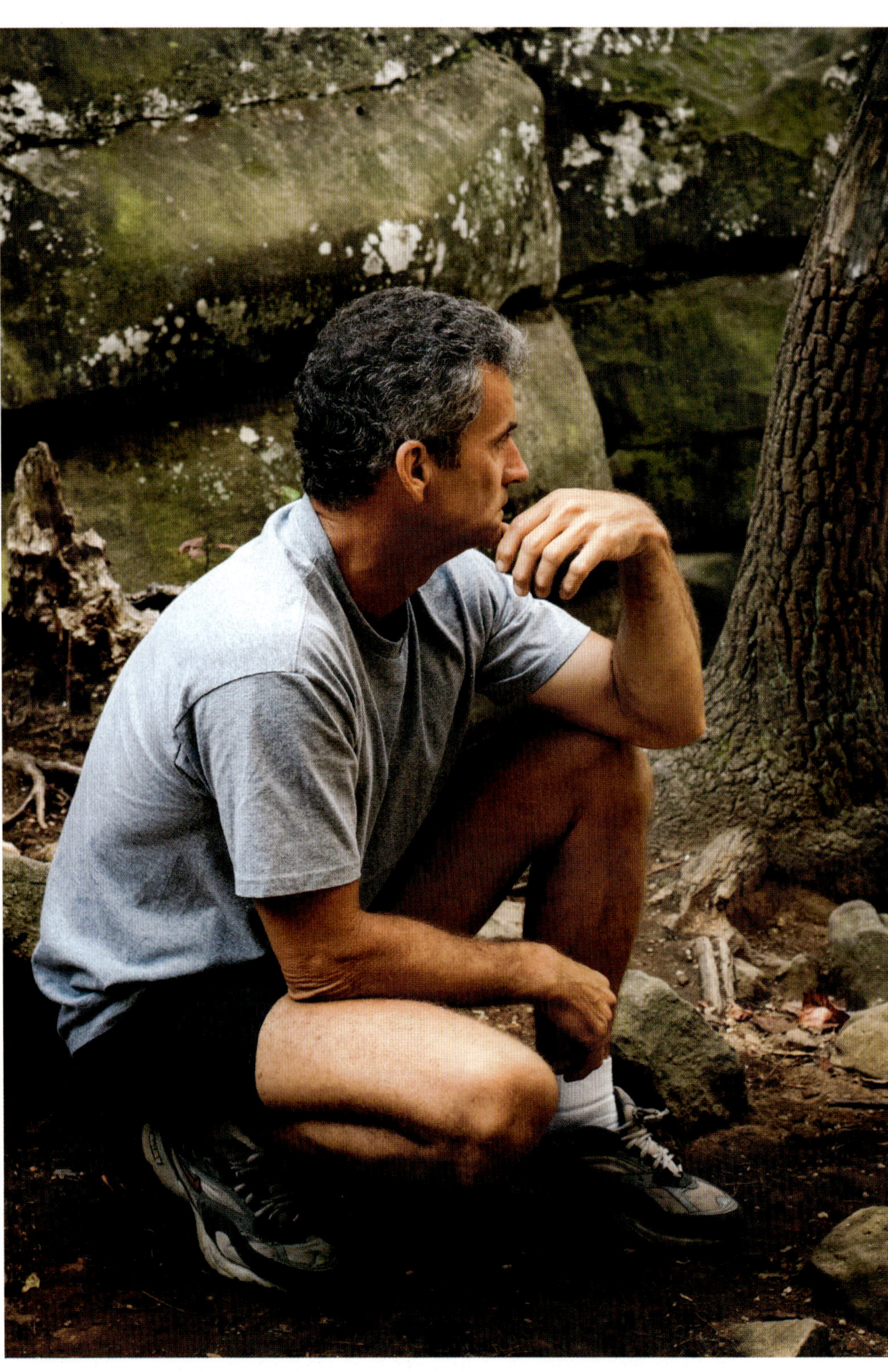

Johnny Arms, "the mayor" of Sand Rock, Alabama

Opposite: Anthony Meeks free-soloing *Heave-Ho* (5.11) at Sand Rock

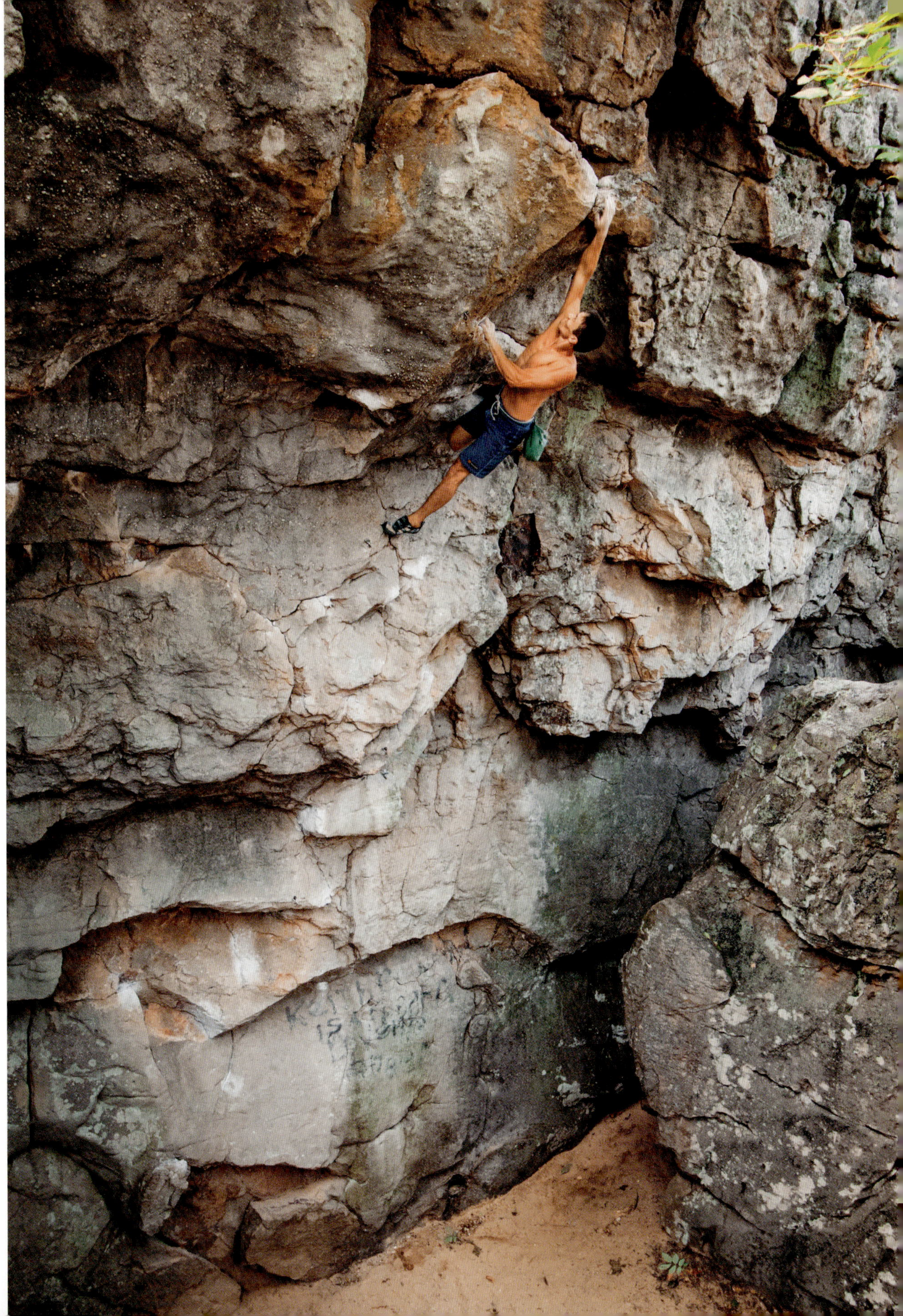

Peter Eiland at Zahnd Wildlife Management Area, Georgia

A climber embracing his German shepherd at Alabama's Little River Canyon National Preserve

Opposite: Jessie playing the banjo at Grandfather Campground near Boone, North Carolina

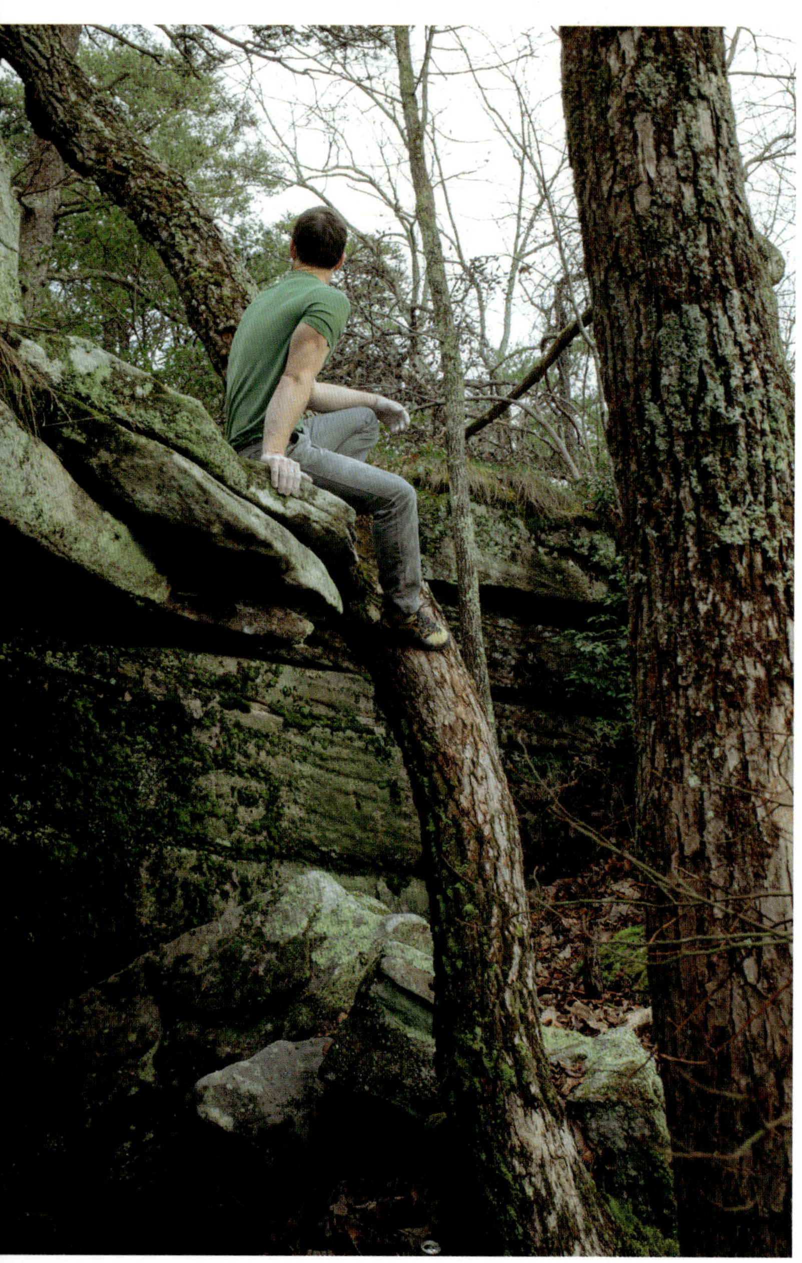

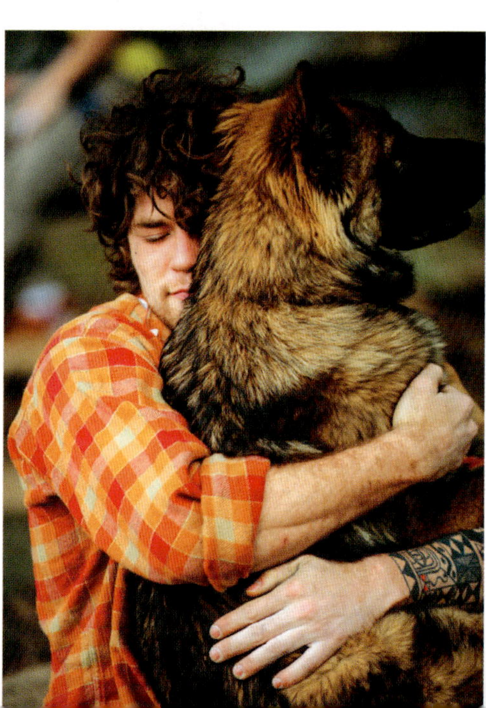

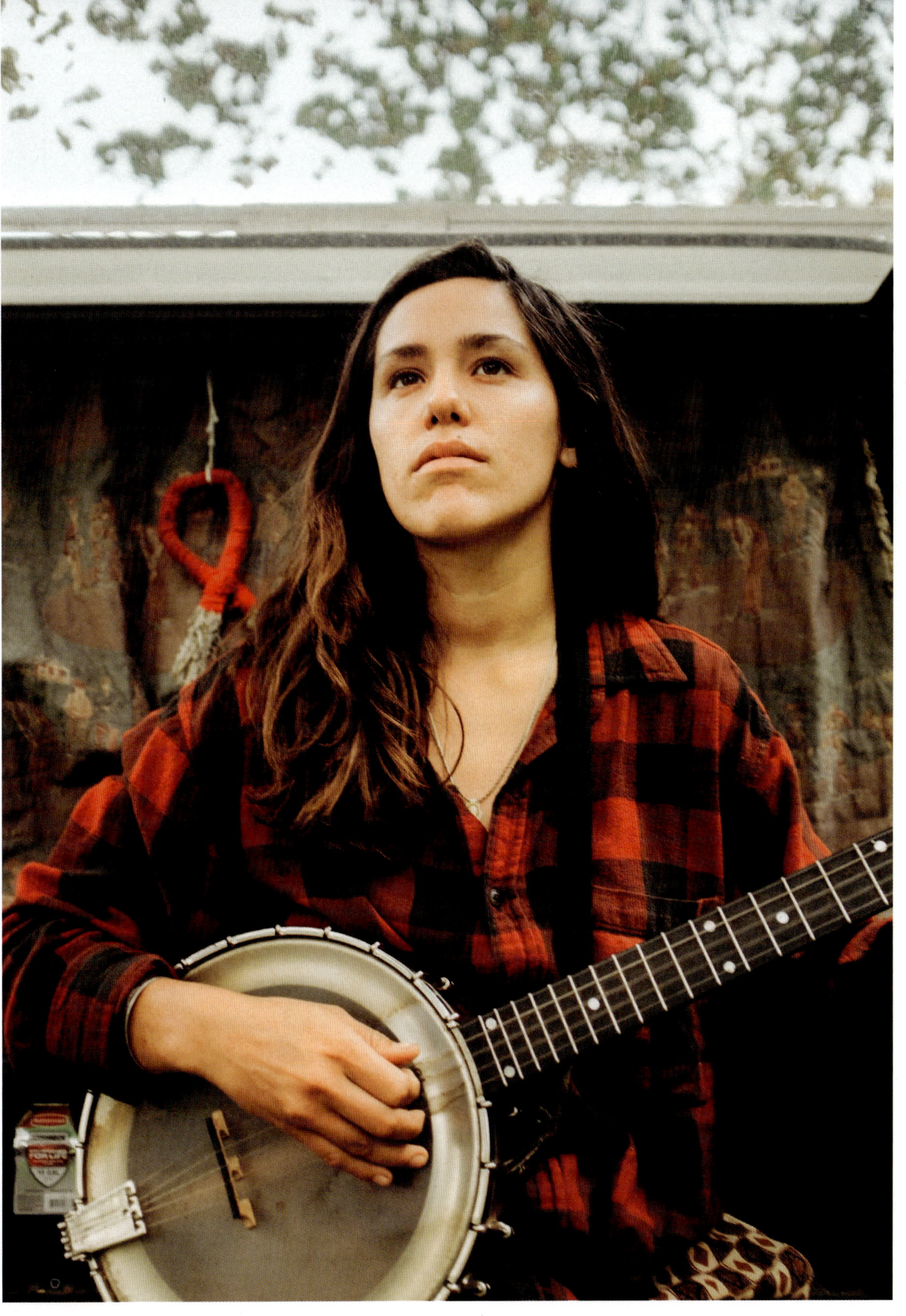

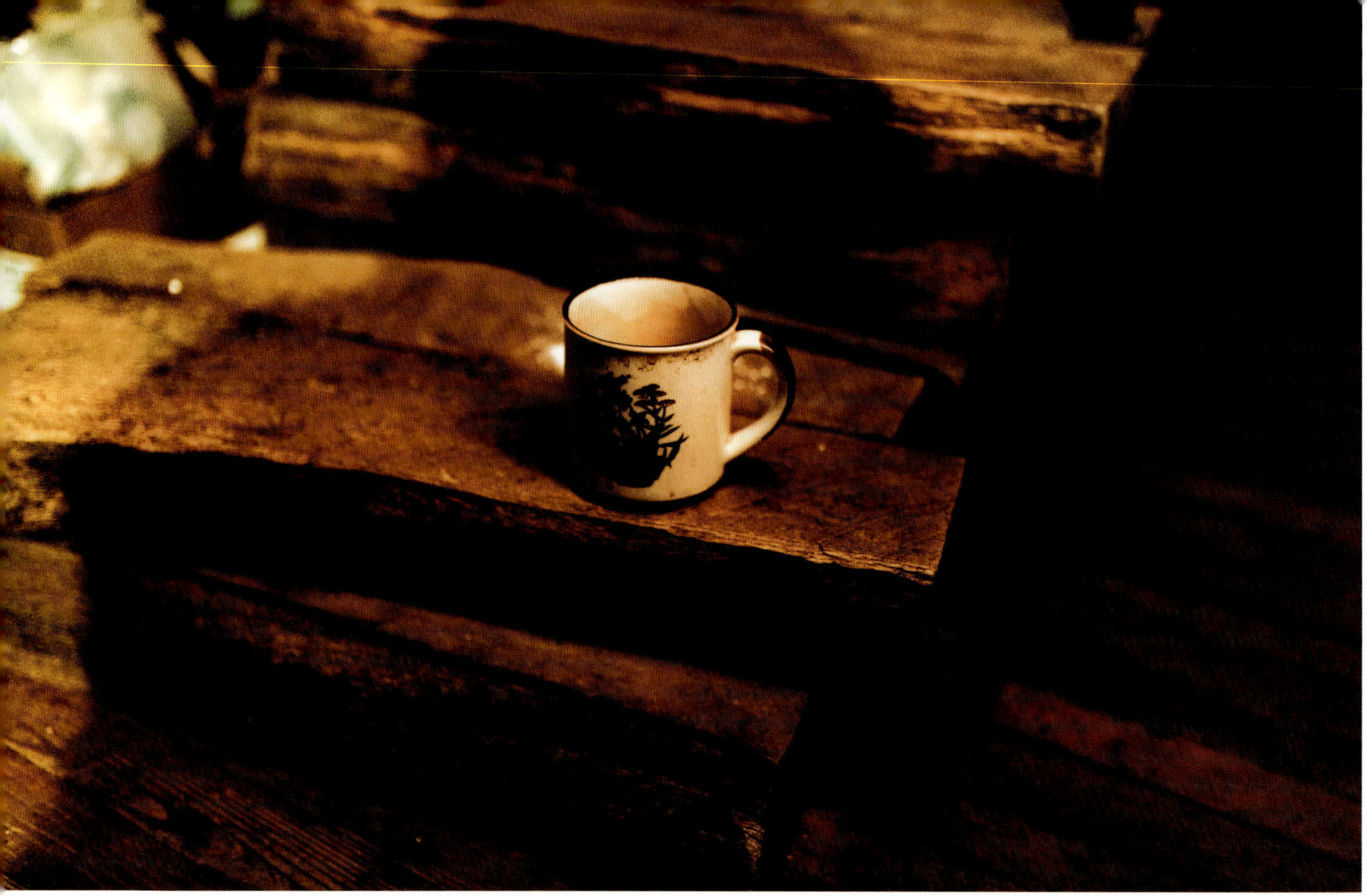

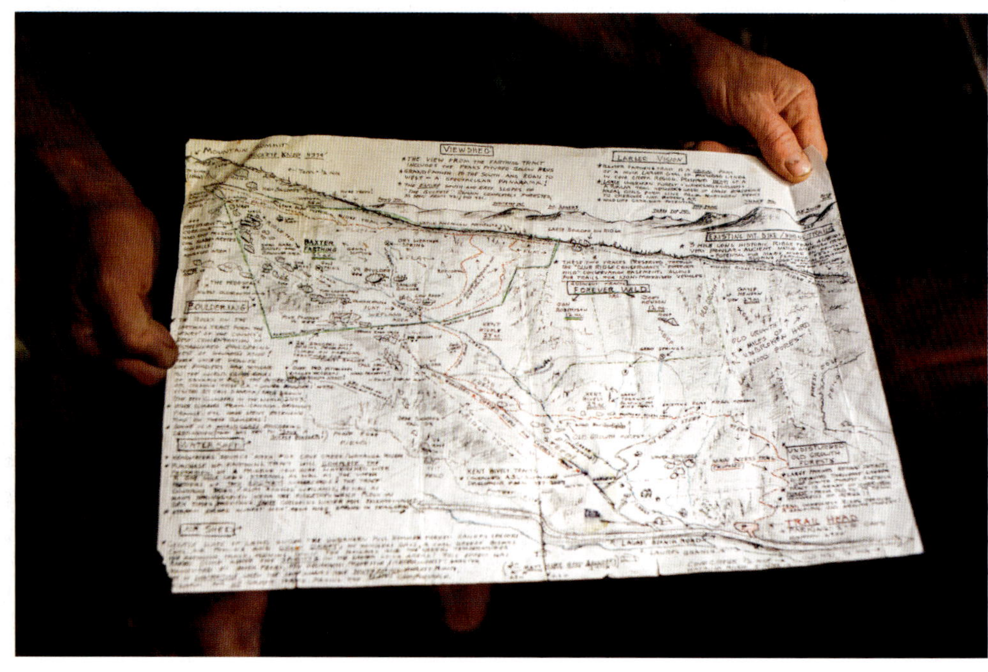
VIEWSHED
LARGER VISION
BAXTER FARTHING
FOREVER WILD
BOULDERING
WATER SHED
UNDISTURBED OLD GROWTH FORESTS
TRAIL HEAD

A CABIN IN THE WOODS

Joey Henson's coffee cup at the Barn near Vilas, North Carolina

Joey holding his hand-drawn map of the Barn Boulders and Buckeye Knob near Vilas

I first encountered climber Joey Henson as a black-and-white photograph in *Stone Crusade,* John Sherman's seminal book about his bouldering road trip across America. In the perfectly composed frame, Jim Horton is halfway through the crux mantle on the Blowing Rock, North Carolina, V6 testpiece *Raw Terror*. His arms are crossed, trapped beneath the weight of his body on the sloping lip, and his expression a balance of effort and fear. From six feet below, chalk-white hands emerge. The spotter's face is in shadow, but the outstretched fingers are unmistakable to me now as Joey's.

In our film about Joey, *The Mapmaker,* my codirector Carlo Nasisse frames the same perpetually chalked hands that now stretch out below Richie Hum as he inches up the thin, mossy face of the terrifying highball *The Nimble* (V10). Through my camera looking down from the top, Joey's six-foot-three frame recedes as Richie climbs ever higher, an intimate stream of encouragement floating up into my microphone: "Keep trying . . . find those stances . . . keep trying . . . I'll catch ya."

Sherman dedicates nearly an entire chapter to his old friend Joey in *Stone Crusade,* but there are no photographs of him climbing in the book. Nor will you find many photos of Joey in old magazines or videos or the internet. Though his climbing exploits are legend, he keeps a low-key existence at the foot of an old-growth mountainside outside Boone in a climber's outpost known simply as "the Barn." It's here that Joey hosts and mentors traveling climbers and where he puts the finishing touches on his imaginatively hand-drawn maps of some of the hundreds of climbing areas he's visited.

Robbie Beeland (left) and Drew Mercer in the Linville Gorge, North Carolina

The school bus at the Barn

The Mapmaker sweetly and honestly captures a complex man and the connections that wind through the cliffs and boulders of his mountains, but there is more to be revealed about Joey in the same way his drawings are intricately detailed but not to scale. They're more mystical than accurate. They sketch a place but also contain Joey's thoughts and dreams about it. As Richie says, "It's kind of a popularity contest among the boulders. The bigger the boulder is drawn, the cooler Joey thinks it is. Even if you're not climber and you're just trying to go for a hike, you can find old-growth forests, or viewpoints, and follow the maps to these beautiful places that Joey keeps secret. He always says, 'If you've studied this map, you know everything that I know.' "

To Joey, physical geography is sacred, undiscovered, and full of magic; the exercise of climbing is less about physical acrobatics and more about connecting more deeply to the landscape and its history. He is as connected to the stone as lichen. Younger climbers learn from him and are charged to carry on traditions of both discovery and secrecy.

In recent years Joey has been exploring and mapping the thousands of boulders in North Carolina's Linville Gorge. Excursions to the gorge with him are usually multiday adventures, with miles of arduous trekking, wild whitewater crossings, and encounters with dangerous wildlife. Access to the area is secure, so he shares his maps with the community, but as with the rest of Boone-area bouldering, there are no guidebooks, and most locals would like to keep it that way. It helps that Joey slows down this process with pen, paper, and word of mouth. "You can't take a photo of every boulder in Linville Gorge," he says, "but you can draw it."

To Joey—a keeper of secrets—the end goal is to save everything and maybe share some of it too. In 2017, he signed an agreement with the Carolina Climbers Coalition to preserve a fifty-five-acre tract of forest above his land renamed the Buckeye Boulders. It's a pristine bouldering area in his backyard that he's cultivated in solitude for decades. The way Joey sees it, after years of advocating for community access to climbing, he's now "walking the walk" by allowing people to park on his property and enjoy the climbing for themselves, with or without a map. ◆

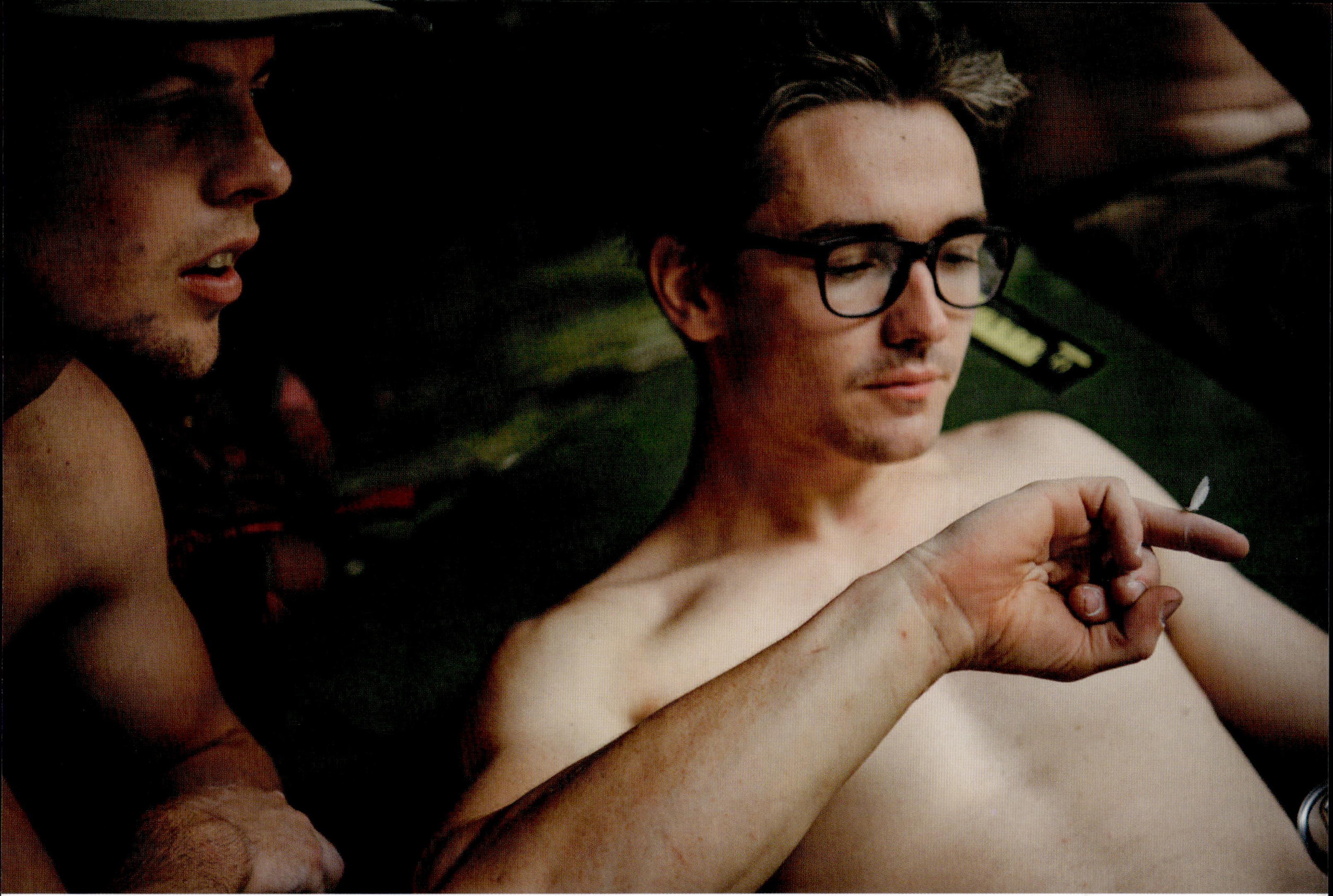

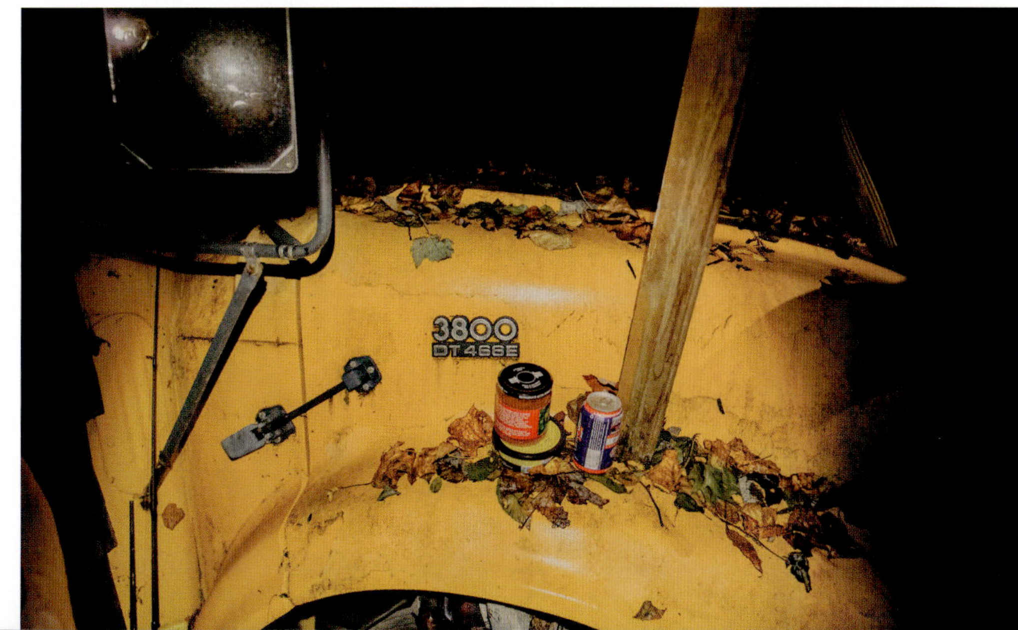
3800
DT466E

Nighttime
at the Barn

Fire juggler
at the Barn

Opposite: Woodruff
Boulder at night

Opposite: Party
at the Barn

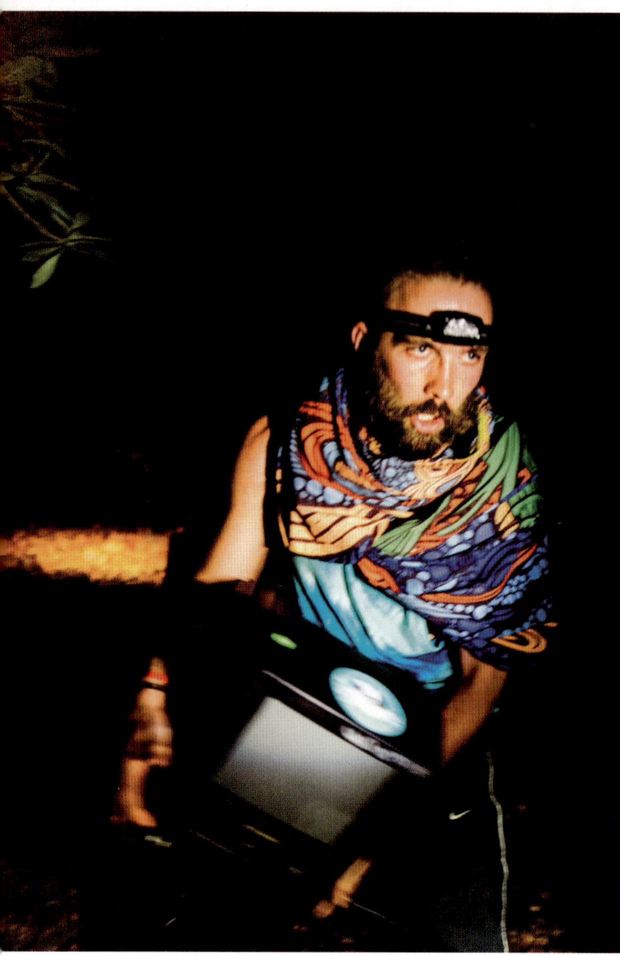

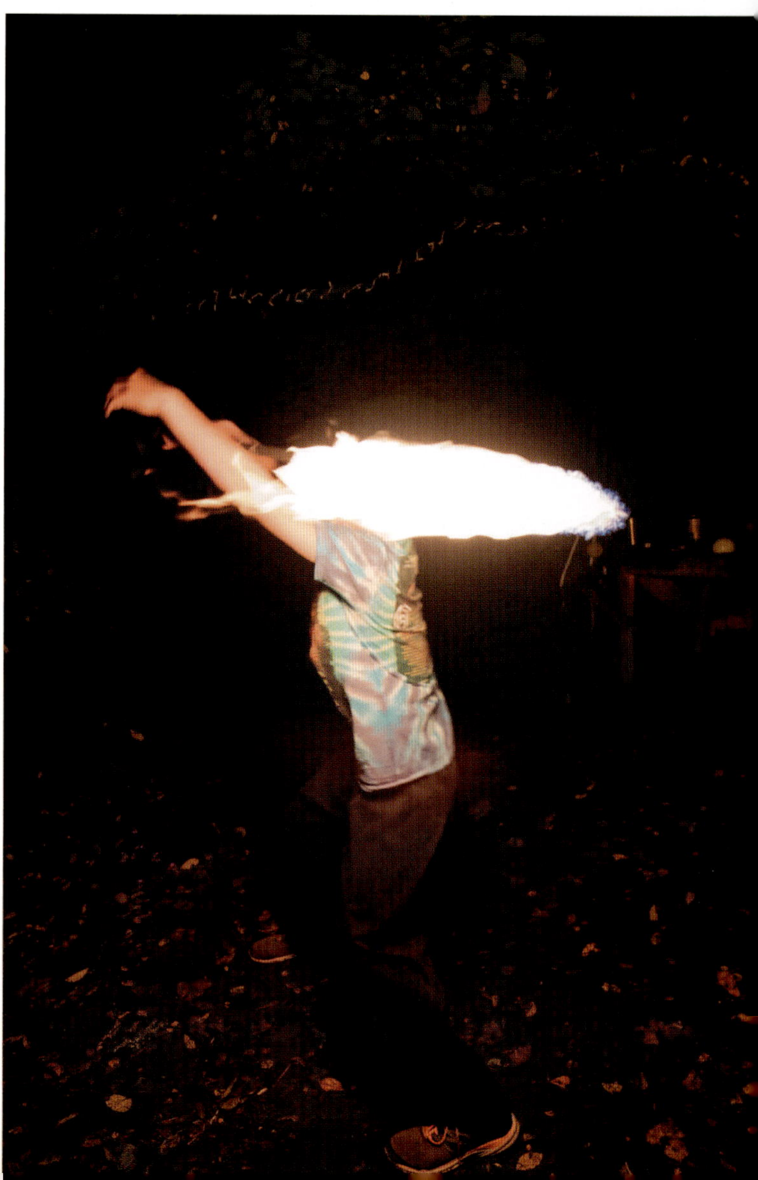

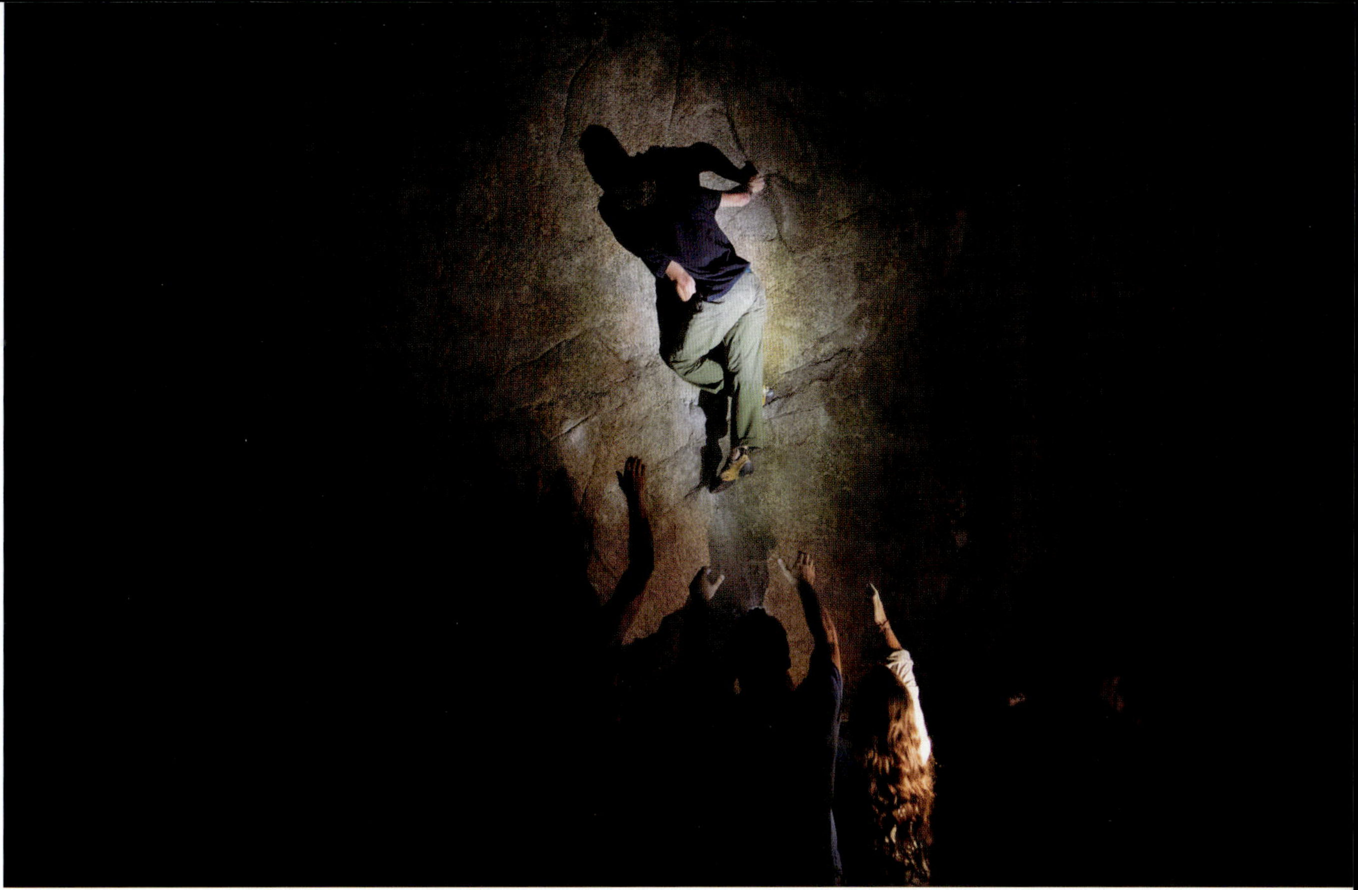

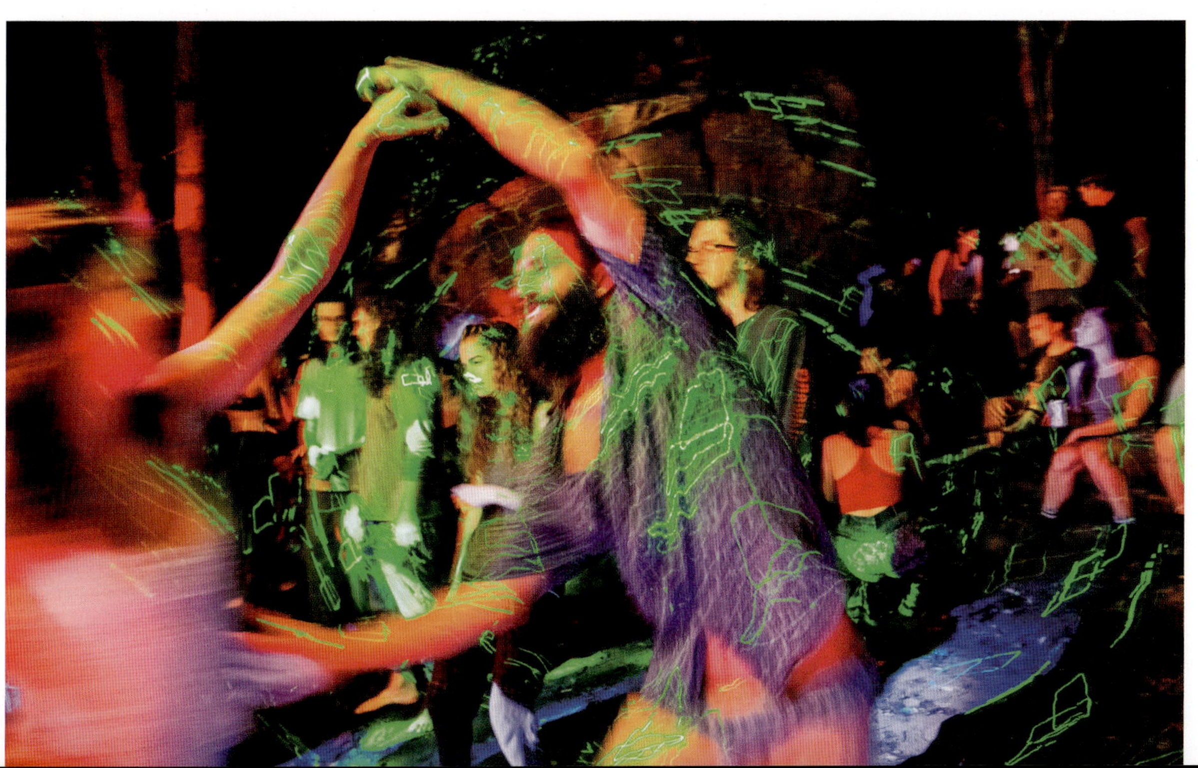

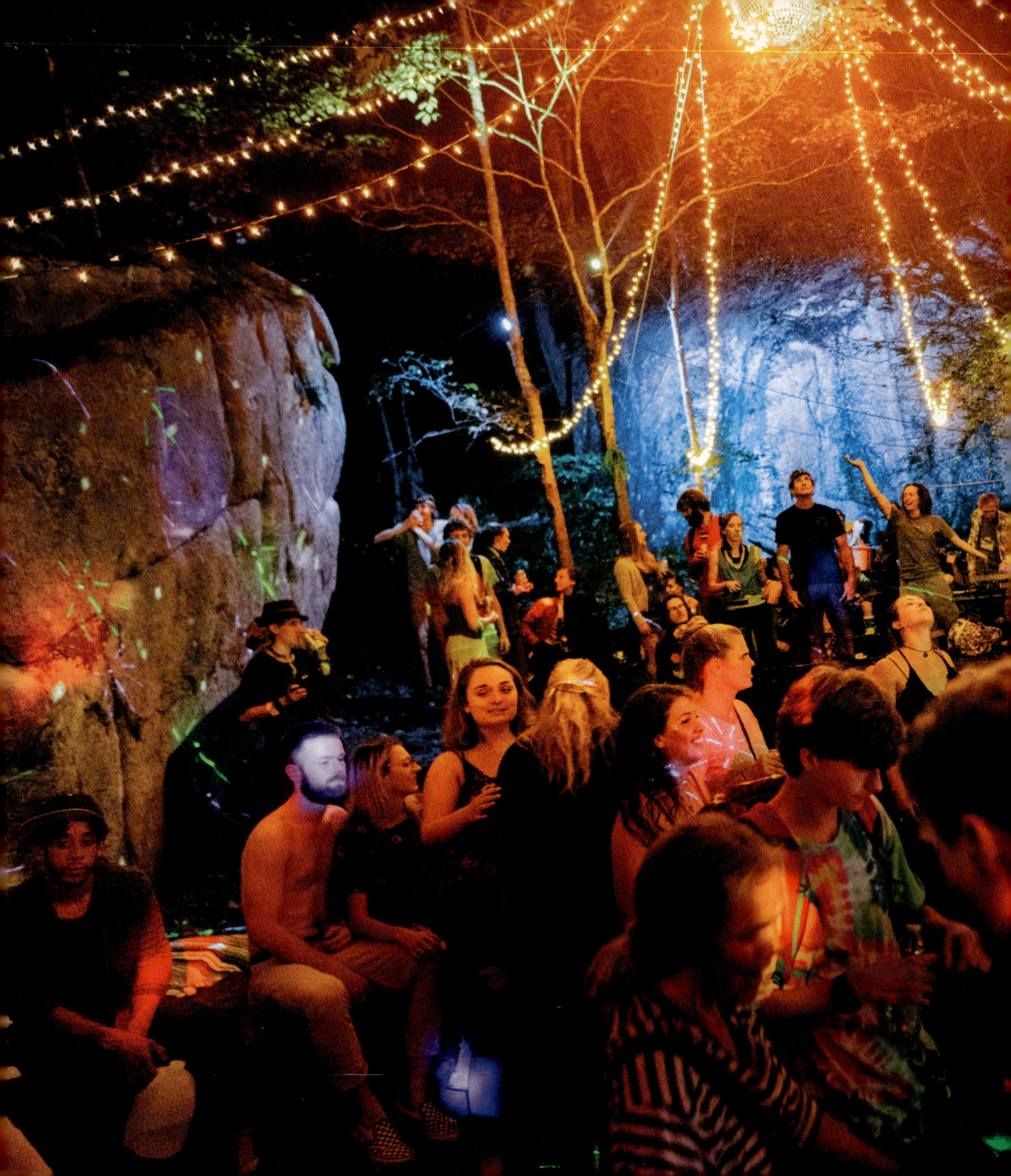

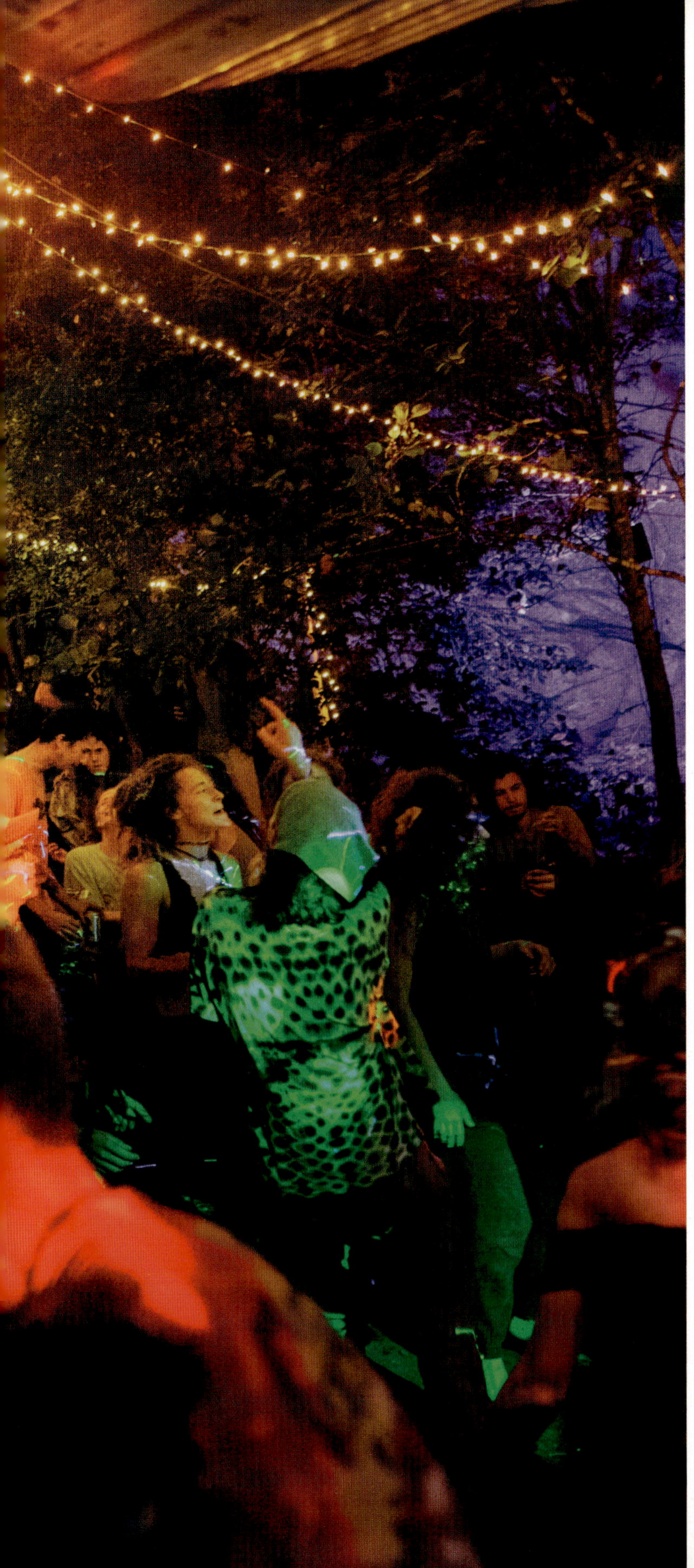

A party at the
Barn near Vilas

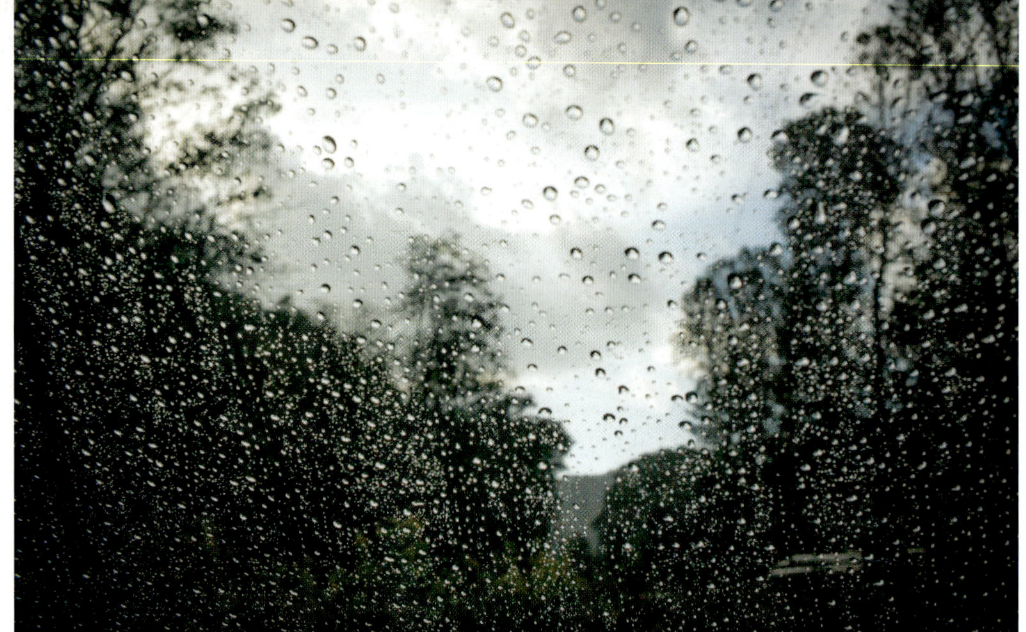

Rainy morning in Vilas

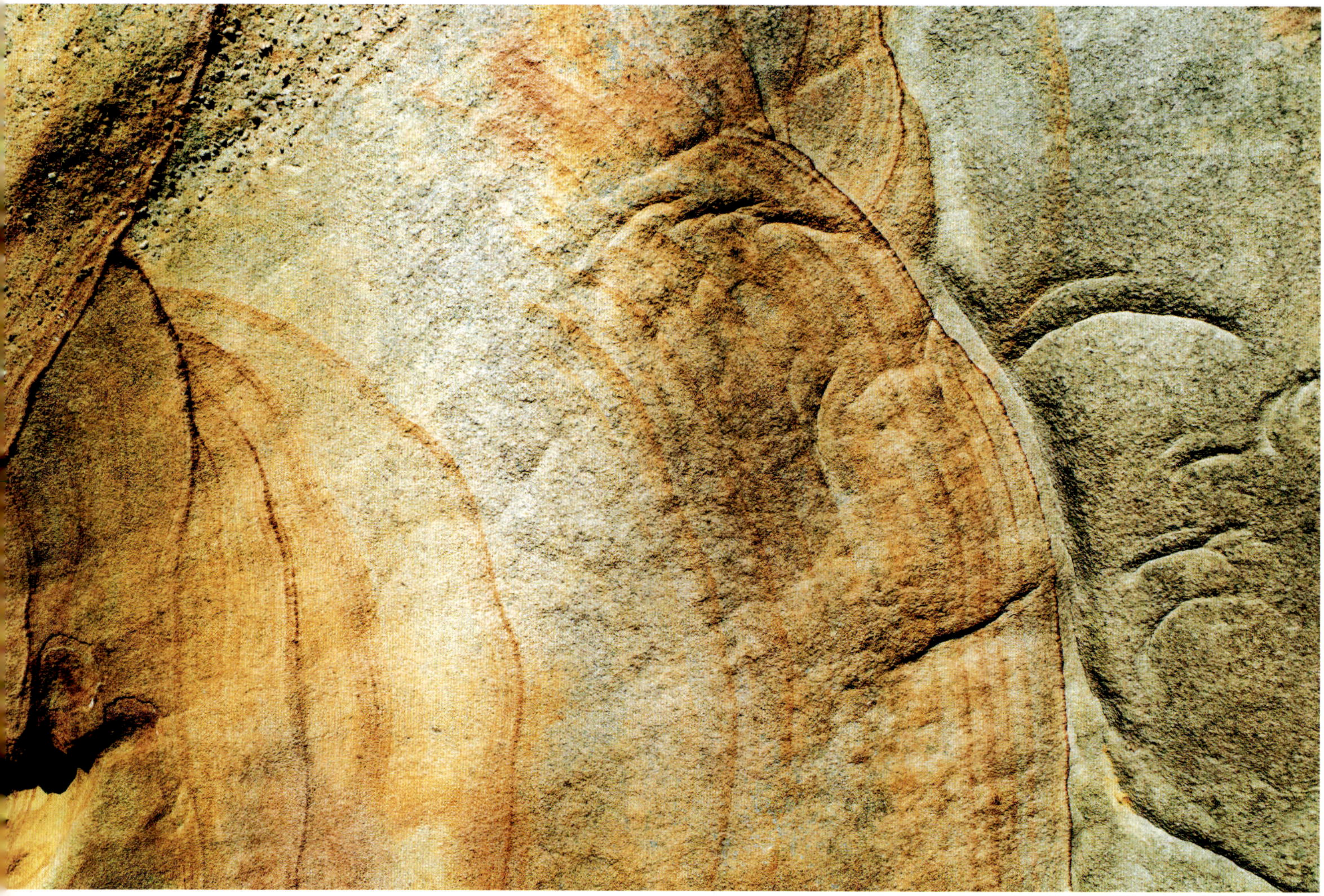

Sandstone detail,
Stone Fort, Tennessee

Opposite: Chad Wykle's
hand after surgery for
Dupuytren's contracture

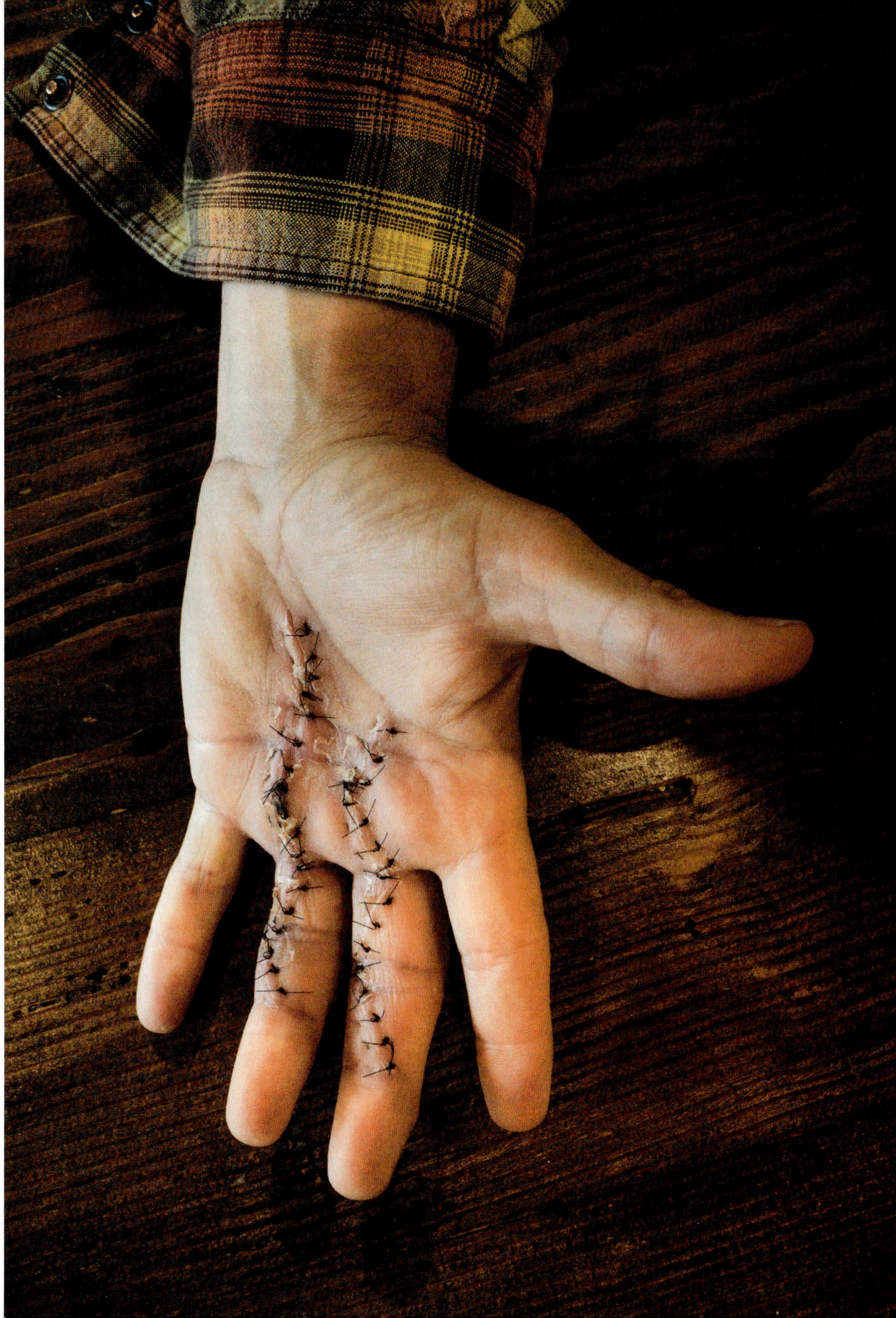

BOULDERING SONAR

US Route 221 stitches together five Southern states from Florida to Virginia. For most of its length it's a sleepy rural highway, but for a thirteen-mile stretch between Linville and Blowing Rock, North Carolina, it comes alive, dancing around the crags and peaks of Grandfather Mountain and tagging up with the scenic Blue Ridge Parkway no less than four times. For climbers, it provides more convenient—and less visible—access to rock than the parkway.

In early 2021, I was in nearby Boone working on a film called *Inner Mounting Flame* about local climber and musician Mike Stam. The title comes from a wild climb Mike had done in the forest off Route 221, which hadn't seen a second ascent in a decade. Boone climber Taylor McNeill had his sights set on a second ascent, and Mike had been mentoring him. Filming an oft-tried but never-repeated climb means a lot of trips, sometimes on a moment's notice. The weather has to be just right, and even when everything lines up perfectly, rest days are nonnegotiable.

We met up with Taylor's friend Nate Draughn at his apartment near the Appalachian State University campus and talked bouldering over hamburgers as late winter snow fell past the windows. Sophia, Nate's soon-to-be-ex girlfriend, was belting out Taylor Swift in the shower, and her dog, Lilo, eyed me warily. It was a typical climbing rest day, with a room full of fidgety climbers doing nothing but talking about climbing. Taylor and Nate decided to explore some unclimbed rock near Sugar Grove. Sophia and Lilo would be moving out within a week.

Taylor McNeill at Boone's Viaduct Boulders

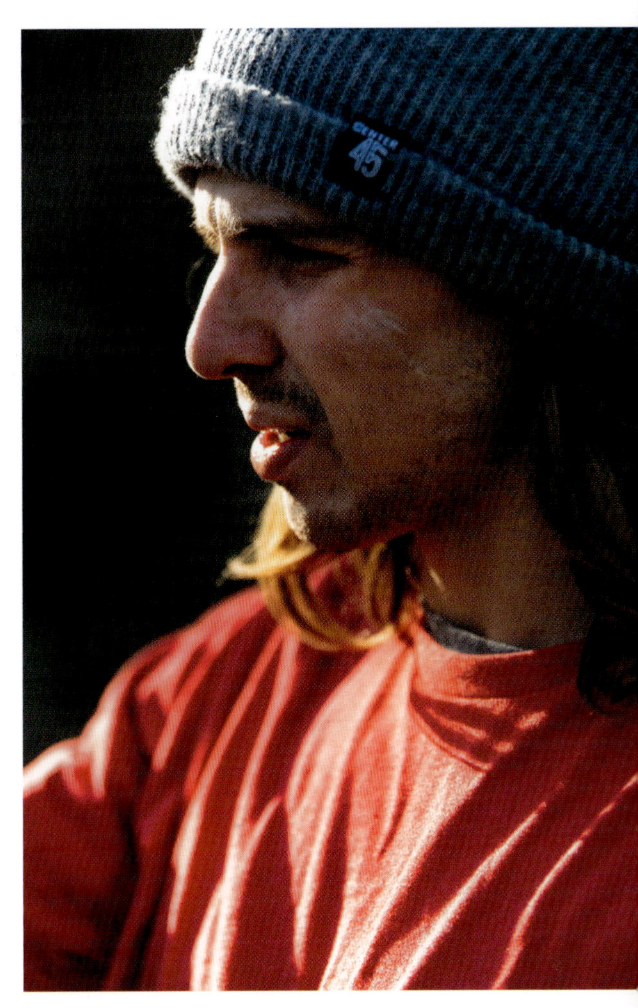

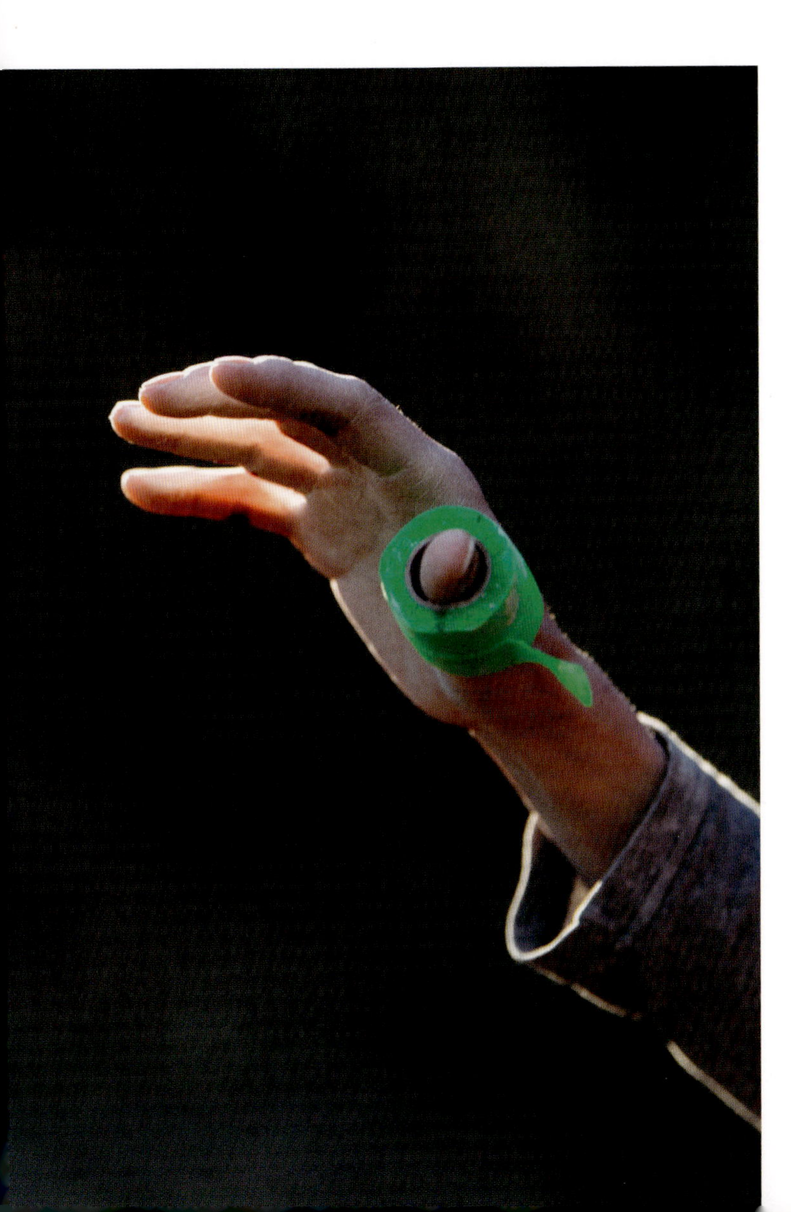

Of course *Inner Mounting Flame* was not the only objective, even when everyone was ready to climb. Other diversions beckoned. The next day, Taylor and I planned to meet up with Nate, who had been working a project off Route 221 by himself all morning. We slept in, took our time getting coffee and provisions at the usual Ingles grocery store, and by the time we parked, peed, and packed down the rough climber's trail off Route 221, it was almost two o'clock.

"Raagghh!" Nate's climbing bellow rose up from the canyon below.

"Yeah?!" Taylor hollered back.

Another scream: "Gahhh!"

"Let's gooo!" yelled Taylor, bounding down the slope.

Back and forth it went: bouldering sonar.

We crashed through the rhododendron to a clearing just as Nate was climbing the last hard moves of *Wet Willy* (V13), watched only by Lilo. I pulled my camera out for a couple of quick shots of him twenty-five feet above the crux, on easier ground. I missed his first ascent—that's what I get for sleeping in.

Nate had recorded the climb on his cell phone, and he and Taylor reviewed it and posted it online from a nearby rock shelter, which made me feel useless as a filmmaker, but I was grateful to absorb the scene. I have to remind myself constantly that it's OK to not record. *Inner Mounting Flame* is not just a film about a single climb or even about climbing generally. It's really about how people are shaped by geography. Almost all my films explore that in one way or another. I want to experience that connection firsthand, even if I'm not the one touching rock, and even if there is no record of it at all.

Boone climbers are surrounded by the classic Southern climbing environment—full of rock shelters and dense forest—but there is a different geographic vibe here in North Carolina's high country than elsewhere in the South. The gorges are deeper and more severe, the exposed walls even more sheer and exposed. Look at a topographic map of the state and you'll see how the gentle rise of the Piedmont from the sea ends abruptly in the Blue Ridge and Great Smoky Mountains, which cut a dramatic diagonal scar north and east. The border with Tennessee is no friendly agreement; it's forced by awesome geology. The climbing has a reputation for being bold, scary, and intimidating.

Nate Draughn on the second ascent of *Bone Saw* (V13), Linville Gorge, North Carolina

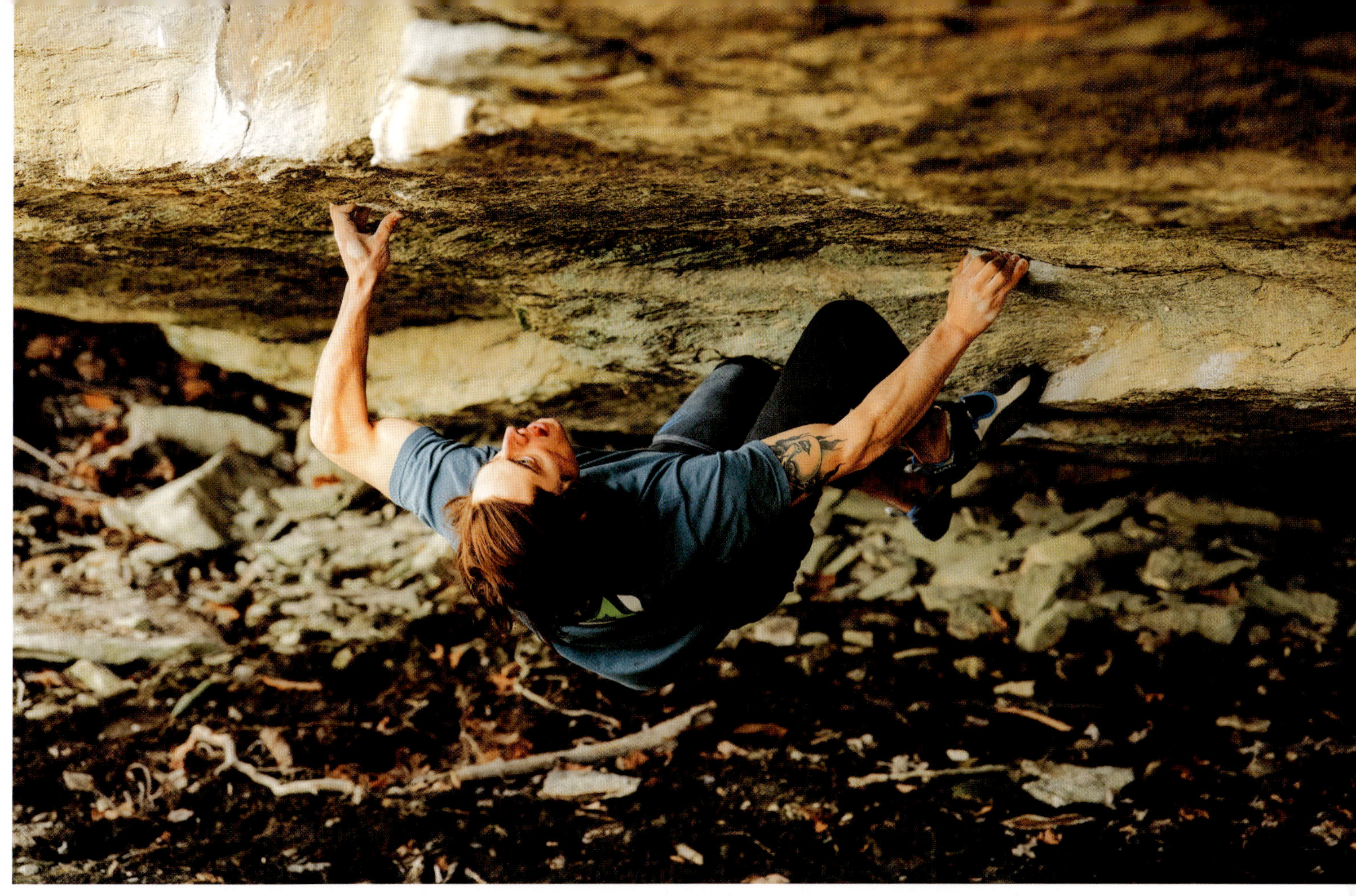

Carolina climbers have always exuded that same character, one that goes hand in hand with fierce traditionalism. Information about this scene was and still is notoriously hard to come by. You had to be in the know to climb anything. First published in the late eighties, Thomas Kelley's third edition of *The Climber's Guide to North Carolina* was more a sharing of history than a fully comprehensive guide. The sketchy, understated descriptions of remote, scary walls were not exactly meant to be a road map to outsiders. When Harrison Shull and Yon Lambert followed up seven years later with *Selected Climbs in North Carolina*, their intentions were more explicit. Along with descriptions of the climbs, they included everything about the style of the first ascent, emphasizing the ground-up North Carolina style, where climbers use "ingenious, daring, or even suicidal solutions to limit their impact, increase commitment levels, and increase sheer difficulty." This kind of philosophical discussion was rare for a climbing guidebook. "In this guide," they wrote, "a route's history and individuality are just as important as its number grade." Above all, it was a warning to future first ascensionists to do their homework and "determine how your contribution will serve as a logical extension of the area's ethic."

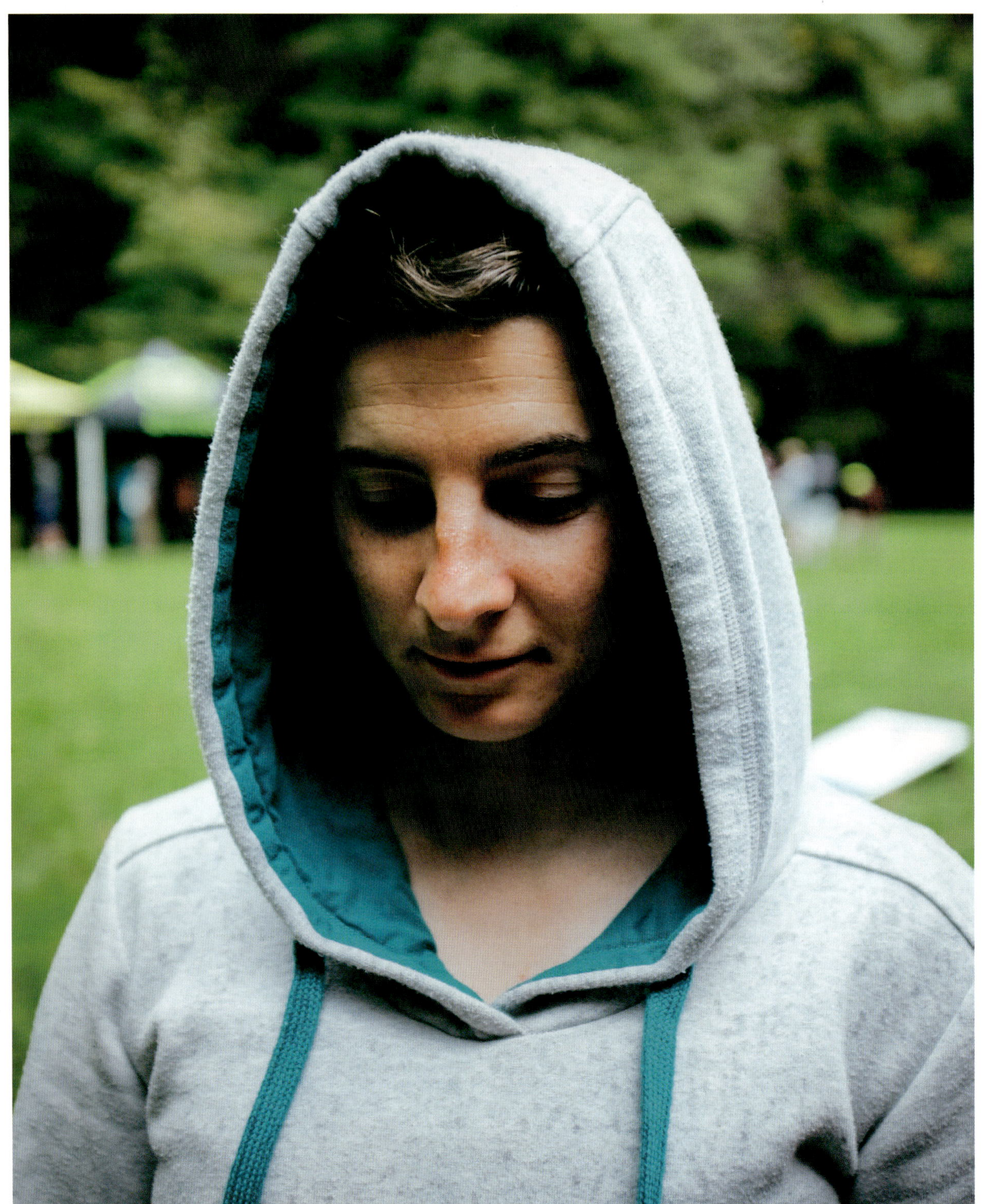

Shull was the prototypical North Carolina insider. Giant in stature and as bold a climber as they come, he was not above getting in your face—or chopping your bolt—if your actions didn't fit the area's time-honored style. But Shull's era also coincided with a growing concern about access. The wild high-country crags faced the same pressures of closure, land development, and overexposure that their counterparts in Alabama, Tennessee, and Georgia were seeing, and something had to be done. It was time to buck the tradition of secrecy for the public good, because, as Shull wrote, "a finite amount of rock calls for special vigilance."

A book can fix traditions for posterity, but direct transmission is still the best way to pass them along. Just like with tall tales and mountain music, the campfire, front porch, or canyon is an essential part of the story. Overhearing the "beta"—directives of a climb, from the moves to the ethics—told by Mike Stam to Nate and Taylor hunched under a rock while the wind howls off Grandfather Mountain is the only Rosetta stone you need to decipher the world of Southern climbing.

Back on Route 221, it started snowing. We rappelled down another gulley to an alcove of rock formations surrounded by broken TVs and mattress springs. Taylor and Nate pulled a blue tarp off the top of one, revealing a giant overhanging pyramid of granite. Taylor gave the smooth arete a dozen tries. As the snowflakes got bigger, it seemed unlikely he would climb it, but I wasn't about to miss it this time if he did. There were a lot of distractions: the cold, the broken TV at my feet, the snow gathering on my camera, Lilo glowering at me. I resolved to keep the camera rolling, just in case.

Taylor made the first ascent of *Apparatus* (V15) on the next go. His victory screams echoed down the canyon. ◆

Jessa Goebel in
Boone, North Carolina

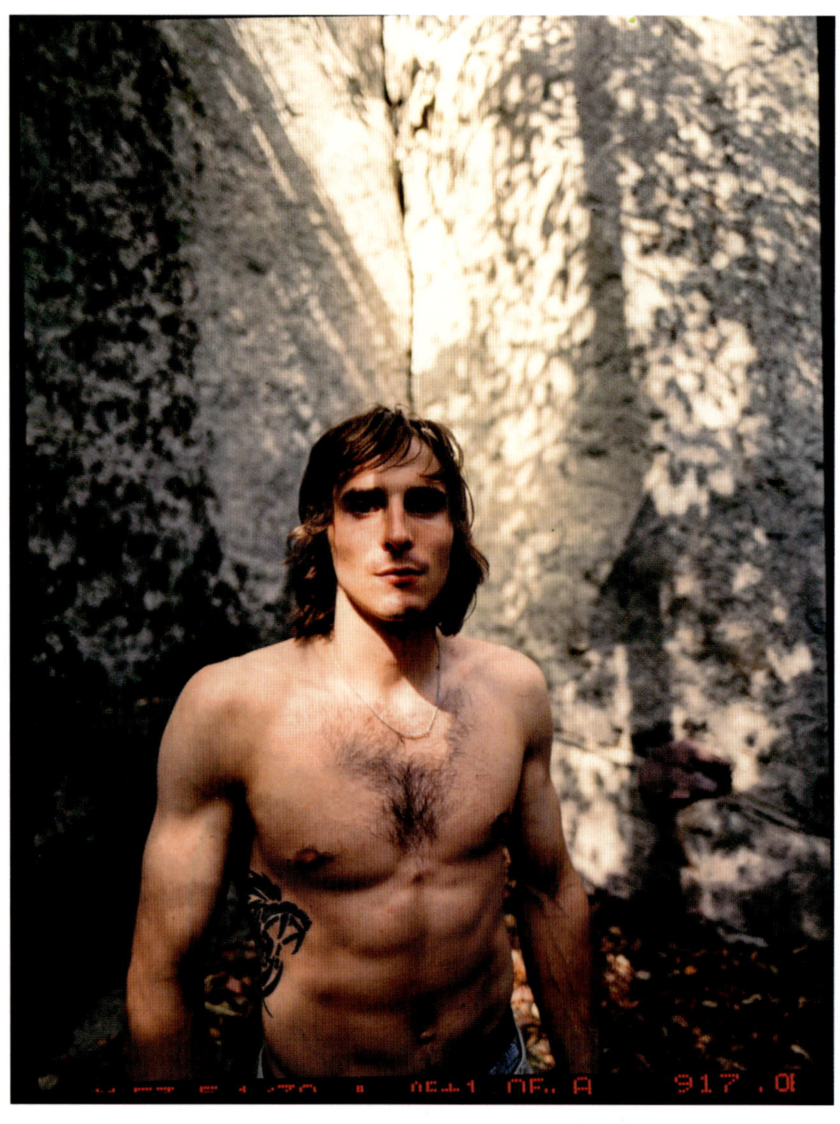

Daniel Woods at Stone Fort, Tennessee

Opposite: Jim Horton, being spotted by Sharif Hassan, on *Heretic* (V3), Hound Ears, North Carolina

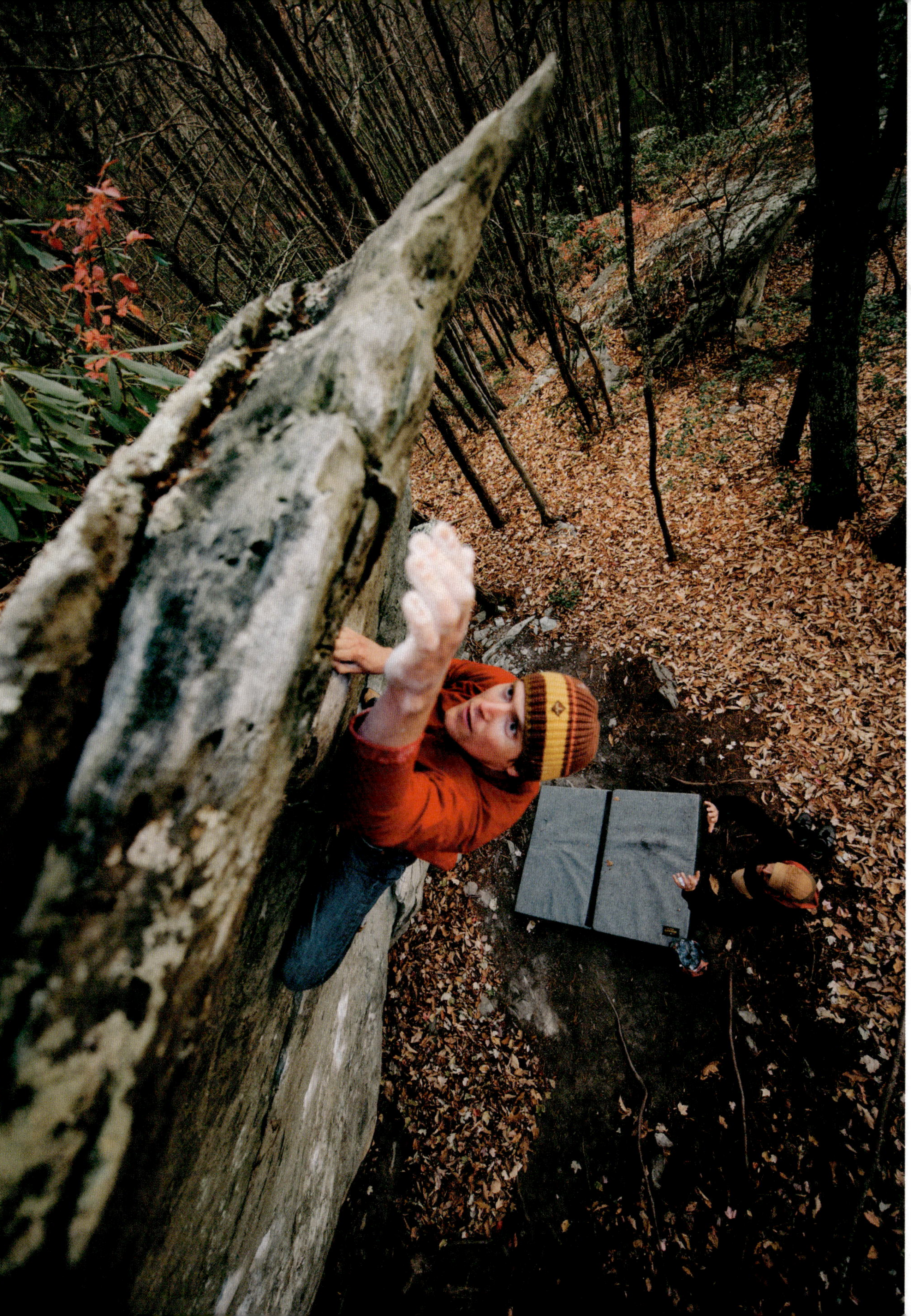

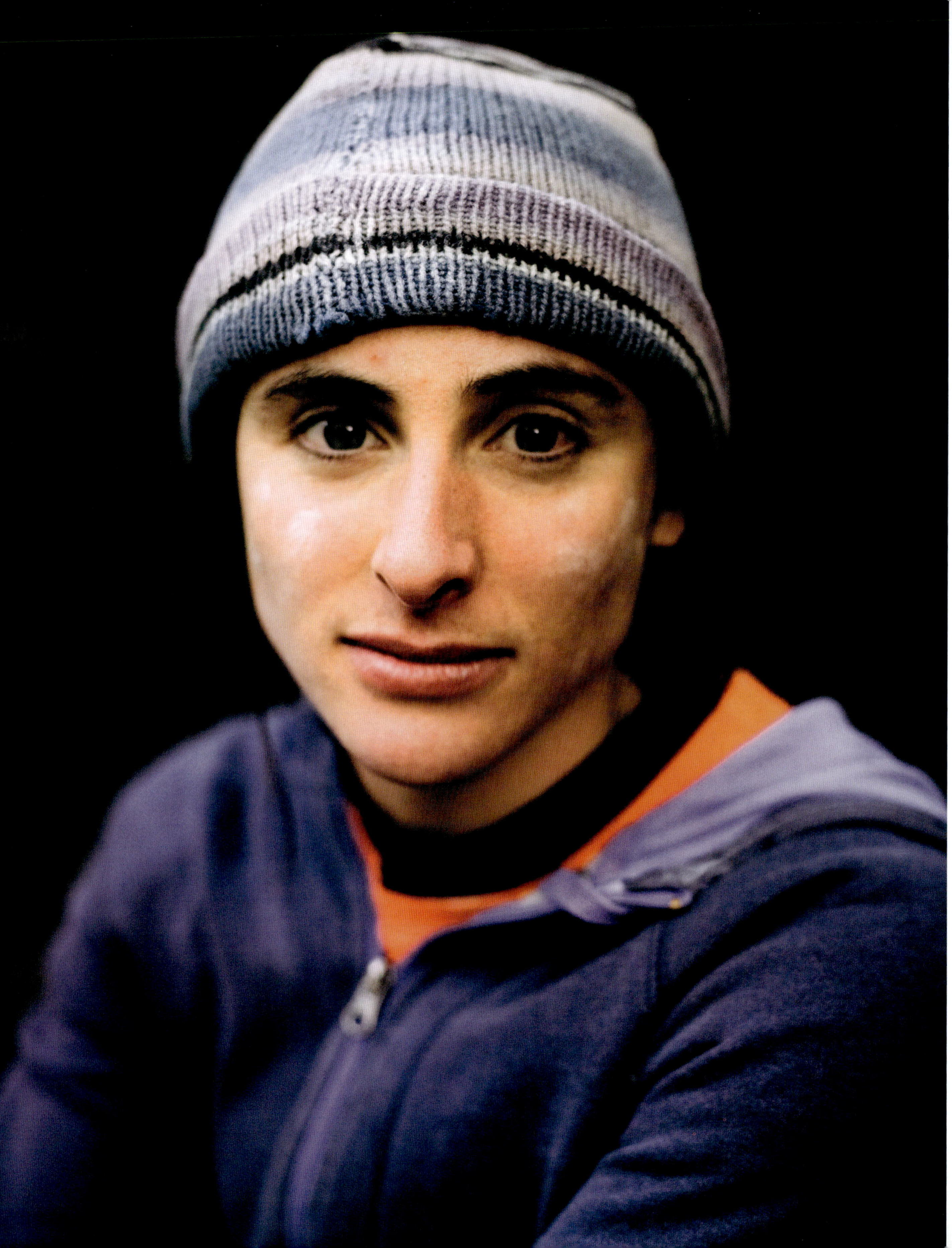

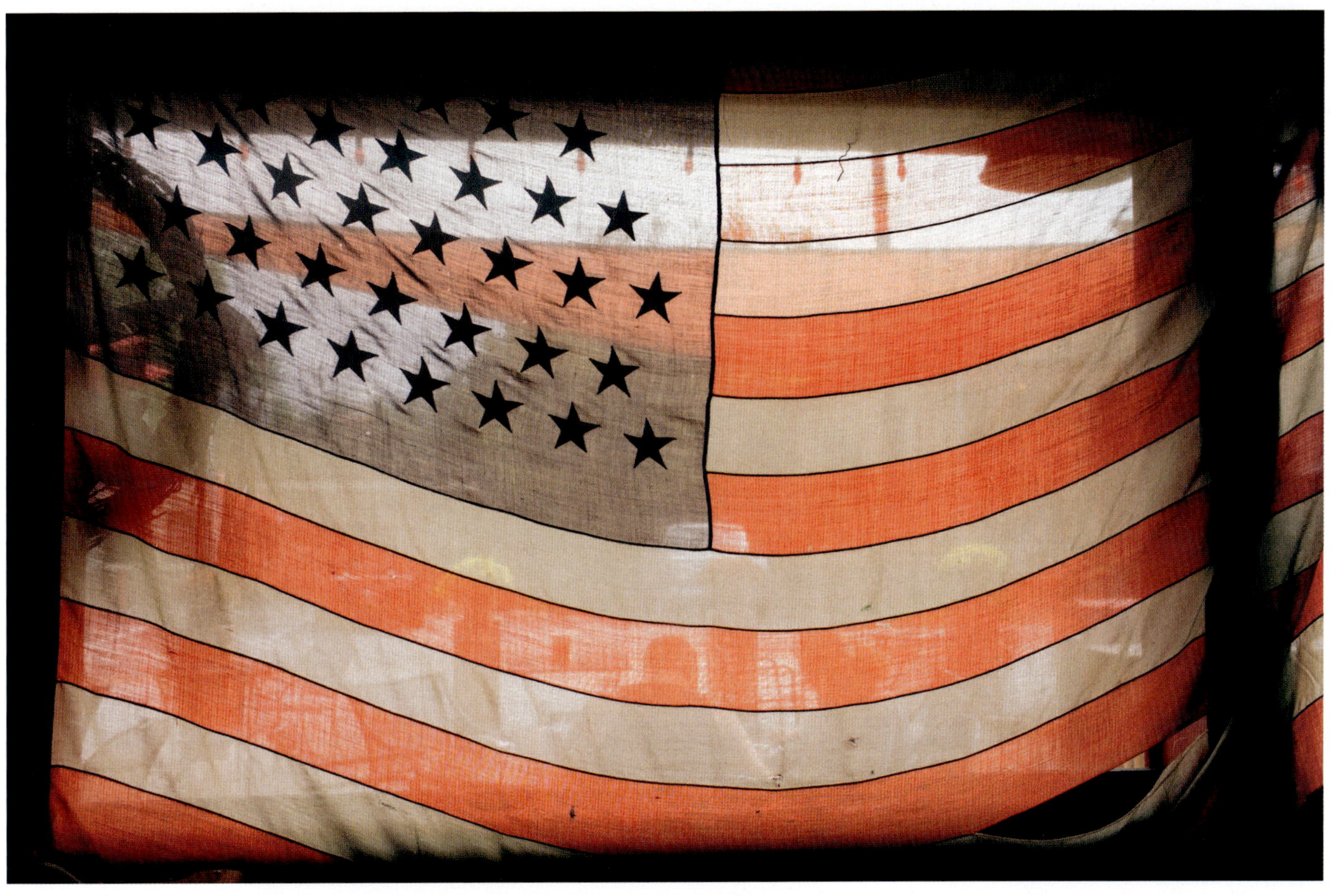

Opposite: Rebecca O'Brian at Hound Ears, North Carolina

Faded American flag in Leipers Fork, Tennessee

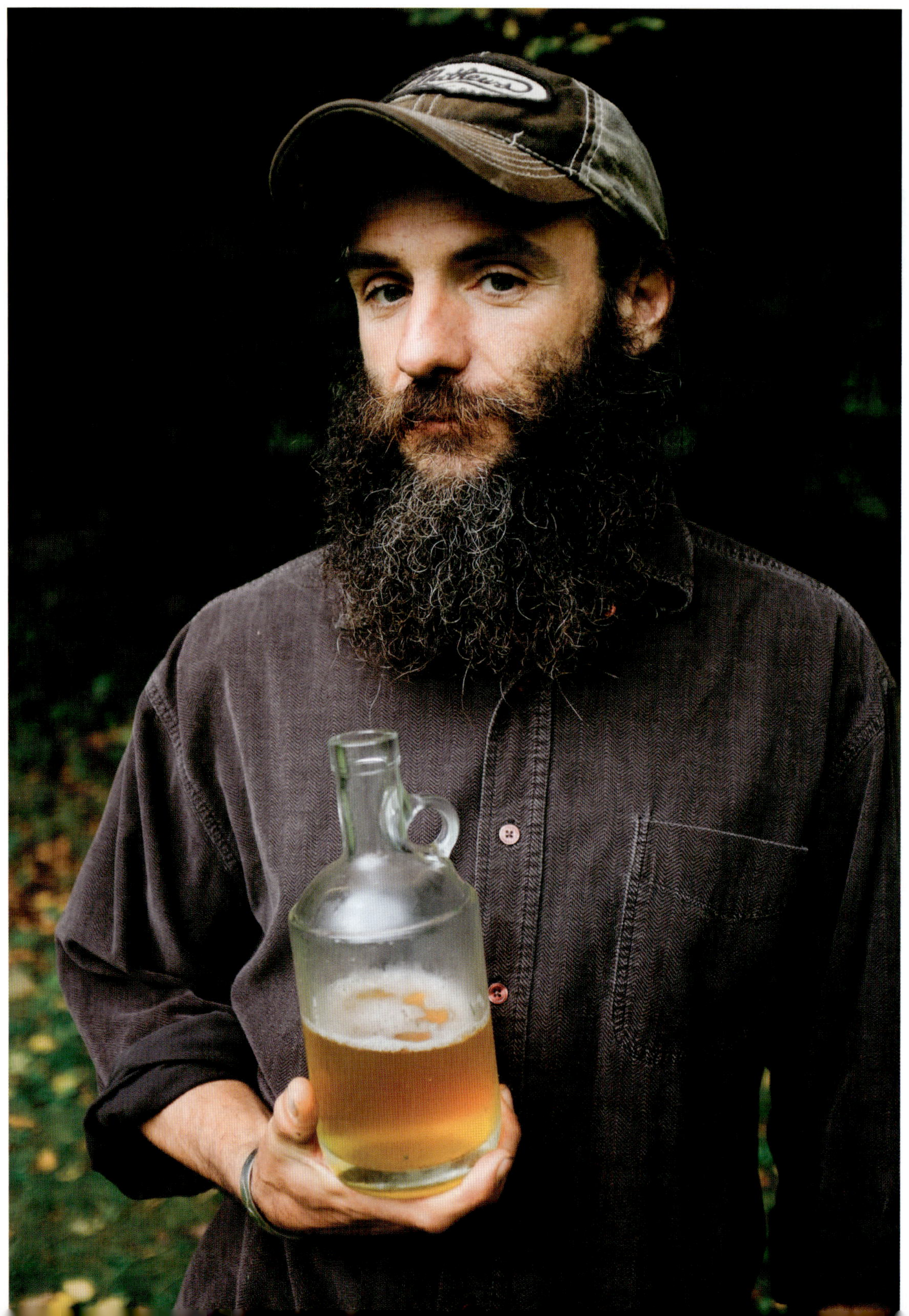

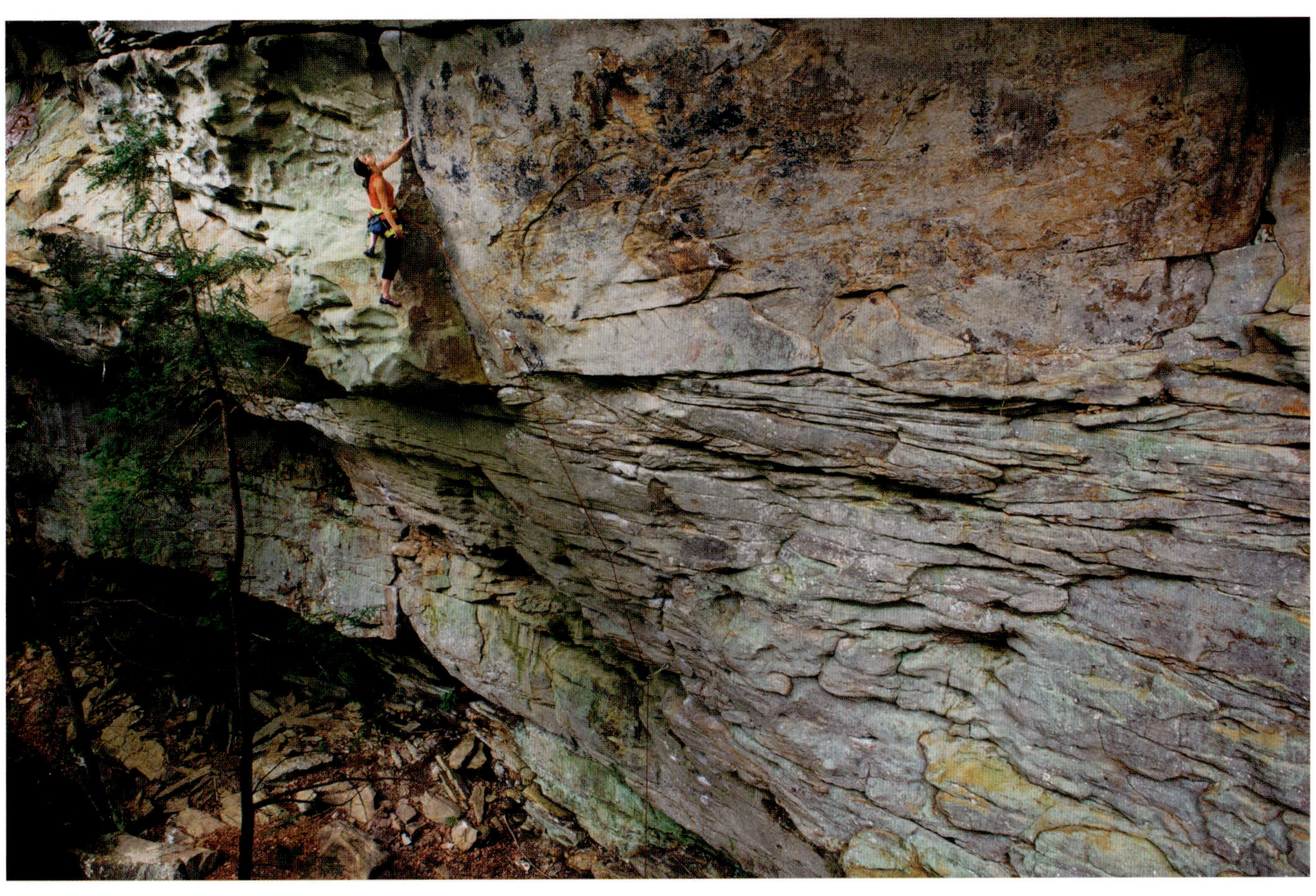

Opposite: Damian Keyes at Grandfather Campground near Boone, North Carolina

Samantha Levy on *Lights of the Dead* (5.11b), Deep Creek, Tennessee

A STUNNING NEW WORLD

I've been moved to tears from the beauty of a place twice in my life. The first time it happened, my wife, Vera, and I were on our honeymoon in a car full of climbing gear and champagne, slowly turning a bend on El Portal Road into Yosemite Valley. It was a perfect bluebird day, and the misty granite walls and forests that unfolded before us with each turn were even more beautiful and dramatic than we both had imagined. It was the opening of a new world for both of us in many ways, and it's a place we're still always scheming to get back to.

The next time was in North Carolina. I was solo this time—with climbing gear but minus the champagne—and it was raining. Coming in from the south, I passed through Boone, then Vilas, and then took US Route 421 up toward the town of Sugar Grove. Winding slowly along Cove Creek and up the Watauga River watershed, the weather suddenly cleared and a bucolic vista of emerald hills lined with creeks that sparkled through the fog was so intense I had to pull off to the side and collect myself. The memory of such a scene is something you end up chasing after for the rest of your life as an artist.

Fishermen are fond of a saying that "God doesn't put trout in ugly places," and I suppose the same can be said about climbable rock, which was what brought me up through Sugar Grove in the first place. Later I'd learn that Joey Henson's barn and his fabled boulders were only a mile away from where I had pulled off, but on that day, I was headed to Kim and Paul Fuelling's house in nearby Mabel. Both are pioneers of high-country bouldering, and on that day my sole purpose was to film them on some local classic climbs.

The Fuellings live at the top of the valley in a sort of mid-century homestead that was once a cinderblock gas station. Custom-remodeled down to the last detail, with furniture as doors, art as furniture, and a skate ramp in the living room, it's a place only a couple of talented, punk-minded artists could conceive of and build together. Being artists, they are always in process. "It's very hard to start a project, and it's very hard to end a project," Kim told me then. "It's like that with climbing too."

Kim and Paul met in art school in Indiana, climbed out West for a while, and were drawn like so many others to the area after going to the first Hound Ears Bouldering Competition nearly twenty years ago. Kim is a painter and Paul is a woodworker, both commissioning pieces for high-end interiors. Paul also builds motorcycles, which they both ride cross-country when not climbing or making art. They keep a furnished Airstream in their front yard, which I try to crash at whenever I visit the Boone area. The climbing has called me back many times, and the lodging is convenient, but it's the beauty of that place and the artist's contact high I am always after too.

I'm particularly drawn to Kim's paintings. They are large-scale, usually oil on panel, vernacular scenes of the rural South. Here is a tobacco barn surrounded by goldenrod, the sky behind rendered in crystalline shapes. Here are two hounds on point, multidimensional lines of perspective leading to lime-colored hills and yellow clouds.

A lot of Kim's work is often inspired by the artwork of the Federal Art Project era, that Works Progress Administration (WPA) experiment in government art patronage and public works programs whose viaducts and hand-built roadways still pervade the scenery of the Appalachians. My great-grandmother Elvira Reilly was one of these WPA-supported artists, an impressionist painter in the early to mid-twentieth century. Like Kim, Grandma Reilly painted from her experiences in Cuba and South Florida. In those scenes, a dozen nuns in various states of relaxation bathe in the southernmost point of Key West, and a group of men crouch in a cockfight pen, one holding what you imagine to be the victor.

Both of my grandparents carried on that tradition, and Grandpa Andrew's painting lessons for me and my siblings left a deep impression. To me, art was always something created by hand in a physical medium. Though I ended up a photographer, I suppose that's where my own project started, and I am still in process.

Lingering in Kim's studio, I slowly turn another canvas, and a stunning new world is revealed. Nothing in photography compares to this experience, but it gets close. The smell of turpentine and linseed oil is both a nostalgic trip back to my childhood and a reminder of everything I'm still chasing. ◆

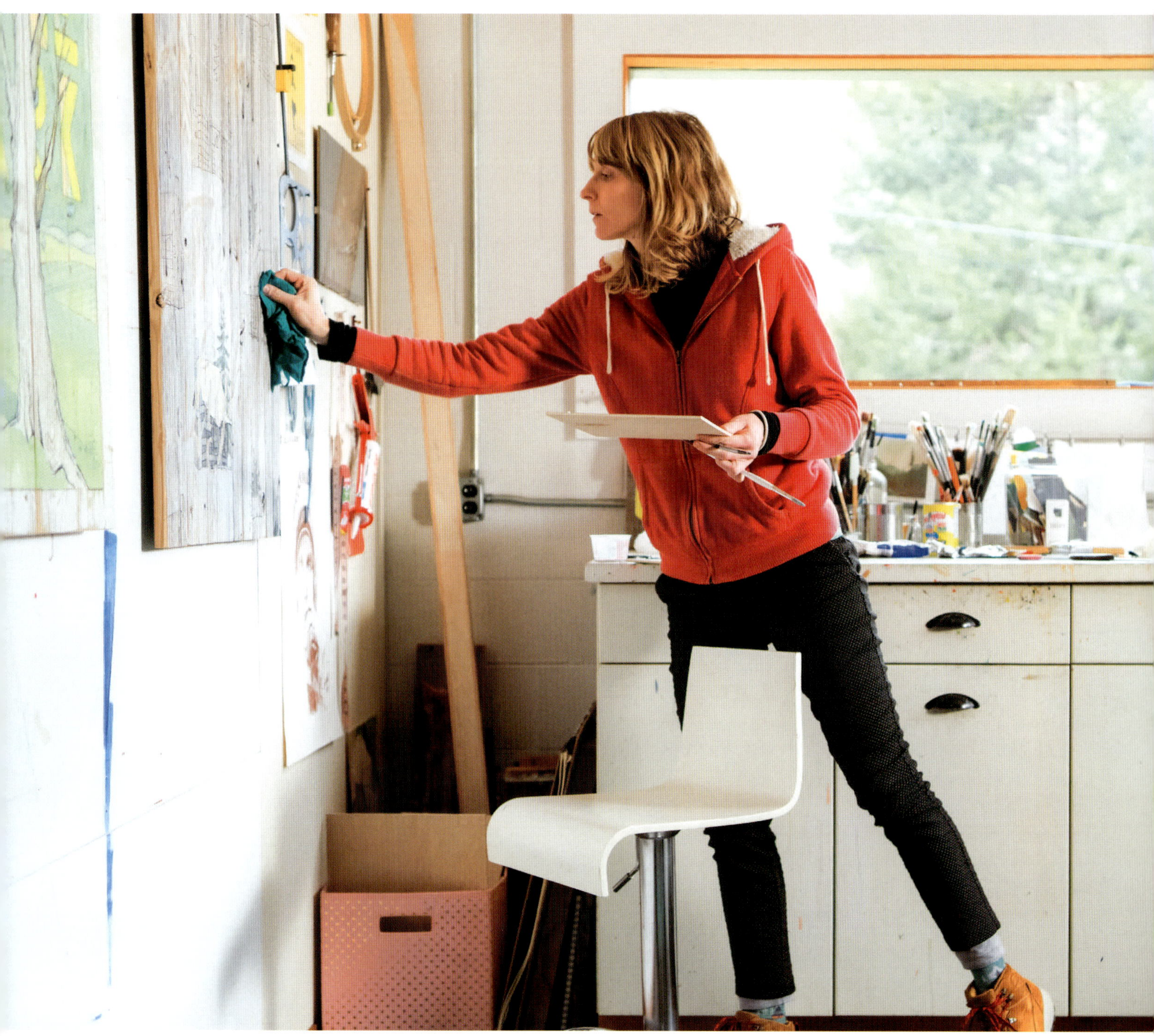

Opposite: Kim Fuelling in her studio in Mabel, North Carolina

Oak trees in Mabel

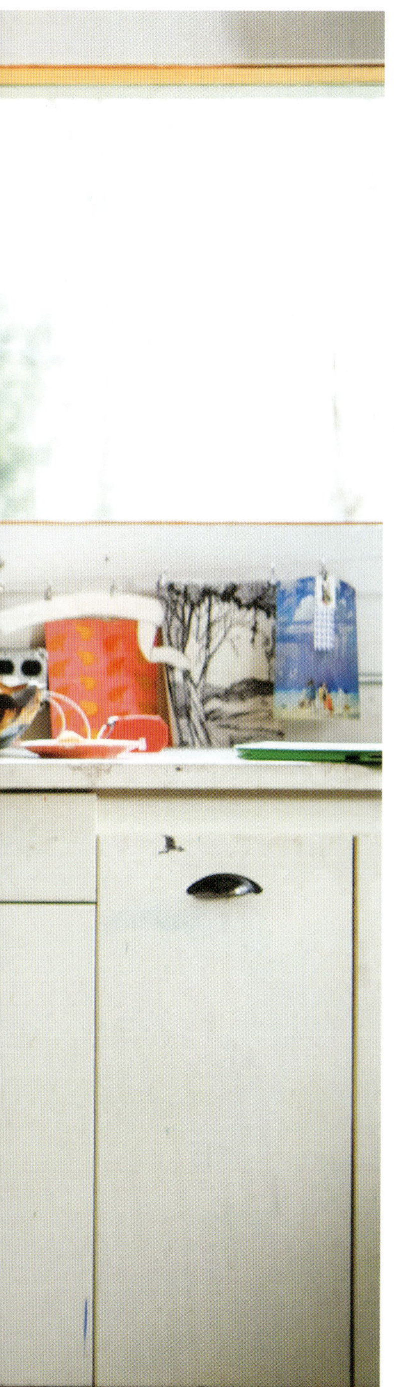

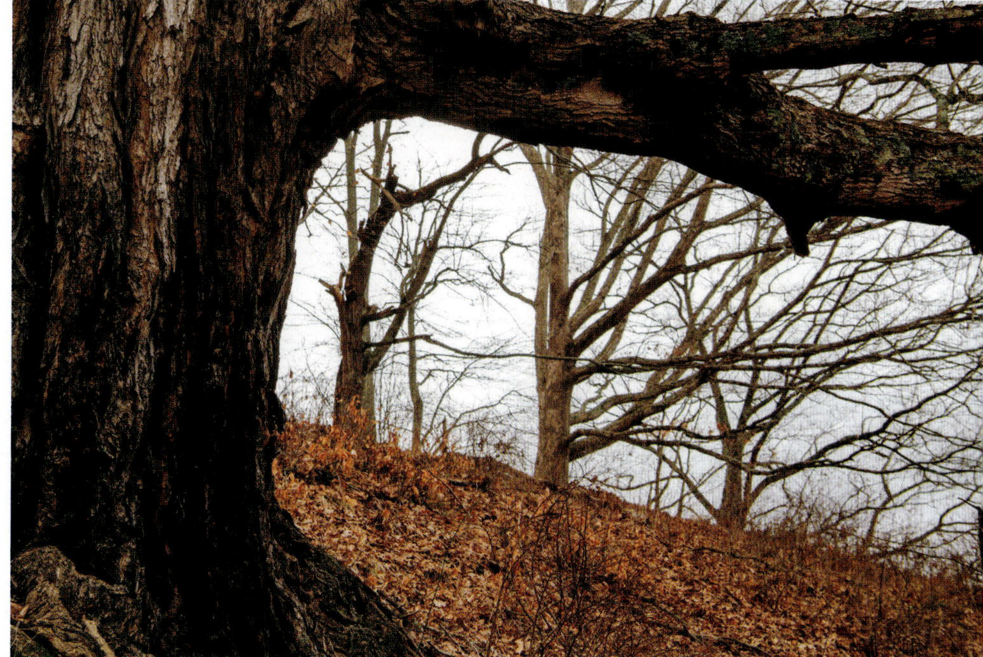

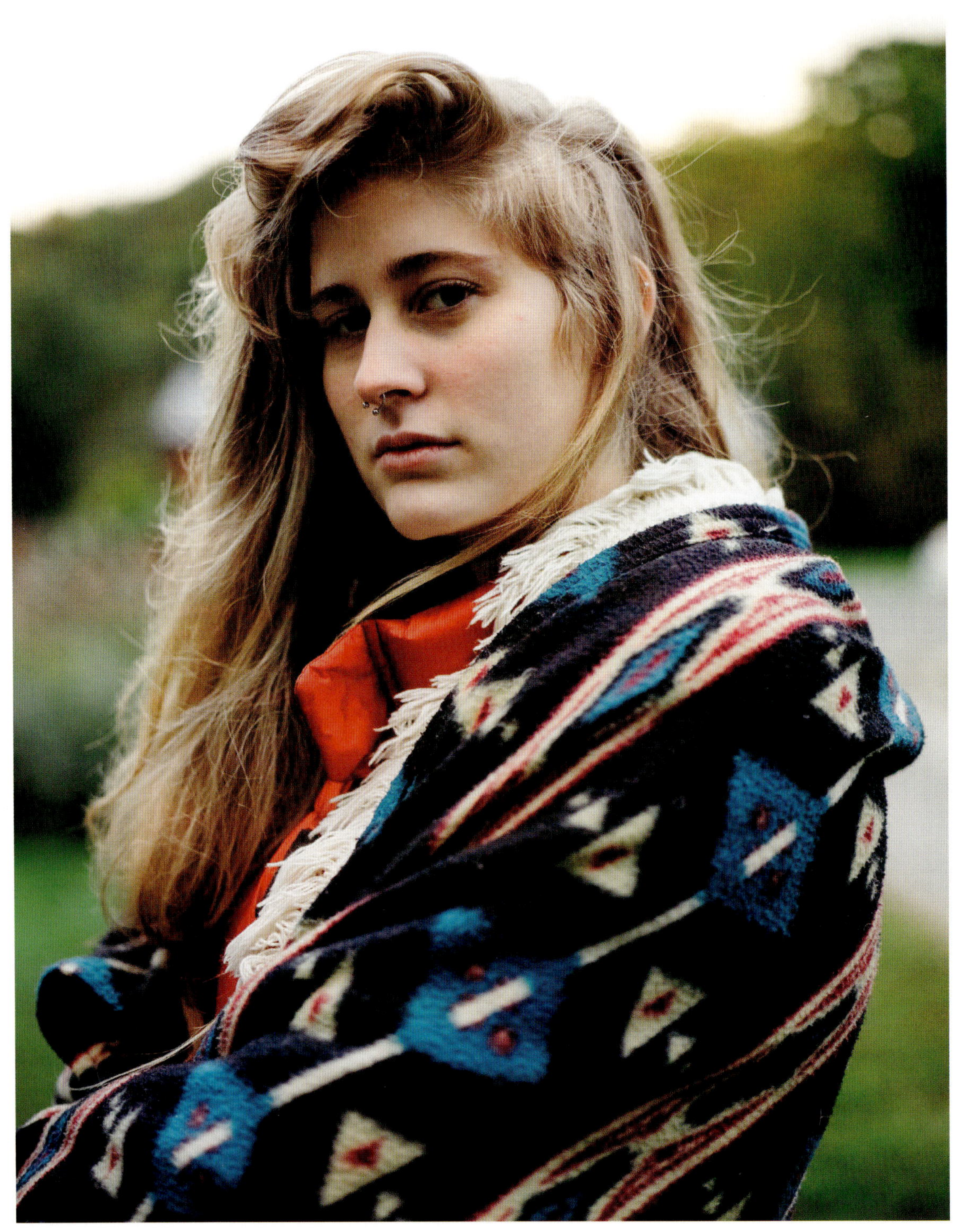

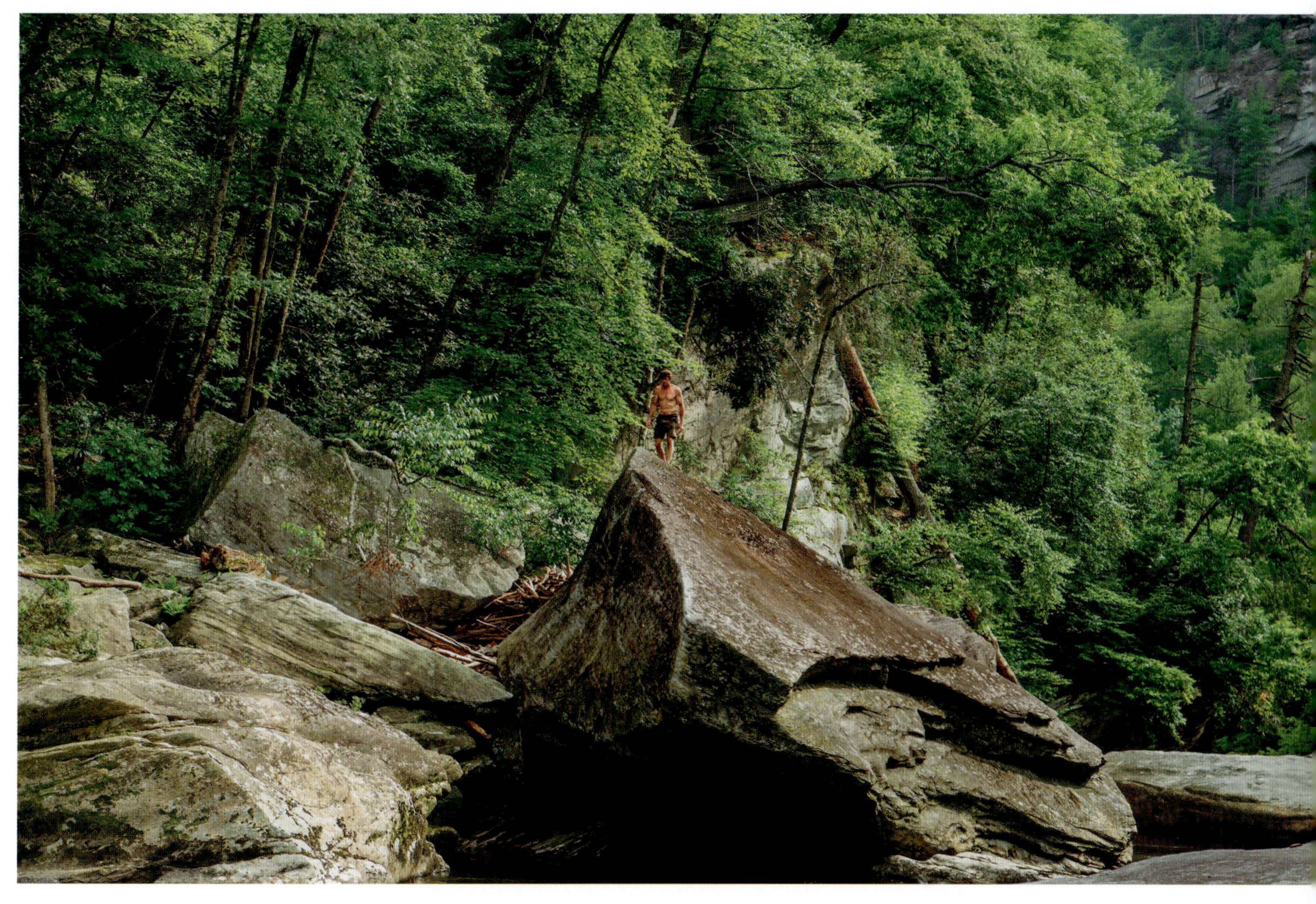

Opposite: Ashley Conrad at Grandfather Campground near Boone, North Carolina

Joey Henson in the Linville Gorge, North Carolina

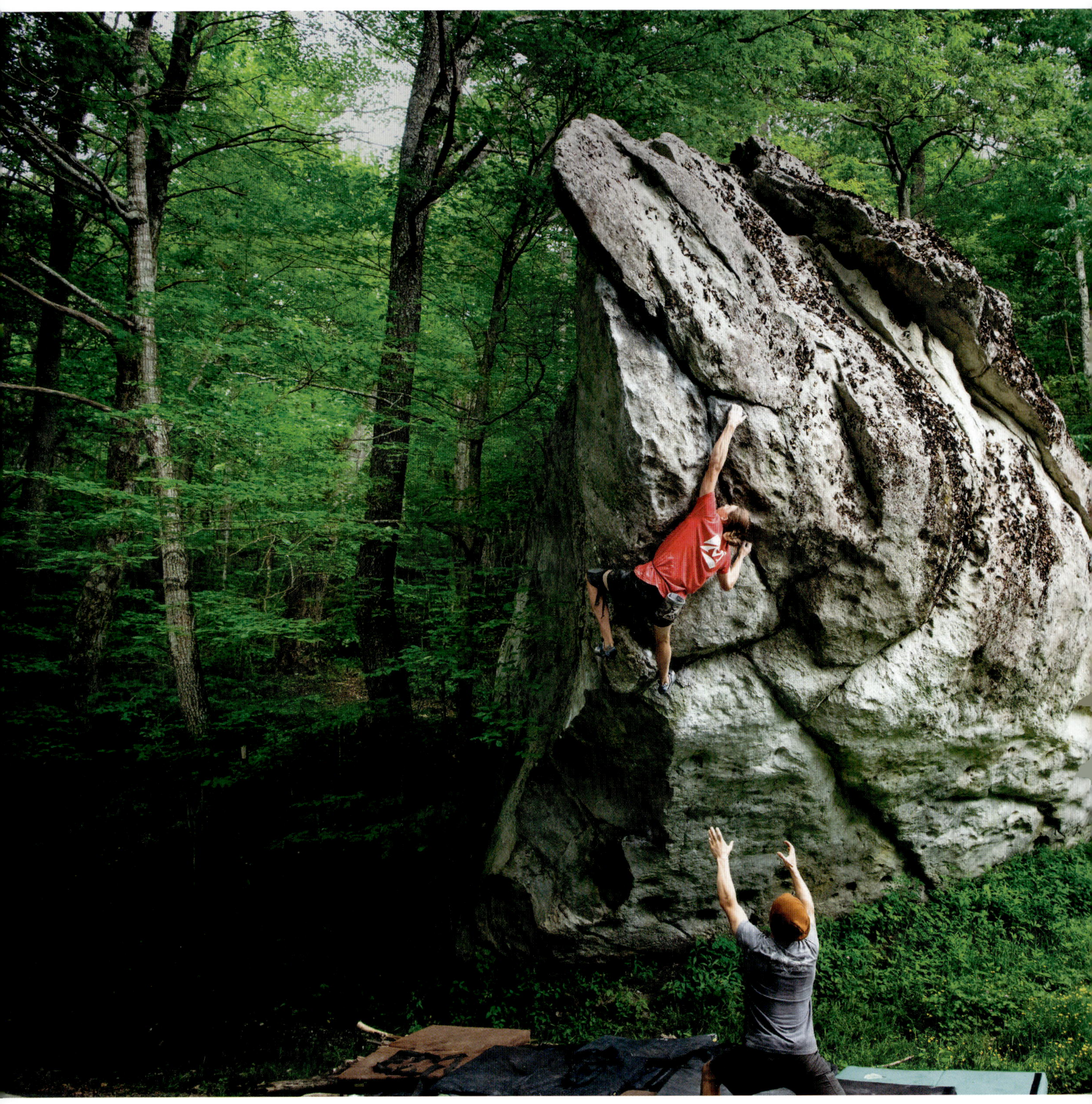

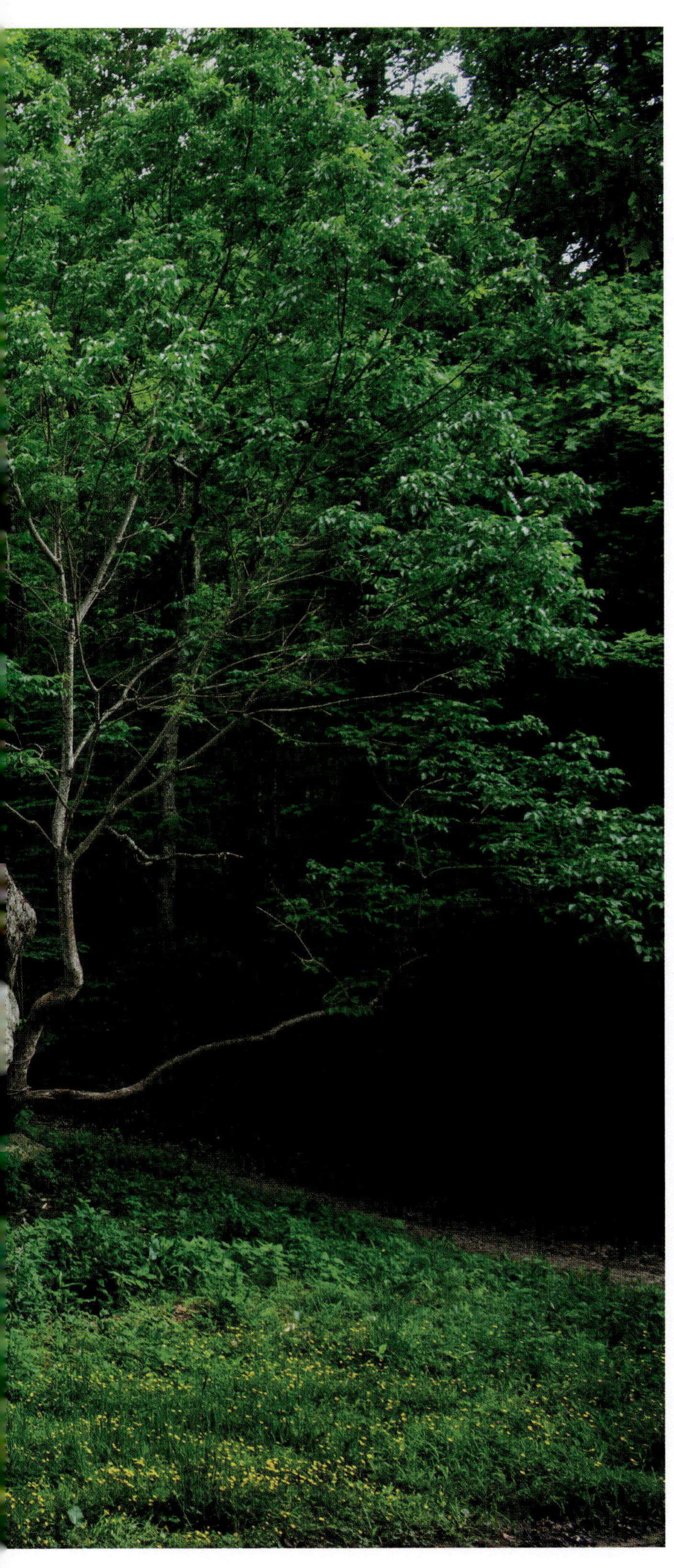

Taylor McNeill, being spotted by Nate Draughn, on *The World Is Not Enough* (V11), along Route 221 near Boone, North Carolina

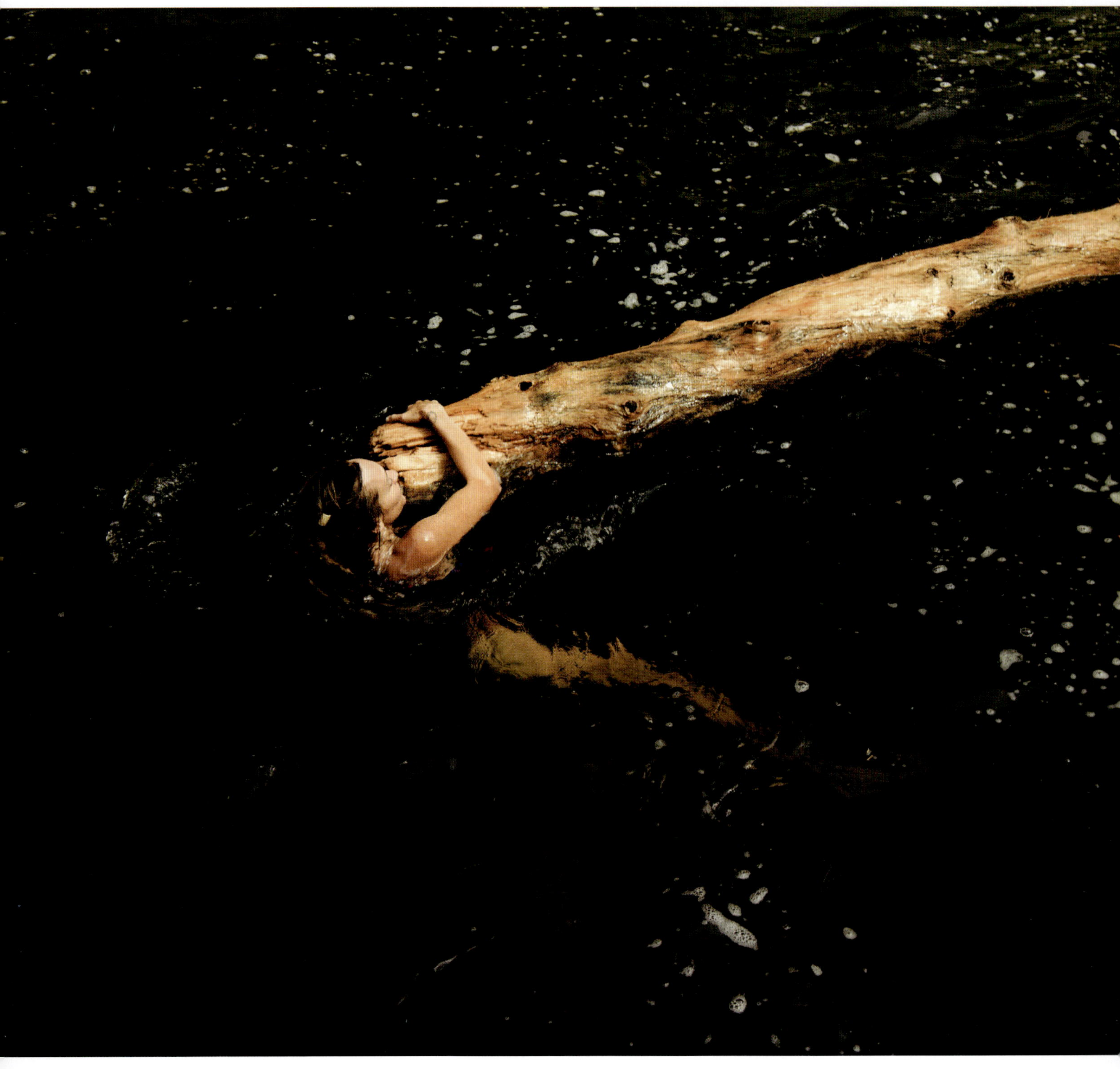

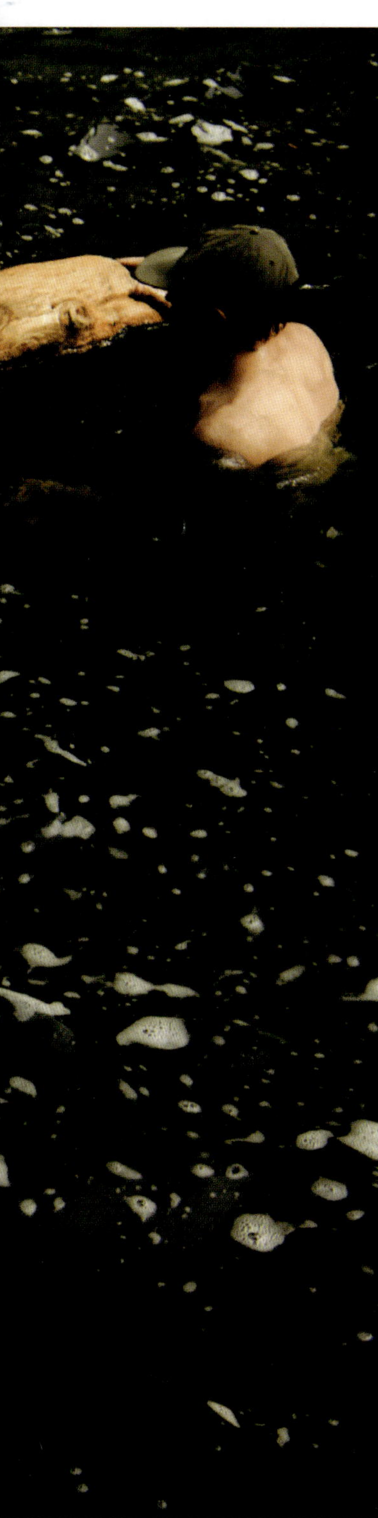

Swimmers in the Linville Gorge, North Carolina

Cutting board in Joey Henson's barn near Vilas, North Carolina

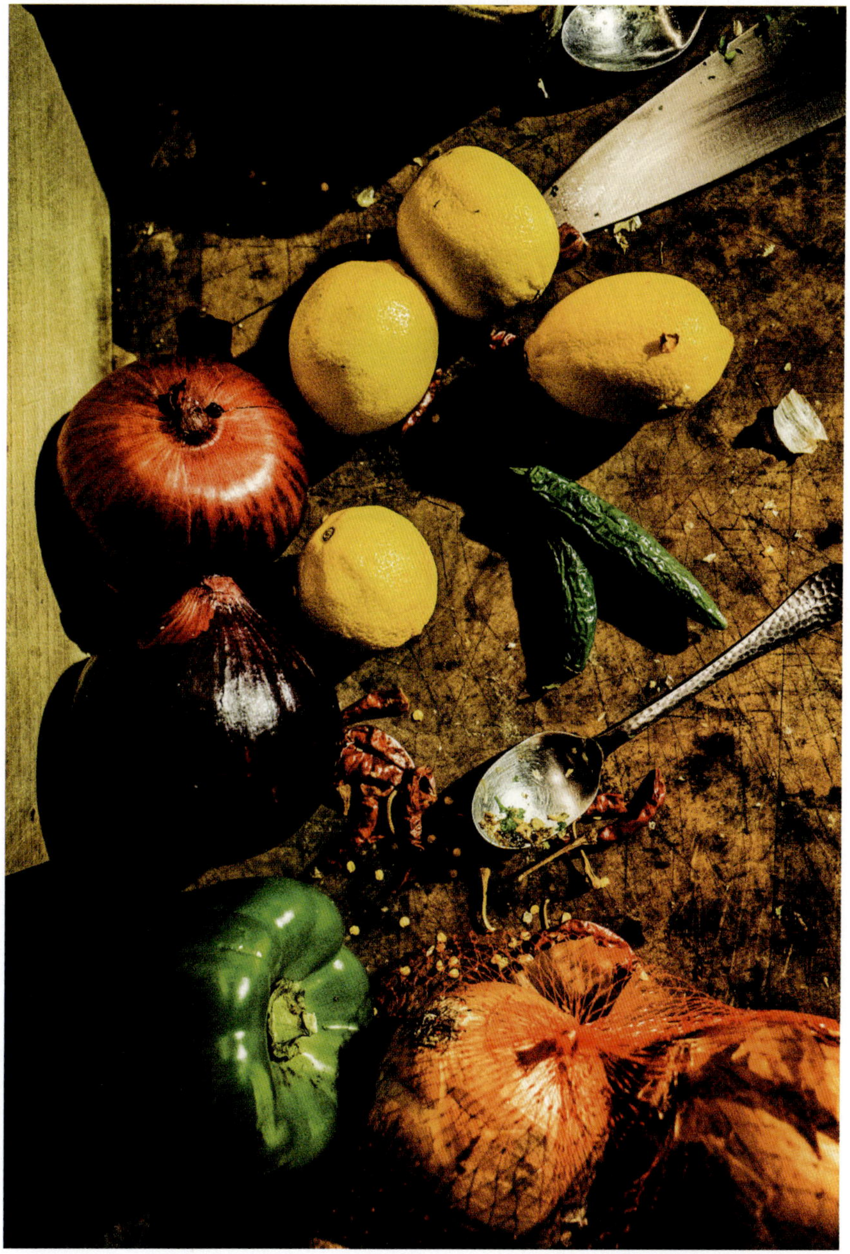

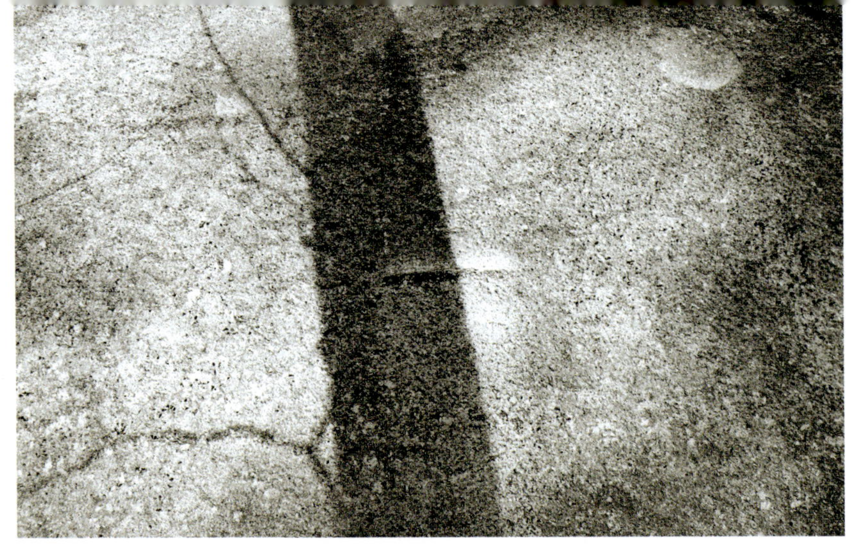

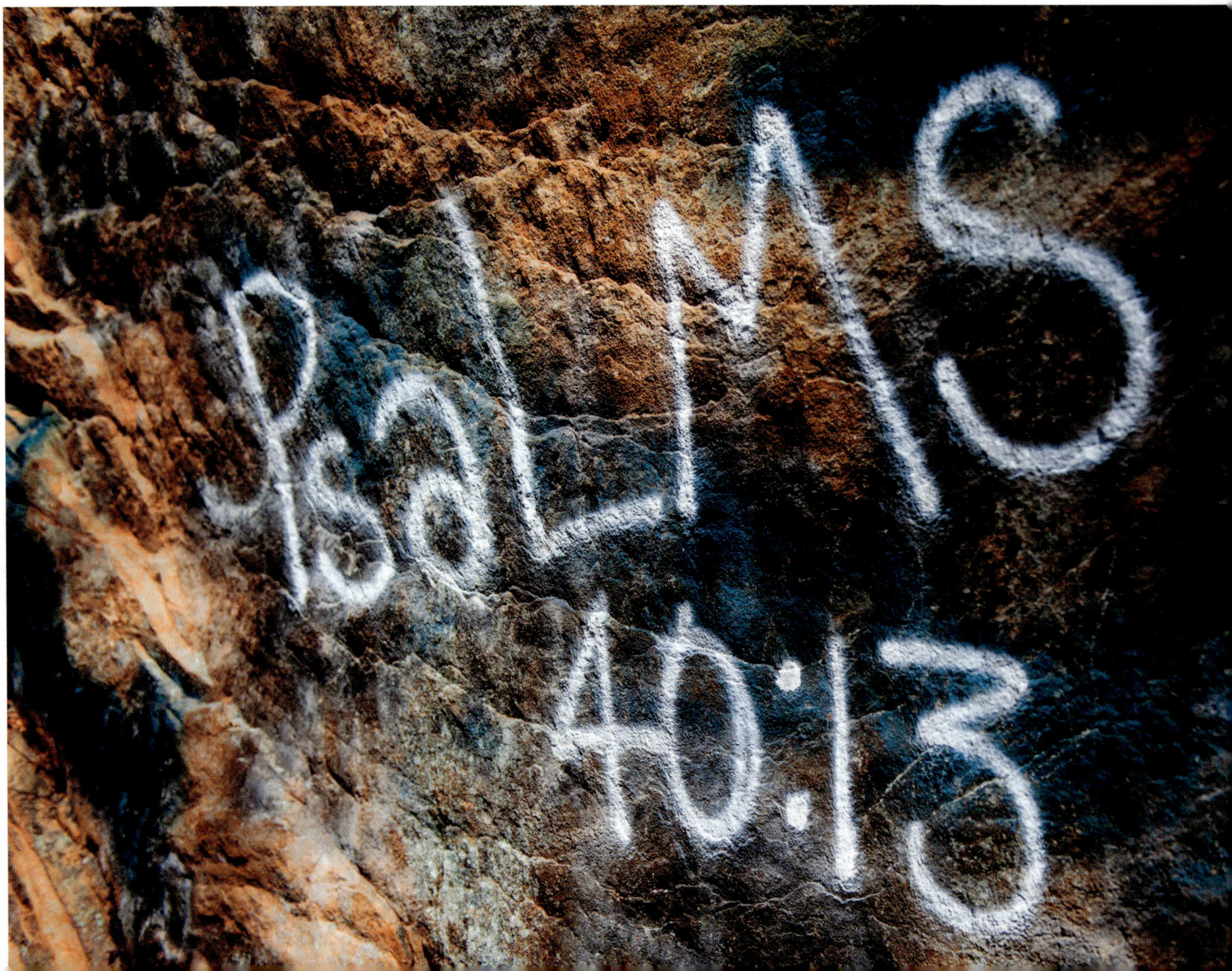

PsaLMS
40:13

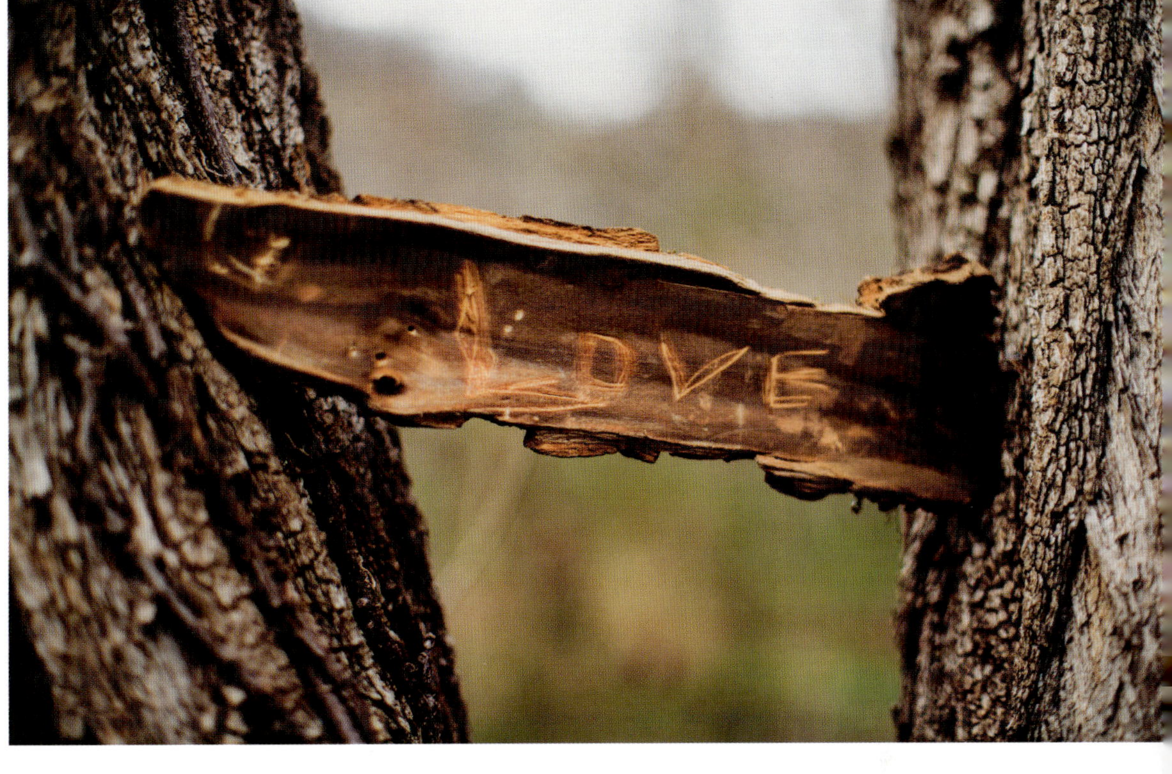

Opposite: Boat Rock in southwestern Atlanta

Opposite: *Be pleased to save me, Lord. Come quickly, Lord, to help me,* near Dayton, Tennessee.

Tree bark art near Chattanooga, Tennessee

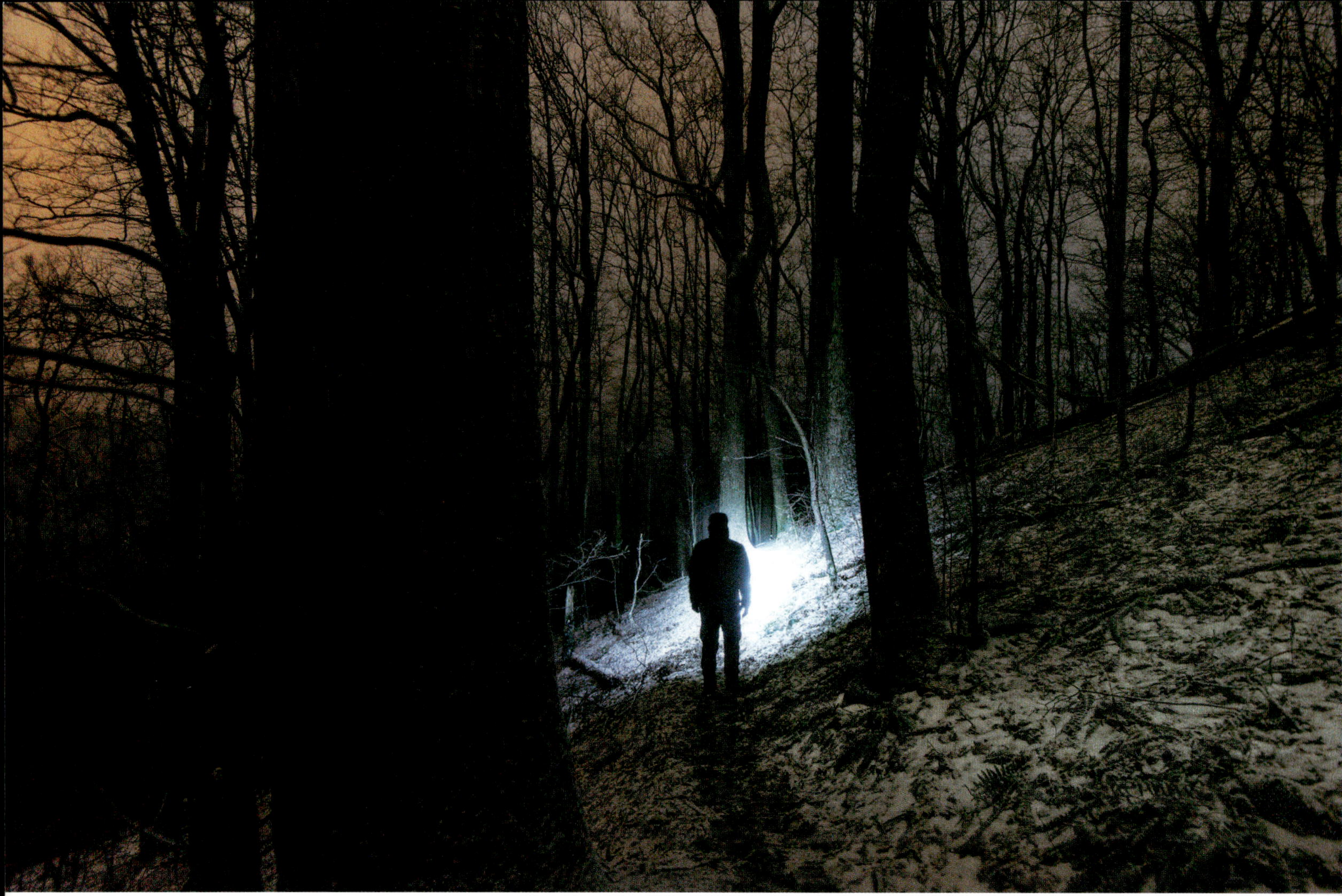

Hiking by headlamp on China Creek Trail, Blowing Rock, North Carolina

Chalk handprints in the Linville Gorge, North Carolina

Opposite: Brad McLeod at Boat Rock in southwestern Atlanta

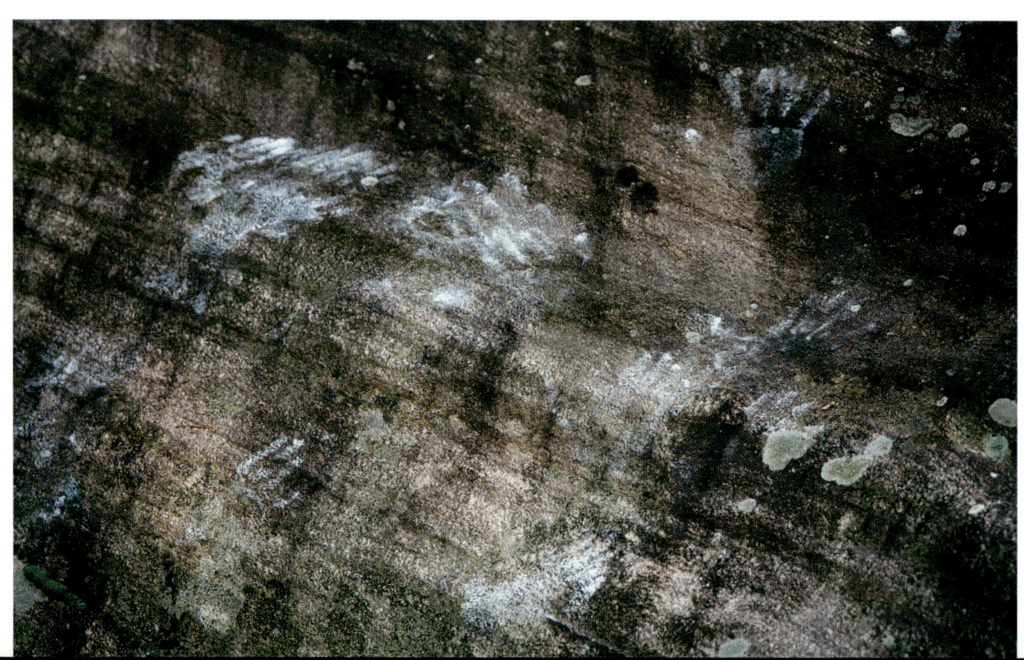

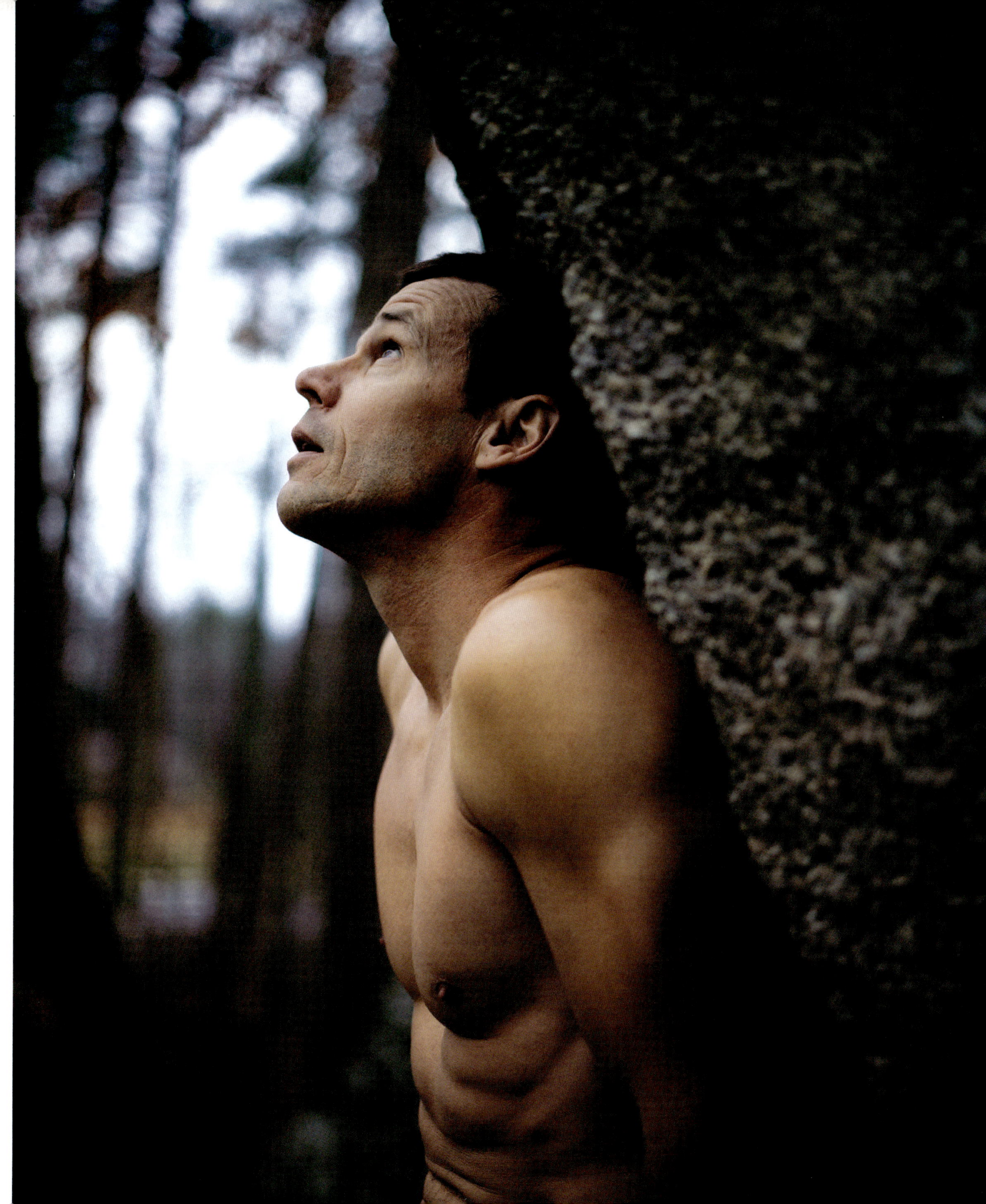

TOGETHER FOREVER

In a semi-forested area of south Atlanta, Daniel Paulete and I explored a field of granite boulders. It had climbing potential, but the trees were tagged for removal. Within a couple months, the rock would be blasted to gravel.

It was February 2008 and my proposed guide to urban climbing in Atlanta shared a similar fate. From the start, there were too few established climbing areas for a guide, but I'd convinced my publisher it had legs. I dragged my research out for more than a year, enlisting friends and chasing rumors of urban rock. The spots we found were either too dangerous, illegal to access, or simply disappearing. In June, the project ended with a brief note from my publisher: "I think it's time to part ways on this project. You may keep the initial advance we paid you, and with that, your obligations under the contract are complete, as are ours."

Daniel and I kept looking. Near the doomed boulder field, we came across an abandoned shack covered by kudzu with daffodils blooming nearby. Tangled in the vines, a handwritten love note began, "I dreamed of me and you being together forever." ◆

Lisa Rands at Stone
Fort, Tennessee

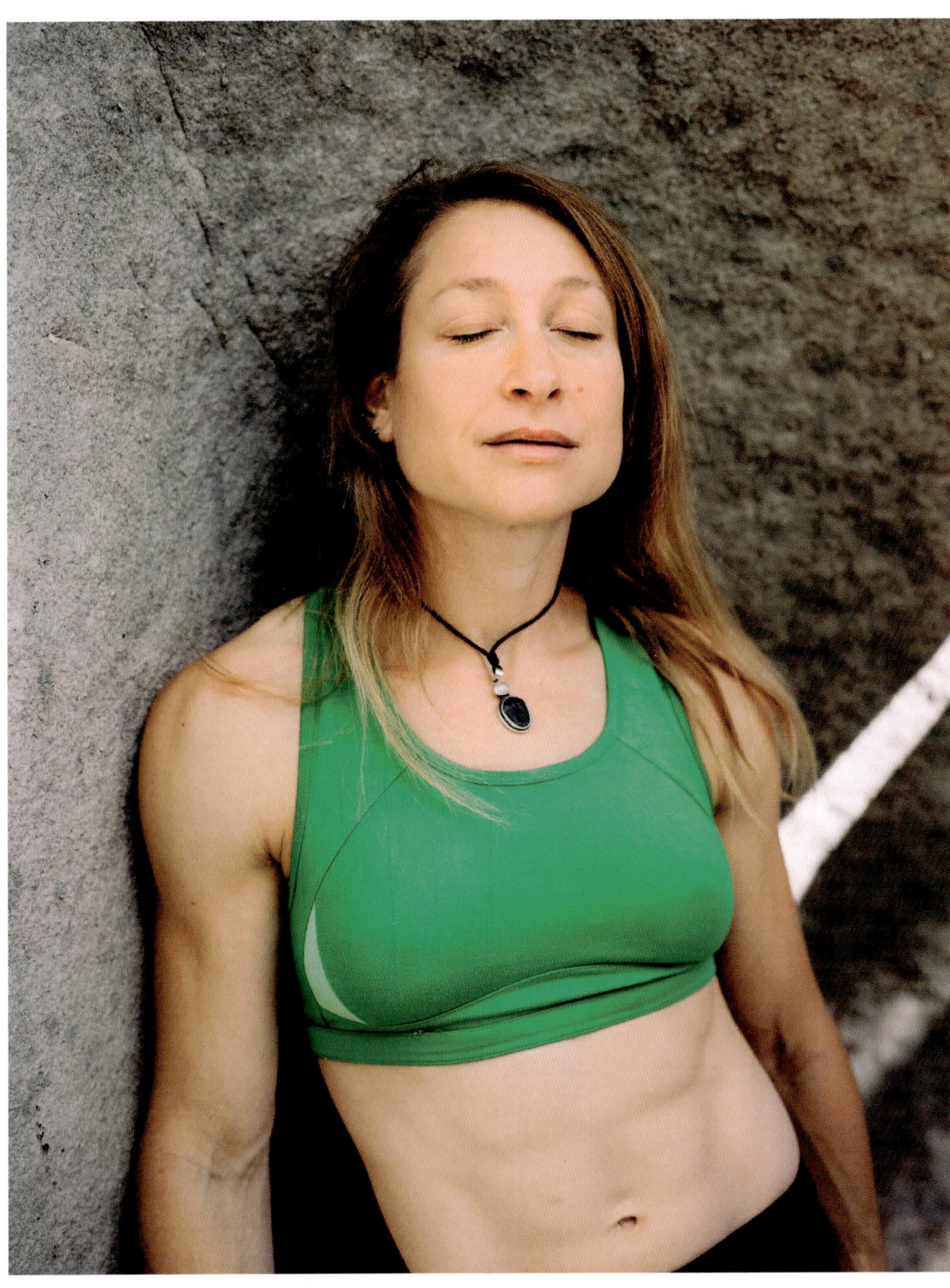

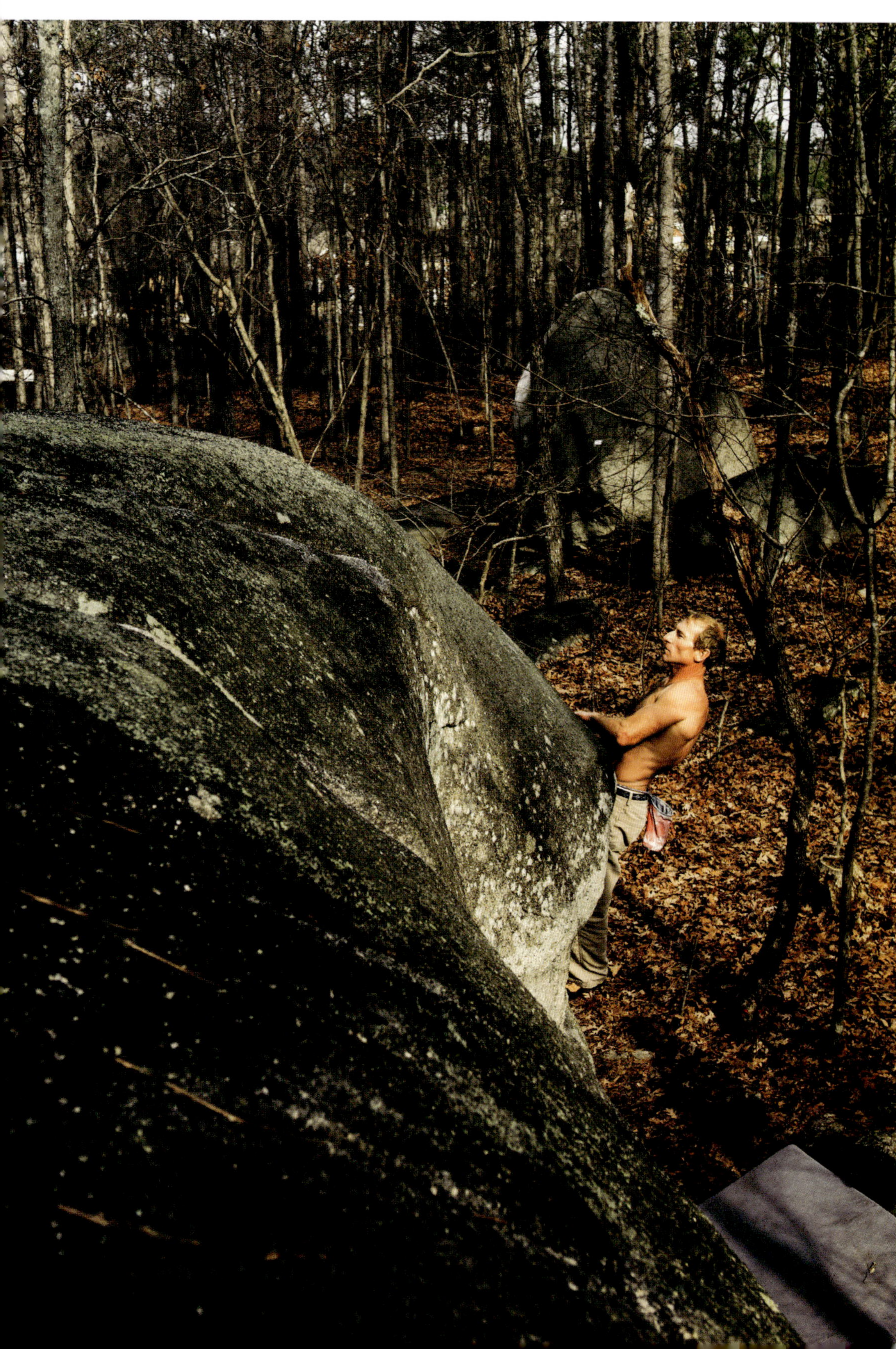

Shannon Stegg on the Firewoman Boulder at Boat Rock in southwestern Atlanta

Opposite: Bob Cormany at Boat Rock

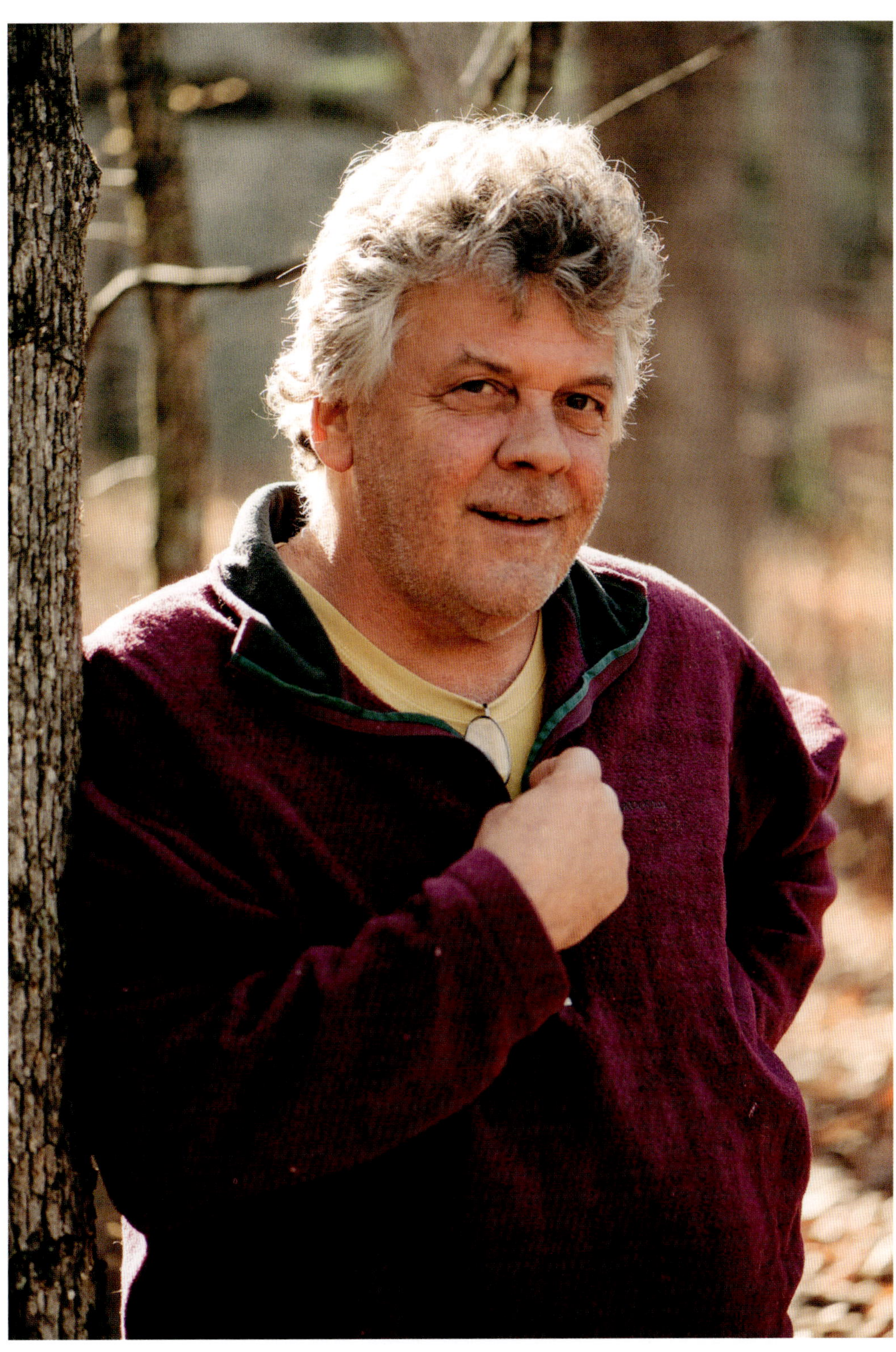

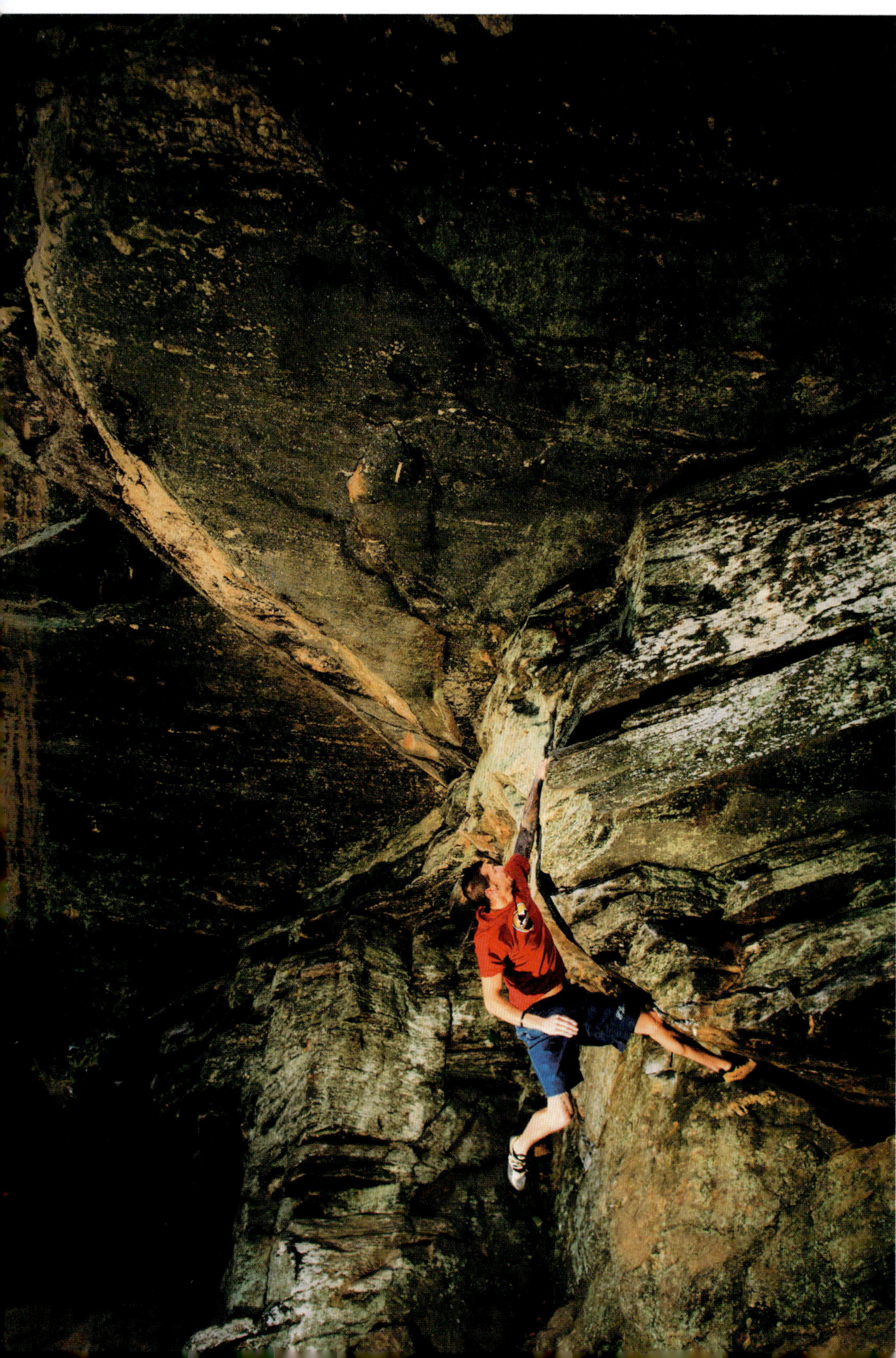

Chris Sierzant on *The Zipper* (5.11d), Atlanta

Opposite: Jennifer Jenkins bouldering at Sand Rock, Alabama

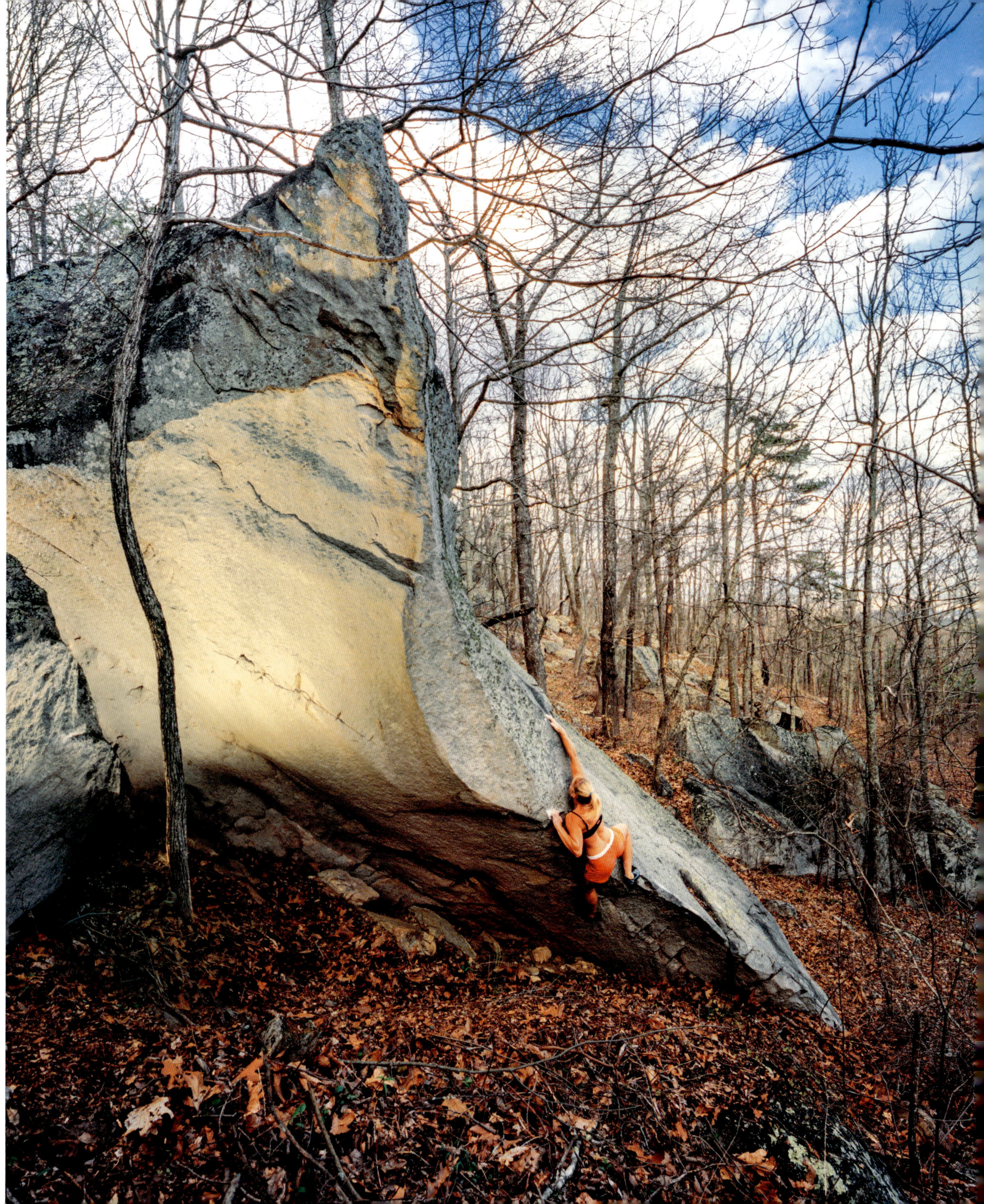

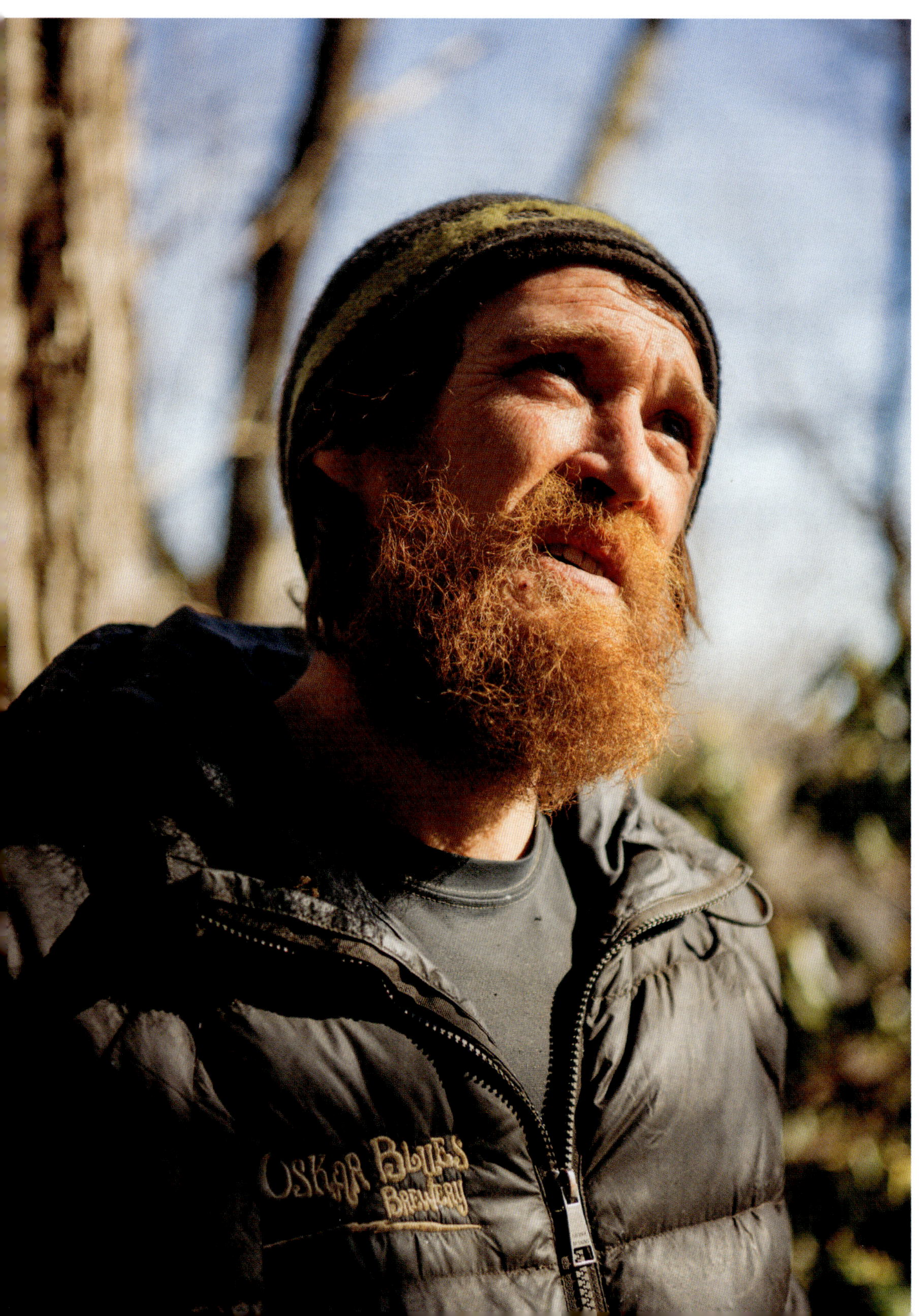
OSKAR BLUES
BREWERY

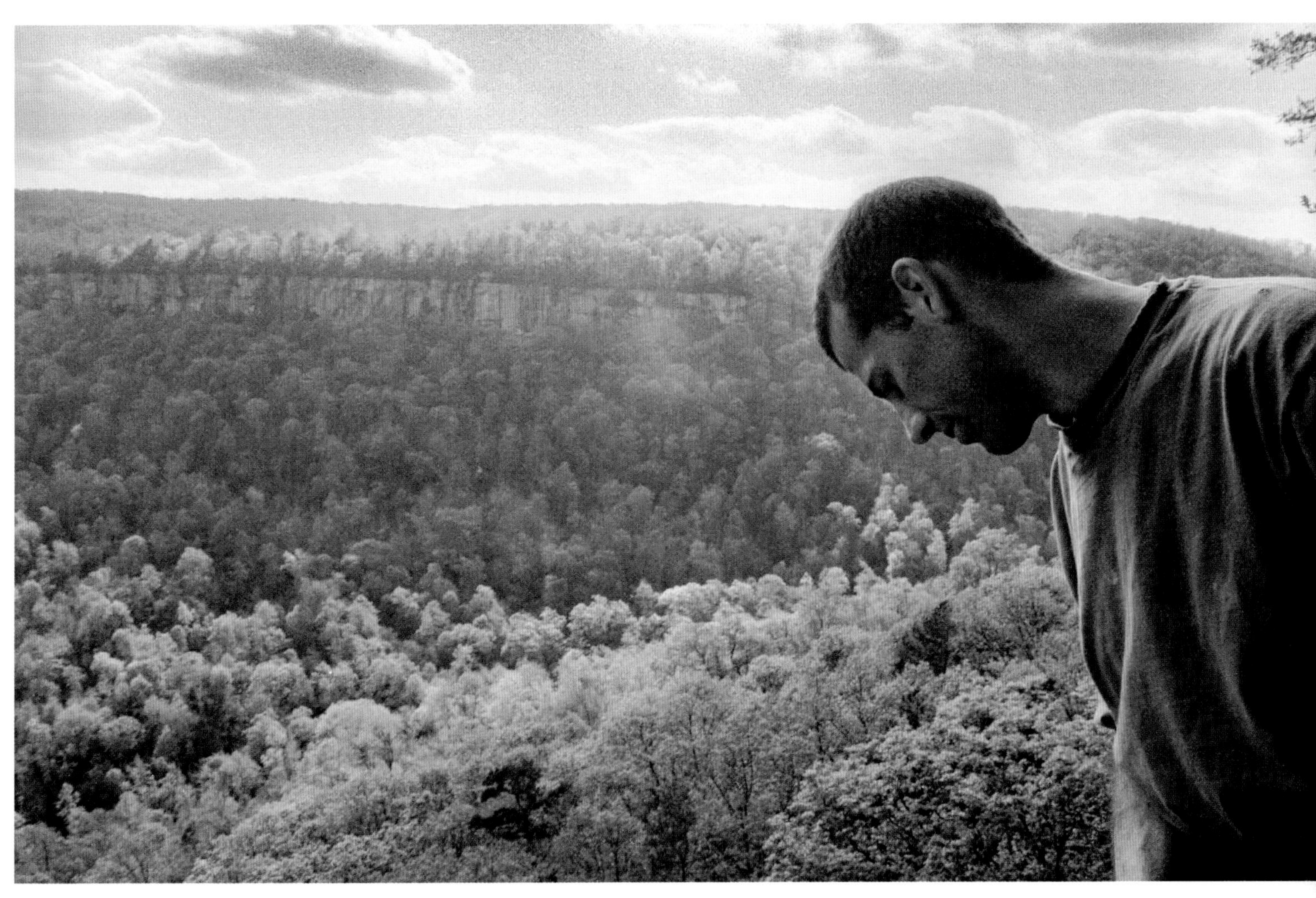

Opposite: Mike Stam in Boone, North Carolina

Thomas Schmidt in Sequatchie Valley, Tennessee

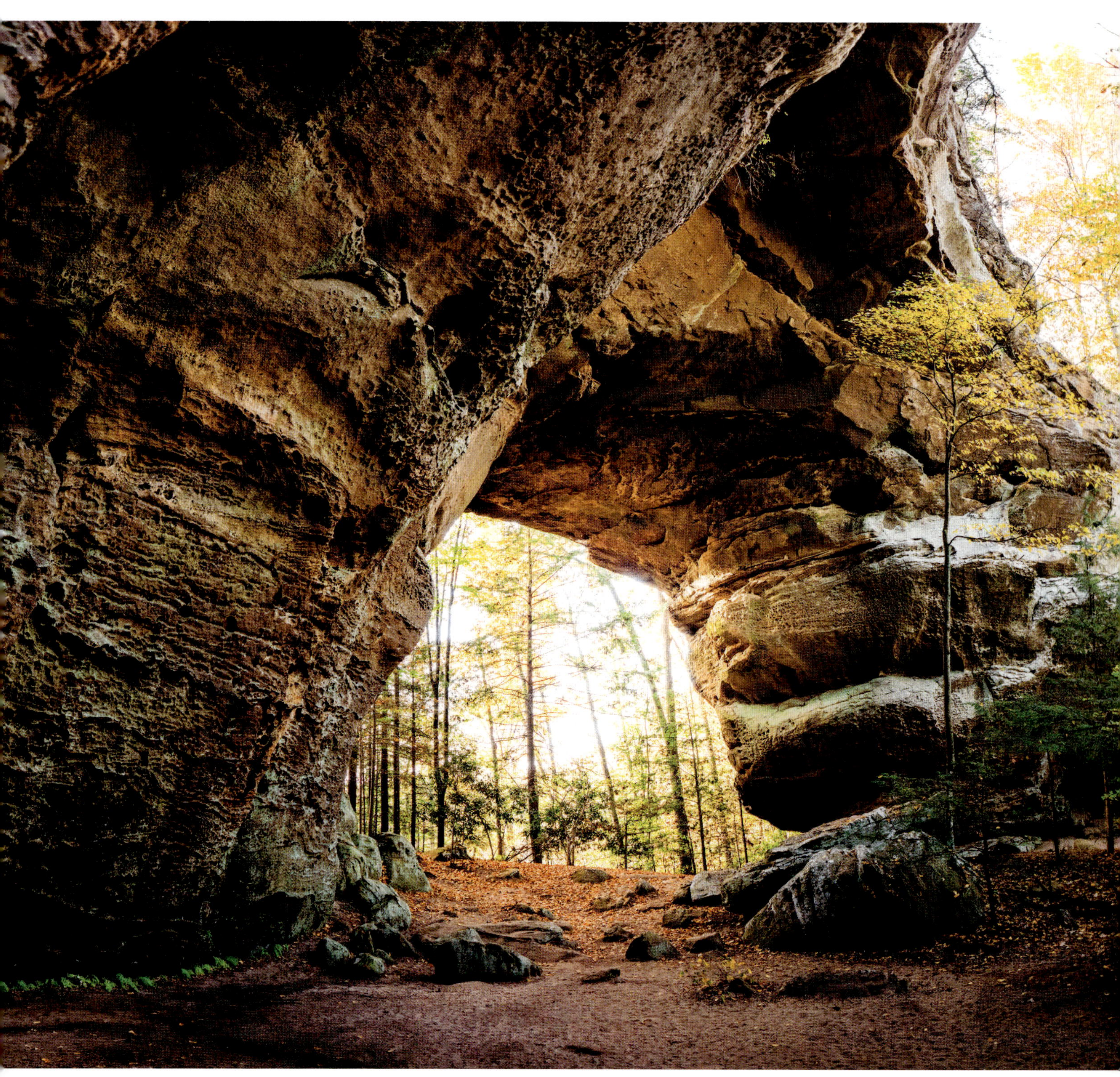

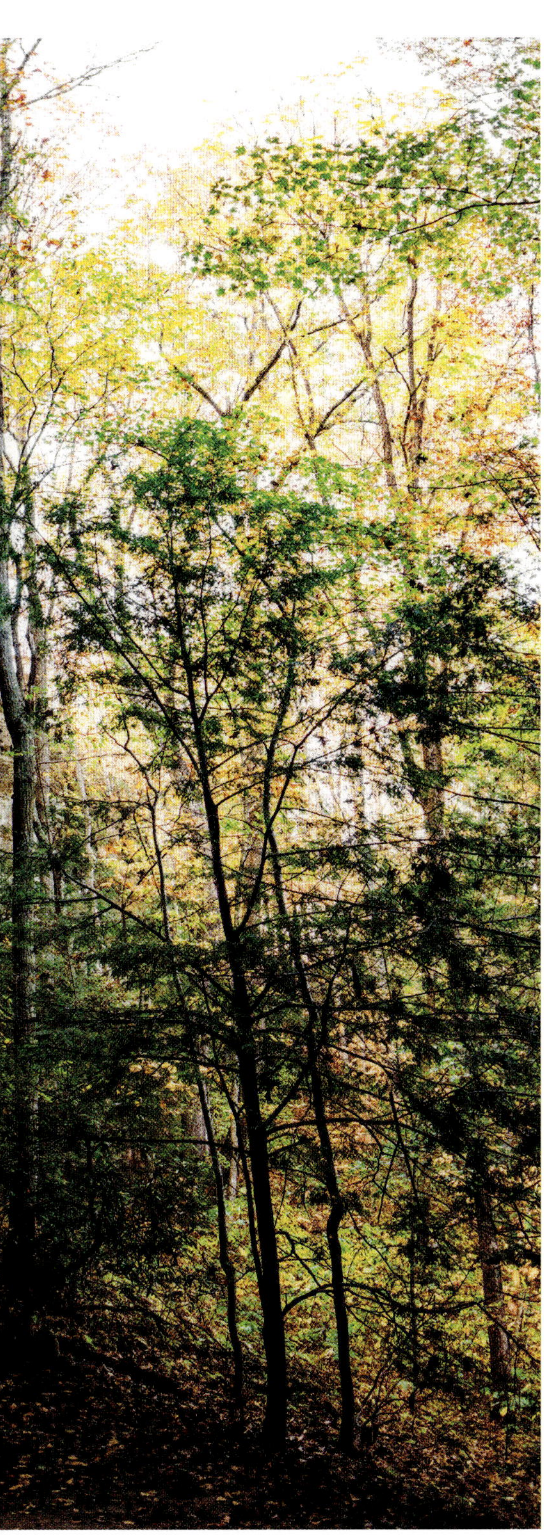

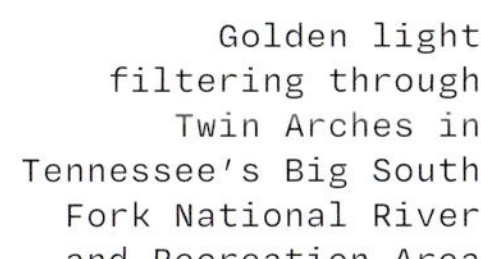

Golden light filtering through Twin Arches in Tennessee's Big South Fork National River and Recreation Area

HOLLER

The Cumberland Plateau is a 150-mile-long shinbone-shaped escarpment rising above east Tennessee, from Kentucky's Cumberland Gap to Signal Point in Chattanooga. If you climb in the South, you've probably found yourself atop the plateau (or more accurately, inside it), clinging to a fine-grained golden sandstone wall above a wild river gorge, or maybe afoot, on the hunt for an untouched wall of rock you once saw shining from across the next canyon. I spent years in the Cumberland Plateau doing just that, but beyond the climbing there is something deeper offered by this landscape that I've come to understand.

"'Rye Whiskey, Rye Whiskey' . . . I think that's what you were just playing." Bobby Fulcher sits on an easy chair in a simple shotgun house in the northern end of the Cumberland Plateaus, banjo in hand. Filmmaker Josh Fowler and I are flies on the wall, filming for a documentary project about the music of the Cumberlands. Across from him, an old woman in a rocking chair giggles, "They called that 'Ol' Dugan in the Loft.'" Bobby smiles and nods, his eyes closed. He strums a chord on his banjo. "Sing it for me."

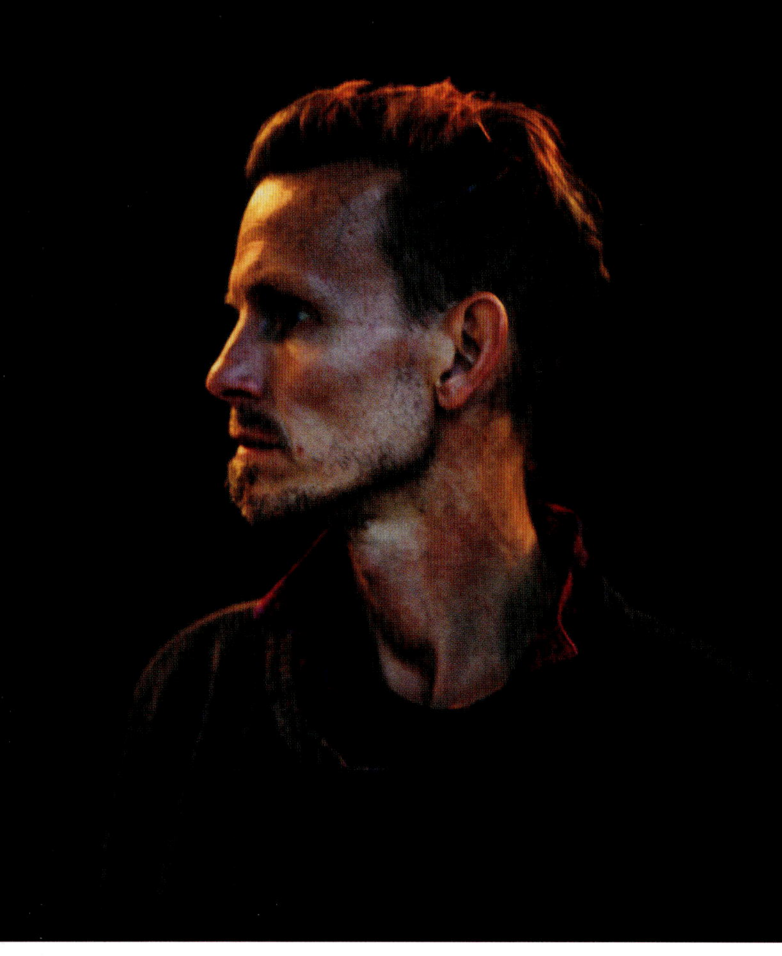

Adam Henry at Horse Pens 40 Ranch, Alabama

Opposite: Anthony Meeks at Deep Creek, Tennessee

The woman begins singing, and Bobby takes up the tune. His reel-to-reel audio recorder lies on a table between them, capturing everything. "Ol' Dugan's in the loft and he pulled his britches off / And he went down the road in his long shirt-tails / Don't you bet them women laughed when they seen ol' Dugan pass / It's a long, long ways away from home."

Outside, the fog coming off the plateau whips around the woman's yard, rattling the window and tinkling chimes that end up on the recording.

I've spent many days like this with Bobby, hearing old-time music on Cumberland front porches and in living rooms. Usually he'll just visit with folks, sometimes whole families he's known for generations, bending over to taste the water in a backyard spring. He'll offer a baked ham and catch up in the parlor over a skillet of cornbread. Inevitably, he'll pull out an instrument—sometimes a banjo, other times a guitar or a fiddle—and they'll all play music together, Bobby's recorder silently rolling in the background.

Bobby has spent the last four decades of his life recording traditional music and documenting local history as an unofficial folklorist of the Cumberland Plateau. Officially, Bobby is the park manager of Tennessee's Justin P. Wilson Cumberland Trail State Park, a footpath that will wind three hundred miles through the entire region when it's done. Locals refer to it simply as the Cumberland Trail, and Bobby envisions his library of obscure and rare recordings—his life's work—woven into the fabric of the trail experience.

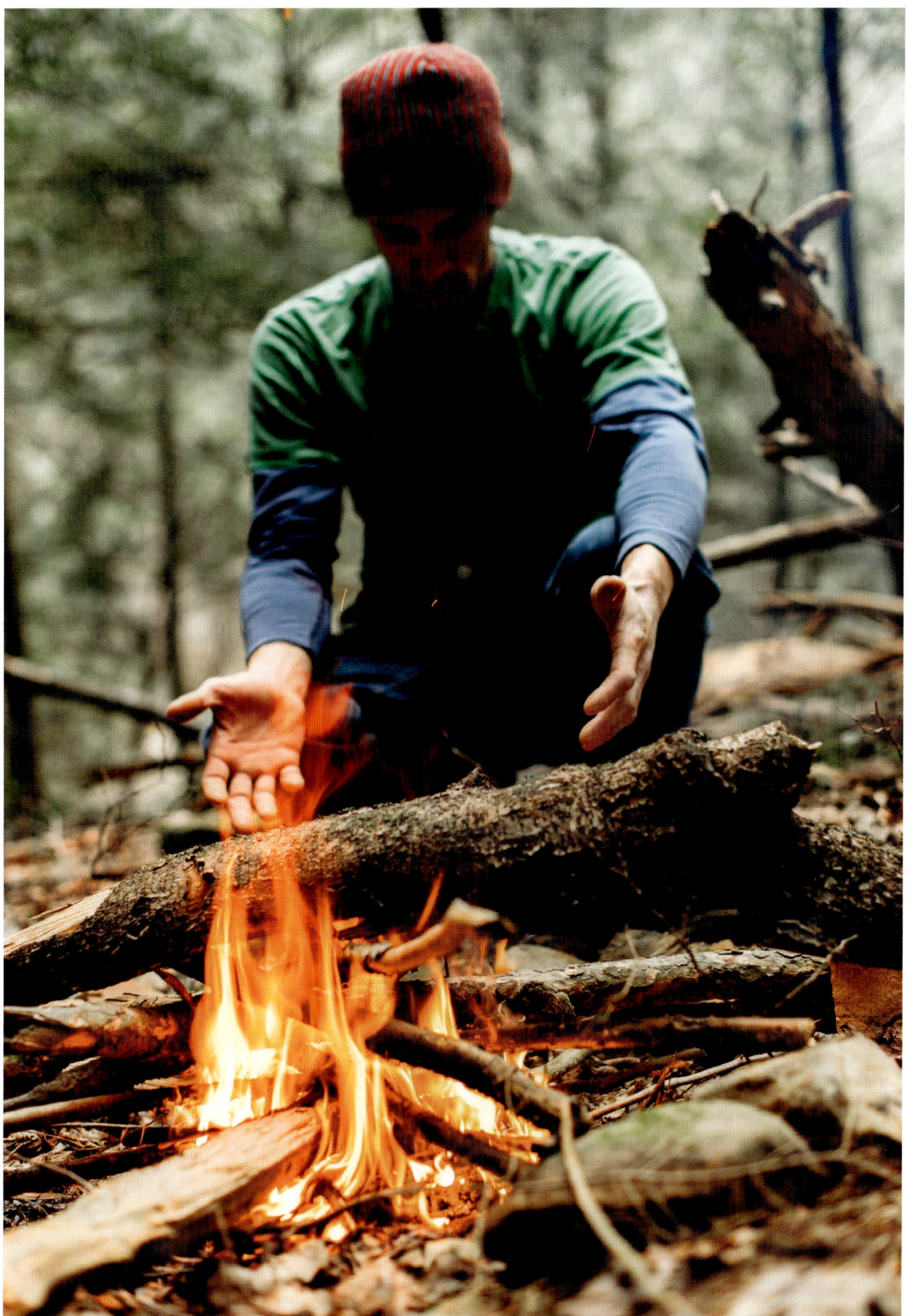

Taylor McNeill along Route 221, Boone, North Carolina

Though his cragging days are in the past, he works closely with local climbers, relying on their rigging expertise for building bridges across gulfs and rivers along the way, and in return mentoring and guiding them as the sport expands through the South. He knows every inch of these mountains and understands how people can be changed profoundly by this landscape—not just through high adventure but also by the simple experience of walking through it. "It takes away the boundaries that the world has for them," as he put it. "You know, these big natural systems, they recreate themselves moment by moment, year by year, age by age. The river scours itself over and over again. The rocks reshape and reform themselves into new figures and new scenes. The plants regenerate. The Cumberland Trail provides an opportunity for people to remake themselves too." Bobby has the true heart of a wilderness rambler. "All I ever wanted," he once told me, "was to sleep in a hollow log."

Filmmaker Carlo Nasisse and I were led into the Big South Fork by Bobby early one morning to catch the sunrise blasting through an immense arch of sandstone. We passed wall after wall of golden rock, once stopping to closely examine an untouched cliff line for its climbing potential. "Now, you leave this one to the 'billies," he scolded, shaking his head. For him, the value of this geography goes beyond its recreational value.

The next night we rough camped in nearby Pickett State Park with Bobby. In our little cave, he explained how the landscape shapes music. The birds and crickets make sounds, he said, and folks imitate it, change it, and integrate it into language and song. They bounce hollers off the sandstone canyon walls, and through geologic alchemy it becomes something that can only be from *this place*. "Go into the woods," he said, "and get that power."

In the dark of the cave, he played an old tune on his banjo, half-singing, half-hooting. I hooted back, hair standing on end, transformed. ◆

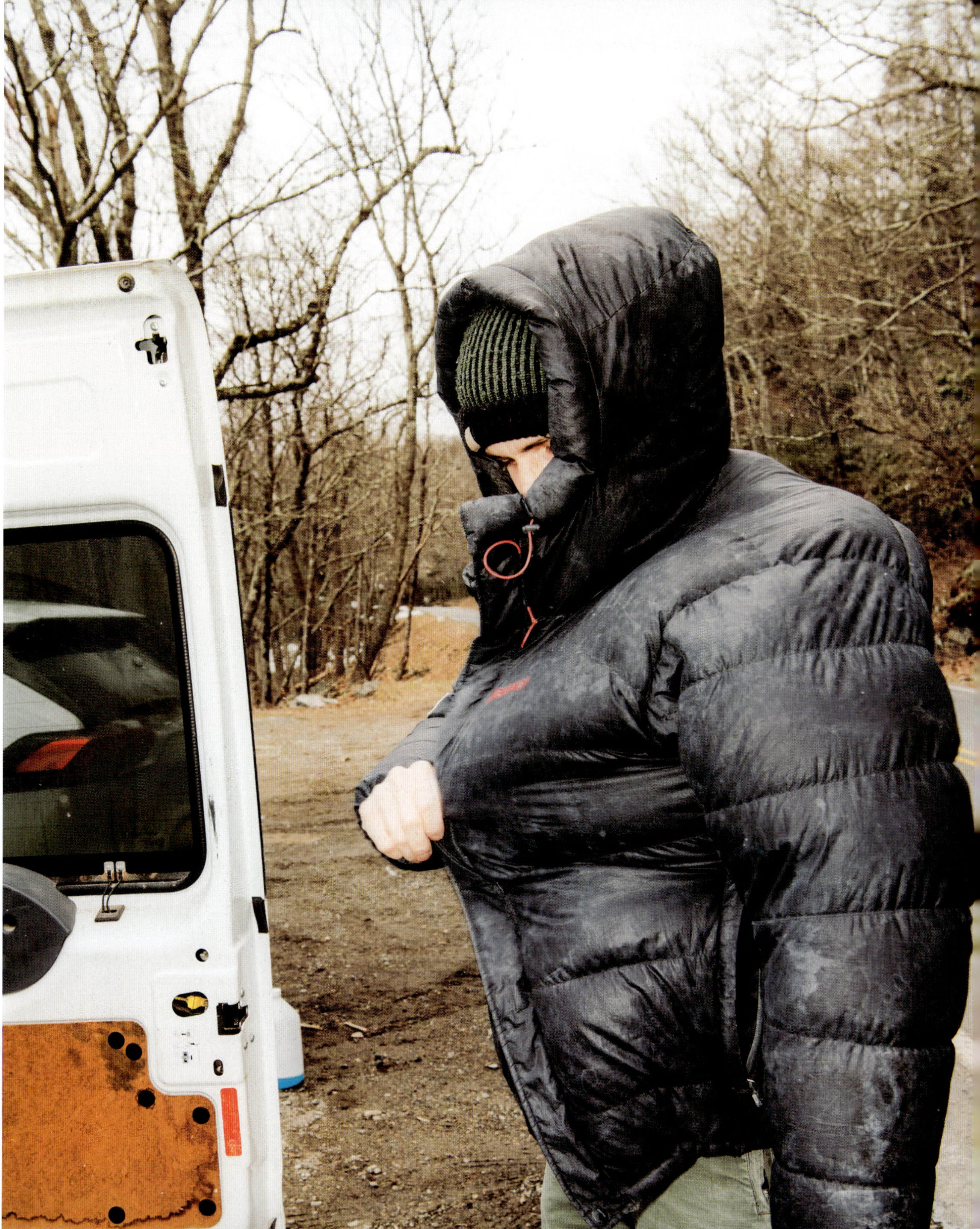

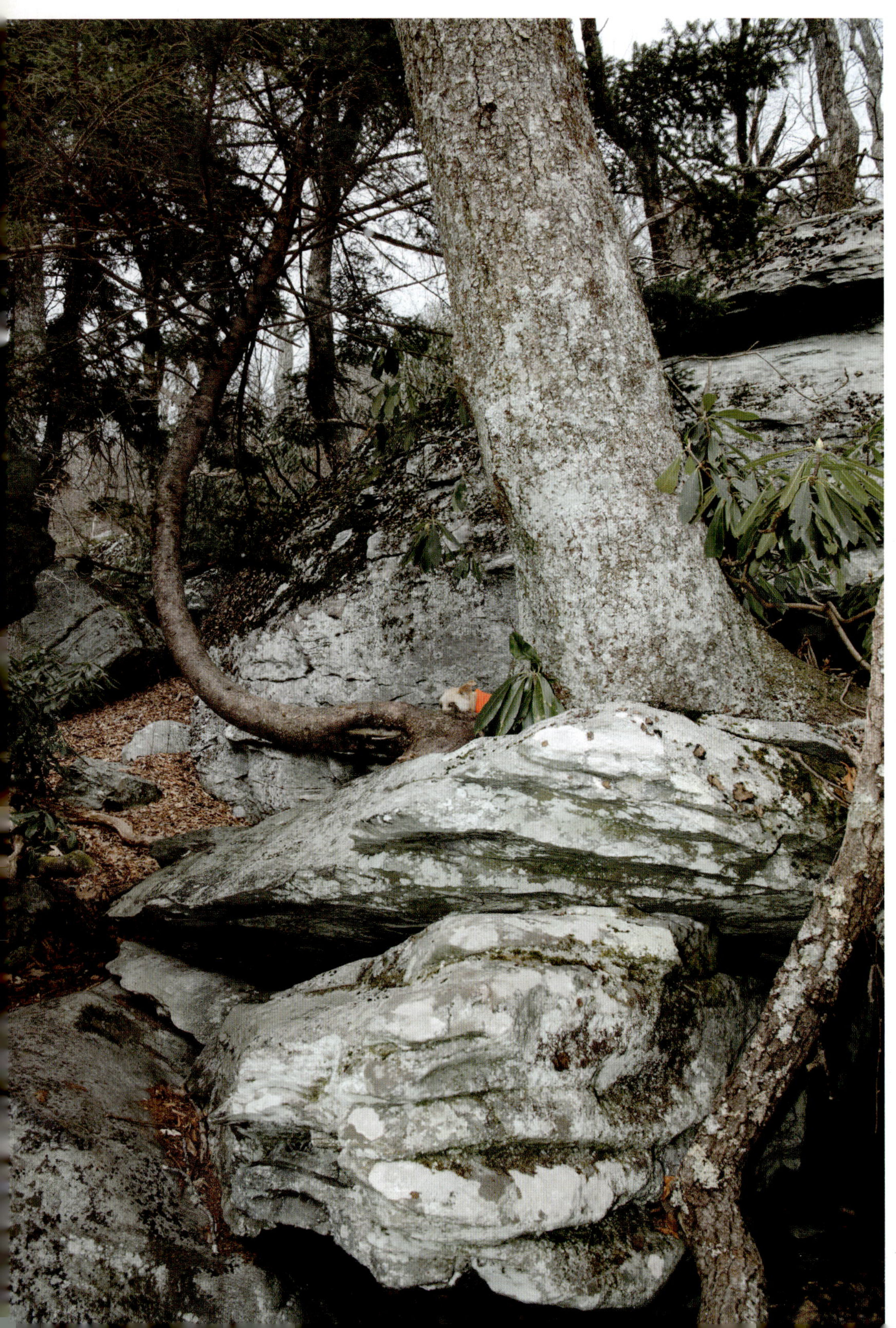

Opposite: Lilo hiding behind a boulder along Route 221, Boone, North Carolina

James Litz at Lilly Boulders, Tennessee

Joey Henson in the Linville Gorge, North Carolina

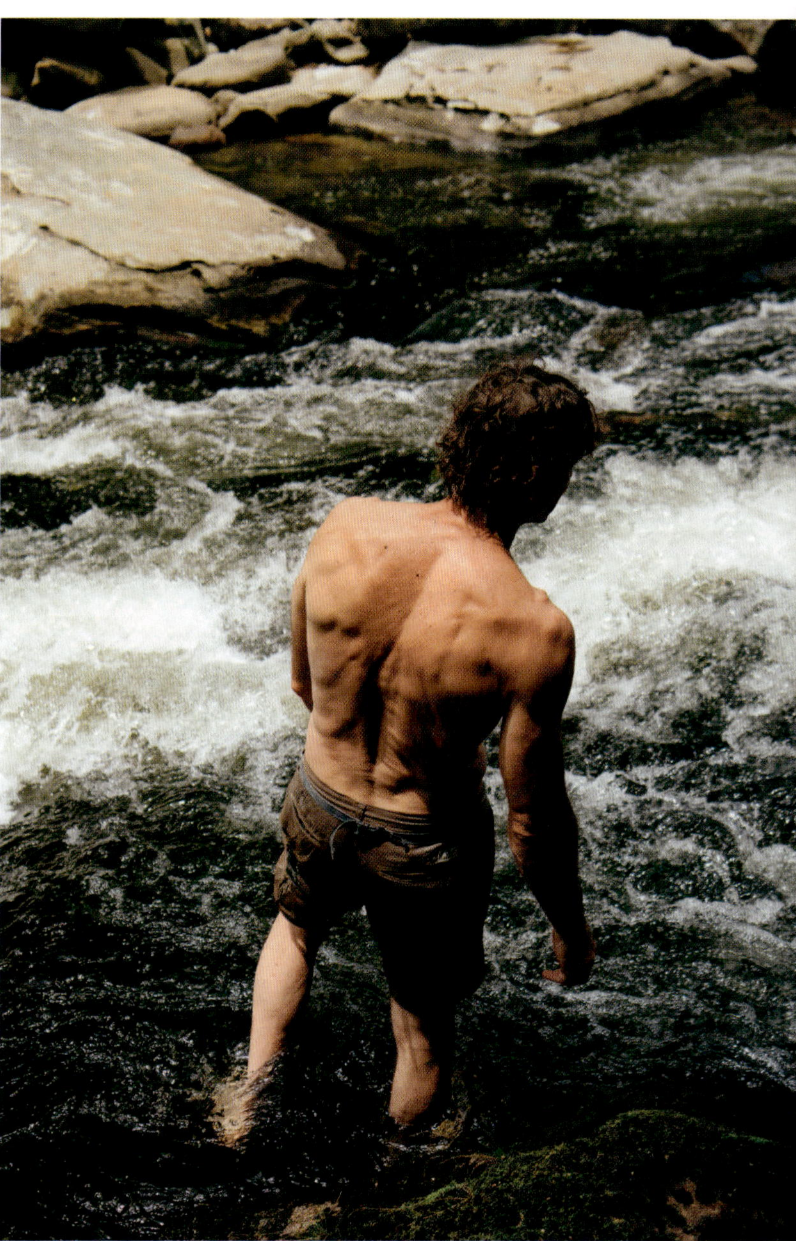

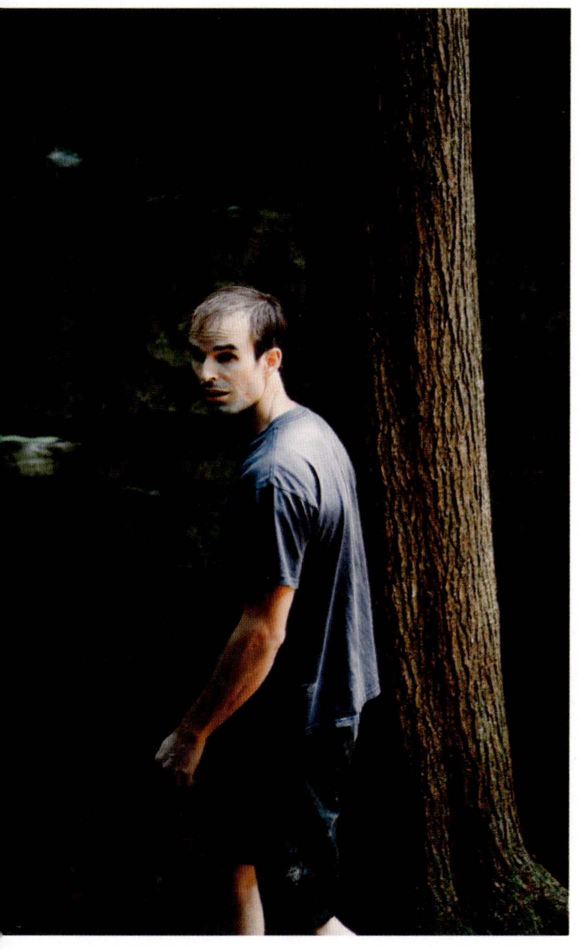

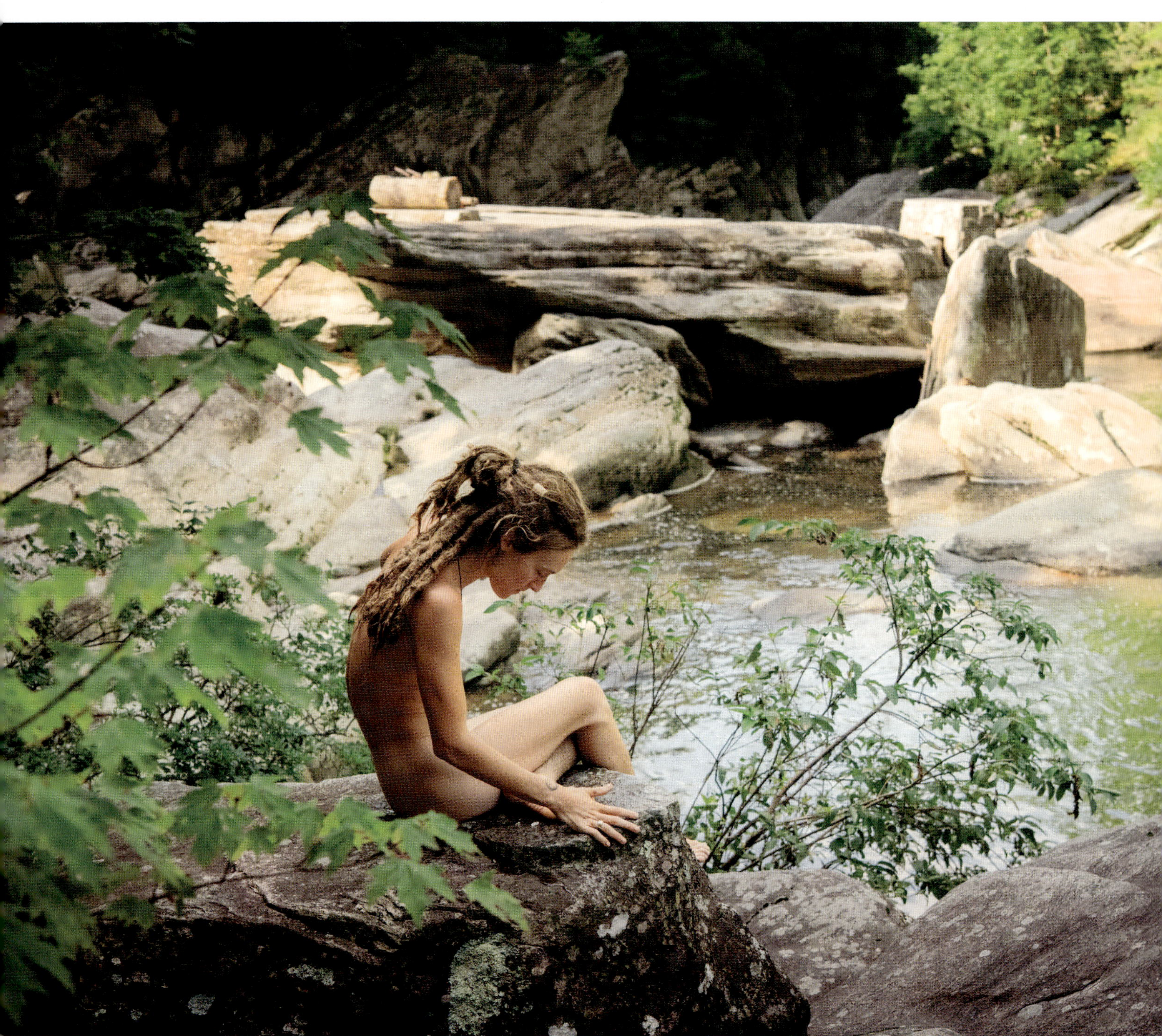

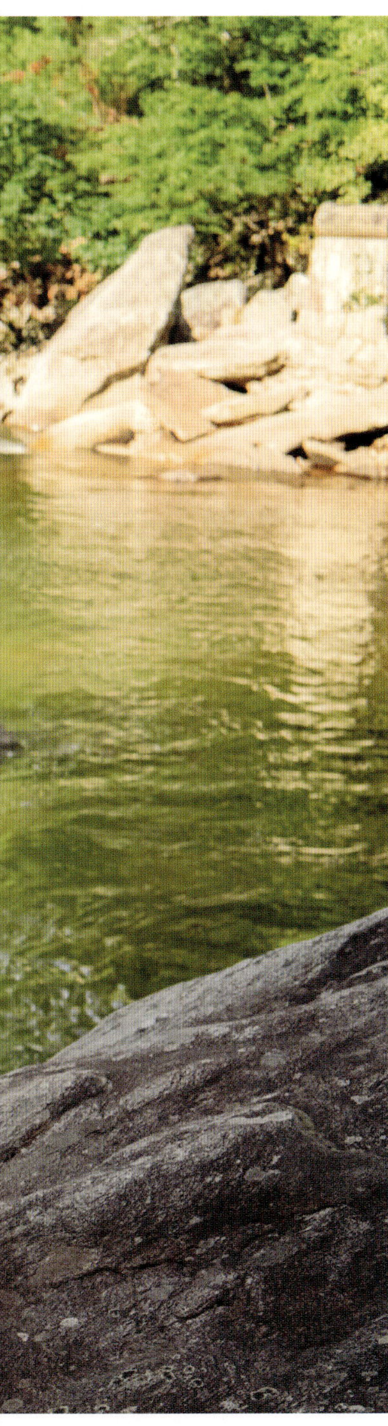

Audrie-Emma Bruce in the Linville Gorge, North Carolina

THE WELL

I recently read a piece in the popular technology magazine *The Verge* about a new Google camera with built-in generative imaging. "As photographs become little more than hallucinations made manifest," declares the author, Sarah Jeong, warning about the erosion of social consensus, "we are *fucked*." In this world, she writes, a photo "stops being a supplement to fallible human recollection, but instead a mirror of it."

It's interesting to me that we are afraid of this mirror. To be honest about our fallibility seems to me a good thing. We have all pretended for too long that, of all the ways to remember, the photograph is superior.

I have far more climbing memories than photographs. The sensory recall of a European road trip is vivid. I can recall the tacky feel of the *pof*-shellacked boulders of Fontainebleau and the scent of wild oregano that we crushed under our hands on a sheer Italian sea cliff. I don't have a single snapshot of a week of multipitch frolicking on Swiss alpine granite towers, but the crunch of boots over glacial snow brings me right back.

In some ways, the photographic record only confuses things. Once you take the camera out, the experience bifurcates. I once enlisted Atlanta climber Zack Pitts to join me and three other friends from Utah on a seven-day mission to climb four desert towers by mountain bike in Utah's Canyonlands National Park. A little out of my depth, I opted to trail behind for telephoto views and sweeping landscapes over the intimate close-ups I might have gotten on lead, ahead of the team.

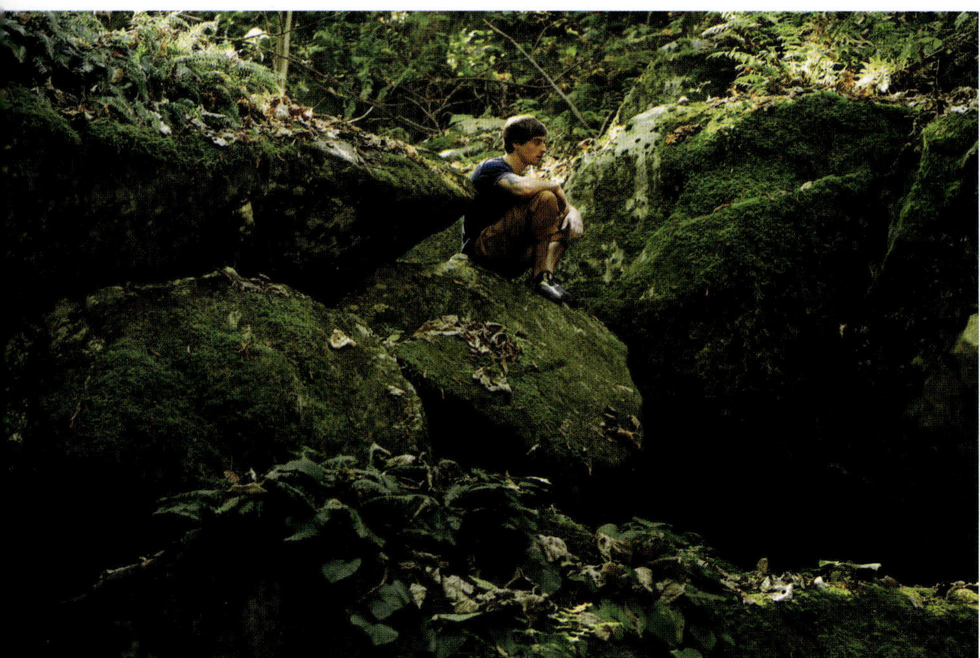

The mountain biking sucked. We ran out of water. At one point I ascended a static line up the first pitch of Washer Woman Tower. I gained a ledge and looked closely at the anchor my partners had attached my line to, a single old piton hammered into the soft sandstone. I reached up and pulled it out of the rock easily with one hand. I wanted to complain to them about the terrifyingly poor anchor, but they were already off to the next pitch, which I dutifully photographed. Perfectly idealized, the image is a different reality than my quiet brush with disaster, another one of so many we experience up against the rock.

Other times, the call to put down the camera is nonnegotiable. Above the rural neighborhood of Jamestown in Alabama hangs a mile-long cliff line. It was underground for decades until the Southeastern Climbers Coalition purchased enough of the land at its base to secure public access around 2005. I visited the area then with my friend Greg Kottkamp and did a little climbing on a beautiful old Eric Zschiesche finger crack called *White Lightning*. From the anchors I could photograph two lines: a lichen-covered blank slab to my right and a steep, intimidating overhanging corner to my left. Both were unclimbed. After photographing Annie Shields on her first ascent of the slab line, *Hearts of Palm* (5.12c), Greg announced he would try the crack line to my left. It was probably the hardest traditional free-climbing line in the area, and it had a dangerously low crux move. Greg and I had climbed together for years. He candidly told me I was the only one he trusted to belay him on this one. I gave up my perfect shooting vantage to climber and photographer John Barr.

Opposite: Nate Draughn at Looking Glass Rock in Brevard, North Carolina

Autumn in Tennessee's Laurel-Snow State Natural Area

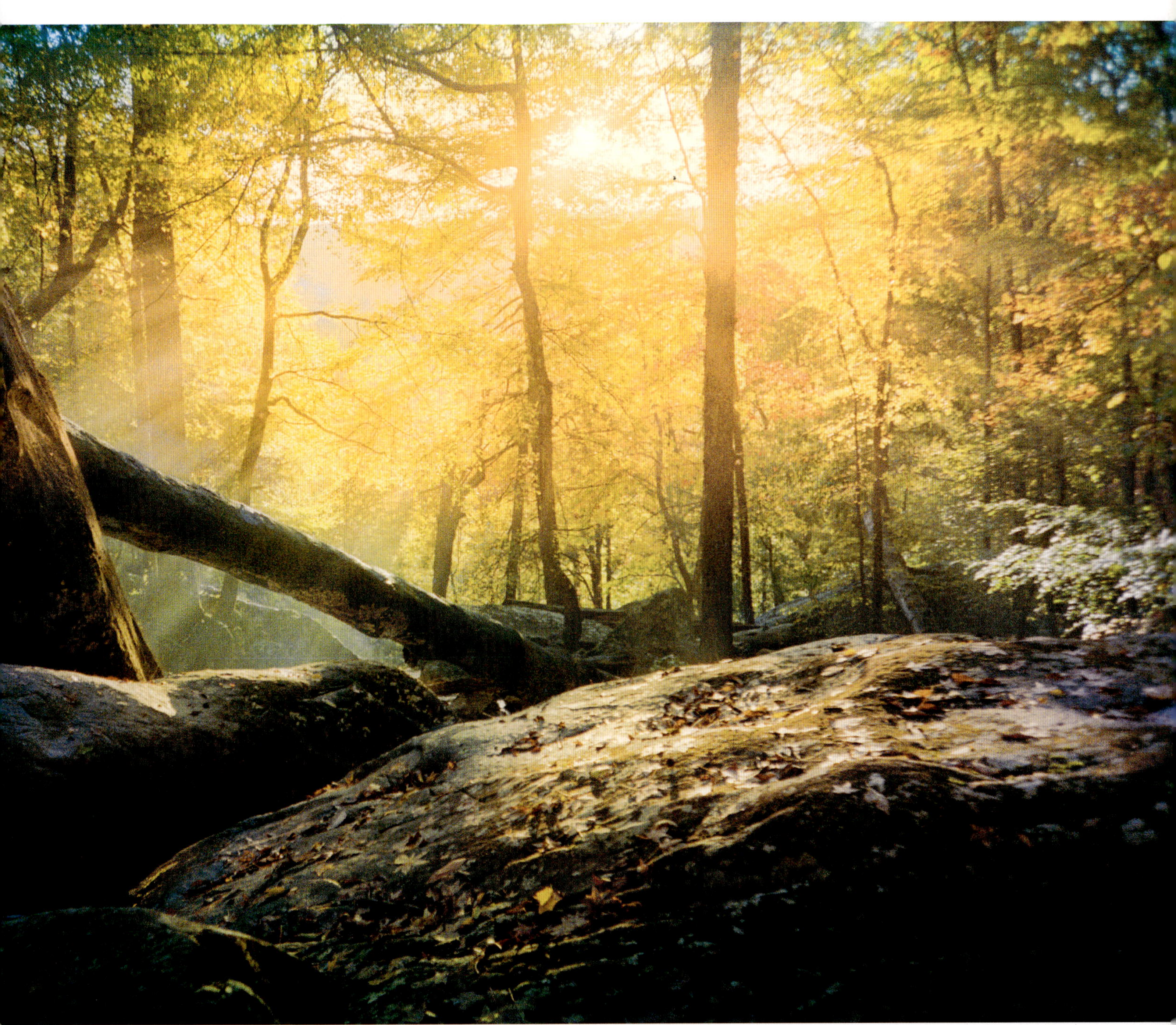

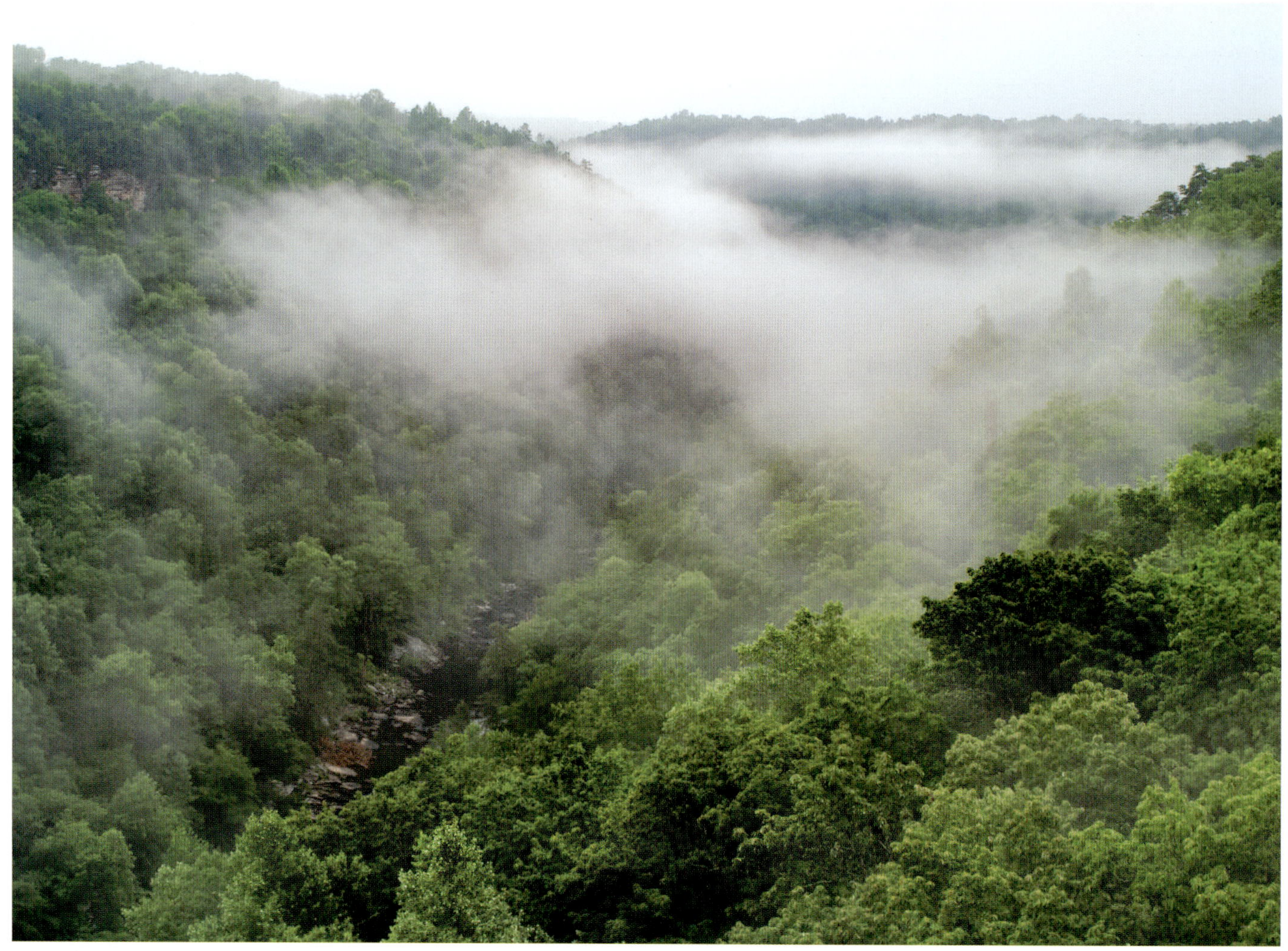

My belay stance was on a ledge a good way off the ground. Greg and I decided that, if he fell from the crux, I'd just jump off. The hope was that his protection would hold, and my daring leap would keep us from crashing into the talus below. If the gear didn't hold, we'd join the graveyard of wrecked cars and appliances at the base. Youthful hubris, maybe, but over the years I'd found Greg to be invincible on the rock. He sent the route on his first try. Barr's excellent photo—proof of Greg's first ascent of *Astro Boy* (5.13)—ended up in the next edition of Chris Watford's *Dixie Cragger's Atlas*.

Fog over Little River
Canyon National
Preserve, Alabama

A few months into the pandemic, I got my two sons out of the house with me on a photo shoot in Boone, North Carolina, for Mad Rock, a climbing shoe company. Theo—ten at the time—was really into climbing and jumped right into the shoot, helping with reflectors and trying the moves on everything. My oldest, Sam, then fifteen, was not into climbing at all. He sat in the shade with his book and observed us from afar. "I realized that most of my dad's job isn't taking exciting photos, or traveling to new locations, but sitting around," he wrote in his journal, "and while you're sitting around, it's hot, buggy, and there's no bathroom for miles."

Theo remembers it differently. The first boulder was taller and scarier than anything he'd seen anyone climb without a rope. The granite was sharp and covered in dry, flaky lichens. He remembers the sound of waterfalls and the smell of rhododendron. The rock at the second location was smoother and damp. He explored some dark rock shelters and caught glimpses of the wild Linville Gorge from the rim.

Both recollections are fallible, yet fully accurate. The photographs from all these experiences are not the record—they are the hallucinations. Like objects brought up from a well, they are only odd glimpses of what's down there in the dark water. I am happy with that. If we lean too heavily on photography as proof, we forget all the infinite interpretations possible below. Maybe these generative cameras will finally sweep away our fixation on photographic anamnesis.

On the release of his novel *Open City*, photographer and writer Teju Cole wrote about his approach in an interview in *Guernica*: "The central thing motivating my photography and by extension my writing is the idea that there was a mythical pre-history of humanity when everything was intact. The process of photography is finding the little pieces and somehow connecting them to each other, introducing them to each other, reuniting little bits of the shattered world."

The realm of rocks and waterfalls and high ledges is a vestige of that intact world, one that can still be sensed roughly and intimately. It doesn't need photographic proof. As climbers, we are lucky to experience it firsthand. ◆

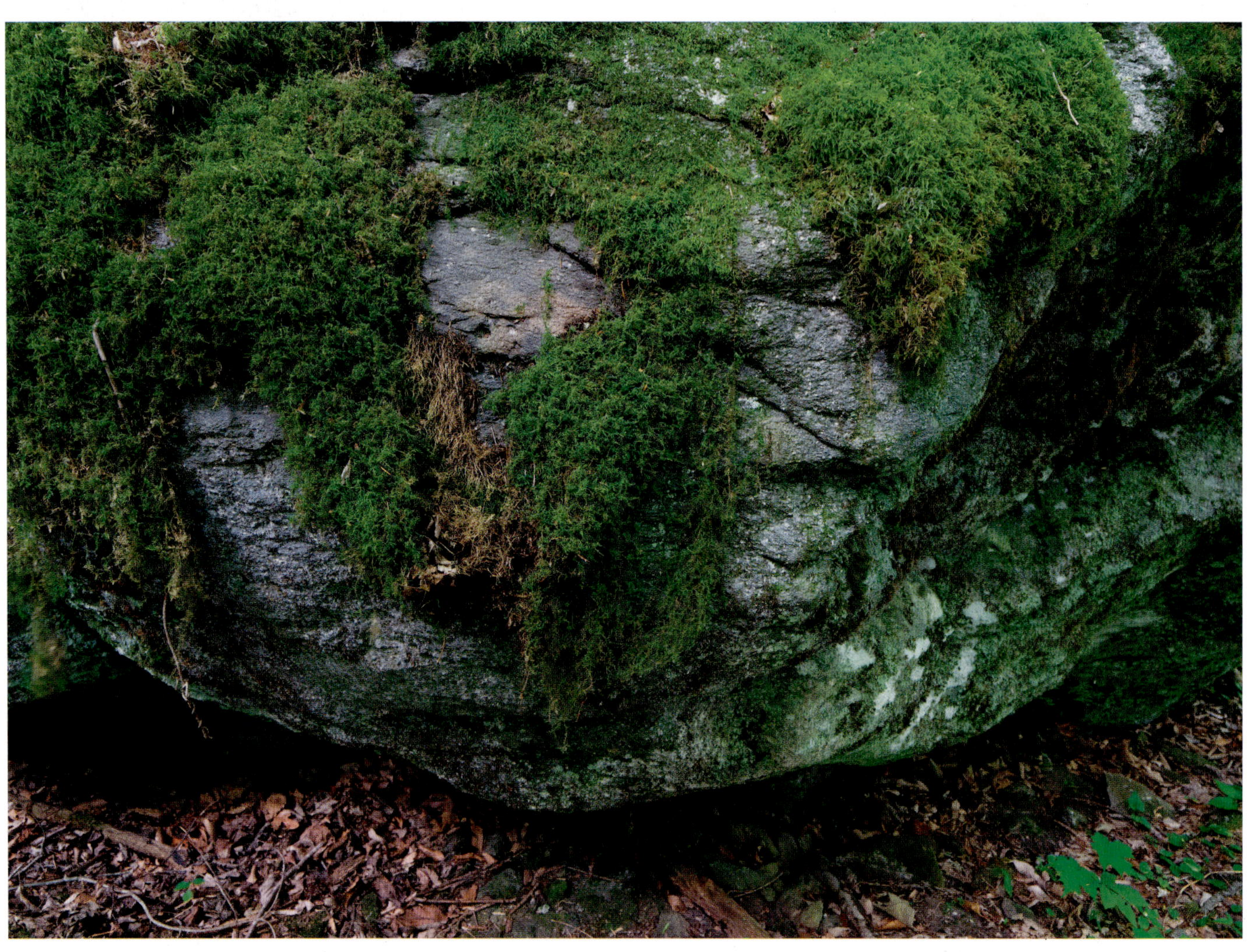

Mossy boulder on Grandfather Mountain, Boone, North Carolina

Opposite: Joey Henson in the Linville Gorge, North Carolina

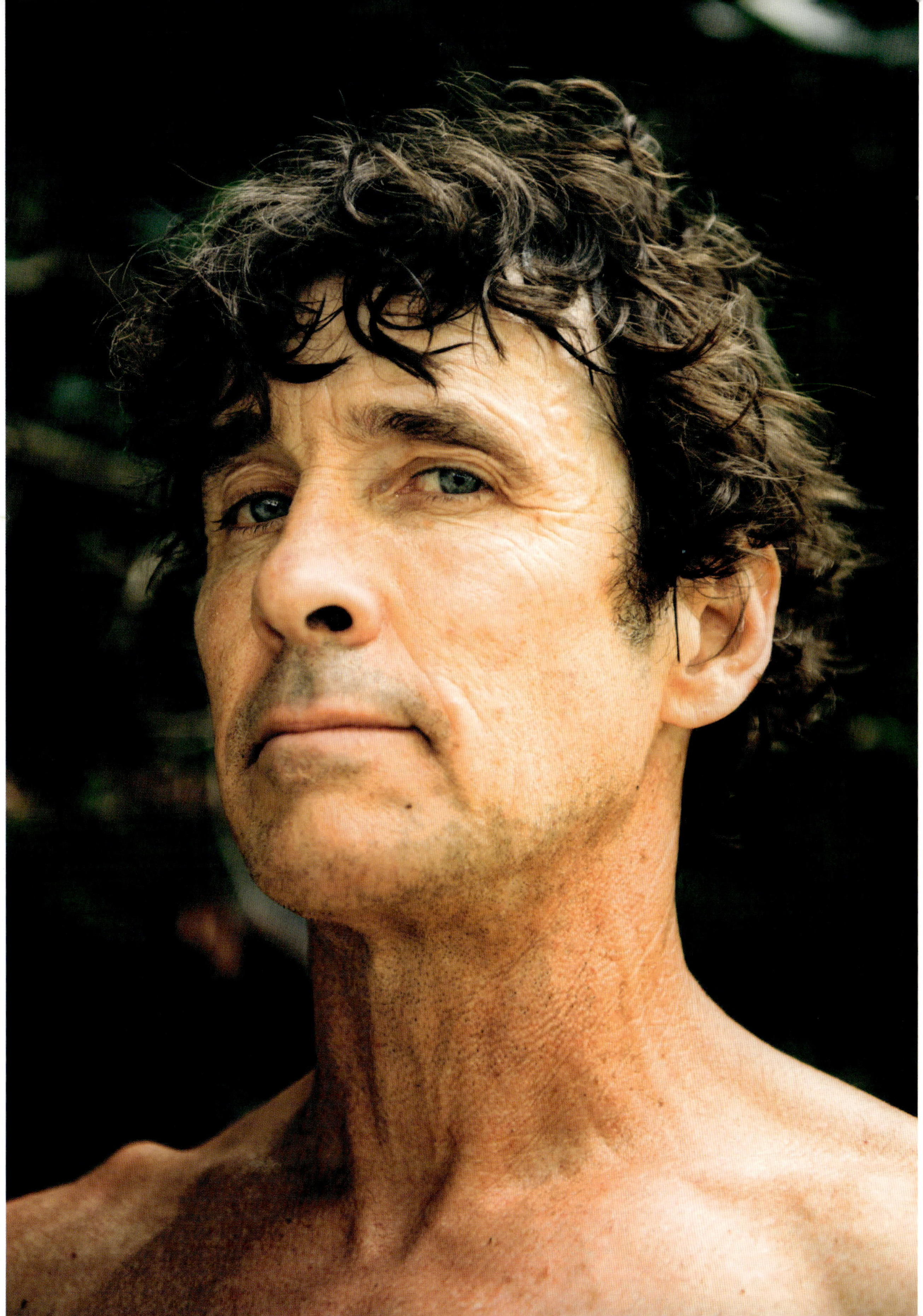

ACKNOWLEDGMENTS

As a photographer and storyteller, I am forever grateful for the generosity and openness of my friends in the Southern climbing community, many of whom are featured in this book.

Thank you also to John Long, Dean Fidelman, Jim Herrington, Jim Thornburg, Peter Essick, and Matt Eich for their early book publishing advice and encouragement, Steve Casimiro for proofing my proto-essays, Bernie Ilgner, Chris Watford, Adam Henry, Dave Wilson, Chad Wykle, Jim Horton, Brad McLeod, and Rob Robinson for sharing their stories and fact checking, and Joey Henson for the beautiful hand-drawn map that graces the book.

My longtime collaborator Josh Fowler was present for many of the moments in this book, and he, along with Greg Kottkamp, and Thomas Schmidt have been my stalwart climbing partners in the South for decades.

Carlo Nasisse understood the vision of this book from the beginning, and has been a steadfast source of creative feedback throughout. My sister Christine—a much better writer than I am—was always there for a critical read-through.

I am forever indebted to acquisitions editor Emily White for believing in *Spare These Stones*, senior editor Laura Shauger and designer Melissa McFeeters for making it sing, and the rest of the amazing staff at Mountaineers Books for so expertly shepherding this project through. I couldn't have dreamed of a better publishing partner.

Thank you to my family, my constant source of revelation and perspective.

The Southeastern Climbers Coalition, Carolina Climbers Coalition, and the Access Fund have been investing in access and preservation of Southern climbing since before I clipped my first bolt on the golden sandstone of Foster Falls in 1996. I heard of their presence early on through word-of-mouth, and on the back page of one of my worn-out guidebooks from those days is a handwritten simple reminder to myself: "Join SCC."

In the decades that followed, I became deeply involved with these organizations, energized by their mission of conservation and community building—a mission that is more important now than ever before. I leave you with the same reminder to join your local climbing organization and get involved. To learn more, visit Southeastern Climbers Coalition at www.seclimbers.org, Carolina Climbers Coalition at www.carolinaclimbers.org, and Access Fund at accessfund.org.

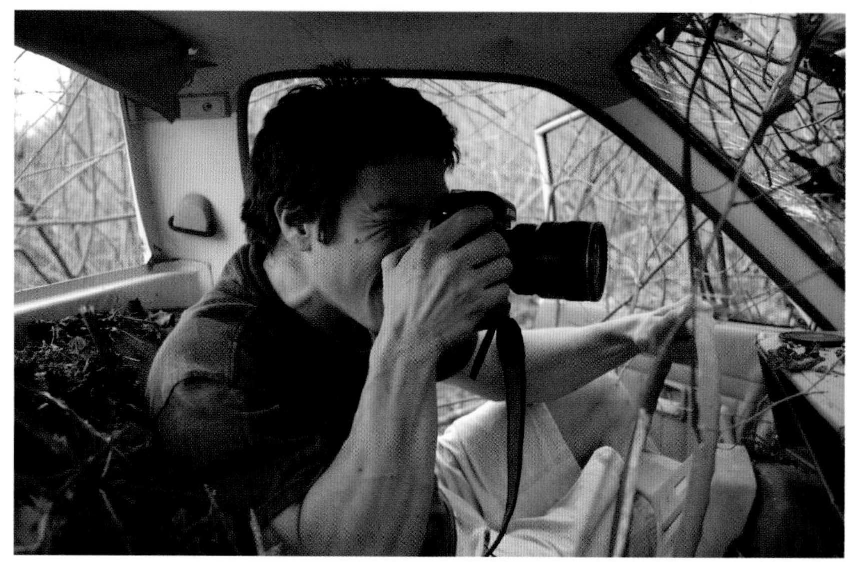

Photo by Greg Kottkamp

ABOUT THE AUTHOR

Photographer, filmmaker, and writer Andrew Kornylak grew up in a small town in southern Ohio. His grandparents were accomplished painters, and his father was an amateur photographer and world traveler. Andrew was the only one who stayed awake for his dad's late-night slideshows. At an early age, he learned to use a camera, a Minolta single-lens reflex handed down from his older brother, a newspaper photographer at the time.

After earning a bachelor's degree in mathematics from the University of Chicago, Kornylak learned to climb, picked up his own camera, and began his career as a participant, traveling and climbing around the US and abroad. Between jobs as a software developer, high-rise window-washer, and climbing instructor, he began producing photography and video for such diverse names as GEO, Discover, *National Geographic*, *Rock & Ice*, The North Face, ESPN, *Garden & Gun*, PBS, Red Bull, and The Nature Conservancy.

Kornylak's work has often been described as innovative and genre-breaking. For him, it starts in the distant past. "It's satisfying to push the envelope, and we are always focused on the future, but it's really important to have a body of work to start from," he says. "I've learned so much from others, but somehow my own work from years ago turns out to be the greatest source of inspiration, and the best foundation for tomorrow's projects. Start early. Build that body of work every day. Trust it. Years later you will revisit it with fresh eyes, and you'll be astonished by some forgotten idea, newly illuminated."

Kornylak lives in Chapel Hill, North Carolina, where he enjoys climbing, playing ice hockey, and projecting photos on the living room wall for his family of five.

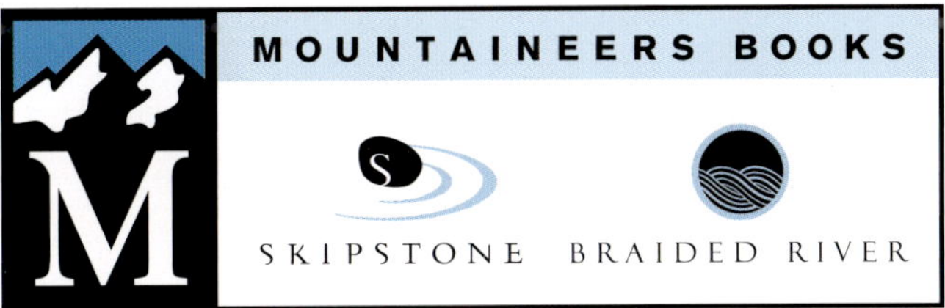

recreation • lifestyle • conservation

MOUNTAINEERS BOOKS, including its two imprints, Skipstone and Braided River, is a leading publisher of quality outdoor recreation, sustainability, and conservation titles. As a 501(c)(3) nonprofit, we are committed to supporting the environmental and educational goals of our organization by providing expert information on human-powered adventure, sustainable practices at home and on the trail, and preservation of wilderness.

Our publications are made possible through the generosity of donors, and through sales of 700 titles on outdoor recreation, sustainable lifestyle, and conservation. To donate, purchase books, or learn more, visit us online:

MOUNTAINEERS BOOKS
1001 SW Klickitat Way, Suite 201 • Seattle, WA 98134
800-553-4453 • mbooks@mountaineersbooks.org • www.mountaineersbooks.org

An independent nonprofit publisher since 1960

YOU MAY ALSO LIKE:

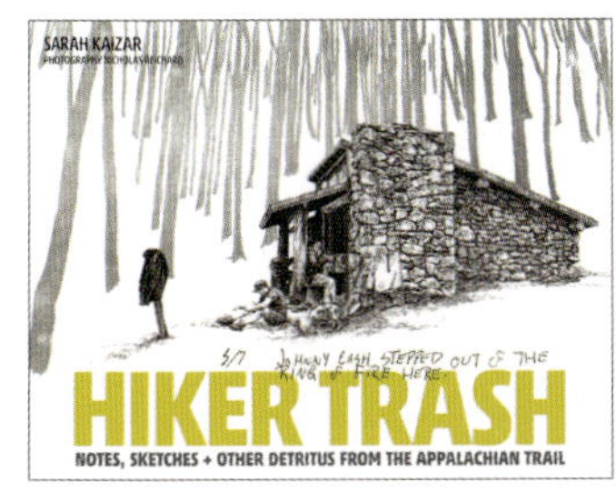

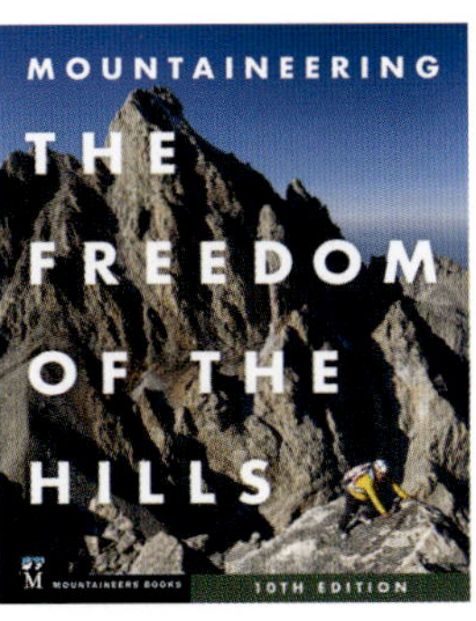

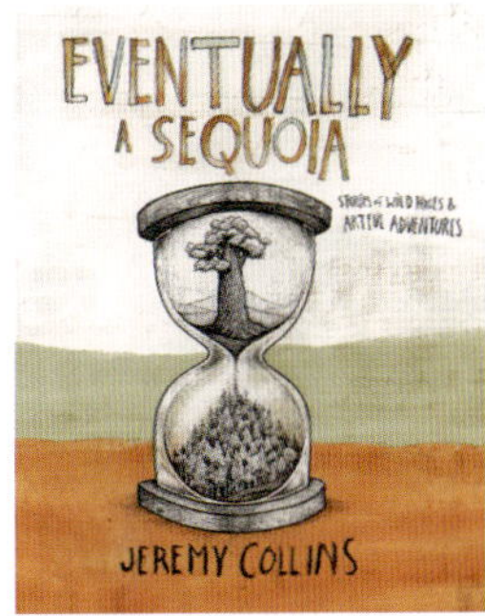

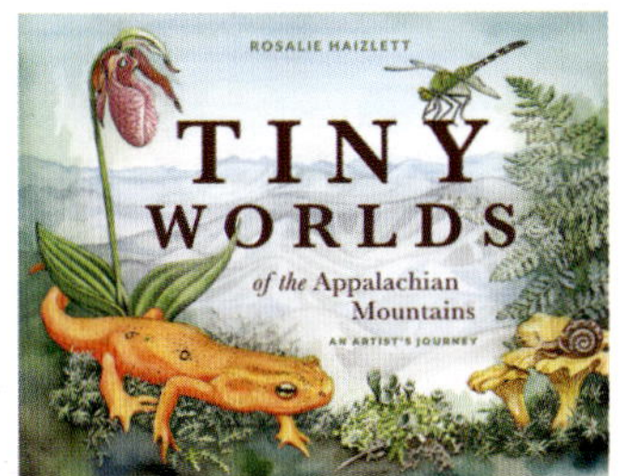

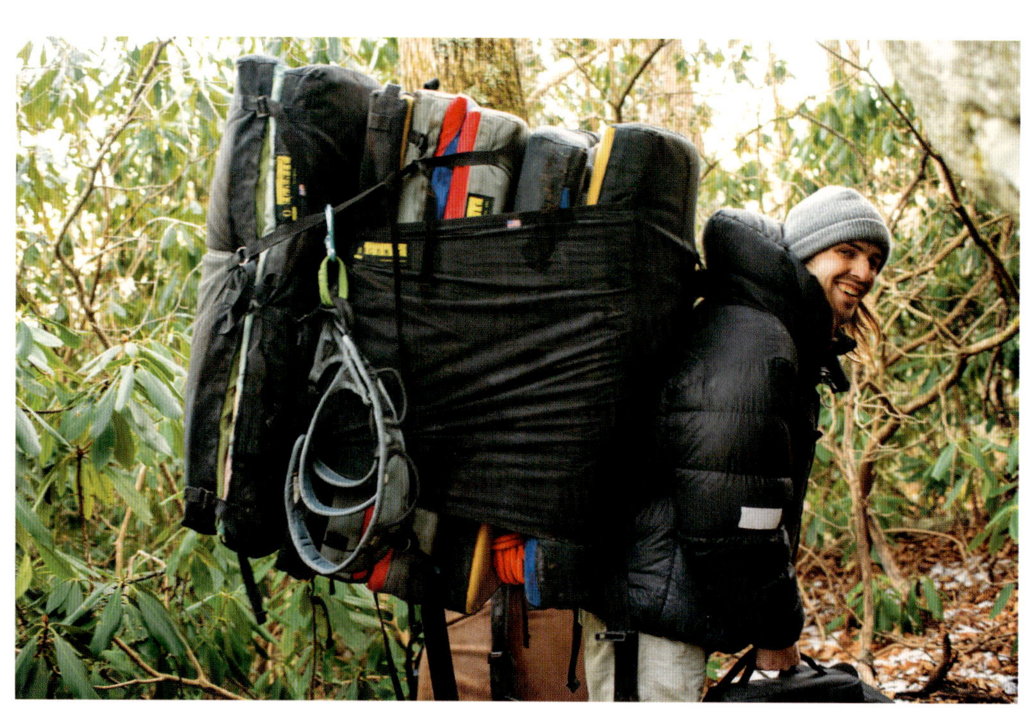